Fifty-Nine in '84

Fifty-Nine in '84

OLD HOSS RADBOURN,

BAREHANDED BASEBALL, AND THE

GREATEST SEASON A PITCHER EVER HAD

EDWARD ACHORN

Smithsonian Books

An Imprint of HarperCollins*Publishers*

HARPER   www.harpercollins.com

HarperCollins books may be purchased for educational, business, or sales promotional use. For information, please write: Special Markets Department, Harper-Collins Publishers, 10 East 53rd Street, New York, NY 10022.

Photo credits appear on page 355.

FIRST EDITION

Designed by Suet Yee Chong

Library of Congress Cataloging-in-Publication Data

Achorn, Edward.
    Fifty-Nine in '84 : old Hoss Radbourn, barehanded baseball, and the greatest season a pitcher ever had / Edward Achorn. —1st ed.
        p.   cm.
Includes bibliographical references and index.
    ISBN 978-0-06-182586-6 (alk. paper)
    1. Radbourn, Charles Gardner, 1853–1897. 2. Pitchers (Baseball)—United States—Biography. 3. Baseball players—United States—Biography. 4. Baseball—United States—History—19th century. I. Title.
GV865.R3A35   2010
796.357092—dc22
    [B]

                                                            2009034296

10 11 12 13 14   OV/RRD   10 9 8 7 6 5 4 3 2 1

To Valerie

"I see," writes a correspondent, "that some fan picks [Christy] Mathewson, [Ed] Walsh and [Rube] Waddell as the three greatest [pitchers]. Matty was a marvel. But when you come to the greatest, it is a matter of choice between Radbourne and [Walter] Johnson. Radbourne, I think, was the greatest pitcher I ever saw."

—Grantland Rice, syndicated columnist, 1924

To this day, I don't think I have seen better pitchers than were Radbourne and Sweeney of the old Providence team, with, perhaps one exception. That was Christy Mathewson. He, I think, would have compared with either of the first two. But they were wonders, and [neither] Mathewson nor any other pitcher who has come since was better than they.

—Frank Bancroft, former manager, 1920

He was brainy and game to the core; he had curves that were as baffling as any sent plateward. He had a fastball that was a marvel; a slow ball that was about as deceptive as any I have ever seen thrown. And, best of all, Radbourne had control that was absolutely marvelous. He practiced weeks, months and even years to acquire perfect handling of the baseball, and when he finally decided that he had learned his lesson he was able to place the ball in almost any spot that he willed.

—Clark Griffith, star pitcher, 1919

He will go down in the history of the game as by far the best pitcher of his day, and his wonderful stamina and record of pitching consecutive games will never be approached, much less equaled.

—Sam Crane, former manager, 1912

Volumes have been written about Pitcher Charlie Radbourne. But why should that prevent me from singing the praises of the gamest man who ever stepped into the box? There is no doubt that Radbourne was as great a little man as ever wore a uniform.

—Hardie Richardson, former player, 1911

Radbourn's wonderful work [in 1884] was, toward the last, the result of grit, pure and simple.

—Wilkes-Barre Times-Leader, January 10, 1911

Each year hundreds of pitchers claim attention of the world; and each year they are promptly forgotten. But Illinois produced a man who, although now 11 years deceased, has a brighter name than any of the multitude.

—Jacob Morse, reporter, 1908

He had a disposition that no one like him possessed and a will power that no one could swerve. I have seen him cry at one time with madness, and yet one kind word from anyone he liked would make him go the limit for that person.

—Ted Sullivan, former manager, 1905

Radbourne was a man of iron nerve, indomitable pluck and great courage. He was also a close student of baseball and a scientific player. He was not a marvel in point of strength, but he had a head filled with gray matter which he never failed to use.

—Rochester Democrat and Chronicle, January 2, 1905

For dead gameness and grit he never had an equal. His heart was as big as ever was encased in human flesh and as tender as a child's. He was obstinate and morose to deceitful people, but one kind word from a friend that he liked and he would wade in blood for him. This was Charles Radbourn, "the king of pitchers."

—Ted Sullivan, former manager, 1897

"Rad" was indisputably the greatest base ball pitcher the world has ever known.

—Sporting News, March 6, 1897

Radbourn was an eccentric fellow in some respects, and one who had to be handled "with gloves."

—Providence Journal, February 6, 1897

"Rad" is a peculiar fellow personally. He is called a crank by many, but at the same time these very ones admit he is a thorough good fellow. This statement, though apparently paradoxical, is quite true. With managers and umpires he is seldom able to get along. Possibly this is due to the fact that his own estimation of his value and importance is not always shared by them, for it must be admitted that Charles Radbourn sometimes is afflicted with what is known in common language as a swelled head. However, all this does not detract from his ability as a pitcher, for when he does "let himself out" there is some excuse for his vanity.

—*Quincy Daily Herald*, May 11, 1890

He is a curious fellow, and to get along with him it is necessary to coax a bit like one would a great big boy. Rad is certainly worth being coaxed.

—*Boston Globe*, April 15, 1888

Every fair-minded man is obliged to admit that Radbourne is the greatest pitcher in the world.

—*Evening Telegram*, Providence, September 1, 1884

Radbourn is the paragon of the season, and a standing wonder of the profession.

—*Cleveland Herald*, September 16, 1884

Radbourn pitches ball as if his very life depended upon it.

—*Cleveland Leader*, September 16, 1884

CONTENTS

PREFACE

In 1916, a baseball writer named Brown Holmes polled ten famous major-league managers, asking them to choose the greatest feat in the game's history. This was before Joe DiMaggio's 56-game hitting streak, or Babe Ruth's 60 home runs in one season, or Carl Hubbell's striking out five future Hall of Fame hitters in a row in an All-Star game. Still, there were many "wonderful feats" to choose from, even then: Tip O'Neill's .492 batting average, Harry Stovey's 156 stolen bases in a single season, Wee Willie Keeler's 44-game hitting streak, Rube Marquard's 19-game winning streak, Ty Cobb's amazing run of batting titles, Walter Johnson's 56 scoreless innings in a row.

When it came time to cast their votes, however, six of the ten managers, including some of the keenest minds in the game—John McGraw, Connie Mack, Pat Moran, Clark Griffith, Jimmy Callahan, and Hugh Jennings—picked another effort as the greatest feat in baseball. They voted for Charles "Old Hoss" Radbourn's astonishing performance in 1884. No other triumph came close in the polling, and for good reason: no pitcher has ever won as many games in a season, and none ever will. And the way Radbourn did it, pitching virtually alone, day after day, in the teeth of agonizing pain, had become the stuff of baseball legend.

The managers of the early twentieth century certainly understood that Radbourn's achievement was extraordinary, almost unbelievable. In the years since, though, Radbourn's story has faded into the mist. Radbourn's plaque remains in the Baseball Hall of Fame, but modern statisticians have tended to downplay his accomplishment, noting that many men of his era pitched plenty of innings and won piles of games. He is hardly a household name, even among fans who know some baseball history. Part of that was Radbourn's own fault. A sullen man, he did little talking to strangers, letting his career tell its own story. When he left the game, he wrote no books or magazine articles about his experience; indeed, when inquisitive fans asked him about his storied career, he mumbled a few words and left it at that. He was such an enigma that no one even could be sure of how to spell his name, both during his own times and for well into the next century. Many went with *Radbourn*, the accepted spelling today, but just as many went with *Radbourne*, with an *e*. He never made clear which was correct. (For the sake of consistency, this book will use Radbourn, except in quotes.)

I learned about Radbourn while growing up in Westborough, Massachusetts, a small town outside the deteriorating industrial city of Worcester. At some point I came across the odd fact that Worcester, of all places, once had a team in the National League—*the* National League. "What kind of game could baseball have been in those days?" I wondered, and I have spent a lifetime reading books, scouring statistics, and squinting at microfilm trying to figure it out. The first edition of MacMillan's *The Baseball Encyclopedia*, published in 1969, when I was twelve, opened my eyes to the rosters and stats of this vanished time, and on page 104 I found the most extraordinary numbers of all—the 1884 season of "O. Radbourn," the book's shorthand for Old Hoss Radbourn. (What a name!) I had to know who this man was, how he could win so many games, what made him tick. When my journalism career took me to Providence, where he had played well over a century earlier, it was as if fate was opening a door.

"The real war will never get in the books," Walt Whitman famously wrote about the American Civil War. I have often thought that was true of nineteenth-century baseball. There have been magnificent works about the period—my dad got me Harold Seymour's *Baseball: The Early Years* when I was a boy, a present I still cherish—and certainly the intrepid members of the Society for American Baseball Research have done brilliant work digging up the past. But so much is gone! Looking at early baseball is an endless search for important pieces that will always be missing from the puzzle. One starts with newspapers, mostly stilted game accounts, told in a foreign language of "cranks" and "kickers" and "dudes." The personal stuff—how players felt, what they said, where they lived, whom they loved—is ever elusive. Trying to re-create that era so that we can all step back into it requires sometimes frustrating, sometimes thrilling detective work, involving census data, record books, microfilm, letters, photos, city directories, family genealogies, obituaries, birth, marriage and death certificates, wills, and more than a few blind alleys. But the more I have probed, the more compellingly human I have found these mysterious ballplayers to be. The story of Radbourn, and of the woman who was the love of his life, seemed particularly poignant as it slowly and reluctantly yielded its long-kept secrets—secrets Radbourn hid from his own family. It is a tale of yearning, struggle, and the achievement of greatness against daunting obstacles.

It was not all that long ago. A while back, I was looking through old baseball souvenirs when I came across some scorecards kept by my grandfather, Edward Welt Achorn, who died decades ago. A scorecard of the May 9, 1905, game between the New York Highlanders (now Yankees) and Boston Americans (now Red Sox) bears in pencil his scrawl of the initials "E.W.A" and "M.L.C."—which can only stand for my grandfather and Mabel Louise Comey, the maiden name of my grandmother, a Mount Holyoke College girl. Long before their marriage, it seems, twenty-one-year-old Edward happily wooed her at Boston's Huntington Avenue Grounds. An even earlier scorecard preserves his attendance at a big September 16, 1904, doubleheader on Ladies' Day between the same teams. He (with his lady, Mabel?) saw Cy Young pitch in the first game for Boston, and Jack Chesbro in the second for New York. Not too shabby! When I looked up the doubleheader in the archives of the *Boston Globe*, I discovered this tidbit: "George Wright, the king of players a few years ago, and John F. Morrill were in the front row." My grandfather, born in the fateful year of 1884, was cheering for the Boston team in the same stands with two men who were teammates of Old Hoss Radbourn, one with Providence's Grays in 1882 and one with Boston's Red Stockings in the late 1880s. George Wright had also played for baseball's first openly professional team, the Red Stockings of Cincinnati, in 1869. In a way, we two Edward Achorns—representing a span of only three generations—thus connect with professional baseball from its very beginnings to the latest pitch.

No, it really wasn't so awfully long ago.

Old Hoss Is Ready

Charlie Radbourn woke up on Friday morning, September 26, 1884, with a knifing ache in his arm and neck. It had not been a pleasant night. He had taken to paying hotel porters to massage his arm and shoulder and apply hot towels and liniment overnight, easing the pain while he fell into a fitful sleep. But the relief did not last long.

After giving up on any more rest, Radbourn turned out of his hotel bed and went to the basin. The sound of downtown traffic boomed below on the Chicago streets—a familiar hum compounded of the clip-clopping of hundreds of hooves, the scraping din of metal wheels on uneven pavement, the whinnying of horses, and the shouted curses of teamsters. Since his throbbing right arm would no longer cooperate, he would have had to use his left hand to lift the folded towel off the top of the stoneware pitcher, pour the water into the bowl, splash it on his tired, lined face, and dry his shaggy, drooping mustache. His muscles on his right side were so weak and sore that he couldn't raise his right hand high enough to button his starched white shirt, thread a necktie, affix his hard collar, and comb down his stiff brown hair. Fumbling with his one good arm, he struggled to get dressed for breakfast.

He could not do it alone. His manager, Frank Bancroft, had taken to rooming with his star pitcher, and he helped Charlie dress, supplying the needed second arm along with words of encouragement. With a pennant at stake, Bancroft wanted to stay close in order to keep an attentive eye on

1

him, smooth Charlie's jagged moods, and make sure he remained productive. The pitcher should have been in good spirits, by all accounts: his heroic work had put his team, the Providence Grays, on the cusp of winning the National League pennant. The National League was by far the best circuit in baseball-crazed America, and capturing its championship was a great achievement, a career-long dream for many players. And yet Radbourn did not seem particularly happy. "He was of a silent, somewhat morose disposition," Bancroft recalled. "I . . . did my best to keep him cheered up by repeating anecdotes and funny stories. But I admit it was a hard task to make Rad cut in with a laugh." A knowing smile was about all Bancroft could elicit from the pitcher. Radbourn often seemed lost in thought, silently mulling over how he would defeat his next opponent. "He thought about little else but baseball, and was always scheming to get some advantage over the other team," Bancroft recalled.

The manager had made it clear way back in the spring that his players were expected to abstain from alcohol through mid-October, the end of the season. Radbourn was a notorious drinker, but he did his drinking discreetly, taking care to show up at the ballpark in condition to win and fill the stands with paying customers, something the pragmatic Bancroft would have appreciated. As soon as the manager left the room, Charlie might well have medicated his aching arm and shoulder and stiff neck with a couple of burning gulps, sending the warmth coursing through his aching body. He was as ready as he ever would be to face the world.

Down in the lobby, hotel guests were milling about, some seated in plush sofas and chairs reading the small type of morning newspapers filled with the usual stories about the hazards and horrors of modern life. There had been a freak accident overnight on the Grand Trunk Railroad between Toronto and Montreal, a derailment that sent cars tumbling violently down an embankment, injuring some passengers severely but, miraculously, killing none. There was an ongoing struggle against bovine pleuropneumonia, which was wiping out cattle in Kentucky and Ohio, terrifying midwestern farmers who could ill afford the loss. And in New Orleans, a lynch mob, infuriated over reports that a Negro had raped a white girl, had besieged a jail, dragged out all of its black prisoners, and—uninterested in such matters as innocence or guilt—hanged the four on trees in the courthouse yard.

Daily life in America was, as always, a dangerous and daunting affair. Other guests talked about the news or their latest business conquests, laughing loudly and spitting streams of tobacco juice in the general direction of spittoons even before drinking their morning coffee. Radbourn might have found his teammates there in the lobby, but on days he pitched he liked to be by himself, thinking.

This was one of those days. Even if he was in no condition to pitch, he planned to try, confident he could at least outsmart enemy batters. But Radbourn had reason to be worried about the frantic messages his body had been sending him in recent days. The pain radiating from his pitching arm and shoulder was excruciating, unremitting now, and it was showing up in his work.

John M. Ward, who had once held the National League record for victories, with forty-seven, until Radbourn broke it, with forty-eight, in 1883, understood well that a team's top pitcher needed unyielding stamina—mental as well as physical—to survive, throwing day after day. It was hard enough to pitch an entire game, he wrote, but it was brutally difficult to throw day after day for an entire season, "during the chilly days of the spring and fall, and under a broiling July sun," an experience so daunting that it "can be appreciated only by one who has gone through it." The man in the pitcher's box confronted more than opposing batters; he had to endure exhausting travel from city to city, "broken rest and hasty meals, bad cooking and changes of water and climate." Water in the 1880s was not always clean, and a visitor who dared to drink it without becoming acclimated to it ran the risk of harrowing cramps and diarrhea. Under such conditions, it was hard for anyone to be ready to pitch anytime he was called upon. "Only a good constitution, a vigorous digestion, the most careful habits, and lots of grit, will ever do it."

Radbourn may not have had the most careful habits, given his fondness for the bottle, and the vigor of his digestion was debatable, but there was one quality Ward valued that he did possess in abundance. Operating on pure grit, Radbourn had done things that season that were nothing less than astounding. Watching him work calmly and effectively in game after game, his teammates at some point gave him one of the most evocative nicknames in baseball history, comparing him with the strong, plodding horses that could be found on the streets of every city in those days before the internal combustion engine, enduring heat and cold with equine patience, loyally lugging their cruel burdens unto death. "Old Hoss—that's what we always called Radbourne," said Bancroft.

But in lugging his burdens, he had all but destroyed his arm. For the first time all year, Radbourn had lost two games in a row, clear evidence that something was very wrong. For weeks now, he had been insisting that he start every Grays game until the pennant was safely won, ignoring his manager's pleas that he sit out some games and get some rest. Bancroft had finally seen enough. On September 25, he forced Radbourn to take the day off, and sent out Eddie Conley, a skinny twenty-year-old Holy Cross student who was earning money for college by pitching in the big leagues. Providence struggled in that one, too, trailing 5–1 going into the sixth inning before coming back to win in extra innings, 6–5.

With one game off to sustain him, Radbourn had a chance to end it all that afternoon of September 26. There was one potentially catastrophic problem: he had no idea when or if his arm would spring back to life—maybe this afternoon, maybe next April, maybe never. And while he was close to clinching the pennant, almost three weeks remained on the National League schedule.

It was no mystery why he hurt. The punishing repetition—pitch after pitch after pitch, day after day, without significant rest—had surely started to wear down his rotator cuff, the complex bundle of tendons that connect the arm to the shoulder, giving the joint its extraordinary flexibility. Even after the pain had set in, searing his shoulder, jarring him awake several times a night, he had continued to pitch. The relentless work had stretched his tendons, making them weak and thin, and possibly opening up a tear.

There was no club doctor to shut him down and make repairs. Even if there had been, physicians knew little about the nature of such injuries, and certainly had developed no regime of surgery or shots to fix the problem. And even those who had a financial stake in star players, the club owners and managers, made few efforts to stop such abuse. They accepted the unpleasant reality that pitchers often dismantled their shoulders trying to win games. That was the cost of doing business. Great players were missed, of course, but there were always plenty of young, strong arms ready to take over.

After lunch, Radbourn headed for the ballpark on Lake Michigan, along Michigan Avenue near Randolph Street. Summer was over, and the day was cloudy and cold, with a chilly autumn wind portending another Chicago winter. While the stands were still empty, Radbourn made his way onto the field, garbed in his dirt-stained, sweat-stiffened flannel uniform trimmed with powder-blue belt and stockings. Radbourn's arm was still dead, almost impossible to lift, and his shoulder muscles were disintegrating and his neck stiff, but that was no matter; he intended to work that afternoon if he could get moving. And so he began the painful process of limbering up, something that had become a daily ritual for him as the season reached its final weeks.

He started about ten feet in front of home plate and lobbed the ball gingerly, underhand, to his catcher. Gradually, as he loosened up, he found he could lift it a little higher. He stepped backward and tried again. As he went along, he rubbed his aching arm vigorously with his left hand, journalist Jacob Morse recalled. "Sometimes his face would be drawn up into contortions, but never a word of complaint left his lips." When he reached the pitcher's box, he could throw with a sidearm motion, and when he got back to second base he was able to get his arm over his head. Finally he could hurl the ball from the outfield to home plate.

By that time the stands were filling up with Chicagoans, a big crowd for a gray Friday, and his teammates were out on the field, glancing his way while they played catch in the gloom, made darker by the coal smoke wafting over from the railroad yard next door. When the Grays saw Radbourn succeed "in making his customary long distance throw," Bancroft recalled, they looked at each other and said, "The 'Old Hoss' is ready and we can't be beat."

Radbourn would demonstrate soon enough whether they were right.

NATIONAL LEAGUE 1883

FINAL STANDINGS

	W	L	PCT.	GB
Boston	63	35	.643	—
Chicago	59	39	.602	4
PROVIDENCE	58	40	.592	5
Cleveland	55	42	.567	7½
Buffalo	52	45	.536	10½
New York	46	50	.479	16
Detroit	40	58	.408	23
Philadelphia	17	81	.173	46

The Importance of Grit

The first of October, 1883, was chilly, and wind whipped through the Messer Street Grounds in Providence, Rhode Island, swirling dead leaves and dust into little flumes against the ballpark's weathered wooden fences. Summer was barely gone, but another dark New England winter was already on the breeze as the late afternoon temperatures dipped into the low fifties, headed for the forties that evening. The acrid, sweetish smell of coal smoke hovered in the air, belched up by hundreds of Providence factory pipes and thousands of small household stoves, leaving a sooty haze that stole some of the meager warmth from the slanting autumn sun.

Not surprisingly, only a relative handful of intrepid baseball lovers—about 350 men, garbed in the standard business attire of rumpled suit, vest, tie, and derby hat—came out for the game, a meaningless exhibition being played on a busy Monday afternoon. This game was a show of gratitude, a postseason "benefit" whose proceeds went directly to the hometown heroes as they prepared to depart for the winter. The young beneficiaries, most of them in their twenties, were glad to have a few extra dollars in their pocket for the off-season. They were not pampered multimillionaires, these professional ballplayers, but workingmen, fellows you might hail on the sidewalk or find standing near the bar in a crowded saloon, grateful to be treated to a whiskey. Even citizens who did not particularly care to see the game bought tickets for the sake of the boys, and

there were twice as many sold as used. As the innings passed and the afternoon grew colder, the men in the stands buried their hands in their pockets
or rubbed them together briskly. Some were inclined to pull out a flask and
steal a warming nip, ignoring the park's no-liquor rule. But they were happy
to be here, to smile and tip their hats to friends, and to savor the setting moments of the 1883 season with some last few cheers for their team.

It was a good one. For the fourth straight year, the Providence Grays had
seriously contended for the pennant of the eight-team National League.
In fact, they had held first place for most of the season, far longer than
any other club, only to stumble at the end, after a nerve-racking struggle.
Though crestfallen, the team's rabid local followers—then known as cranks
or fanatics (a word later shortened to fans)—knew they were fortunate to
claim this celebrated club as their own, when much bigger cities had to
make do with much bigger losers.

On this afternoon, both they and the team's biggest star were in for a
surprise. The umpire was keeping a secret that would make news halfway
across the continent.

Most of the small crowd had come here on horsecars, trams that glided over
railroad tracks imbedded in the streets, each car tugged along by two stout,
sweat-streaked horses. It took twenty minutes to get out to the Messer Street
Grounds from downtown, on a route that ran down the center of the city's
glitziest avenue, Westminster Street, past glittering stores, ornate stone office buildings, and tree-lined neighborhoods of handsome mansions before
reaching the West Side, former farmland now filling up with narrow, two-
story frame houses and brick schools for a burgeoning middle class headed
by men putting in ten-hour days in factories and offices. To the sprightly
rhythm of clip-clopping horseshoes on paving stones, interlaced with the
driver's periodic curses and clanging of his bell to warn traffic away from
the tracks, many passengers passed the time by perusing the city's two-cent
papers.

Buried deep inside the paper were some late news dispatches—one
about the steamer *Colorado*, which had left Buffalo bearing freight for Chicago, only to explode, scalding and dismembering an unspecified number

of crew members; another about a brazen train robbery on the Atchison, Topeka, and Santa Fe Railroad. The eastbound Cannonball passenger train, leaving at night from Denver, had stopped a few hours into its journey at Coolidge, Kansas, 470 miles west of Kansas City. When it started up again at about 2:00 a.m., three desperados appeared and ordered the engineer to halt. When he refused, they shot him dead and fatally wounded his fireman with a bullet in the mouth. Such stories were dramatic but hardly astonishing. Every afternoon's paper was packed with similar vignettes of the chaos and peril of life in 1880s America.

Pain and peril were no strangers to the men on the field at the Messer Street Grounds that afternoon. Mostly poorly educated members of the working class, fond of drinking, cursing, and carousing, adorned with bristling mustaches that they grew to advertise their toughness, they were hard characters who played to win, resorting to cheating and violence if necessary. And to maintain their grip on their prized jobs, they played hard, risking grave injuries.

At the end of the fourth inning of their benefit game, the Grays were getting up from their bench, ready to jog back onto the field, when the umpire shouted over to them. He ordered one of the players to report immediately to home plate. Everyone stopped.

The marked man was the toughest of this surly crew, the team's biggest star, pitcher Charles Radbourn. In his fourth National League season, he was a familiar figure on America's ball fields, with his thick shoulders and squat neck, his bushy brown mustache under his prominent nose, and the rim of his light gray cap characteristically thrust down low, framing the pale, shining eyes that glared out from underneath. Charlie was only twenty-eight, but his face was already lined and leathery, with the look of a man who had struggled fiercely to get ahead. A proud and pugnacious veteran of many baseball wars, he was not known to suffer foolish umpires gladly.

Though primarily a pitcher, he had been stationed in center field that afternoon, in deference to his dead right arm, earned through months of overwork in a desperate and ultimately futile quest to drag the Grays to the pennant. No one could fairly blame Radbourn for Providence's swoon over the final five days of the season, as he fought off excruciating, penetrating pain. Stouthearted to the last, he had given his all with almost nothing left to give.

Now that the long struggle was over and there was nothing more he could do, something was up. With a look of skepticism, he reported to the plate. The ump—his teammate Lee Richmond, an unusually cultured ball-player educated at Brown University, filling in as arbiter that day—broke into a wide grin.

"Mr. Radbourn," Richmond cried out in a stage voice intended to reach the grandstand, "permit me in behalf of your many friends to present to you this elegant testimonial as a token of their respect for you as a gentleman and a ballplayer."

Richmond pulled out a small case made of embossed plush. Radbourn accepted the object with a nod and carefully opened it. Inside was a stunning present, worth far more than the money he would be taking home as his share of this benefit game: a shiny gold watch, a solid-gold chain, and a charm in the form of a ten-dollar gold piece. On the timepiece's shimmering cover were the raised letters *C.R.* Snapped open, it revealed a cursive inscription: *Presented to Charles Radbourn by his many friends in Providence, October 1, 1883.* The magnificent gift had been purchased two miles away at C. Robert Linke's elegant jewelry store, at 77 Westminster Street, for nearly $200—an eye-popping tribute in an age when the average major league salary stood well under $2,000. News of the honor traveled all the way to Radbourn's home state of Illinois, where the *Peoria Daily Transcript* noted proudly that the recipient of the gold watch had once pitched for the local team.

The little circle of players at home plate passed around the gift, admiring its "solidity and beautiful finish." The *Providence Journal* predicted that it would "be highly cherished by the modest pitcher, who has fairly won the magnificent keepsake by his uncommon skill as a ball-tosser and quiet, gentlemanly deportment on and off the base ball arena."

That last bit was a case of laying it on a bit thick. Radbourn possessed uncommon skill, to be sure, and was a man of few words—fellow pitcher George Washington Bradley rated him "a good, quiet chap"—but he was also a whiskey-slugging son of a butcher, a stubborn adversary who was prey to wounded feelings and sullen moods, and more than capable of dealing out nasty insults. As another reporter noted, Radbourn had a "naturally jealous disposition" that often left him with a bad "case of the sulks." In truth, he was no more of a conventional gentleman than most of the other young men who had clawed their way into this ill-reputed profession.

Indeed, even among the rabble of ballplayers he was an odd character, with a rebellious streak that suggested something stormy and swirling beneath the placid surface of his quiet demeanor and dogged work ethic. For one thing, Radbourn wanted nothing to do with the trappings of celebrity. Most pitchers liked to warm up in front of the grandstand, basking in the adulation of men and (especially) women gathered there. Charlie scorned such men as grandstanders who loved the glory but often failed to earn it when the going got rough. He chose to prepare himself for battle without distractions, off to the side, out of sight. Similarly, most players, greedy for fame, were delighted to have their pictures taken. Whether on the field or in the studio, they froze in position dutifully—knowing the slightest movement would produce a blur—in front of bulky, boxy cameras attached to rigid tripods. The resulting images, captured on wet plates of glass, were used to mass-produce black-and-white photographs that made their faces and forms famous, displayed on saloon walls, stuffed into cigarette packs to stiffen the package and protect the product, or hawked to baseball fanatics from storefront windows.

Radbourn found a memorable way to mock the ritual. On April 29, 1886, when the two teams gathered on the field at New York's Polo Grounds in front of a grandstand festooned with red, white, and blue bunting for a ceremonial photograph marking the season's opening day, Charlie dutifully rested his right hand on the shoulder of the teammate sitting in front of him. But at the last minute, wearing a straight face, betraying his intentions only with his twinkling eyes, he lifted his left hand above his teammate's other shoulder, firmly thrust out his middle finger, and held it rock steady so that it would remain sharp and clear in the captured image, a bird defiantly flipped at eternity. The photographer, who had gone to great pains to position the two teams and umpire just right, snapped the picture without noticing Radbourn's antics on the far left. Charlie was seemingly the first man in history whose use of the obscene gesture was preserved on film. He may well have been the second, too. The following year, posing for his photograph on an Old Judge Tobacco baseball card, Radbourn placed his hands on his hips and, wearing a bland expression, subtly extended the middle finger of his left hand. *Click.*

All the same, there was something about him that set him apart as a leader. No one was as dead set on winning, or as resolute against the blows of pain and disappointment. "Radbourne was a man who never despaired of victory, no matter how the tide of fortune flowed," his sometime teammate Hardie Richardson noted. "He did not know the meaning of the word 'quit.'" When his team was losing badly, he turned to his mates on the bench and told them, calmly and quietly, "Well, we'll get them yet, see if we don't." He believed he could defeat anyone, and infused confidence in his teammates. Baseball writer Sid Mercer noted that "Radbourne, never particularly wonderful in a physical way but always wonderful as a pitcher, was able to keep his fellow players in that frame of mind where they were sure they could not be beaten when he was in the box." He had a "bulging notion of personal success which after all is worth more than anything else in base ball," Mercer wrote. "For dead gameness and grit he never had an equal," said Ted Sullivan, one of his managers. Sullivan never forgot the sight of him walking to the pitcher's box with "that sullen, dogged, and indifferent appearance, which was ever characteristic of him."

He had become a great pitcher in spite of a body that seemed ill designed for athletic brilliance. He stood only five feet nine inches and weighed 168 pounds—average for the time, but slight for a top athlete. Nature had unkindly denied him the long whiplike arms and big, powerful legs that helped some men heave a baseball extraordinarily fast. He had made up for it with an indomitable will. Radbourn put in hours of lonely practice, mastering new pitches. When no catcher was available, he worked on his own, obsessively firing at bottles perched on stools, knocking them off repeatedly, until he was certain he had achieved command over everything he threw, with the capacity to consistently tease the edges of the strike zone. "Any delivery without control," Radbourn noted, "is no delivery at all"—an admirably concise summary of the pitcher's art. He possessed in abundance what modern major-league pitching coaches call the three C's: confidence, concentration, and command of the strike zone. "Radbourne often appeared carelessly indifferent in the box, even when pitching [the] most important games, but he was not," manager Sam Crane recalled. "It was his absolute confidence in himself that made his position in the box appear careless." Clark Griffith, a future major leaguer who lived near Radbourn as a youth in Illinois, got his most important lessons in pitching from the quiet master. "I'd say the two greatest things he showed me were the curve ball, how to throw it, how to use it, and the importance of grit."

He may have worked as loyally as a horse, but he felt little if any devotion to his supposed masters, the men who paid his substantial salary. As far as Radbourn was concerned, the capitalists who ran professional baseball were grasping thieves bent on stealing what was rightfully his. He was not far from wrong, because the owners, operating on narrow profit margins and trying to stave off bankruptcy, did indeed collude with each other to squeeze Charlie and his fellow players to the fullest extent possible. One way they did it was through the reserve clause, an ingenious part of the standard player contract. It was the brainchild of the president of the National League's Boston club, Arthur Soden, a frugal, chilly, clean-shaven Yankee who brought his lunch to work every day to spare the expense of restaurants, and spent his off hours as the president of the Boston Chess Club, springing clever traps on less devious opponents. Under the clause, which the owners adopted in 1879, a player was chained to his ball club even *beyond* the strict term of his contract. When his contract expired, he could negotiate a new one only with his own team, and no other. The system blocked him from selling his services to the highest bidder through a free market, and kept him from seeking a new life in another city with another team.

The owners insisted they needed the reserve clause to protect their investment. It wasn't cheap to discover and develop talented players, and if stars were free to pick up and leave at the end of a season, a club's value could plummet overnight. Moreover, baseball's business model depended on the loyal patronage of local customers, developed through years of cheering for their favorite players. If those stars fled, the bonds of affection would be broken. These arguments held merit as far as they went, but they could not obscure a vital truth: the reserve clause was brutally unfair to players. It depressed their salaries by eliminating competition for their services. Meanwhile, an owner could blithely sell his rights in a man to any team at any time, sending him far from his family and friends without his permission, while pocketing the selling price, giving absolutely nothing to the player involved—whose blood, toil, and talent were what made him valuable in the first place.

No fool about financial matters, Radbourn thought this business of "owning" a human being bore a suspicious resemblance to an evil institution supposedly abolished in America two decades earlier. "The only difference between the league and slavery is that the managers can't lick you," Radbourn complained bitterly in an interview. "They can have you down so fine that you have no say in the matter at all. I sign a contract with a club, and they can hold me forever, if they see fit, or so long as I want to play ball." A reporter later wrote of him: "He was a sort of anarchist and was never happy unless scoring the magnates for their so-called oppressive measures."

Radbourn particularly resented being trapped in Providence, the smallest market in the National League, and one that generated far less revenue for player salaries than such baseball-crazed megalopolises as New York and Chicago. Before the 1883 season, in fact, Charlie had attempted to flee to the American Association, a new major league challenging the National League's hegemony, and one that did not yet observe the reserve rule. Radbourn signed with the Browns of St. Louis, America's sixth biggest city, a baseball hotbed that had three times Providence's population. But fate intervened. Before the season began, the American Association reached a peace accord with the older National League, under which the leagues pledged to respect each other's contracts and to recognize the hated reserve clause. The men who had jumped that winter were summarily ordered back to their teams, and the disgruntled Radbourn returned to pipsqueak Providence. At the end of the season, he flirted with the idea of holding out, hoping to force the owners to give him his release, but he eventually relented and signed for $3,000 for 1884. That was excellent money, to be sure, but it was still less than he might have made in New York or as a free agent.

With the sullen, dogged determination that was his hallmark, he kept looking for a way to break free without sacrificing his professional career. All exits from Providence seemed closed. Still, Radbourn had a habit of accomplishing things that no one thought he could.

*   *   *

The gift of the gold watch on that cool October afternoon symbolized Radbourn's new status as baseball's greatest pitcher. Throwing in more than three-quarters of the Grays' games, Charlie had achieved in 1883 something no other man ever had—winning an astounding forty-eight games, a new major-league record. "The greatest all-round pitcher in the League is Radbourne, sure," asserted Sam Wise, shortstop of the champion Boston club, Providence's bitter rivals, in a postseason interview. "That man is as steady as a rock, seldom makes a mistake, watches his bases like a hawk, pitches alternately a fast and slow but always puzzling ball, and is a fine batsman." Rhode Island fanatics agreed completely. After Charlie handed over his luxurious present for safekeeping, the crowd burst into prolonged applause. Radbourn, "nervously doffing his cap," jogged back onto the field.

But though he had turned in one of the great seasons in baseball history, Radbourn was still unsatisfied. It stuck in his craw that, after months of toil, he had been bested at the end, denied a championship flag, the one great professional achievement that still eluded him. Worse, he had to face the cold reality that the dream might not even be attainable anymore. He would be twenty-nine in 1884, old for a professional pitcher, especially one who had thrown as many innings as he had over the previous four years. Moreover, something was seriously wrong with him this time, something that might be beyond the healing powers of a winter of rest. Charlie could barely lift his right arm. He had always survived on grit, but he might have pushed himself too hard this time, inflicting permanent damage on the muscle and cartilage he needed to speed a baseball past a hitter. He would have to wait to see whether his arm and shoulder came back to life.

As the applause subsided on that fading October afternoon at the Messer Street Grounds, few in the crowd knew of the frightening risks Radbourn had taken to earn that watch. And the pitcher, as much as he was suffering now, had no idea of the dark and painful days that awaited him on the other side of winter.

I Am a Pitcher

On an October day thirty-five years earlier, a young English couple wrapped up their infant daughter, Sara, and stepped out of the door into one of the loveliest landscapes in England. Dressed in their finest clothing, they walked beneath yellow leaves along a tranquil, tree-lined path that ascended a green hill. At the crown stood a splendid chapel near a great columned mansion with a stunning view of the winding Avon River and the ancient city of Bath, a former Roman enclave that had long been a fashionable retreat for the British aristocracy, who came to drink and bathe in its healing sulfuric waters—and, of course, to see and be seen. At the foot of that sloping hill, nestled in a narrow valley that ran all the way to Bath, gleamed a peaceful Arcadian glade spanned by a lovely Palladian bridge, a delight to the eye in its classical order and decorum, its golden stone reflecting in the bright blue water. Charles Radbourn, if not his new wife, knew almost every inch of this fantastic estate, called Prior Park. He had spent part of his youth right on these grounds, a little paradise in the midst of a rich and prosperous region of England, an island nation whose mighty empire spanned the globe.

Prior Park was the eighteenth-century creation of Ralph Allen, a bold, ingenious businessman who had made a fortune reforming the British postal service and then turned his wealth to personal and public good. Famous for his charitable works, he was an enlightened thinker and patron of the arts, the friend and benefactor of the portrait and landscape painter Thomas

Gainsborough and the novelists Henry Fielding and Samuel Richardson, all regular guests here. The famous landscape gardener Capability Brown had helped design Prior Park's majestic, sprawling gardens, with advice from another of Allen's friends, the great poet Alexander Pope.

To neighboring farmers who spent their lives at wearying toil, Prior Park loomed on the horizon like something from a fairy tale. "There was an air of grandeur in it that struck you with awe and rivaled the beauties of the best Grecian architecture," Fielding wrote of the noble house, "and it was as commodious within as venerable without." Allen had built it as a kind of showplace for the creamy-hued stone he was quarrying in the region, another source of his expanding wealth. More playfully, he had demonstrated the virtues of his stone by constructing on a nearby hill a "sham castle," a one-sided illusion of walls, towers, and turrets, recalling the glories of medieval England. From a distance it looked like something straight out of the age of chivalry.

The delightful Mr. Allen had died in 1764, taking with him much of the financial wherewithal and drive to maintain his magnificent estate. In 1829, the property was sold to Roman Catholic bishop Peter Augustine Baines, a farsighted cleric who turned it into Prior Park College, a Catholic

Grounds of Prior Park, with Bath in the distance

seminary and lay university. He hired a hardworking man from Chilton, one George Radbourn, to serve as Prior Park's gardener, a job that entailed the impossible task of maintaining grounds that a much larger staff had once overseen. Still, Radbourn handled the task to the bishop's evident satisfaction, and held the post for years. He raised four sons here, living in a handsome stone outbuilding called the Lower Lodge, along the base of the Carriage Road.

By autumn 1848, the gardener was getting old and sore, and the cycle of life in his family was turning. His second-oldest son, twenty-year-old Charles, had just married Caroline Gardner, also twenty, in Bath. Caroline became pregnant months before the wedding, and though the two stayed together for life, one of them may have been a reluctant partner at the start, since the ceremony waited until the third quarter of the year, alarmingly close to the birth of their first child, on September 9. Now, on October 8, 1848, the husband and wife, with baby in arms, took the short and pleasant stroll up the hill, past autumn trees, to Prior Park's Roman Catholic chapel. There, beneath its soaring stone arches, its deep stillness stirred by the priest's echoing voice, Charles and Caroline—under their Latin names, Caroli and Carolinae—had Sara Maria Radbourn christened.

By 1851, the three were living down below in the busy city, along with a lodger, at 2 Beaufort Square, in Bath's Walcot neighborhood. Charles was working as a butcher, his lifelong trade. But even in this bucolic land, life was changing, growing disturbingly less secure for those who owned small farms or raised livestock in the district. The Great Western Railway, built between 1838 and 1840 to link London and Bristol, had generally reduced the cost of transporting goods but had also flooded the market in London, forcing down prices and putting at risk the region's small farms, which lacked the efficiencies of scale. By the early 1850s, the restless Radbourns— not only Charles, but also his brothers James and George—wanted something better for themselves and their progeny than they could find anymore in their green and pleasant land.

They invested their savings in steamship tickets for the perilous two-week trip to the hustling, rambunctious country across the sea, where millions of African Americans still suffered in the chains of slavery, but where free men who had the gumption to think big could make something of themselves. Like millions of fellow immigrants, Charles, Caroline, and little Sara arrived at the bustling port of New York City in 1854, from where they headed upstate to help ply the family trade of raising and butchering livestock. They settled with their fellow Radbourns just outside Rochester, a thriving manufacturing center of thirty-six thousand, known as the "flour city" for its extensive milling operations. It was there, on December 11, 1854, that Caroline gave birth to the second of their eight surviving children— Charles G. Radbourn, a boy destined for lasting fame in a sport that was thriving downstate among the clerks and lawyers of New York City.

But Charles and Caroline were not yet settled. In 1855, they picked up yet again and struck out for the West, joining the extended Radbourn clan in rough-hewn central Illinois. When the young family arrived in the town of Bloomington, it still bore the ramshackle appearance of a frontier village, built along a wide, rutted, and alternately muddy and dusty main road, where hogs rooted in the muck. All the same, it attracted a good number of people doing business, among them an ungainly, grotesquely tall lawyer— made still taller by his frayed stovepipe hat—from nearby Springfield. This prairie attorney, a former one-term congressman by the name of Abraham Lincoln, seemed to be in town constantly, as he took on cases at the county courthouse, told off-color jokes—uncouthly punching his listeners under the ribs for emphasis—and plotted strategy with local members of the emerging Republican Party, all the time contemplating what to do about the inescapable issue that was rapidly tearing the country apart.

It was in Bloomington, on May 29, 1856, at a political convention in Major's Hall, upstairs from Humphrey's Cheap Store in a three-story brick building at the corner of East and Front streets, that the forty-seven-year-old Lincoln gave his first great speech denouncing slavery, revealing a passion and eloquence that stunned and stirred his listeners. It was a Bloomington friend named Jesse W. Fell, founder and publisher of the *Bloomington Pantagraph*, who urged Lincoln to challenge Stephen A. Douglas to a series of debates as a candidate for the U.S. Senate in 1858. When Lincoln stopped by Bloomington that year to rally his supporters between the debates, thousands turned out, and the English-born Charles Radbourn might well have taken time off to be among them, witnessing this great American spectacle, perhaps bearing his young namesake on his shoulders. It was Bloomington, too, that produced Judge David Davis, the Lincoln crony who managed his forces so brilliantly at the 1860 Republican National Convention, securing him the nomination and ultimately the presidency. Lincoln's path to greatness, in short, wound repeatedly through the place that Radbourn called home. It was no surprise that this muscular young region—then known as the Northwest—had stepped up as a major player in American politics and culture. For years, the North and South had roughly balanced each other in the tussle over slavery and economics. Now, this land of wide-open spaces that was filling up daily with brash and ambitious men seemed poised to decide America's fate—or as Senator Douglas boldly predicted, to "speak the law to this nation and to execute the law as spoken."

In the midst of this boiling political ferment—smack between Lincoln's great address at Major's Hall and his debates with Douglas—the June 1, 1857, edition of Jesse Fell's *Bloomington Pantagraph* carried an advertisement with the woodcut of a great, beefy bull and a headline proclaiming, "NEW MEAT MARKET." It announced that Charles Radbourn had opened his store on Front Street, next door to Mason's Livery Stable and just down the road from Major's Hall, and would be "happy to wait on customers. He will keep a full and excellent supply of Fresh Meats always on hand." Soon the butcher with the broad West County English accent was serving a steady stream of women in hoopskirts and men in long coats and top hats. Tax records from the Civil War era show him owning cattle, calves, hogs, and sheep, obviously for slaughter. The close-knit Radbourns were getting ahead in America. Before the end of the decade, the old gardener of Prior Park, George Radbourn, and his wife, Sarah, had come to America, too, and were living in Illinois with their sons Charles and James.

Little Charlie, their grandson, effectively grew up on the great, sweeping prairies that surrounded Bloomington. Charles senior taught his oldest boy how to hunt at an early age, and by his teen years, the quiet and intense young man was already displaying rare athletic ability, including keen concentration, a steady hand, and a deadly aim that provided the family table with a stable supply of fresh game. From the start, he wanted to be better than other men, and he set about doing it—in hunting as in baseball— without fanfare. All of the Radbourn men loved to hunt and fish—perhaps because, as the pitcher's nephew asserted many years later, they "didn't like people too well" and yearned to roam free of them. Radbourn's cousin Henry Radbourn was so determined to escape his fellow man that he fled to Montana, where he homesteaded on a ranch in the vast open spaces. One morning, when he staggered out of bed to relieve himself off the front porch, he saw a wisp of smoke on the distant horizon. "Damn," he muttered, scowling, "they're crowding in on me again!" There may have been an element of exaggeration in that family legend, because Henry was social enough to play for the Helena ball club, and even came into town from his dusty ranch one April afternoon in 1884 to talk baseball with the editor of the *Daily Independent*, informing him that he was "anxious for another crack at Butte," Helena's bitter rival for the territorial championship. Still, Henry's nephew had it right that the Radbourns were "neurotic, sort of" in their desire to escape into themselves.

Certainly, Charlie Radbourn came of age with an unusual fondness for the silent woods and fields and for the animals, wild and domesticated, that kept him company. Later in life, he kept a kennel of thoroughbred pointers that he carefully trained, delighting in their companionship during his many hours trooping about the countryside. "Radbourne's reserved, almost churlish disposition was never displayed toward his dogs. To them, there was no limit in his affection," wrote E. E. Pierson, one of the first writers to research his life. Charlie even seemed to feel affection, or at least humble respect, for the animals he hunted. Though he avidly tracked wild creatures, developing his skills as an expert marksman, he shot at them only when they were in motion, giving them a sporting chance to survive. On one occasion, young Radbourn captured a quail with a broken wing; he brought it home with him, rather than kill it as a spoil of the hunt. Tenderly he set the broken bone, nursed the bird back to health, and gave it to a friend, who kept it in a cage. When he passed by the cage, Radbourn liked to sing out to the bird, using the bobwhite call he had learned to imitate with eerie perfection during his hours in the echoing woods. "Without fail, the prisoner would respond," and "would flutter towards him as if desirous of showing its affection towards the man who had repaired the damaged pinion."

Charlie's schooling was perfunctory at best, brought to a swift end so that he could work to help support the family. His younger brother William went only as far as the third grade, and William's son Carroll doubted Charlie received more than two or three years of formal education. Unlike the doggedly self-taught Lincoln, Radbourn lacked the obsessive drive to overcome the limitations of a miserable country education. The census of 1870, taken when young Charlie was fifteen, noted that he could read but could not write. Nevertheless, when he applied himself to the avocation that would make him famous, Radbourn displayed a fierce will to distinguish himself that was highly reminiscent of his fellow prairie legend.

Radbourn never forgot where he came from. During the 1884 season, a man approached the great pitcher in a hotel lobby. "Gee, Old Hoss, ain't you ever going to tire out?" he asked. "Tire out?" Radbourn snapped at him. "Tire out tossing a little five-ounce ball for two hours a day? Man, I used to be a butcher. From 4 in the morning until 8 at night I knocked down steers with a 25-pound sledge. Tired of playing 2 hours a day for 10 times the money I got for 16 hours a day?" That was not a complaint; just an acknowledgment that life was hard and that men were supposed to shut up and bear it. Though he spent his youth smeared with blood and offal, knocking down many more steers than books, Charlie harbored no resentment against his father. He remained a homebody all his life, homesick while he was away, always yearning to get back to his siblings and parents. And while other ballplayers squandered their fortunes, Radbourn pinched pennies and scrupulously saved, stockpiling the pay from his first few years in the National League to buy his father a house on West Washington Street. When he wasn't busy bludgeoning cattle, Charlie tried his hand as a brakeman on the Indiana, Bloomington, and Western Railroad, a dangerous and physically draining job that involved running along the roofs of moving cars. But as the mania for a new sport raged throughout the Northwest during the 1860s and '70s, he began making better money doing something he genuinely loved—playing baseball.

"Ever since Charley was big enough to toss a ball his ability in handling the ball has attracted attention," the *Pantagraph* recounted in 1883. His earliest clippings were not particularly edifying, however. Radbourn began playing with Bloomington's superb amateur team in the mid-seventies, along with his cousin Henry, not yet gone to Montana. On the night of August 30, 1876, the eve of an important game against archrival Springfield, the twenty-one-year-old Radbourn was not to be found resting up at home; he was in a downtown saloon named Schausten's, getting seriously sloshed. The episode ended up in the paper as part of a scandalous story. Two gamblers named Ed Stahl and Jim Conners were in the hot, crowded bar that night, working to guarantee a big payoff the next day for their bets on Springfield, and when locals pointed out to them the players on the Bloomington team, the pair approached a tipsy Radbourn and offered him $25 to throw the game. "He does not deny that he may have said that he would take the money, but, being drunk, was not responsible for his words," the *Pantagraph* reported, which, however much it exonerated Radbourn as a cheater, hardly seemed a high recommendation for his character. At some point during the next several hours, Charlie and his cousin Henry sobered up enough to make it clear to the gamblers that they wanted nothing to do with selling out their teammates and their town. Still, when Springfield won the next day 4–1, rumors swept through the crowd that the gamblers had successfully "sugared" two other Bloomington players, a charge that caused "great excitement" near the backstop where gamblers congregated at the end of the game and on the town's streets that night, where many more men were angrily counting their losses.

The scandal, one of many signs that gamblers had infested baseball and were rapidly hollowing out its integrity, was not enough to destroy Radbourn's professional career. By 1877, the *Pantagraph* asserted, "Charley was decidedly the best pitcher in the state." His gritty will to excel and his exceptional timing and coordination were obvious to the trained eyes of baseball men, and in 1878, at twenty-three, he left home for the first time, going forty miles away to earn his living as a member of the new Reds of Peoria. With a population of twenty-seven thousand, the Illinois city was hardly a mighty metropolis, but it managed to draw the region's top talent to a team that, impressively, included four future major league players. The Reds played no set schedule, traveling instead from place to place like itinerant actors, riding in sooty trains and dusty carts, grabbing food when and where they could. They took on any and all comers, from ragtag town teams to major-league clubs, offering midwestern farmers and merchants a brief respite from tedium and drudgery. The club made little if any money, since travel costs gobbled up most of the proceeds generated by small crowds. But the experience made a better player of Radbourn, who in his silent manner studied the ways of baseball professionals. A strong hitter, he opened the season as a right fielder, but the highlight of his year was his appearance as a relief pitcher against the National League's Chicago club, after their big men pounded the starter out of the box. Though the Reds lost 9–0, Radbourn struck out five batters.

By the time the wandering Reds folded that summer, someone else had his eye on Radbourn. Ted Sullivan, whose nose for talent later won him jobs as a major-league manager and scout, was a short, peppery twenty-eight-year-old from County Clare, Ireland, and cofounder of the four-team Northwestern League, with franchises in Rockford, Illinois; Omaha, Nebraska; and Davenport and Dubuque, Iowa. From the start, he had resolved, shrewdly, to fill his Dubuque club, nicknamed the Rabbits, with Peoria's best players, who were little known because they had played in no league. His most serious rival was Rockford owner James McKee, who got the jump on him by stocking his team with top-level talent, including several members of the National League's defunct Milwaukee franchise. "Gentlemen, I have the strawberry shortcake team of the league," McKee boasted at the circuit's annual meeting, where his fellow baseball entrepreneurs, frantic to catch up, were anxiously thumbing through copies of the *Spalding Base Ball Guide* and the *New York Clipper*, looking for players to fill out their rosters. "My heart was throbbing for fear that somebody would mention my hidden treasure—namely Radbourne and the Peoria players; but no, they were looking to the East for men that had [high pitching and batting] averages," Sullivan recalled. At one point, McKee even asked him about Radbourn, but Sullivan managed to put him off. As soon as the meeting closed, Sullivan hightailed it to the railroad depot. "The train could not come fast enough to take me to Bloomington to see 'Rad' for to have lost him would have broken my heart," Sullivan recalled. As soon as the train wheezed and clanked to a stop at the station, he hustled to the Radbourn house, and was greeted by Charlie at the door. Radbourn seemed reluctant to leave his family again, but finally told the highly persuasive young manager, "Ted, I will go, but I have to get $75 a month."

The contract survives, showing the club misspelled his name, this time as "Radburn," while granting him his $75 each month—half of it on the first, half on the fifteenth—from mid-April to mid-October. Sullivan built a superb team loaded with future major leaguers. Yet even in that crowd, Radbourn quickly struck Sullivan as something special. He had a "defiant air" in the pitcher's box, not unlike that of heavyweight boxing champion John L. Sullivan when he climbed into the ring and stared down his opponent. "You can call it hypnotism, magnetism, or some other 'ism,' it was there just the same," the manager recalled. "He was like the mighty oak with a will power that would accomplish anything he would undertake. He had the endurance of an ox." By then, the outlines of the mature Radbourn had come into sharp focus. He was fiercely dedicated to his craft, focused on winning, strangely indifferent to vulgar applause. "There was little of the dress parade and show-off to Charlie," Sullivan observed. Already, he refused to warm up in front of the crowd to "show his form," preferring to "sneak away with his catcher to one side of the stand." Many times, Radbourn made Sullivan smile as they sat on the bench together, watching some Adonis show off his speed and curves for the ladies in the grandstand. "Look at him now," Radbourn muttered scornfully, "he's got everything, but when the game starts he'll get a colic."

Radbourn, determined in his quiet way to triumph over all the poseurs and pretenders, quickly emerged as the league's star pitcher, proving embarrassingly dominant. After he shamed Rockford's strawberry shortcake team by throwing an 8–0 shutout, some of its players loudly promised under Radbourn's hotel window that "they would settle his ambition as a pitcher"—presumably with violence—if he dared to show them up again. Radbourn, who had overheard the threat, went to bed that evening but could not stop the wheels from turning in his head. At midnight he got up, went to Sullivan's room, and banged on the door. When the squinting, sleepy-eyed manager opened it, Radbourn asked his permission to pitch all of the remaining games against the Rockford club, especially the ones played on their home field. "I thought it was a strange and novel request at that hour of the night, when he could have asked me in the morning, but that was Radbourn's way," Sullivan said. As the manager recalled, Radbourn shut out Rockford again the following day, and beat them the rest of the season, leading the Rabbits to the 1879 Northwestern League pennant. No one, it turned out, thwarted his ambition to be a top professional pitcher.

He proved so overpowering, in fact, that some spectators literally could not believe what they were seeing. In one game against a crack amateur club, Radbourn struck out batter after batter, snapping curveballs past them. As Sullivan recalled years later, the hometown umpire eventually stopped calling strikes, accusing Radbourn of pitching with a trick ball. He won anyway.

By then, the twenty-five-year-old pitcher had come to the attention of John P. Sage, president of the National League's Buffalo Club, nicknamed the Bisons. Sage signed him for the 1880 season for the princely salary of $750, $300 more than he had demanded from Dubuque. In three years, the grandson of an English gardener and the son of a butcher from Bath and Bloomington had worked his way up from hometown star to baseball's highest level. If he just performed to his ability, the big money he craved would be coming his way. Expected to share pitching duties with Jimmy "Pud" Galvin, the rookie impressed the club's young player-manager Sam Crane from the start. "He said very little, but was a hard worker. He had a square, firm chin and was evidently a youngster of firm determination," with "such broad shoulders that he appeared almost humpbacked," Crane recalled. The manager thought Radbourn was something like Galvin, compact and strong, though they had their physical differences. "Jimmy's bull neck sunk into his wide spread of shoulders like the head of a mud-turtle into its shell. Radbourne was cleaner built than Galvin, however—on smoother and less heavy lines, and I knew that he had the pushing power—the punch."

Baseball had not yet developed the costly machinery of spring training. The players got started in late March right in the chilly North, braving the remnants of winter. To shelter players from Buffalo's springtime sleet and snow, the Bisons, for example, rented a vast brick regimental armory in the city. Though its cavernous drill hall was spacious enough for throwing and running, it was far from ideal. "The armory was like an ice house, dark and gloomy," Crane remembered. Determined to prove himself to his bosses, Radbourn threw hard in the frosty room, day after day, clouds of his breath visible in the cold air, trying to ignore the pain that started radiating from his shoulder. Buffalo had no hot water or rubdowns available, and Radbourn kept his mouth shut, hoping to work through the hurt as he warmed up. It was a disastrous decision. He dealt himself a serious injury, ruining his effectiveness before the season even began. "I warned him and so did the more experienced Galvin, to 'go light,' but it seemed impossible to restrain his youthful exuberance," Crane remembered.

Desperate to nurse himself back to health, Radbourn played a few regular-season games in the outfield and at second base. But without a functioning shoulder, it was no use. Poorly performing players were a luxury few teams could afford, and after only six games, when Radbourn was hitting a pitiful .143, Crane had to break the bad news: Buffalo had released him. Radbourn took it without betraying emotion, though he bitterly resented the team for giving up on him. Now, far from rocketing to the top of his profession, he was heading home to face well-wishers and neighbors as an embarrassing failure, back to the reek of death and the screaming animals of his father's bloody trade, perhaps, having been deemed unsuitable for the big time. His family would get none of the money he had counted on earning. But when boarding a passenger car with his fellow nobodies bound for Illinois, while the steam engine hissed in anticipation of the journey, he turned to Crane and made a memorable vow. "I will show these Buffalo people this: I am a pitcher. You watch me."

It was not an idle threat. After slowly, doggedly rebuilding his strength, Radbourn rejoined amateur teams in the Bloomington area and finished the 1880 season in what Crane called "a perfect blaze of glory." By 1881, he was back in the National League, this time pitching for the Providence Grays, winning twenty-five games that year, then thirty-three the next, then forty-eight—all the time taking "especial delight in walloping the poor 'Bisons.'" Building on each success, he worked fervently, crafting new ways to beat hitters. "Radbourne was continually inventing some new delivery and trying to get control of it," recalled Harry Wright, his manager in 1882 and 1883. During that time, Radbourn introduced what was called a "dry spitter"—a knuckleball that fluttered to the plate and was brutally hard to hit (and catch).

With Providence, Radbourn quickly emerged as one of the game's greatest stars. In trying to capture Radbourn's greatness, Crane, like Sullivan, turned to a universal symbol of strength and endurance. "He was as strong and sturdy as an oak," Crane said, "the most willing worker of any pitcher who ever lived, and he was the idol of his fellow players, as well as of the fans in Providence and all over the circuit." On August 27, 1882, Radbourn ended one of the longest games in major league history, breaking an eighteen-inning scoreless tie against Detroit at the Messer Street Grounds by slamming a towering fly ball that cleared the left-field fence near the foul pole, giving him a home run and the Grays a 1–0 victory. For decades, aficionados regarded it as the greatest baseball game ever played. The 1883 season simply cemented his reputation as the best pitcher in the game.

But nothing Radbourn had ever done would compare with what he was about to do in 1884.

CHAPTER 3

Raging, Tearing, Booming

If Radbourn felt beat up at the end of the 1883 season, he had good reason. Professional baseball in the 1880s was not the pastoral game of myth—green, lovely, and languid—but a nasty, brutish, fast-paced affair, populated by profanity-spewing young men in dirt-smeared uniforms who had few qualms about using violence to get their way. One of them was a pitcher named Hugh Ignatius Daily, and he came close to killing Charlie Radbourn in 1883.

Daily, son of a laborer who had fled the potato famine in Ireland, was a scarred and bitter man, swarthy and scowling—"an inveterate growler," in the words of the *New York Herald*—and altogether a nasty piece of work even by the standards of 1880s baseball. A rangy, six-foot-two, hard-throwing right-hander for the pennant-contending Cleveland club, he possessed a wicked fastball and snapping curve—along with a propensity to cheat, in particular by stepping out of the pitcher's box, a six-by-four-foot flat rectangle that predated the mound. What really set Hugh apart, though, was a remarkable physical attribute: he played major-league ball without the benefit of two hands. His right arm was muscular, with a hand that gripped a ball or bat powerfully, but his left arm ended in a sawed-off stump, the result of a boyhood shooting accident that necessitated amputation. Daily survived in baseball by holding his bat halfway up, swinging with one hand, and by manipulating his stump, trapping the ball against it when fielding. Though he sheathed this wad of skin and bone in a protective chamois skin, all this pounding and chafing often made it tender and sore, which failed to improve his mood any. The press, reflecting nineteenth-century sensitivities about such matters, commonly referred to him as "One Arm" Daily.

During one game, One Arm chastised his catcher, a hard-boiled, hard-drinking Irishman named Tom Deasley, for returning the ball to him too fast. "Don't speed them so hard at me, Tom. Arch 'em down. Jest lob dose balls; dey crack against de stump of me arm, and give me a twitch," Daily cried out. Sometime later he motioned Deasley out to the box, presumably to discuss signs. While the enemy team looked on, hoping to pick off their signals, the pitcher asked Deasley to edge even closer. As Deasley leaned his head near the pitcher's shoulder, Daily brought his stump up in a flash, delivering Deasley a stinging, eye-watering blow in the chin. "After that visitation of Daly's [*sic*] stump to his face, Tom always took Daly's cue and 'arched 'em down,'" teammate Tom Brown recalled. Deasley, four inches shorter, many pounds lighter, and significantly saner than Daily, thought better of retaliating, even against a one-handed man.

In 1883, Daily was nursing a particular grudge against Radbourn for the crime of demonstrating he was the better pitcher. At the end of July, with Providence and Cleveland locked in a tense struggle for first place, Radbourn opened the series by throwing a sparkling no-hitter, the first and last of his career, embarrassing Cleveland in front of its home crowd, 8–0. It was very nearly a perfect game. "Only one man smelt first base," as one newspaperman put it, and that on an error. Cleveland evened up the series by winning the next game, but Providence took the third, to shove Cleveland back into second place, one-half game behind.

By then, Daily had seen enough. His moment for revenge came when Charlie strode to the plate in the fifth inning of the July 30 game, with Cleveland holding a narrow 3–2 edge. Staring at his nemesis, One Arm reared back, ran to the front of the pitcher's box, and fired a fastball at Radbourn. The ball slammed into Charlie's upper chest with horrific force, and he buckled over in pain. In short order, it "raised a lump on his chest," the *Cleveland Herald* reported. Though he almost never left a game he started, Radbourn was unable to go on. Radbourn could not even take first base; there was no penalty yet in the National League for hitting a batter with a pitch. Manager Harry Wright turned over the pitching duties to his latest acquisition, a twenty-year-old Californian named Charlie Sweeney. The kid quickly let loose a flood of four more runs, and that was that. Daily won the game, 7–2, thrusting Cleveland back into first place by one-half game. Worse for Providence, Radbourn—who might have been killed by the traumatic blow near the heart and neck—was too sore and stiff to play for days. The missile had done its work.

Bereft of Radbourn's iron arm, the Grays lost their next games, at Buffalo, by scores of 3–1, 9–2, and 16–11. "Four straight defeats is a bitter pill," the *Providence Evening Press* lamented, adding sarcastically: "How much we are indebted to Mr. Daly [*sic*] for these disgraceful defeats at Buffalo, by reason of his disabling Radbourn, of course cannot be exactly known." The Grays proceeded to lose eight straight games—a severe blow in a ninety-eight-game schedule. That they survived in the race at all was a testament to the will and endurance of Radbourn, who returned to the lineup as soon as he could move, and played harder than ever.

As harsh as it was, professional baseball merely mirrored the tough, aggressive United States that was emerging in the 1880s, rising from the obscene slaughter of the Civil War and the tenacious depression that followed it. The world had never seen anything quite like this crude and pugnacious country, whose self-made men of industry readily embraced the popular philosophy, drawn from Darwin's discoveries, that life was a ceaseless struggle, and only the fittest could survive.

"The old nations of the earth creep on at a snail's pace," steel magnate Andrew Carnegie observed; "the Republic thunders past with the rush of the express train." That was a fitting image, for railroad barons, using Carnegie's steel, were laying track across the continent at an astonishing pace, never since matched, moving more people and goods faster than ever before. The railroads changed just about everything: where people worked, what they ate and wore and read, even how they perceived time and space. Once-isolated villages were now linked to the great wide world, and the gentle rhythms that had marked rural life for centuries were forever interrupted. The telegraph, its wires strung alongside railroad tracks, sent the latest news and business decisions flying from one end of the country to the other, making great corporations and combines possible. It also spread baseball game results, which could now be posted within minutes on distant ballpark scoreboards and, within hours, in stories and box scores in newspapers, run off by the thousands on high-speed presses. In fact, major-league baseball was possible only because of railroads, which let clubs from big, far-flung cities play each other according to a reliable schedule.

Bell's amazing telephone, carrying voices to homes and businesses along metal wires, was starting to transform daily life, as growing numbers of Americans hooked into the network. In 1883, for the first time, phone lines linked the great business centers of Chicago and New York. By then, many New York buildings were lit with Thomas Alva Edison's miraculous incandescent electric bulbs. Up north in Rochester, George Eastman had invented a process for manufacturing rolls of camera film, which would eventually replace bulky photographic plates. Another Rochester man, George Selden, had filed a patent for an automobile that would run on an internal combustion engine. The modern world was unfolding before Americans' astonished eyes.

That brash spirit of achievement had its dark side, of course. Shrewd leaders of industry were dedicated to destroying their competitors, not only by inventing the modern business world through corporations, constant streamlining of operations, and exploitation of information technology but also by manipulating stock prices, restraining trade, and buying up corrupt legislatures.

From the perspective of the average person, the United States had metamorphosed almost overnight into a weird and wondrous place. Between 1860 and 1880, the population exploded by a staggering 60 percent, soaring to 50 million people. Foreigners swarmed in, of course, but millions of American-born men and women were also on the move. Sick of the poverty and dreary toil of rural life, they were flocking to cities. Until the mid-nineteenth century, the vast majority of Americans had lived on farms or in placid little towns, where the pace of life was slow and behavior was constrained by habit and the prying eyes of neighbors. In 1830, the United States had only ten communities with more than 19,000 residents. By 1880, the number had exploded tenfold—and the largest, New York, had boomed from 200,000 to 1.2 million souls.

This strange new America—urban America, with its noise and bustle, its ferocious competition and crime, its diverse cultures, its opportunities for risqué behavior with anonymity, and its ever-changing fashions, novelties, and entertainment—thrilled and amazed the newcomers. Amid the infernal racket of traffic, horse-drawn buses crammed with people clattered over the pavement as fares jumped on and off without waiting for the driver to stop. Garish posters lured passersby to minstrel shows and sporting events. Street vendors, inured to the stink of rotting garbage, horse piss, and manure, worked every corner, shouting their wares to pedestrians. Lunchrooms were everywhere, with men inside wolfing down their food and hustling back to work.

Because the cities attracted both rich and poor, they displayed towering disparities, which some took to be symptomatic of the age's cruel indifference to all but the almighty dollar. Out on the streets, filthy and neglected children begged for coins and homeless vagabonds hawked penny newspapers as handsome carriages rolled by. Stifling tenements, wooden death traps, stood not far from the brick and granite mansions of the nouveau riche. City dwellers complained of speeding drivers, filthy streets, sky-high rents and taxes, rapacious pickpockets and rip-off artists, and corrupt police officers paid off to ignore predators.

As its standard of living soared, America became, in the eyes of its critics, crass and shallow. Dandies frittered away good money on tight striped pants and handsome jackets, and fashion-conscious ladies, rejecting the simpler ways of their mothers, indulged themselves in expensive boots, bustles, and bright dresses of silk or satin. Divorce was on the rise, and families disintegrated, as women increasingly earned money on their own, no longer relying solely on men for support. Prostitutes by the thousands worked city sidewalks, brazenly taking perfect strangers by the arm and saying sweetly, "Charlie, how are you?" or "Where are you going?" Saloons reeking of tobacco juice, sweat, and stale beer were packed every night with drunken men and painted whores. Some particularly dubious establishments offered sex shows in the back, for a fee, sometimes through a peephole.

Crime flourished, not only in the dark alleys and red-light districts, but also in the nation's city halls and capitol buildings, where it often seemed that America's celebrated democracy had been instituted mainly for the purpose of extracting bribes, providing jobs for henchmen, and defrauding the citizenry. Elections were stolen—even at the highest level, many asserted, as in 1876, when the so-called fraud of the century put the apparent loser, Rutherford B. Hayes, in the White House. Racism flourished, too, as white Americans—especially in the defeated but defiant South—used threats and violence to turn back the gains millions of blacks had made after the Civil War. "The moral atmosphere is more than tainted, it is rotten," said Frederick Douglass, the nation's foremost African American leader and voice of conscience. "Avarice, duplicity, falsehood, corruption, servility, fawning and trickery of all kinds, confront us at every turn." And no one seemed to have any power to stop it.

Meanwhile, city dwellers, keen for diversion and excitement, had fallen in love with a spectator sport that in many ways perfectly embodied America's violent, thrill-seeking, winner-take-all culture.

It began, gently enough, with an age-old children's game that was played under any number of rules, often improvised on the spot, involving the simplest of sporting goods: a stick for a bat, a hand-wrapped ball, and rocks or posts that could be deemed bases. When the Puritans crossed the ocean to America in the early 1660s, the English culture they brought with them included such games. Fellows from close-knit communities along the Atlantic seaboard enjoyed a variation called "town ball"—aptly named, since a fair proportion of a town gathered to play it, with twelve to twenty men on a side. Another variant was called "base ball"—as in *A Little Pretty Pocket Book*, a children's book first published in London in 1744. It featured a delightful little poem, "Base-Ball," as apt a description of the game's charm as was ever penned:

> The *Ball* once struck off,
> Away flies the *Boy*
> To the next destin'd Post
> And then Home with Joy.

Jane Austen, in her 1803 novel *Northanger Abbey*, named "base ball" as one of the pleasures that her headstrong teenage protagonist preferred over books.

During the 1830s and '40s, young white-collar urban Americans—clerks, merchants, brokers, doctors, bank employees, and insurance salesmen, who finally had the time and money for leisure pursuits—adopted the children's game and reshaped it to their own ends, molding it into a respectable adult escape. They gave it a formal structure through rules, and formed social clubs so that they could play it regularly, first against each other and, in later years, in matches with other clubs, often as an excuse to hold extravagant postgame banquets. The most famous of these early organizations, the Knickerbocker Club of New York City, had an unusually well-thought-out set of rules, which worked so well that it became standard, the basis for the modern game.

Decades before golf became an American addiction, baseball was a way for young men to build business and social contacts while enjoying fun and exercise on the freshly mowed fields in and around their cities. It was originally prized for its powers to restore the harried man, as an oasis of order and calm in a jittery society, a respite from the grinding tension of America's pitiless, money-grubbing culture. "Let us go forth awhile, and get better air in our lungs. Let us leave our close rooms. . . . The game of ball is glorious," wrote Walt Whitman, who had become acquainted with the sport in the 1840s as a Brooklyn journalist. "I see great things in baseball; it's our game—the American game. It will take our people out of doors, fill them with oxygen, give them a larger physical stoicism. Tend to relieve us from being a nervous, dyspeptic set, repair these losses and be a blessing to us."

In the 1850s, a visitor to the Elysian Fields, a popular pleasure resort in Hoboken, New Jersey, observed weary working people spread out on the grass, enjoying an hour's rest, "to them the highest happiness," from "the week's ceaseless toil." And near them, "the centre of the lawn has been marked out into a magnificent ball ground, and two parties of rollicking, joyous young men are engaged in that excellent and health-imparting sport, base ball. They are without hats, coats or waistcoats, and their well-knit forms, and elastic movements, as they bound after the bounding ball, furnish gratifying evidence that there are still classes of young men among us as calculated to preserve the race from degenerating." The vibrant game caught on, spread to the raw Midwest, to the South and all the way to the Pacific Coast—and, by the late 1860s, was in Americans' blood, part of their lives and lore, their poetry and songs. It was already called the National Pastime.

Meanwhile, amateur clubs had made a fascinating discovery: Americans were willing to part with cash to watch young men play this bat-and-ball game exceptionally well. And since winning teams reaped more money than losers, helping to defray club costs while swelling members' pride, managers began securing the best players by paying for them. Such hiring had to be done furtively at first, since it violated clubs' rules and the established code of gentlemanly conduct. But once professionals were in, the amateur gentlemen quickly found themselves tossed from the lineup. And with money now at stake, this gentle, slow-paced pastime became as nervous, rushed, violent, and ruthless as the society at large. Brash young men fought hard for the relatively few jobs available. In only a few years, adjustments to the rules dramatically speeded up play. Swift, deadly throwing entered the game. Bloody injuries became common. By 1881, the *New York Times* noticed, it had become "rather more dangerous to play base-ball than to fill lighted kerosene lamps."

Whitman spoke for many when he mourned the infiltration of cutthroat competition into his lung-expanding, restorative "American game." The shift to brutality and aggression horrified him, as did the transformation of pitching: from the old style of tossing, giving batters a fair chance to hit, to the new approach of using curveballs, mixed speeds, and other subterfuges to bamboozle the hitter. "The wolf, the snake, the cur, the sneak, all seem entered into the modern sportsman," Whitman lamented. Harvard University president Charles William Eliot fully shared the dismay of the good gray poet. "I think base ball is a wretched game," he confessed to a reporter. "I call it one of the worst games, although I know it is called the American national game." In an 1884 piece, the *Sporting Life*, a popular weekly, offered a checklist of the acts of "low trickery" that had come to be employed by professional ballplayers, including "slyly cutting the ball to have it changed, tripping up base runners, willfully colliding with fielders to make them commit errors, hiding the ball, and other specially mean tricks of the kind characteristic of corner lot loafers in their ball games." Good old-fashioned American sportsmanship seemed a thing of the past—in baseball as in business and politics. "Injuries were often intentionally inflicted," said Connie

Mack of his playing days in the 1880s, "and there was rarely a player on one team who would say a good word of a man on a rival nine."

But the strategic use of violence and guile only piqued the interest of ticket-buying Americans. The game seemed a perfect expression of their late nineteenth-century culture, in its brilliant interplay between individual achievement and teamwork; in the increasingly specialized skills of its participants; in its ready translation into fascinating, complex statistics; in its symbiotic relationship with a sensationalistic press; in its strong link to gambling; and, to some extent, surely, in its cheating and aggression. Before the decade was out, Mark Twain described baseball, only half in jest, as the perfect image of 1880s America, "the very symbol, the outward and visible expression of the drive, and push, and rush and struggle of the raging, tearing, booming nineteenth century!"

Ballplayers knew full well what miseries they risked by playing such a game. There was little protective equipment—no batting helmets, no batting gloves, not even fielding gloves, which did not come into universal use until the 1890s. Fielders caught the hard ball *barehanded*—taking stinging, hard throws and spearing hot line drives with their unprotected or, as they put it, "meat" hands. Everybody knew that was a hazardous business. "The ball is a combination of cast iron and India rubber nearly as hard as a cannon ball, and propelled as rapidly," one writer observed in 1884, only half joking. "To occupy the grand stand of a base ball park is a dangerous proceeding, while the players take the ball and their lives in their hands at the same time." In 1882, a thrown ball shattered the left forefinger of Phillies shortstop Mike Moynahan, and the mangled digit had to be amputated at the first joint. Moynahan, undeterred by the loss, returned to the game as soon as the stump healed over.

The barehanded outfielders in the 1880s were every bit as good as the top fielders of the twentieth century, Chicago sportswriter Byron E. Clarke asserted, with this major difference: "they got hurt more and were always getting their fingers broken." Cliff Carroll, the graceful left fielder of the Providence club from 1882 through 1886, displayed his mauled and misshapen hands in a 1911 newspaper photo, under the heading "FAMOUS

NATIONAL LEAGUER CARRIES PROOF OF LONG CAREER ON DIAMOND." Bare-handed play made for a nerve-rattling brand of baseball, since no one could feel certain that a sprinting fielder would hold on to a spinning fly ball or a wicked liner.

To survive in baseball in that era, professionals needed more than talent. Cunning and fearlessness were prerequisites. Most club owners limited their rosters to twelve or thirteen players, about all they could afford on the slim profits that went with drawing two thousand customers per game. If a man was not up to the intimidating task of standing at the plate while fastballs whistled past his unprotected head, or catching blazing line drives with his bare hands, or making quick decisions on the fly, he was liable to be abruptly replaced. So men played with abandon, suffering constant scrapes and bruises and subjecting themselves to broken bones, torn ligaments, and gashes from shoe spikes. A long season of it placed a severe strain on even the most resilient players. Most were addicts of what they called "fruit cake," or chewing tobacco, and they spat streams of brown spit everywhere while fueling themselves on nicotine, which helped to relieve pain. The bitter, prematurely aged faces that stare out from early team photos and baseball cards bespeak the stress and physical toll men endured in that profession.

Like most working Americans, players had no union and thus few protections against the will of management. They were "owned" by their club, blocked from signing with a team willing to pay them more. If they attempted to break their contract or otherwise failed to toe the line, they could be placed on the owners' dreaded blacklist and effectively banished for life. If an injury waylaid them, management could, and often did, halt their pay, as Cleveland center fielder Al Hall discovered when he shattered his leg in a ghastly collision with teammate Pete Hotaling on May 13, 1880. Hall received the courtesy of an ambulance ride to Cincinnati Hospital but from then on was on his own, without salary or medical insurance. He never played again, and died in a Pennsylvania insane asylum five years later. From the owners' perspective, a man who could not play deserved no pay.

No matter how long a player served his team, he received no pension and was on his own once the cheering stopped. Some ballplayers were educated in college or trades and could look forward to some sort of career after baseball. Some had the native sense to set aside part of their money

for the harsh world that awaited them. But all too many lacked both education and sense, blowing everything they earned, and more, on women and
drink while the going was good. The *New York Times*, among others, was
distinctly unimpressed, describing the typical ballplayer as a "worthless, dissipated gladiator; not much above the professional pugilist in morality and
respectability." Boisterous and arrogant, clueless about how to behave in
polite company, ballplayers were "more or less despised and looked down
upon," recalled Sam Crane. "They graduated from the 'dump' and the big
salaries they received gave them an altogether exaggerated opinion of their
own importance." Mothers were horrified when their sons revealed a burning ambition to join these traveling hooligans. The courtly Connie Mack
helped make baseball respectable and was an American icon by the time
he retired as manager of the Philadelphia Athletics in 1950, but when he
got his start in the 1880s some of his higher-toned neighbors considered it a
step *down* for an Irish immigrant's son and shoe factory worker to become a
professional ballplayer. "Baseball was mighty glamorous and exciting to me,"
he remembered, "but there is no use in blinking at the fact that at that time
the game was thought, by solid, respectable people, to be only one degree
above grand larceny, arson and mayhem, and those who engaged in it were
beneath the notice of decent society."

However dishonorable and dangerous this profession was, young men
struggled to get into it, because the alternatives were often even less pleasant. They hailed from the hard-luck farms of the Midwest, the claustropho-
bic coal mines of western Pennsylvania, the sweatshops of New England,
the festering slums of New York and Philadelphia and San Francisco. They
were all too aware that their fellow workingmen frequently ended up smothered, crushed, or horribly mutilated in industrial accidents—some 35,000
Americans killed and 536,000 injured each year, on average, from 1880 to
1900, by one estimate. Daily newspapers were filled with stories of on-the-
job horrors—severed fingers and hands, scalding burns, and cracked skulls.
There was no safety net for the injured or the poor, other than meager
handouts by local churches or by corrupt politicians and gang bosses who
expected some favor in return. Those lucky enough to avoid injury on the
job might put in ten or even twelve hours a day in a factory doing tiresome,
repetitive tasks that made their neck, arms, and back ache, or outdoors per-

forming hard labor such as digging ditches, carting bricks, or laying rail, often under a blazing sun. Construction jobs in the cold, wind, and ice were even worse—though a man felt fortunate to get any work at all in winter, the season of dread and starvation.

With the money they earned, blue-collar workers could do little more than survive. In 1880, a long, hard day's work earned a farm laborer a pittance, an average of $1.31. Blacksmiths made $2.28 per day, on average; carpenters, $2.42; masons, $2.79; printers, $2.18; woolen-mill operatives, $1.24; shoemakers, $1.76. By those standards, a ballplayer's salary of $1,000 to $2,000 a year—roughly $10 to $20 per game—was princely. But it was not just the money that drew young men to baseball. Decent society might disparage the profession, but there were thousands of Americans who keenly appreciated the talent, guts, and artistry required to survive at the game's highest level. The sport offered many men born into the working class their only means of rising above the common herd, of winning respect in a money-obsessed society. Fastidious mothers, college presidents, and snobby editors at the *Times* might view a professional ballplayer with nothing but disdain, but, as the *Buffalo Commercial Advertiser* observed, the "small boy worships him, the young girls dote on him, and his friends and neighbors look upon him as immense, perfectly elegant, the howlingest kind of a swell."

Baseball in the 1880s was, in its essence, already the game we know. The marvelous, magical mathematics were set in place: ninety feet between the bases, nine innings, nine men in the field, each taking his turn at bat, three outs to a side, three strikes and you're out.

The game already centered on its compelling war-within-a-war: the test of wills between the pitcher and the batter. Like his counterpart today, the 1884 pitcher relied mostly on a hard-thrown ball to get the better of his opponent. But, just as now, he needed more than raw power to be effective; he had to confuse the hitter with curveballs and sliders, and with a confounding mixture of speeds and locations. The pitcher asserted his dominance by firing high, hard fastballs to brush back any hitter brazen enough to crowd the plate or get too comfortable. He looked runners back to the bag, guarding against stolen bases. Ballplayers already knew how to steal bases by getting a jump on the pitcher's motion, and to slide to evade the tag. Hitters carefully studied the man with the ball, forming educated guesses about what kind of pitch he would throw next, and swinging hard for it. They had learned how to hit to the opposite field, to sacrifice themselves with ground balls in order to move runners along, and to employ the hit-and-run play. Fielders backed each other up, threw to the cutoff man, and shifted to match the strengths of hitters. Baseball called for top physical skills—keen eyesight, strength, coordination, and speed—but it also demanded the ability to think under pressure. The basics, in short, were well established by 1884.

In some ways, though, the game looked startlingly different from the modern version. Notably, the pitcher worked from a rectangular box, its front edge only fifty feet from home plate, rather than from today's raised mound with its rubber slab in the middle, sixty feet six inches from the plate (part of the game since 1893). Home plate was square, positioned like a diamond, its bottom two sides tucked against the baselines, its top two sides forming a point toward the pitcher. The modern five-sided home plate—designed to make it easier for umpires to read strikes—waited until 1901. A pregame flip of a coin gave the winning captain the choice of whether to bat first or last, instead of today's practice of having the visitors bat first.

As long as he remained within his box, the 1884 pitcher could take a running start and heave the ball toward the batter, who had no batting helmet to protect him and precious little time to decide whether to swing, hold up, or hit the dirt. "The pitcher would turn his back and take a hop, skip and jump, swinging his hand below his hip, in a sort of underhand delivery," Connie Mack recalled. "But . . . that ball came mighty fast, especially with all the momentum worked up by the hop, step and jump behind it." John M. Ward, a star player who was himself traumatized by being struck by a pitch, wrote about how terrifying it could be to stand in at the plate that close to the man throwing the ball. "The batter who has once been hit hard—and all of them have—will never quite forget the occurrence, and will forever after have the respect for the ball that a burned child has for the fire," he wrote. One of Ward's former teammates had been raked on the head with a fastball that left a long, ragged scar he would carry for the rest of his days. "An inch lower," Ward noted, "and the blow might have cost him his life." But a batter could not afford to think of such things at the plate. "It is absolutely necessary . . . to first conquer one's self, to fight down fear and forget everything except that the ball must be hit."

Foul balls did not yet count as strikes; the National League did not start penalizing hitters for foul balls until 1901, and the American League two years later. That made life harder for 1880s pitchers, Ward recalled, "because the batsman could stand and pound away until the man in the box became exhausted," without a strike being called. "I remember many occasions when the man at bat had fouled five or six times—in the good old days—and I've seen tired pitchers grit their teeth and keep putting 'em over."

Pitchers also had to deal with *two* strike zones—one between the shoulders and belt, and one between the belt and knees. A batter stated his preference when he came to the plate—the zone that played to his strengths as a hitter—and the umpire adjusted accordingly. The umpire thus might begin the game with a cry of "Striker-up! Low Ball! Play!" Pitchers needed pinpoint control to thread that needle. (In 1887, a single zone between the chest and knees finally replaced the two.) Only one umpire worked each game, creating plenty of opportunities for crafty players to cheat—and supplying a very lonely target for belligerent players and spectators.

In most cases, only two men split pitching duties for a team, rather than today's eleven or twelve. Under the rules of the time, substitutions could not be made once a game began, except in the case of debilitating injury. So it was generally a good idea to stow away the second pitcher in the starting lineup, usually playing in the outfield, in case the starter weakened and could not go on. Pitchers thus were expected to be good batters and skilled fielders as well as excellent throwers. Radbourn, for example, was a hard hitter who typically batted fourth in the Grays lineup. In 1884, in addition to pitching, Charlie played in the outfield and at first base, second base, and even shortstop. In the decades that followed, as rosters expanded and baseball amended its rules to permit midgame substitutions, pitchers became mere throwing specialists, weak hitters good for little more than bunting, and certainly incapable of filling in at such a tricky position as shortstop. But baseball fanatics long remembered the tough, well-rounded athlete who pitched in the 1880s—"a fierce-eyed, big-mustached warhorse" who won at least as many games as pitchers did decades later, "fielded better, and could hit right up with the other fellows, besides filling in at three or four other positions in the time of need." That description, penned by sportswriter William A. Phelon in 1914, fit Radbourn to a T. Nonetheless, pitchers were expected to finish the games they started, and players and the public considered it something of a humiliation for a man to surrender his place midway into the contest.

Radbourn had some advantages over his modern counterparts. Pitchers threw from a point closer to home plate and were therefore more intimidating. The baseball was harder to drive for distance—it had a hard rubber center rather than today's light, springy cork one—and smart pitchers could let up at times, since a batter was unlikely to blast a three-run homer. Outfielders played remarkably shallow by modern standards, so much so that a hitter who plunked the ball in front of the right fielder faced the distinct danger of being thrown out at first. Even so, a pitcher could not let up too much. Professional hitters could do serious damage, and home runs over the distant fences were not unknown.

Hitters used long, heavy clubs that they often purchased themselves, and when it was their turn to hit they pulled their own bat from a tall wooden box kept at the end of the bench. In 1884, the best hitter of the American Association's Louisville club, Pete Browning, paid a visit to a local woodshop run by J. F. Hillerich, who specialized in crafting stair railings, porch columns, and butter churns, to see about getting a new bat. Hillerich fashioned him one by hand. When Browning collected three hits with it, legend holds, he returned for more, bringing his teammates. It all led to Hillerich and Bradsby, the company that has sold more than a hundred million bats since Browning paid his fateful visit—its most famous line being the Louisville Slugger, supposedly named after Pete. Similarly, Grays batters in 1884 patronized a busy woodshop at 41 Harrison Street in Providence, not far from the park. The owner made them big, thirty-five-inch-long ash clubs painted black at the end of the barrel and stamped with his name: Burlingame.

Because premium-quality baseballs were an expensive item ($1.50 apiece, retail), with a limited supply provided by the league, a single ball was supposed to suffice for an entire game. A spectator who caught a foul ball was obliged to toss it back to the playing field immediately, lest a player, usher, or hired policeman wrestle it away from him. Neighborhood boys knew that they would be gladly waved into the ballpark for free for returning any ball hit out. Even the rules made much of conserving precious baseballs. Umpires were required to wait a full *five minutes* when a ball was lost before resuming play—just in case somebody turned up with it. Rhode Island was so small, some people joked, that a ball hit out of the Messer Street Grounds was liable to be knocked out of the state, "and the play is delayed until extradition papers can be obtained from the Governor." In 1884, the Boston Unions hit on the bright idea of employing *two* baseballs per game. When one ball was hit over the fence, the second could be immediately put into play until the first one was returned. "Tedious delays are thus avoided," the *Sporting Life* enthused. This was considered a radical innovation.

A baseball that had been pounded and abused all afternoon certainly added to the challenge of hitting and fielding. In the eighth inning of a rain-soaked exhibition contest between Cleveland and the Metropolitans of New York in August 1882, for example, the ball turned into a wobbling oval of mush every time it was hit high in the air. Even when it ripped open in the ninth inning, the umpire refused to replace it, per the rules, until the half inning was over. On another soggy afternoon in August 1880, before a paid attendance of ninety-one in an official National League game, Buffalo's Pud Galvin retired one Worcester batter after another, aided by a ball that grew mushier and mushier, until by the end it was, in the words of one account, like "a leather bag filled with jelly." It made a "spatty" sound when it fell into a fielder's hands—something, the reporter noted, like what you would hear "if a flap-jack or mud-pie had fallen from a height on some hard, flat substance." Naturally, the Worcester batters found it virtually impossible to drive the jelly bag out of the infield. Galvin that day secured the first of his two major-league no-hitters—a mighty feat that would be duly engraved on his Hall of Fame plaque in Cooperstown, with no mention of the sodden circumstances. Though batting last had its strategic advantages, captains who won the pregame coin flip sometimes elected to hit first simply because the ball was harder at the beginning of the game, and easier to drive for distance.

If a beat-up baseball helped pitchers, so too did the starting time of games—late in the afternoon, at 3:30 or 4:00 p.m., to accommodate businessmen looking for an invigorating diversion at the end of a tough workday before trudging home to the family. Since there were no ballpark lights yet, the arrival of dusk made it difficult—sometime dangerously so—for the hitter to see a ball turned nearly black with accumulated dirt, grass stains, and tobacco juice.

But such advantages weighed little against the one massive disadvantage for a pitcher in the 1880s: a punishing workload that all but killed his arm. A top man might well start more than half of the games his team played, and once he started, he was expected to pitch all the way through the ninth, or even on into extra innings. Radbourn, for instance, completed sixty-six of his sixty-eight starts in 1883; Pud Galvin finished seventy-two of seventy-five. Those thousands of fastballs and hard curves placed an agonizing strain on a man's arm. Under such punishment, many young pitchers lasted only two or three seasons, quickly stripping their gears beyond hope of repair, since there was no reconstructive surgery available. Owners found it cheaper to discard a used-up man and sign a new one than to protect a loyal veteran by carrying extra arms on the roster.

Providence, for instance, had to wonder how much longer Charles Radbourn could go on. For all his success, he had thrown a mountain of pitches between 1881 and 1883, working in more than 1,400 innings during those three years, 632 of them in 1883 alone. (Today, 200 innings a season is considered a grueling workload.) Radbourn was nearing the end of the standard life of a big-league pitcher, approaching the point of becoming just another old hoss past his prime, one who could expect to be, like the four-legged variety, worked until he dropped.

Fortunately for the Providence club, if not for Old Hoss, there was a fresher and stronger arm on the roster, a young pitcher who was every bit as good as Radbourn, just waiting to take over.

Lucky Man

In January 1884, the new manager of the Providence club, an enterprising New Englander named Frank Bancroft, decided to make a quick trip south, to attend to some business before spring training got under way. Wishing to travel in style, he booked a stateroom on the six-year-old, 2,200-ton, 275-foot-long luxury steamer *City of Columbus*, which departed from Boston's Nickerson's Wharf at 3:00 p.m. on Thursday, January 17. Some eighty-seven passengers were aboard, many of them well-to-do Bostonians eager to escape frigid New England for a warm vacation in Savannah, Georgia, and they spent a pleasant first night at sea smoking and playing cards in the ship's cozy, well-appointed public rooms, despite choppy seas, a rising wind, and bitter cold outside.

But at 3:45 a.m., after the captain had gone below to get some rest, leaving the wheel to his second mate, something went horribly wrong. Passing around the cliffs of Gay Head, on the island of Martha's Vineyard, the steamer smashed into a ledge of jagged submerged rocks, known as Devil's Ridge, and stuck. The captain, rushing from his room, hastily roused the passengers from below and was explaining to them their predicament when water rushed into the cabin, forcing them to the main deck. There, a big wave crashed over the rapidly sinking steamer, sweeping scores of shrieking men, women, and children out to sea, where they drowned or quickly perished of exposure. A couple of dozen men managed to climb onto the ice-encrusted rigging, shivering and clinging desperately for life, while they watched their fellow passengers die. The victims' wailing cries for help, drowned out by crashing breakers, went unheeded.

It is likely the Grays' new manager would have perished along with the 103 passengers and crew lost. But Frank Bancroft was "proverbially a lucky man," in the words of the *Sporting Life*. At the eleventh hour, the manager changed his mind about the trip and canceled his stateroom, deciding to remain in Boston. Instead of going down with the ship, Bancroft enjoyed a busy and profitable winter, digging through a mound of personal business and getting ready for the 1884 season. Frank was a born Yankee—shrewd, addicted to work, incessantly angling for money, and adept at driving a very hard bargain. A seasoned National League manager, he knew how to assess talent, how to promote a team, how to keep churlish investors happy, how to charm members of the press with funny baseball stories, and how to make a good deal of money in a business where profit margins were typically narrow to nonexistent.

Still, it was unclear whether he knew how to coax better performance out of the Grays than Harry Wright, already a legendary manager who was heading off to run the Philadelphia club. It was Wright who had pieced together most of this outstanding Providence lineup and had very nearly captured pennants with it in 1882 and 1883. Harry had done a masterly job, in particular, of keeping Charlie Radbourn producing at or near his peak. Now it was Bancroft's turn to handle the moody veteran, and the new manager probably feared the worst, given the plan he was turning over in his head that winter. Bancroft intended to radically restructure the Grays' pitching rotation, greatly reducing the prominence of the proud competitor who was the team's highest-paid player.

Cheating death might seem like enough of a lucky break for any one man in one winter, but Bancroft was only getting started. Soon after the *Columbus* sank, he won a lottery, taking home the handsome sum of $250—about $5,900 in today's inflated currency. Meanwhile, Bancroft was preparing to cash in on an entertainment craze sweeping America. That February 11, he and his brother Julius proudly opened their indoor roller-skating rink, the Adelphi, in his adopted city of New Bedford, Massachusetts, thirty miles east of Providence. Thanks to Bancroft's influence, the Adelphi quickly attracted celebrities—star ballplayers Harry Stovey, Charlie Buffinton, and

Paul Hines, among others—looking for a fun way to stay in shape during the cold months and flirt with pretty young women who might need a steadying arm. Fond of publicity stunts, Bancroft spoke about hosting a baseball game played on roller skates before the winter was out.

He had other schemes afoot. In his contract negotiations with the Grays, Bancroft had obtained the scorecard concession at the Providence grounds, and he immediately set about boosting sales by shifting to a new and more beautiful card, to be designed and printed by the Strobridge Lithograph Co. of Cincinnati, famous for its dazzling, color-drenched circus posters. Each card was to be adorned with a sketch of a Providence player, rotated throughout the season until every Grays player had been featured. As it turned out, the public loved them—in a sense, early baseball cards—deeming them "works of art," recalled William D. Perrin, a Providence *Evening Bulletin* reporter who zealously collected the full set as a lad. "Many Providence people kept the entire collection," Perrin noted, but "the thief of time, or some other variety of robber, broke in and took away the prized possession" of the reporter himself, who still lamented their loss forty years later.

While beefing up his own bank account during the off-season, Bancroft worked dutifully on schemes to fill his employer's coffers. He partnered with the Providence and Worcester Railroad to help boost attendance on Wednesdays and Saturdays, arranging with P & W agents to sell coupons at depots along the line good for both fares and entry to the ballpark. He toiled for hours, hunched over a well-worn copy of the National League schedule, making detailed arrangements to plug up open days with exhibition games against minor-league and local clubs—an approach that left players exhausted but swelled the owners' profit margin.

That was the bottom line of the business called baseball, after all, and that was Frank Bancroft's hallmark. He got along with his men, all in all, and generally kept them focused on winning, but he was most admired in baseball circles for his knack of building teams on a tight budget, cramming games into already crowded schedules, and raking in money. The *Sporting Life*, in profiling baseball's top managers in January 1884, called him "the most successful manager in the business"—with the emphasis on business. While the great Harry Wright concentrated on disciplining and training his players, "Bancroft thinks of nothing but the dollars and cents." Indeed, he delegated most of the on-field strategy to his team captain, leaving himself free to focus on financial matters. "In other words," the *Sporting Life* explained, "he looks upon a base ball nine as though it were the same thing as a minstrel or theatrical company, who had no purpose in life but to 'make money,' and generally Bancroft accomplishes the latter purposes." He had, indeed, managed theatrical events, as well, including Sunday concerts at the Grand Opera House, in New Bedford. The "New Bedford Yankee," the *Detroit News* observed, was "as 'slick' as they make 'em."

In his role as manager, Bancroft slogged away from dawn until late night, handling endless tedious details, placating club directors, making travel connections, herding players on and off trains with one eye on their baggage, or bending over a desk in his hotel room by gaslight, adding and subtracting rows of numbers, arranging for exhibition games, and corresponding with insiders to obtain the latest information about promising prospects. The exhausting days took their toll. Though only thirty-seven at the start of the 1884 season, Bancroft looked like a man well advanced into middle age. Of average height, he had a long, pale, gaunt face, with beady, bright eyes but drooping lids, thinning hair, and a ridiculously bushy brown mustache that swept over his mouth like a miniature Niagara Falls. Posing for a photograph alongside his players—rail-thin and ramrod straight in his light derby hat, high collar, and conservative dark suit, one hand thrust between the buttons on his narrow chest like some factory-town Napoleon— he seemed more like a fretful clergyman than a commanding leader. But his intelligence, his baseball savvy, his innate decency, and his ability to get things done earned him the respect of ballplayers. "Personally, he is a man of good address, sharp and alert and of pleasant manners and with no nonsense about him," a newspaper reporter observed in 1879. "He is not loud-mouthed or boisterous in his criticism, but treats his men in a gentlemanly way, expecting the same consideration in return." Some of his players, it turned out, lacked the character to reciprocate.

He was not above playing a trick or two to help his team. In late July 1883, when managing the Cleveland team, he found himself in a quandary, facing the powerful Providence Grays in a big game with two of his starting players on the shelf. "He was at his wit's ends to know how to arrange matters so as to get a chance against his formidable opponent," the Providence

Evening Telegram recounted. When a light rain began falling at noon—not enough to cancel the game—Bancroft knew what to do. "He hurried to its assistance," ordering his groundskeeper to unroll the fire hose and thoroughly inundate the field. "When the Providence men arrived, the ground was examined, and it was declared that it was too wet to play on." Cleveland had lived to fight another day.

Although not a rigid teetotaler, Bancroft refused to drink even a glass of lager during baseball season, and he extracted a temperance pledge from his players after making his own. Alcohol abuse was the bane of nineteenth-century managers. Players were known to show up for games with fearsome hangovers or even half drunk, which, not surprisingly, impeded their performance. "Boys, I'd rather pay the coin out of my own pocket than be compelled to fine you, but it will cost every man who gets drunk this year just $25 for the spree," Bancroft recalled warning his players before the 1883 season. The stiff fines sobered up his first baseman Bill Phillips, who later thanked him for imposing them. "For the first time since I began playing ball, I'm winding up the season with a bank account!" Phillips told him. Whether the Grays would listen was another matter. In 1882, Providence's directors found themselves forced to fine Jack Farrell the whopping sum of $200, and Vincent "Sandy" Nava $100, for "conduct prejudicial to the interests" of the club—code for heavy drinking. Harry Wright, a soft-spoken, gentlemanly fellow with a professorial beard and wire-rimmed glasses, had tried to restrain the Grays' worst offenders, with mixed results at best. On one road trip, the manager took a room directly across the hall from two of the Providence club's biggest boozers, with the idea of setting a trap to catch them breaking curfew. Harry saw the men to bed and pretended to retire himself. But when all was silent he rose quietly, opened his door without a creak, tiptoed across the hall, and tied a string to the doorknob of the boozers' room. The other end he strung under his door and tied to some paper that would rustle if the men opened their door. Harry waited until nearly dawn for a peep of activity, and finally drifted off to sleep. When he awoke, he discovered that nothing had moved the paper. Yet when he ventured from his room, he found the other end of the string tied to his own doorknob—and the beds in the room across the hall undisturbed and bare of ballplayers. "Figuring the joke was on him, Harry let the players get away with it," a reporter noted.

The new manager would endeavor to do better. While insisting to a reporter that "every man in the team is a clear-headed, sensible person" who would not "jeopardize the interests of his club by any careless indiscretions"— a white lie at best—Bancroft warned that the strength of any ball club rested on the "harmony, temperate habits, and [players' keeping] an interest of the club at heart." Put another way, disharmony, drunkenness, and selfishness could crumple even a first-rate team like the Grays. Bancroft intended to do all in his power to prevent such a calamity.

From the start, Bancroft had been a survivor in the midst of trouble. He was born on May 9, 1846, in rural Lancaster, Massachusetts. Only three days later his young mother died. Raised on his grandfather's farm, the ambitious boy pitched on his school's ball club and ran away at the age of fifteen, several months after the bombardment of Fort Sumter, to seek glory in the Civil War. Throwing his family off the trail by enlisting under the alias of Henry F. Colter, Frank served as a drummer boy with Company A of the 8th New Hampshire regiment, arranging ball games during his off-hours while assigned to the Department of the Gulf. Reenlisting in 1864 as a bugler, Bancroft was transferred in early 1865 to the 8th Battalion Mounted Infantry. While six hundred thousand young Americans perished in the war, many after suffering ghastly wounds and amputations, the teenager survived more than three years inside a whirlwind of bullets, grapeshot, horror, and disease—that famous luck again—to muster out, safe and sound, on October 28, 1865.

He went into the hotel trade and, by dint of hard work and crafty investments, became by his early thirties proprietor of his own large establishment, the Bancroft House, at the corner of Union and Acushnet avenues in New Bedford. A rabid follower of Boston's Red Stockings, Bancroft was determined to bring first-class baseball to his own city—and, not coincidentally, fill up his hotel rooms with visiting ball clubs. In 1877, hoping to whip up local interest in the club's one hundred shares of $15 stock, he hired baseball's greatest star—George Wright, the dashing shortstop of the champion Red Stockings, and kid brother of Harry Wright—to appear in New Bedford and make a show of helping to lay out the new grounds. George's arrival was a banner day for Bancroft, who met him at the local depot with a splendid carriage drawn by a pair of gray horses, specially hired for the occasion. He set Wright alongside him on the driver's seat, exhibiting him like a trophy, and drove him through the city's principal streets. With his curly dark hair, gleaming smile, and pork chop sideburns, George had emerged as baseball's first superstar, and he drew waves and applause from the citizenry as he passed by. Bancroft "felt prouder over having the famous shortstop for a companion than he would have been had he been sitting beside the President of the United States," one reporter recounted. Bancroft got his backers, and New Bedford got its team, its field fenced and graded, and a small grandstand built, under his management.

Some of Bancroft's moneymaking schemes fared better than others. Over the winter of 1877–78, he hit on the idea of turning his ball field into an outdoor skating rink and charging admission to a "Siberian Carnival." Bancroft duly built up an embankment along Kempton Street and persuaded the city to crank open the fire hydrants. "I went to bed dreaming of skaters and, of course, shekels at the gate," he recalled. But early the next morning, his doorbell rang and a breathless friend informed him there was "hell to pay" on Kempton Street. The water had seeped through the sand under the street, and tenants across the way found their cellars flooded, with every loose object in the basement floating about. Bancroft rushed to the ballpark to find that the water had run out from under the ice, which had settled and cracked to pieces, "and the Siberian carnival was a dream only." Meanwhile, city officials were demanding a big sum for the wasted water. Luckily, Frank had political pull, and a councillor named "Wash" Cook persuaded officials to withdraw their claim on the grounds that the baseball manager and hotel owner was a "public benefactor."

Two years later, businessmen in the booming industrial city of Worcester, Massachusetts, lured the benefactor away to create its own professional ball club. Bancroft did such an impressive job building a profitable franchise that the team won an invitation to join the National League in 1880. He repeated the process in Detroit, three times Worcester's size, creating a club from scratch in 1881 that finished fourth in the eight-team league, and went on to post a winning record in 1882 while clearing $25,000 in profit for the owners.

Along the way, Bancroft tried all means of innovative schemes to make money. In late 1879 he employed several of his Worcester players and secured corporate sponsorship for an extended postseason jaunt that would include a groundbreaking trip to Cuba. Bancroft, like his fellow American entrepreneurs, believed in spreading his product around the world. The players donned bluish gray uniforms with red caps, stockings, and belts and "H.B." in big letters across the chest. That stood for Hop Bitters, a wildly popular patent medicine manufactured by Asa T. Soule of Rochester, New York, and marketed as the "Invalid's Friend and Hope." Soule, who made a fortune off the concoction, asserted that Hop Bitters cured "All Diseases of the Stomach, Bowels, Blood, Liver, Kidneys, and Urinary Organs, Nervousness, Sleeplessness, and especially Female Complaints." While such claims were patently absurd, his customers—many of them elderly ladies who were thought to be strict teetotalers—enjoyed their thrice-daily jolt from the amber-hued bottle, perhaps because its secret ingredients included an alcohol content above 40 percent. As his Hop Bitters team made its long journey, the manager filed lively reports to newspapers back home, keeping baseball, the miracle cure, and Frank Bancroft in the public eye.

After a stormy passage of five days from New York, Bancroft's men arrived in Havana on December 18, finding the Spanish colony in a tense mood. A Cuban revolution called the Ten Years' War had just ended in the rebels' defeat, and Spanish officials remained deeply resentful of the United States over its clandestine role in the war, including an incident six years earlier in which a former Confederate blockade runner, the *Virginius*, had been caught transporting would-be rebels and ammunition to Cuba. When Spanish authorities summarily executed fifty-three members of the crew and passengers, including a number of Americans, the United States came close to declaring war. By the time the Hop Bitters arrived, hundreds of Spanish soldiers patrolled the streets of Havana, Bancroft noted, and they showed "in every conceivable way but that of actual violence their hatred of Americans." They did not take well to his distribution of American flags with the name Hop Bitters imprinted on them, fearing they would "encourage the Cubans to rebellion," and for a time authorities took Bancroft into custody to ask him what he was doing.

Anti-Americanism was only one of the troubles Bancroft confronted.

He discovered that his hosts refused to honor the $2,000 guarantee they had promised him before he made the trip. Moreover, he could sell tickets to his games only if the government granted him permission, and greedy authorities wanted 50 percent of the gate share, so much that the Hop Bitters would have lost money. Worried that Bancroft might turn around and leave, wealthy baseball fanatics and the country's railroad lines and carriage owners, who expected to earn a good deal transporting spectators, kicked in enough to make it worth the Americans' while to play. On December 21, some three thousand Cubans turned out for the first of two games, Bancroft reported, "a good sprinkling of whom were ladies, who manifested their appreciation of the sport by clapping their tiny hands and waving their handkerchiefs, the men yelling like so many wild Indians and gesticulating at a fearful rate." The supposed Cuban all-star team—good fielders but poor hitters—proved no match for the professionals, even after Bancroft loaned the team two of his best players, Curry Foley and Charlie Bennett. In a second game, the Hop Bitters again throttled the local stars. This one drew a festive crowd of five thousand, "nearly one-half of whom," Bancroft observed, "were the fairest senoritas the isle could boast of." On that warm December day, a refreshing breeze from the Gulf danced over the sunny ball field, reminding Bancroft of mid-June in New England.

Though Cuba in the 1870s had its drawbacks—the risk of yellow fever high among them, not to mention the hostility of the authorities—the players made the best of it. "The boys are all well, and amusing themselves by sightseeing and killing Cuban fleas and mosquitoes," Bancroft reported. In the evening, the Americans put on impromptu concerts, "the chief features being Foley's Irish eccentricities, Bushong's ballads, and a quartet composed of Knight, Whitney, Irwin, and Bushong in camp-meeting melodies and national airs." The latter, not surprisingly, were "very distasteful" to the Spanish soldiers roaming about. However tense it was at times, Bancroft's jaunt to Cuba ignited interest in baseball, helping it overtake the Spanish import of bullfighting as the island's favorite sport.

Accepting an offer of $1,800 to manage the Cleveland club in 1883, Bancroft opened the season with another classic piece of aggressive promotion. During a spring training trip to Washington, D.C., he secured an invitation to the White House, where he and his men met one afternoon with the president himself. A man's man who enjoyed the fine things of life, including fishing, good cigars, and well-made clothes, Chester A. Arthur was said to own eighty pairs of pants, the kind of detail that earned him the sobriquet "the dude president." At six feet two inches, the dapper, bewhiskered President Arthur stood taller even than most of the well-muscled players. Shaking hands all around, the president complimented the men on their appearance and dutifully smiled when informed there were no office seekers among them. Before Bancroft and his athletes left, Arthur offered a classic politician's bromide, pointedly disagreeing with those Americans who rated players nothing but drunks and brutes. "Good ballplayers," Arthur declared, "make good citizens." That wasn't necessarily true. Eleven days later, one good ballplayer, Terry Larkin of the Baltimore Orioles, went on a drunken spree, shot his wife, Margaret, through her left cheek, fired a bullet through a door at police officers trying to break in and save her, and then tried to commit suicide at the hospital by slashing his own throat. Still, the White House visit pumped up interest in the Cleveland club and brought readers out to the ballpark.

Under Bancroft's stewardship, the Cleveland club blossomed and for the first time made a serious run for the National League pennant. It fell apart after ace pitcher Jim McCormick twisted his ankle on the base paths and then badly strained his pitching arm. One Arm Daily, never known for enduring difficulties with good grace, was forced to pick up the slack for his missing colleague, and he grew increasingly resentful of the penny-pinching Bancroft for refusing to pay him extra money for the extra work. It all came to a bad pass on September 1 at Chicago's Lake Front Park, where the White Stockings throttled the Blues 21–7, effectively ending their pennant hopes. "Nine very gloomy men walked with Manager Frank Bancroft to the Union depot in Chicago to take the midnight sleeper for Cleveland," said one report. No sooner had they boarded the train than a ruckus broke out. Daily and a twenty-year-old pitcher named Lem Hunter tussled over stowing a valise, and the argument quickly escalated to savage words. The rookie angrily chastised Daily for his halfhearted performance in that afternoon's slaughter, calling him a "duffer," while the one-handed veteran shot back that "he could fight as well as he could play ball, and any man that fought with him would have to bring a candle and stay all night, for he was a stayer, every time." Finally, teammates separated the pitchers and coaxed them to shut up and sit down. Within moments, though, an actual fistfight erupted between shortstop Jack Glasscock and second baseman Fred Dunlap. Bancroft had to jump between the two and push them apart, to keep the members of his star double-play combination from doing serious injury to each other. Both Daily and Glasscock threatened to kill Dunlap for the slights they had endured. "This disgraceful episode occurred in the near presence of ladies," said a story wired across the country. When asked for his impression of the fight, Bancroft's response was characteristically laconic: "Too bad."

Late in the 1883 season, Bancroft began signing his men to contracts for 1884. But, to his growing irritation, he still had not heard from his bosses about his own fate, though he had turned a $15,000 profit for the team. While awaiting a contract, he received a telegram from J. Edward "Ned" Allen, secretary of the Providence club, offering him the job of manager. "Wire lowest terms," Allen instructed Bancroft.

Bancroft showed the telegram to some of his trusted players. They advised him to make the jump. "There is championship stuff in that team, and with good luck you ought to capture the rag," one told him. Like Radbourn, Bancroft had never won a National League pennant, something high on his list of professional goals. Moreover, Providence was a thirty-minute train ride from his home in New Bedford, and he had personal reasons to be close. In the spring, his thirty-one-year-old wife had died of pneumonia at his Bancroft House hotel, leaving him with a young son to care for. Bancroft's sister had taken the boy under her wing during the regular season, and she had recently married a New Bedford man. "To be near his boy," Bancroft noted, he was "prepared to sacrifice something." Even so, Bancroft had enjoyed his time in Cleveland and had no particular wish to betray his employers. He decided to wire back to Allen an almost outlandish demand: $2,500 a season—$800 more than he was earning at Cleveland, and more than many star players made—plus the scorecard concession. A reply came back: "All right; your terms are accepted." He could hardly turn down that kind of deal.

Cleveland's owners felt themselves ill used when they got the news, but they respected Bancroft's work and tried to keep him on, matching Providence's outlandish offer. Bancroft, who had not wanted to go in the first place, promised he would remain in Cleveland if he could secure an "honorable release" from his pledge to the Grays. He headed for Providence, "all primed for a row over the contract." Ned Allen was there to greet him warmly. "I suppose you are all ready to sign, Frank?" he asked. Frank wasn't, and explained he was staying in Cleveland because the club had met Providence's offer. Allen took the news calmly. "Oh, well, take this contract, scratch out just what you like and hand it back," he said. Bancroft, honorbound or not, simply could not resist. He asked for still more, and the Grays again accepted his terms. Having benefited handsomely from a bidding war for his services, he wired Howe: "Impossible to get my release." The lucky man had skillfully played one team against another to boost his income dramatically, while going to a team that had an even better chance of making him a pennant-winning general. Even so, the *Cleveland Herald* took his departure well. "Mr. Bancroft," it noted, "will always be remembered here as a successful, hard-working manager and a good and thoroughly honest and genial gentleman."

Having managed National League teams since 1880, Frank knew the Grays players well. This was not one of the teams he had to build from scratch. It was a perennial pennant contender, loaded with talent—"a splendid baseball machine," in his own words. But when he arrived in Providence, he discovered the machine that looked so splendid from a distance was in fact clattering and smoking, which may have explained Wright's decision to bolt to Philadelphia. Raw egos had divided the club into bickering factions, and know-it-all stockholders were taking sides, angrily squabbling over how to best manage the team, and complaining that the players were out of shape and drinking too much. Despite holding first place for much of the 1883 season, the Grays had drawn only 1,252 per game—61,341 for the year—while generating a meager profit of $3,098.19. As the season drew to a close, rumors swept the city that the club's president, Colonel Henry B. Winship, planned to issue a hefty dividend to stockholders and pay for it by starving the team, slashing the roster from fourteen to eleven players. The owners had a devious end game in mind, many feared—a secret plan to sell off the remaining men and fold the club. They were suspected of having purchased an interest in the more lucrative Narragansett Driving Association, which operated harness racing at the nearby Narragansett Park track, preferring to deal with a sport whose four-legged athletes—though pampered, skittish, and prone to bite—were not nearly as fractious and self-serving as professional ballplayers. In the ensuing uproar, Winship resigned his post, pleading that his business demanded too much of his time anyway. The directors returned stove merchant Henry T. Root to the club's presidency, a move that delighted league president Abraham G. Mills, who considered Root "one of the very best men the League ever had." He wrote to Root, expressing relief that the Providence helm "is in your good Roman grip." Another man he greatly admired, Ned Allen, became the club's new vice president and, as chairman of the board, its most energetic executive, pursuing an aggressive strategy of spending money to secure such profit-generating talent as Bancroft—and secure with him, if possible, the 1884 pennant.

The players were no happier than the squabbling directors. Charles Radbourn and his pal Cliff Carroll initially refused to sign their contracts for 1884, planning to hold out, and gave in only under pressure and financial emollients from Allen. At the same time, stockholders, players, and reporters were arguing over the handling, or mishandling, of Providence pitchers: namely, Harry Wright's decision to work Radbourn half to death in 1883, when there was a young pitcher available who could have spelled him. Some thought that a two-man rotation would have given the Grays the strength they needed to capture the pennant instead of falling short in the final week. Others, Wright obviously among them, believed it made sense to use baseball's best pitcher in as many games as possible. The dispute created tremendous ill will among both players and stockholders, leaving a wound that had yet to heal when Bancroft arrived.

Bancroft put on a good face over the winter, regaling the press with optimistic accounts of the team's health and pennant prospects for 1884. Preseason predictions had Providence in another close pennant fight against the two previous champions, Boston (1883) and Chicago (1880, 1881, and 1882). Just which of those three superb clubs would win was anyone's guess. "It is unnecessary to flourish any trumpets or make any loud statements of what we intend doing," Bancroft told the *Sporting Life.* "I prefer to let the work speak for itself." But beneath the brave exterior, he quickly realized he had stepped into a highly dysfunctional business family, riddled with rude, obnoxious men who didn't know as much about baseball as they thought, and who stood to make his life unpleasant for months to come. Well before the season began, he had come to the realization that, whatever extra money he might earn, jumping to Providence had been a serious misstep.

"I made a bad error leaving Cleveland. They were the best people I ever worked for," Bancroft moaned to Wright in March, adding anxiously, "Don't show this letter to *any one*."

But it was too late to back out now. He'd have to do the best he could.

Treasure from the Gold Country

Charlie Radbourn spent part of every winter in his hometown of Blooming-ton, and his friends and family knew that he loved to be off, indulging his love for hunting in the Illinois woods, cherishing the deep silence, broken by the crunch of snow underfoot, the sudden flutter of wings, and the crack of a shotgun as he caught a winter bird in flight. Indeed, he had perfected the art to such a great degree that, during the previous winter, he had issued an extraordinary statement to the newspapers:

> Believing that I am best wing shot in the world, I hereby challenge any man to shoot against me, in the field, for $1,000. The above amount, or any part of the same, is ready to be put up in any responsible stakeholder's hands whenever this challenge is accepted.
>
> Yours,
> Charles Radbourne,
> Bloomington, Ill., January 13, 1883.

One thousand dollars was an enormous amount of money for the time—one-half to one-third of a star ballplayer's salary, and well more than the common laborer received for a year's work. That he had that kind of loot lying around, ready to put up for such a stunt, was a remarkable testament not only to his fiercely competitive spirit and his confidence in his abilities as a crack shot but also to his penchant for hoarding his money. One W. D. Pearce of Ashland, Missouri, reportedly responded, but what happened after that is not clear.

Radbourn kept coming back every winter to the silent woods and snowy fields of central Illinois and the warm hearth of his close family. Here, each year, he restored his strength and got ready for the new season. Every year of baseball was grueling, but this coming season, he must have sensed, would be particularly tough. He had seriously damaged his arm, grinding down the cartilage connecting his muscles and bones, by overworking himself in 1883. And in 1884 he would be confronting something possibly worse: another Charlie, a younger, taller, more muscular, brilliantly talented pitcher out to steal his glory.

Unlike the older Charlie, this one was entering the 1884 campaign with a fresh, strong arm. Only twenty, he combined a scorching fastball with a cracking curve and a towering belief in his own greatness. He seemed destined for stardom—and soon—with or without the vaunted Radbourn at his side.

Charles W. Sweeney was born on April 13, 1863, some three thousand miles from Providence, in another city by a sheltering bay. San Francisco was a wildly booming metropolis during those years, its population nearly tripling between 1860 and 1870 despite the aggravation, cost, and outright danger of getting there. People flocking from Europe or the East had to take an arduous and risky months-long ship voyage around Cape Horn, the icy, wind-whipped tip of South America; or cross the sweltering Isthmus of Panama through lush jungle, swatting voracious mosquitoes that spread malaria and yellow fever; or traverse the Great Plains on wagon trails, perhaps the most dangerous route of all, braving thirst, starvation, and Indian attacks. By the time Sweeney was born American innovation and energy were starting to shrink the distance. A new cross-country telegraph, supplementing the Pony Express, had vastly improved communications, while a transcontinental railroad linking San Francisco with the East, long stalled in Congress, was finally being built. All the same, the railway would not be completed for another six years, and for years to come San Francisco would retain many of the qualities of a raw and violent boomtown.

People had risked everything to get here for one reason: to get rich. San Francisco's population had exploded after the discovery of gold in nearby Coloma in 1848. Within six years, three hundred thousand people flooded to California, among them Charlie's Irish-born parents, Edward and Mary Sweeney. Edward identified himself in the 1860 federal census as a farmer, his dreams of instant riches from gold mining having been thwarted, evidently. But before the decade was out, he—like many low-skilled Irishmen in the nineteenth century—had made enough friends, or greased enough palms, to obtain a steady job as a city policeman, one of many positions necessitated by a booming population of greedy adventurers with a strong taste for theft, gambling, and prostitution. Equipped with a nightstick and revolver, Officer Sweeney walked some very dangerous and gloomy streets, using as much force as he dared employ against the city's loathsome characters.

In July 1869, he was called to a dark saloon, where an Irish immigrant named John McDonald had supposedly shot himself. When Sweeney arrived, "a crimson stream was gushing" from the victim's chest. The barkeeper had heard an explosion in the back room but said he thought nothing of it, believing a firecracker had gone off. The barman deemed it suicide, though McDonald had seemed in a happy frame of mind earlier in the day. Such things happened often in 1860s San Francisco, and no one investigated terribly closely.

In June 1871, Officer Sweeney arrested a teenager named Cornelius Dunn for using profanity in the vicinity of a church picnic at the City Gardens, hauling him aboard a Folsom Street horsecar for a plodding trip to the station. The car had only made it as far as Ninth Street when a violent street gang of about twenty teens, bent on rescuing their friend, intercepted the vehicle, seized possession of it, and forced off the passengers—including the fuming, red-faced officer. Sweeney pulled out his revolver, supposedly intending to use it as a club, and found the gun wrenched from his hand. Fortunately for him, civilians rushed to his aid and helped him beat back the young thugs, while Sweeney recovered his weapon. Most escaped, but Sweeney arrested two, who were subsequently fined $40 each, no small sum in 1871 (Dunn got a $15 punishment for swearing). "Parents who permit their sons to train with the Hoodlums," the *San Francisco Bulletin* lectured, "will find it a very costly business—more expensive than sending them to school."

Even by the standards of nineteenth-century policing, which permitted a generous degree of brutality and corruption, the pitcher's dad proved to be a bad fit for the job. The elder Sweeney was the subject of repeated complaints to the Board of Police Commissioners for his tantrums, abusive language, and outright violence toward the public. On a Sunday evening in June 1874 he finally went too far. One Thomas Gorman—perhaps the same Thomas Gorman who regularly appeared in the paper for such activities as using vulgar language, committing adultery, disturbing the peace, and, in 1878, plunging a knife into a man's chest—was sitting in a saloon on Market Street when Sweeney strolled in with some friends to get a drink. A conversation of some type began, and Gorman intemperately called Sweeney a liar in front of his party. The policeman leapt up "in a moment of impulse" and knocked Gorman to the ground. "That was the whole transaction," Sweeney testified at his hearing. But the details provided by one Detective Jones made it clear that the officer's attack was much more savage than that. A bloody mess, Gorman dragged himself off the saloon floor and staggered to the police station to complain to the sergeant on duty that one of the department's own "had knocked him down, and stamped on him." The ruffian's face was bruised and his wrist wrenched. His gaping head wound was so bad that the officers sent him over to the city prison to get it sewed up.

Gorman had calmed down considerably by the time of the police commissioners' hearing. Concluding upon further reflection that it might not be a particularly brilliant idea to threaten the career of a homicidal policeman with an uncontrollable temper, Gorman insisted at the hearing that he "was quite as much or more to blame than the officer." But the commissioners had heard enough about Sweeney. They voted to drum him out of the force.

Charlie Sweeney thus grew up in a household with a father prone to prowl bars, explode with rage, and defend his honor, such as it was, with deadly violence—all attributes the old man passed on to his more famous son. It's not clear how much schooling Charlie received, though his pen-

chant to write letters in later life suggests he was better educated than Radbourn. In any case, by the age of seventeen he was working. The 1880 census
recorded his occupation as apprentice butcher—the same unpleasant job
that Radbourn had been forced to take as a youth. But then, the two shared
many similarities: Both hailed from large families; both grew up in rugged communities away from the cultured East; both were children of immigrants; both were touchy men with oversized egos. And both found a
remarkable way to escape from the bloody, brutal business of butchering—
by entering the hard profession of baseball as pitchers.

By the age of eighteen, Sweeney had grown into a rangy, slender, ambitious ace for the San Francisco Athletics, one of four professional teams in
the area's thriving baseball scene. Already, he was eager to break free and
begin a more lucrative career in the East, where some of his fellow Californians had gone for better money with the top professional nines. In May
1882, Sweeney boarded the Pacific Railroad for the first leg of a week-and-
a-half-long journey all the way to Providence, enduring dust and heat, bad
food, and the risk of Indian attacks while crossing sprawling buffalo ranges.
When he finally reached little Rhode Island, tucked into an obscure corner
of New England, he managed to get into one National League game, playing right field for Harry Wright's Grays, while Radbourn pitched—a tryout
under regular-season game conditions, so that the manager could get a
sense of the man's demeanor and physical ability against top competition.
Quite probably the teenager came highly recommended by Grays players
Jerry Denny and Sandy Nava, both of whom had grown up and played pro
ball in California. Sweeney had a dismal debut, going 0 for 4 and flub-
bing one of his two chances in the field. Though he surely impressed the
Providence manager with a show of his explosive fastball, Wright sent him
back to California for seasoning. "Under more favorable auspices, he would
undoubtedly have made a better showing," the *Providence Journal* observed
sympathetically.

While Sweeney matured, Wright started the 1883 season with a pitching
rotation of Radbourn and Lee Richmond, a southpaw who a few short years
earlier, while finishing up his undergraduate studies at Brown University,
had ranked among the game's elite hurlers. His meteoric rise and fall was a
sadly common trajectory for young pitchers. Working for Frank Bancroft's

Worcester club on the Thursday afternoon of June 10, 1880, Richmond beat Cleveland in a four-hit, 5–0 shutout. After the game, he hustled to Worcester's Union Station to catch a train back to Providence for the Brown commencement activities the following day, including a Friday night senior-class supper at the Music Hall downtown. On Saturday, he took the morning train back to Worcester, where, that afternoon, he pitched the first perfect game in major league history, beating Cleveland 1–0. Richmond went on to make a league-leading seventy-four appearances while striking out an impressive 243 batters. His future seemed limitless. But, like many young hurlers, he overdid it, ruining his arm with too much work. Two years of mediocre performances followed. By 1883, Richmond, a used-up man at twenty-six, was attempting a comeback as a backup hurler for the Grays. But as soon as the spring began, his well-rested arm began to ache, and Richmond had to face the cruel reality that he was finished as a pitcher, his effectiveness forever destroyed by too many hard curveballs. Wright telegraphed California, urgently summoning Sweeney.

By then, the hotheaded young Californian was already locked into a contract, wearing the red and white of the San Francisco Niantics. That spring he was cementing his local reputation as that scariest breed of pitcher: excessively fast and excessively wild. Sweeney "has but one aim," the *San Francisco Chronicle* observed, "and that is to fire the ball in as hard as he can." During his first game of the 1883 season in California, he had surrendered only three hits, but lost 8–2 because of his five wild pitches and seven passed balls—a clear sign that his poor catcher could not keep up with his frightening speed. With the help of a top professional catcher, and slightly better control, Sweeney might easily become one of the game's premier pitchers.

If his contract posed any impediment to his departure, Sweeney quickly removed it. On May 14, pitching against the Californians, he sent a message to his employers that there was little point in trying to make him stay. Before the second inning was over, it was obvious that Sweeney was trying to lose—"throwing the game" without a shred of integrity or concern for his teammates. "He was reproved, but still continued offending," the *Chronicle* reported, "and was therefore expelled from the Pacific Coast circuit on account of insubordination and unprofessional conduct." As Sweeney saw things, expulsion was his ticket to freedom, and local newspaper reports of his conduct would hardly make much difference to the National League if he quickly established himself back East as a reliable player. But had anyone cared to notice at the time, the incident revealed shocking disloyalty and an absence of character that might well harm his new team if Sweeney was again faced with a stark choice between honor and self-advancement. At any rate, he was soon a continent away, giving the sore-armed Radbourn a desperately needed break.

The 1,035 patrons on hand at the Messer Street Grounds on June 11, 1883, did not expect much of the fresh-faced twenty-year-old who strode to the box for his big-league pitching debut against the intimidating lineup of the first-place White Stockings. But Sweeney walked off the field one hour and fifty-three minutes later to the crowd's ringing cheers, having fashioned a 6–2 victory. "His swift and deceptive delivery completely mystified the defending champions," the *Providence Journal* crowed. While surrendering three walks—that wildness again—Sweeney held Chicago's hard hitters to a paltry four singles. Here was a man, at last, who might prove a worthy partner for the overworked Radbourn. "He was cool and collected at critical points, and his handling of the sphere was as speedy and regular at the finish as at the opening," the *Journal* noted, adding approvingly that his pitches "came in at times with the rapidity of cannon shots." A reporter who saw him for the first time that month noted there was nothing particularly showy about his windup, but what he delivered was impressive. "He has great pace and good curves, and gets his grip on the ball while holding it on his shoulder."

At five feet ten and a half inches and 181 pounds, the new pitcher burst on the scene as a prime physical specimen of American manhood, handsome, tall, and strong, certainly in comparison with the shorter, weedier, and slightly hunchbacked Radbourn. Sweeney, the reporter observed, threw much like Boston's great Jim "Grasshopper" Whitney, another towering, rather dangerously wild flamethrower who had starred in California, and "the management are satisfied they have secured another treasure from the gold country."

In short order, Sweeney assumed cult hero status in Providence. He was a boisterous, showy character, even as a rookie. "Sweeney was a bullheaded chap, fond of swiftly going companions, while Radbourne was just the opposite," one reporter recalled. Soon after the young pitcher arrived in Providence, a handsome man walked into a fragrant cigar store run by a Grays fan and announced he was none other than Charlie Sweeney. Chatting with the dealer about what great sports Providence people were, he leaned over the glass cases loaded with a splendid array of fine cigars and confessed that he was temporarily short on cash. Might he get a box of superior smokes on credit until the Grays' payday? The owner, of course, was only too happy to comply, and sent the celebrity off with a hundred of his finest cigars. He never saw the visitor again—who, it turned out, was not the pitcher after all. "One look at the real Sweeney convinced the dealer his education in baseball had been sadly neglected," *Providence Evening Bulletin* reporter William Perrin recalled.

Yet Wright used the young pitcher surprisingly sparingly in the weeks that followed. Writing forty-five years after the 1883 season, Perrin still bore a grudge against the manager for stinting the California kid. Wright's management of his pitchers, he noted, "was a mystery to the rest of the country." While Providence sat Sweeney on the bench and forced Radbourn to bear a crushing burden, the other three clubs in contention each regularly rotated two high-quality starters, an approach that clearly helped Boston's Red Stockings capture the pennant. "Here is the rock," Perrin contended, "on which the Grays split."

Something made Wright wary of using Sweeney. One rumor sweeping Providence was that the veterans detested the rookie and refused to give him their full support when he took to the box. Certainly, throughout his career Sweeney displayed a disconcerting knack for irritating his teammates with his strutting demeanor, nasty asides, and tirades over the slightest provocation; more than once in his career, his snide words led to fistfights. From the moment he had set foot in Providence, the brash rookie had acted as if he were taking over as the club's ace. Still, when a reporter cornered Wright on the train from Providence up to Boston at the height of the pennant race in September, the manager felt compelled to deny the gossip: "There is not a man in the Providence team who does not try as hard to play and do as well when Sweeney or Richmond pitches, as they do when Radbourne does."

Whatever the reason, Wright left the California kid on the bench, game after game, after bringing him all the way east. For all his raw talent, Sweeney compiled a mediocre 7–7 record while recording a worse earned run average than the league as a whole. He was wild, hard on the catcher, walking too many men. A case could be made that Radbourn, even when pushed to the brink of collapse, was the better money pitcher in crucial games. But there may have been more to the story than that. Wright, a self-made expert in the psychology of competitive athletes, with far more pennants to his credit than any manager alive, may have kept Sweeney in the shadows for the sake of his brilliant veteran's fragile ego. Even though Radbourn evidently complained bitterly about having too much work, Wright managed to keep him focused on pitching and winning by making it clear to all that the veteran was his essential man, the ace.

Bancroft, trusting his own instincts over those of even Wright, resolved that the 1884 campaign was going to be entirely different. He had studied Sweeney in action in 1883 and had concluded that Wright did not just have a fine prospect on his hands—he had one of the best pitchers *ever*. Sweeney would make the leap to greatness, Bancroft felt certain, as soon as he learned to mix up his pitches a little and get them over the corner of the plate more consistently. Sweeney had been working on those tasks by pitching winter ball in San Francisco, his 1883 expulsion evidently having been rescinded. In January, Bancroft informed the sporting press that, come the regular season, Wright's policy would be scrapped, and Sweeney, who had "demonstrated that he is thoroughly competent to alternate with Radbourn," would do so, "thus guarding against overworking the latter, as was the case last year."

Radbourn would simply have to learn to share the glory with this brilliant young pitcher.

Sweeney was far from the only player who felt compelled to work during the off-season. Few ballplayers were rich enough to lounge about, particularly if they had mouths to feed. Big-league pay ran from April to October. The game's notoriously improvident men—notably the hard drinkers and womanizers—often ran out of cash before spring, sometimes far from home, and were reduced to begging for an advance on the next season's salary. Albert G. Spalding, a former star pitcher who was president of the Chicago club, seemed particularly harried by requests that winter, and his patience was wearing thin. One of the moochers was slugging center fielder George Gore, who had led a team called the Gore Combination on a barnstorming tour through Texas and Louisiana. "It seems unaccountable to me that the players who go to New Orleans require so much more money than players who go to their homes and do nothing," Spalding chided Gore. Expressing the hope that the men would make no plans to descend on New Orleans the following winter, he warned, "You must make this last $100.00 do you until the season opens." Gore's teammates Mike Kelly, Silver Flint, and Ned Williamson, three of the game's biggest stars, also hit up the boss for fat advances. "Have already advanced you seven hundred dollars with the distinct understanding that no more would be requested. I cannot comply with your request," Spalding snapped at Williamson on January 16. He added tartly on March 7: "Attempting to keep Williamson in funds is a good deal like poring [*sic*] water into a rat hole, you do not know the depth, consequently can form no sentiment as to the amount required to fill it." Sure

enough, as soon as the 1884 season was over, Williamson was back, pleading for more. "The fact is, I am heavily in debt—about $500—through my own extravagance and folly, and I need the advance money to enable me to square up, turn over a new leaf and begin over again," he told the Chicago-based periodical *American Sports*.

In early 1884, Williamson and Flint's profligate ways threatened to bring scandal down on their team. A Florida man named Charles R. Jeffreys had written an angry private letter to Spalding, complaining that he had been flimflammed by the two well-paid stars. He had loaned them $50 apiece—about $1,100 in today's

George Gore

money—in March 1883, and they had yet to repay him, in spite of repeated promises to do so. Jeffreys had actually hunted them down during a series in New York City and wrung from them a pledge that they would reimburse him on their next payday, which never seemed to arrive. "Now I do not want any trouble about it, but I am a poor man and can't afford to lose it," Jeffreys told Spalding. The victim added a naked threat: he would go to the newspapers and denounce the dishonorable Chicago club unless he got his $100 back immediately. Spalding dashed off a letter to Flint, warning him, "It will be unpleasant for you, as well as for us, to have a matter of this kind paraded in print and I hope you & Williamson will devise some way to settle this." But he also tendered some friendly advice to Jeffreys: "Of course, it is very unpleasant for us to have men in our employ who treat their friends this way, yet as you become more acquainted with Ball players as a class, you will not be quite so liberal in your loans to them."

While no comparable records for the Providence club have survived, Bancroft surely had to deal with his own improvident players who were short on cash. Several men showed up in Providence before the April 1 reporting deadline—and while a number of Grays players were highly dedicated to their craft and liable to arrive early to get in shape, some were doubtless there for money to tide them over for the winter. Bancroft rented a local gymnasium and got them working out.

Between their weight lifting, sit-ups, and twirling of Indian clubs, the players spent a good deal of time discussing some significant changes made by National League owners during their winter meeting. For starters, the 1884 schedule had been expanded from 98 games to 112. Those fourteen extra games would mean a more tiring season for every regular, and make a two-man pitching rotation more of a necessity than ever. Meanwhile, the pitch count had been adjusted. For years, the league had been experimenting with it, feeling its way toward the best balance between offense and defense. Now, to speed up the action, the owners had trimmed the number of balls required for a walk from seven to six—en route to establishing the classic four balls/three strikes formula five years later.

The most revolutionary change involved pitching motion. For the first time, National Leaguers would be given full freedom to throw overhand. Under 1883 rules, pitchers had been barred from raising their arm above shoulder height, though scofflaws had snuck in overhand throws anyway. They usually got away with it because the lonely umpire found it easier to look the other way than endure endless bickering with an angry pitcher and his overheated teammates.

The sports journals bristled with debate over the new rule. George Wright, whose glory days went back to the elegant era of straight-arm underhand throwing, thought baseball had been damaged irretrievably by shifting so much power to the pitcher. It had become much less of a *team* game; almost everything depended now on the quality of the pitcher—and of his catcher, who had to possess both the bravery and the dexterity to receive such cannon fire. The influence of the other seven fielders had shrunk dramatically.

"How pleasant it used to be to witness a game," Wright sighed. He could well remember his teammates Asa Brainard and "Dug" Allison performing as pitcher and catcher: "Asa standing gracefully with his feet crossed, ball held in front of him, [would] take a look over his shoulder to see if the boys were all ready, give his 'siders' one or two strokes and deliver the ball into Dug's hands with a smack. And Dug would take it so easily, give a shake of his head, jump around behind the batsman, and return it to the pitcher." The ferocity of 1880s competition, alas, had stomped all over the classic grace of early baseball. "The way the game is played now you will see the pitcher get into the most agonizing of positions, look at the catcher, lift his foot two or three times, give his belt one or two pulls, and away goes the ball. If it is an inshoot you see the batsman flying out of his position to avoid being hit and let the catcher have a chance to stagger under the ball, which is thrown in as if shot from a gun. I think the League has carried matters to extremes when they allow a pitcher to throw a ball as he pleases. There is many a player on a nine who can throw a ball so swiftly that no batsman can hit it."

George had a point. Pitchers were indeed shattering the game's traditional balance, making themselves vastly more dominant through the use of feverish speed and devilish tricks. What George did not seem to grasp was that they were going to do it no matter what the rulebook might say, that the umpires were not equipped to stop them, and that the owners were only accepting reality by codifying baseball's continuing metamorphosis into the intensely competitive modern game. George's pragmatic older brother Harry seemed much more philosophical about it all. "It will affect the batting very little, because the pitchers cannot throw the ball any harder than they did towards the close of last season, when the umpires uniformly neglected the rule and allowed the pitchers to do as they pleased," he observed. In any case, the batters would quickly adjust to the "firers." The new freedom might even protect pitchers' arms by prompting them to throw more overhand fastballs, resorting less to the hard curveball, "which is a fearful strain on certain muscles of the arm, and which toward the close of the season quite cripples many effective pitchers."

Charlie Radbourn, who had risen to the top as a sidearm man, would have little use for the rule change. He might pull out the occasional overhand throw from his bag of tricks, along with throwing sidearm and underarm, dancing around the pitcher's box, and mixing up fastballs and junk curves. But the new rule would be a huge boost for Charlie Sweeney, who relied much more on the blunt weapon of speed to dominate the batter. With the overhand rule in place, all the stars were aligning to get the golden boy in position for a glorious season.

Brimstone and Treacle

There was something suspicious about them, very suspicious. As they stepped off a passenger car behind a steaming engine in late March 1884, the three young men—grubby, rumpled, unshaven; rather nasty-looking, in truth—caught the eye of the police detective stationed at the Washington, D.C., depot. Three years earlier, a madman had leapt from the shadows at the Baltimore and Potomac station and pumped two bullets into the back of President James A. Garfield, leading to his death two months later, and since then the Washington police had been decidedly less blasé about strange characters in public places. Moreover, there were all sorts of rumors afloat about anarchists and unionists willing to use powerful incendiary bombs to strike at the heart of the established order. These three strong, rough-edged young men—one of them nineteen (operating under an alias, it turned out), one twenty, one twenty-five—looked like they might be trouble. They left the depot with big trunks and boarded a horse-drawn vehicle. The detective thought it best to tail them, just in case.

He soon saw they were headed in the general direction of the White House. Before they reached it, they swung north onto Ninth Street, pulling over at number 413, in front of a joint named Scanlon's. It was a well-known saloon and billiards hall owned and operated by Michael B. Scanlon, a glib and gregarious forty-year-old from Cork, Ireland, married to an Irish lass named Nancy. Scanlon had risked his life for the adopted country he loved, as a soldier in the Union army, enlisting as a teenager to fight the minions

of wealthy southern planters, who in the eyes of many Irishmen were no better than dirty British aristocrats. Having survived the war, the enterprising
youth turned to the business of sports. He scraped together enough money
to open his pool hall, while arranging baseball matches on the White Lot, a
pleasant expanse of green between the South Lawn of the White House and
a truncated Washington Monument, still under construction and awaiting
its capstone. The games drew thousands of spectators, including on occasion the seventeenth president, Andrew Johnson, who delightedly sat with
his staff in chairs along the first-base line, seeking relief from the cares
of one of the most unpleasant presidencies in history. President Johnson
loved this booming American sport so much that he ordered the Marine
Band to attend games and serenade the crowd. In 1870, Scanlon oversaw the
construction of the city's first enclosed ballpark, the Olympic Grounds, at
Seventeenth and S streets. And now, in March 1884, he was manager of the
Washington Nationals of the new Union Association, a third major league.

The officer saw the three shady men go inside and decided to investi-
gate. Scanlon roared with laughter when he learned that his friends had
been followed. They were dubious characters, all right, but hardly dangerous criminals or revolutionary conspirators—just hard-drinking ballplayers, covered in the dust and grime of a wearying train trip from San
Francisco. Two of them were members of the Providence club: pitcher
Charlie Sweeney and third baseman Jerry Denny. They had spent the winter earning extra cash in the Bay Area by playing ball—Denny when he
wasn't toiling in the noisy, greasy boiler shop of the Central Pacific Railroad
Company at Oakland Point, trying to earn enough to support his wife and
young daughter. The third was a nineteen-year-old catcher and upholster-
er's apprentice who played as Mike Creegan rather than use his real name,
Marcus Kragen, to cloak his career from an upright German-Austrian family that most decidedly did not approve. Scanlon signed Creegan to his
own Nationals, and it seems highly probable he took the opportunity of
this little get-together to pitch Sweeney and Denny on the virtues of violating their Providence contracts and jumping to the Nationals. If so, they
resisted his blandishments. Though slow to come on from San Francisco,
they would rejoin their teammates, as planned, in the coming days.

By then, most of the boys were already gathering in Providence from

Jack Farrell, 1884 Grays scorecard

near and far for the start of the long season. Catcher Sandy Nava returned from New Orleans, where he had been playing ball as part of the spendthrift Gore Combination. Shortstop Arthur Irwin had a shorter trip, a fifty-minute train ride from Boston, where he had spent many sweaty hours at the South Boston Athletic Club's gymnasium, working on his endurance and coordination by playing spirited games of handball with his former Worcester teammate Lon Knight. The Bloomington boys Radbourn and Cliff Carroll arrived early, as did center fielder Paul Hines, up from his home in Washington, D.C., to skate at Bancroft's rink and join the boys in the gym. Venerable Joe Start, a balding, clean-shaven man with a ruddy complexion and bracing blue eyes, was back for another year in the vital role of team captain, directing strategy on the field. At forty-one, he was the National League's oldest player, and one of its most revered, having earned the nickname "Old Reliable" not only for his nearly flawless work as a barehanded first baseman but also for his integrity and steadiness under pressure.

Only one stubborn player was still absent without leave, seemingly unimpressed with the club and its new manager: the Grays' hard-drinking, hard-fighting, heavyset veteran second baseman Jack Farrell. Bancroft sent him a "peremptory order" to report, which finally jostled him. Nicknamed "Moose," the twenty-six-year-old Farrell was an unpleasant character, with close-set, frowning eyes and a bushy mustache, a man fully capable of irritating friend or foe. Boston second baseman "Black Jack" Burdock quite enjoyed torturing his Providence counterpart and "was never happier than

when sliding down to second base, digging fat Jack in the shins or rubbing
the bark off his knees." Farrell, fed up with the abuse, retaliated by deposit-
ing sharp stones along the path where Burdock slid in hard. After his skin
had been shredded a few times, the Boston star rethought his strategy.

Minus Farrell, Sweeney, and Denny, the Grays opened their exhibition season on the damp, raw, windy afternoon of March 29 at the Messer Street
Grounds, taking on Brown University's nine. It was a few days shy of six
months since the Grays had last taken the field here, on that chilly October
day when Radbourn opened the plush case and removed his gold watch.
The crowd this afternoon was similar in size: about three hundred stalwarts,
braving intermittent drizzle and wind gusts that were so fierce that they
shredded awnings downtown. Still, the crowd was eager for baseball after
the void of the winter months, and looked forward to seeing Radbourn work
against the Ivy Leaguers.

Curiously, the great pitcher trotted out to second base instead, while a
scrawny kid took the box—one of Bancroft's new men, Paul Revere Radford, who at twenty-two was not much older than the college boys he was
facing. Radford was born in the Boston neighborhood of Roxbury, the son
of a man with the equally patriotic moniker of Benjamin Franklin Radford,
a self-made man of means, manufacturer, banker, and four-term selectman
in the Boston suburb of Hyde Park. "Strong and sturdy, resolute and determined of will," as one observer described him, Benjamin Franklin had sired
ten children, yet still found the time to proudly watch his son Paul Revere
play ball. "He is possessed of considerable wealth," the *Journal* noted, "and
is desirous that Paul should develop into a first-class professional player."
The boy, though nimble and smart, did not cut quite as impressive a figure as his dad. Standing five foot six and weighing only 148 pounds, he
had been saddled with the nickname of "Shorty." Still, he was coming off
a memorable rookie season in 1883, playing right field for his hometown
team, Boston's Red Stockings, and making spectacular catches that helped
them capture the pennant. The problem was, Paul Revere could barely hit
a lick—.205 that year—and Boston declined to retain his services for 1884.
Bancroft grabbed him not only for his sparkling defense but also for his

potential as an emergency pitcher, remembering he had done good service as an amateur hurler back in Hyde Park. Thrilled to be staying in New England, close to home, Radford had spent the winter working out hard in his father's handsome barn on Fairmount Avenue, which he had converted into a gymnasium.

Now he was heading to the pitcher's box in his new team's first exhibition game, while the club's best-paid star acted the role of utility infielder. Radford displayed a "swift and quite puzzling" delivery, and he seemed "to have command of the various curves," holding the college athletes to two runs over five innings. With the game essentially in the bag, the Grays leading 7–2, Bancroft signaled for Radbourn to come in and test his arm.

Right away, it was apparent something was terribly wrong. The bitter lesson of the dark, cold armory in Buffalo had taught Radbourn to go easy in spring, and he knew better than to pour it on against college kids on a windy March afternoon. But even so, Radbourn was a mess. The great pitcher had nothing and merely tossed the ball to the plate, surrendering seven runs over four innings to the rank amateurs, barely staving off an embarrassing defeat, as the Grays edged the collegians, 10–9. The pain and weakness that had dogged Radbourn during the waning days of 1883 seemed to be back, and it was not clear when or even whether he would return to form.

The Grays hustled from the field in the dying light to catch the horse-cars downtown to the Union Depot, where they grabbed an evening train to frosty Boston, then boarded a midnight steamship for a two-day trip to the Virginia peninsula. Radbourn had plenty of time to stare at the sea, brooding about his career. Bancroft, characteristically, had chosen to take his club far away from Providence, turning spring training into a moneymaking extravaganza, whatever it might cost the men in aggravation and exhaustion.

Most teams, for better or worse, stayed close to home in April, making do with trying conditions—even the mighty White Stockings of Chicago, whose park was right along Michigan Avenue, on the bone-chilling, wind-whipped lakefront, where winter conditions often persisted well into spring. The men sat on the bench, shivering in their overcoats, and when called on to run, they waded around the bases through mud, slush, and at times snow. When they were not slogging through the muck, some spent hours wrapped in blankets and carpets in a sweltering room in the clubhouse that had been turned into a sweatbox. A reporter sent to study the operation that spring entered a dark chamber and, straining to adjust his eyes, barely made out a makeshift bed on the floor. In it were "two motionless forms" that turned out to be pitcher Fred Goldsmith and third baseman Ned Williamson. "There they are," Mike Kelly informed the reporter with a wink, "all that is left of 'em. Rather more than a bunch of toothpicks, but not much." Williamson, fattened up by his New Orleans trip, popped out from under the heavy covering, his face "as red as a beet and swathed in perspiration," and Goldsmith "poked out an equally moist and blooming countenance." In an adjoining room was "a mammoth stove in full blast," and

Ned Williamson

a pile of wraps used for the operation—"scattered blankets, rugs, old bat bags, canvas-flaps and the like." It was a primitive treatment, but the ballplayers swore by its effectiveness in melting away flab and purging toxins from the bloodstream—namely, the residue of months of heavy whiskey drinking. Williamson, determined to sweat as much as possible, wrapped himself in a mangy chunk of carpet that had once served as the bed of Champion, the big black Labrador of the club's late owner and president, William Hulbert.

Bancroft would have none of that. He had arranged an ambitious schedule of lucrative April games along the eastern seaboard. The Grays would be on the move for the whole month, catching trains and horse-drawn buses, eating hotel food and living out of suitcases. They would start out in Virginia, then work their way gradually up the coast, collecting gate proceeds as they went, returning to Providence in time for the May 1 regular-season opener.

As Bancroft's luck would have it, that month turned out to be an unusually good April to be away from New England. The weather remained stubbornly cold up north, long after the calendar promised warmer days. Boston's Red Stockings opened the baseball calendar every year with a traditional exhibition game on Fast Day, a centuries-old Puritan holiday of prayer, fasting, and thankfulness as New England's killing winter gave way at last to spring; and while Fast Day games were often played under robin's egg skies, in breezes fragrant with early wildflowers and sun-drenched earth, this year's April 3 contest got snowed out. The field was buried under six inches of heavy powder and then doused with a long, raw rain that covered the ground with "the vilest slush imaginable," the *Boston Globe* reported. "All those who could do so stayed in-doors, and those who were obliged to go out did so with a mental protest. Everyone looked as uncomfortable and sour as Boston people ever allow themselves to be." And for the next several weeks, the weather remained cold and damp. Modern climate scientists know why. The massive explosions of the island volcano of Krakatoa in Indonesia on August 26 and 27, 1883—blasts that could be heard three thousand miles from the scene—had shot fine dust into the upper atmosphere, cloaking much of the Northern Hemisphere and impeding the sun's radiation, causing global cooling that persisted throughout 1884. The Grays felt it even down south. Some thirteen years later, Sweeney still bitterly remembered the misery of pitching in "cold weather, with snow on the ground" during the trip.

Sweeney remembered it well because he got stuck with the hard work. Radbourn was unfit for duty. Fighting stiffness in his arm, he thought it the better part of valor to bide his time that cold April and let Sweeney do virtually all of the pitching. Initially, at least, the young hotshot seemed only too happy to comply, demonstrating his excellence and signaling that a new generation was ready for the money and glory now that Radbourn's day was fading. The old warhorse, though suddenly overshadowed by a young star, had learned from hard experience that baseball careers had a way of vanishing overnight, and his best hope was to be patient and nurse himself back to health. Part of the treatment was to dose himself morning and night with an old folk remedy from his parents' native England—a regimen, he was convinced, that would preserve his arm for the long season. Each spring, Radbourn swallowed copious amounts of a thick brown syrup made of sulfur and molasses. Variously called "brimstone and treacle" and "Grandma's spring tonic," the mixture was thought to "thin the blood," which had supposedly thickened during the winter, making one sluggish and tired. It also functioned as a laxative and suppressed the appetite. (In Charles Dickens's novel *Nicholas Nickleby*, the starving students of Mr. Wackford Squeers's school are frequently dosed to reduce their porridge consumption.)

Radbourn was apparently over another health threat. George Washington Bradley, a top professional pitcher who at times traveled with him, recalled many years later that Charlie went through a bout of obsessive eating. "Whenever we would stop at a railroad station, or wait for a bus he would buy apples or something and would munch away," Bradley recalled. It turned out that Radbourn had a yards-long tapeworm wending inside his intestines—a common enough affliction in the nineteenth century, usually the result of eating undercooked meat, particularly pork. Fortunately, Radbourn managed to expel the loathsome creature with the help of a doctor's toxic drugs.

While his blood was thinning out, his bowels getting purged, and his shoulder healing, Radbourn watched Sweeney perform brilliantly in game after game—against amateurs in Hampton, Virginia, and a fine Eastern League team in Richmond; against the American Association's Baltimore Orioles and Washington Nationals (not to be confused with Scanlon's Washington Nationals); and against an assortment of professional and semipro teams in Lancaster, Wilmington, Trenton, Reading, and Harrisburg. Radbourn was nowhere to be found in most of the month's box scores, while Sweeney, in the words of the *New York Times*, "proved such a success that he even pitched on days when Radbourn was to toss the sphere, and was paid extra for these games." Before the season opened, the paper reported, "Radbourn and Sweeney became jealous of each other." Though Radbourn loved to pitch and was never a man to shirk his duty, it is hard to avoid the suspicion that, at some level, he was darkly hoping the insufferable youth would burn out before the season even started.

If so, he hoped in vain. Sweeney was brilliant, fully justifying Bancroft's public declarations of faith in him. In Baltimore, some twenty-five hundred fanatics turned out to watch the young pitcher, putting $900 in Bancroft's pocket. Local businessmen liked the team so much that they tendered the manager a formal offer of $10,000 to move the Grays to Baltimore, which Bancroft declined on behalf of the directors back home. The landlord of the Stevens House in Lancaster, meanwhile, declared Bancroft's men the finest-looking and most gentlemanly ball club he had ever hosted in his hotel. By the time the Grays arrived in Brooklyn to play that city's Association club, their spring record was a dazzling fourteen wins and no losses, and the players were growing hungry for an undefeated spring.

Brooklyn, then America's third-largest city, behind New York and Philadelphia, had been a baseball hotbed since the earliest days of the organized game, though it had dropped out of the major leagues in the 1870s. In 1883, an enterprising journalist and real estate speculator named Charles H. Byrne joined forces with three other men—his brother-in-law Joseph A. Doyle, a nasty customer who ran a gambling house on Ann Street in lower Manhattan and was tight with Tammany Hall, the powerful Democratic political machine; George Taylor, city editor of the *New York Herald*; and Ferdinand A. Abell, the operator of a society club (read: gambling parlor) at Narragansett Pier in Rhode Island—to found a new professional Brooklyn club and enter it in the Inter-State Association, one of baseball's top minor leagues. With Doyle and Abell's money—nobody seemed to worry too much about the taint of potential gambling corruption—the group built an impressive twenty-five hundred–seat stadium between Third and Fifth streets and Fourth and Fifth avenues and named it Washington Park, after General George Washington—most fittingly, since the field marked the approximate location of the Continental Army in the Battle of Long Island, as it fended off a much larger British and Hessian force before retreating to Brooklyn Heights. Indeed, an old stone house that had served as the general's impromptu headquarters still stood on the grounds, and was fitted out for further service as the Brooklyn team's clubroom. (Rebuilt after a fire, it lives on today as the Vechte-Cortelyou House.)

The club had proved to be a gold mine. Harried businessmen, not only from Brooklyn but also from lower Manhattan, flocked to games. Fifth Avenue horsecars disgorged well-dressed men who had crossed the Hudson River on the Fulton, Wall, and South Street ferries; some also made their way to the park across the new Brooklyn Bridge, despite the public's trepidation that it might fall down. Suddenly rich, the owners found they could afford to beef up their club with outstanding players, notably by looting the league's bankrupt franchise in Camden, New Jersey, and the reinvigorated Brooklyns went on to capture the Inter-State pennant. The club and its crowds were so impressive that Byrne and company received an invitation to move on up to the American Association in 1884. The Brooklyn men planned to demonstrate during the April exhibition season that their boys could compete at the major-league level, and the team could make a loud statement along those lines by beating the famous Providence club of the National League.

The Brooklyn owners didn't particularly care about making their point by winning fair and square. Before the two-game series began, Bancroft was disturbed to learn that they had hired as umpire one John Daily, a local man who had a record of notorious bias toward Brooklyn. Bancroft anxiously wrote to Byrne, explaining his objections and asking him to select someone else, adding he would happily accept any other umpire in New York or Brooklyn. "I feared there would be unpleasantness if he was allowed to umpire in his usual local manner," Bancroft said. When Byrne curtly refused, Bancroft reluctantly went along, worrying he would lose the lucrative games in that big city if he pushed too hard.

But the bitter disagreements were only beginning. Before the first game, Bancroft met with Byrne's brother-in-law, team manager Doyle, to go over ground rules. The Providence manager was willing to play under American Association rules with one big exception: Bancroft wanted Sweeney to throw overhand, now permitted in National League games. As one reporter noted that spring, Sweeney "pitches as a round-arm cricket bowler delivers the ball. The ball leaves his hand above his head, takes a most decided drop and is very puzzling." In the presence of Providence club vice president Ned Allen and Paul Radford's proud dad, who had accompanied the Grays on their entire April tour, Doyle agreed, and the set got under way on April 19. A big Saturday throng of some three thousand people crowded Washington Park and extended the Providence nine a cordial welcome. Brooklynites, remembering Joe Start's glory days with the old Brooklyn Atlantics way back in the Civil War era, presented the venerable captain with a splendid basket of flowers, an explosion of spring colors. Start bowed to the crowd, which bathed him in prolonged applause. Then he and his Grays uncharitably crushed the local team, winning their fifteenth straight by an embarrassing 15–0 margin, clubbing twenty-one hits and refusing to yield even a single run for the home crowd to enjoy. Manager Doyle, getting angrier as he watched the game go on, took the drubbing personally, deeming it a needless humiliation of his boys and his partners.

Finding that his liberality to Bancroft had proved too costly on Saturday, Doyle angrily withdrew his permission for overhand throws before the second game on Monday, insisting this time that Sweeney follow American Association rules that required him to keep his arm below his shoulder. He warned Bancroft that umpire Daily would start calling balks the moment Sweeny's arm went over his head. Bancroft pulled the young pitcher aside and told him to throw underhand, but to keep an eye on the Brooklyn hurler. If he began throwing overhand, so should Sweeney.

By the time Providence had taken a 5–0 lead, Sweeney had developed a crick in his shoulder, no doubt from using a different motion than he

Joe Start, 1884 Grays scorecard

had employed all spring. Providence had little choice but to send Sweeney out to right field, trading places with Radford. Working against hardened professionals rather than college boys, Shorty this time surrendered eight runs, while the Grays struggled to keep pace. That made it a new game—8–8 as the sixth inning began—with the crowd roaring and bellowing with joy, heaping insults on the Providence men. The unthinkable was happening: the Grays were in danger of losing their perfect spring record to a second-rate expansion club in a lesser league.

But it was not over yet. Start

and Farrell were keeping a close watch on Brooklyn pitcher Bill "Adonis" Terry, who was clearly throwing overhand. Though they were quick to point out the violation, Daily maddeningly refused to call the hometown pitcher on it. After Radford surrendered two more runs in the sixth, Start—slow to anger, but a bear once roused—called Sweeney back to the box and told him to throw just as he liked, overhand or not. Back in his comfort zone, Sweeney proceeded to force one Brooklyn player to fly out, and another to ground out. Each time, though, Daily declared a balk, to the Grays' astonishment and outrage, and gave the runner his base. When Daily succeeded in filling the bases, Start tore into the umpire, insisting he had no right to issue such punishments, since the Grays had never agreed to play by Association rules. Still, the hometown arbiter refused to budge, and the frenzied crowd began whooping insults at the Grays. Start had had it. He called Bancroft down from the rowdy grandstand and recommended that the Grays end the game there and then, pack up their bats, and leave. It was pointless to continue if the umpire was going to call every out a balk. Bancroft, worried about preserving his gate share, advised Start to keep playing and see what happened.

Bancroft, meanwhile, began frantically searching the stands for Doyle. Finding him, he pleaded with his counterpart to overrule his umpire's gross unfairness. Doyle, still fuming about Saturday's humiliation, was unreceptive, to put it mildly. As a gambling-hall owner and Tammany Society henchman, he felt nothing but scorn for Bancroft's fastidiousness, and flew into a profanity-laced tirade at the Providence manager. "The language used by this man (who was enraged because we had not allowed his team to make a single run in Saturday's game) was heard by many persons in the grand stand, but I will not mar your columns by repeating it," Bancroft noted primly in his account to the *Boston Globe*.

Back on the field, Start was pleading with the Brooklyn club's captain to install another umpire for the final innings of the game, giving both teams a fair chance. At that point, someone in the crowd shouted, "Five minutes are up!" Doyle ordered umpire Daily to award the game to Brooklyn, and he dutifully cried out, "Play!" When the Grays failed to take their positions, the umpire bellowed that the game was forfeited to Brooklyn, and with that decision went all the bets—the thousands of dollars that had been wagered, making some unsavory gamblers big winners that afternoon against very long odds. To the hoots and howls of the crowd, Brooklyn scurried off the field with its tainted victory, while the Grays remained, prepared to resume play under National League rules if Brooklyn had the guts to try. Brooklyn team officials vanished as well, making off with the large sack containing Providence's share of the gate receipts. Finally, persuaded no one was coming back, the Providence men packed up their bats and left, hissed by the crowd that lingered.

For days, the dispute played out in the press. Henry Chadwick, writing in the *Brooklyn Eagle*, contended the Grays "lost prestige" and "deserved what they got" for refusing to play one of the two games under Association rules. He reported that Joe Start had brazenly ignored Bancroft's orders to play on and that the manager had been compelled to fine him $25 for insubordination, a charge Bancroft vehemently denied. "While deploring any 'kicking' during a ball game, I desire the captain always to protest when being robbed," Bancroft said. The umpire was "requiring us to put out *five* men to get the side out, and showing from the first that if he could help them any, the Brooklyns should have the game." Brooklyn, in turn, angrily canceled all the remaining exhibition games Bancroft had scheduled with the team, and owner Byrne refused even to hand over his guarantee of $100 to the Grays for playing the Monday game. "This is not a question of dollars and cents; it is a positive question of principle. We maintain that any club guilty of such behavior as the Providence people indulged in should suffer some penalty," Byrne puffed, pompously claiming the moral high ground while cheating the Grays out of their fair share of the gate.

For his part, Bancroft fiercely defended his men's honor. "I dislike very much to raise the cry against umpires so early in the season, but I cannot stand everything," Bancroft wrote to the *Sporting Life*, adding he would leave it to the public to decide who was right. "One thing is certain," he noted. "The Providence Club and Capt. Joe Start have established a reputation for gentlemanly deportment off and on the field, which is too solid to be battered down by such partisan reports as have been ventilated by the over-zealous friends of the Brooklyn Club."

Sweeney, who had just celebrated his twenty-first birthday on April 13, was back throwing overhand again two days after the Brooklyn debacle, at

Manhattan's Polo Grounds. He pitched the Grays to a 7–2 victory against the Metropolitans, one of the American Association's best teams. After the Grays beat the Mets on Thursday, 13–6, with help from Radford—there was still no sign of Radbourn in the lineup—Sweeney returned on Friday to defeat New York 14–2 with a sparkling four-hitter, for a sweep of their three-game series.

Having dominated four American Association teams on their long tour, the Grays finally returned home to Providence, where they beat Brown University two more times. Radbourn, working as umpire on April 29, let his prankish side take over. To the amusement of players and spectators, he began calling outlandish strikes against his teammates "out of pure mischief," while helping the college boys by calling balls when they came to the plate—still not enough to sway the result. On April 30, the eve of the start of the new National League season, the Grays traveled to Bancroft's hometown of New Bedford for the final spring warm-up. In honor of the local man made good, umpire Frank Whitney made a little speech before the game and presented Bancroft with the splendid gift of a gold-headed ebony cane. At the Kempton Street field that Bancroft had once disastrously flooded, his club slaughtered the home team, 17–5.

The best part, from Providence's perspective, was the performance of Radbourn. All those doses of brimstone and treacle, combined with some solid rest, seemed to have done some good. Pitching, at last, from the fourth inning on, the ace threw beautifully, allowing no runs and demonstrating that he was, as the *Providence Evening Press* noted, "in fine trim" to start the home opener the next afternoon.

For Bancroft, April could hardly have been more successful. He had put a good deal of money in the team's coffers. Beyond the purely mercenary considerations, his Grays had played in twenty-three preseason games and won twenty-two. Sweeney had been nothing short of spectacular, pitching in nineteen games and winning all of them, except for the forfeited Brooklyn game, which he could hardly be blamed for losing. From the moment the club returned to Providence, Bancroft could not stop talking about his young phenom, lavishing praise on Sweeney's "drops and curves" as "the most marvelous he had ever seen." Meanwhile, Radbourn, the team's supposed star and $3,000 man, had become a distinctly secondary figure. Bancroft assured reporters that Charlie's arm wasn't seriously lame; the veteran was simply getting over the soreness he felt every spring, a pain that vanished when the weather got warm. Nevertheless, thanks to the emergence of Sweeney, it now seemed feasible that the Grays would compete for the pennant even if Radbourn's arm never got better.

After the New Bedford game, Bancroft went home, threw himself in a chair, and mulled over the opening of the National League season on the following afternoon, May 1. Cleveland was coming to the Messer Street Grounds, and Bancroft, eager to beat his former club, wanted to start the campaign with his best man, the pitcher he relied on to win the big games.

It wouldn't be Charlie Radbourn pitching on opening day for the Grays after all. It would be Charlie Sweeney.

Pneumonia Weather

After a frigid, rainy April, May Day arrived as the poets described it: bright, cheerful, inspiriting, "ushered in with a clear sunshine, and by the singing of the birds," the *Providence Journal* reported. Though it was a workday, a Thursday, the members of the Pawtucket Bicycle Club took a five-mile run into the capital city that morning, perched atop their wobbly, newfangled machines—no easy task, given the bicycle's massive front wheel trailed by a tiny one, and the holes and ruts in the dirt streets they had to navigate. Others enjoyed a picnic in the park or a jaunt in the woods with their families. Still others made their way via railroad, horsecar, and foot to the Messer Street Grounds for the 3:30 p.m. inauguration of the 1884 National League campaign.

They came to a classic wooden ballpark in the city's West End, not far from the stunning Victorian mansions being built by the city's new industrial elites along Broadway. Providence had the smallest fan base in the National League—104,857 residents, less than a third of the population of Boston, one-fifth that of Chicago, and a minuscule one-twelfth that of New York. All the same, Providence people loved their baseball, and the city's fanatics were perhaps America's most rabid.

Variations of the still-developing game had been popular in the Ocean State since at least the early nineteenth century, but the "New York" version—our baseball—really took off when Cincinnati's famous Red Stockings toured New England in 1869, setting the standard that young men yearned to emulate. Several years later, the Rhode Islands made their debut as the state's first all-professional club. They played at Providence's first enclosed grounds, Adelaide Park, off Broad Street on the South Side, memorable for its bleaching boards—what later generations would call bleachers—along the right field line, built around a huge spreading tree. (The origin of the term is obscure, but bleachers may have gotten their name from the pounding sun's propensity to bleach the color out of the uncovered wood.) When the gate opened on scorching summer afternoons, hundreds made their way to the shade under the branches. On occasion, a ball that had been hit into the tree bounced from limb to limb until it plunked on top of the head of a spectator.

In 1878, city fathers fashioned a better team and secured a slot for it in the National League, replacing the troubled Hartford franchise. The new club broke away from the traditional white uniform, choosing instead steel-gray shirts, knickers, and caps, trimmed with light blue, and its fanatics promptly nicknamed the team the Grays. As part of the upgrade, the club built a new park, nestled into a neighborhood of subdivided fields that were quickly filling up with attractive homes and a new elementary school, near the end of the Westminister Street horsecar line.

For the next several seasons, the Messer Street Grounds played host to one of the elite teams in baseball. The *Providence Journal* posted telegraphed updates of games in its plate-glass front window in the financial district downtown, drawing throngs of men and women who blocked the square, indifferent to police whistles and the curses of indignant drivers. "Businessmen left their stores, lawyers ran out of court, and doctors neglected their patients to stand on the hot pavements to 'see how the Grays are coming out,'" William D. Perrin recalled. When the Grays captured their first National League pennant in 1879, Rhode Island was overjoyed. In the four seasons that followed, the Grays remained one of the league's dominant teams, finishing second or third.

For some, the Grays became an outright obsession. During the summer of 1883, a delusional Providence man named Jimmy Murphy hung around the Messer Street Grounds day after day, begging every player or manager who crossed his path for a chance to pitch. The irritated professionals told him, in so many words, to get lost. But before their morning practice on

June 27, Charlie Radbourn and his clique—including his Bloomington crony Cliff Carroll—suddenly relented, inviting the man inside to show them his stuff. Jimmy was thrilled. He strode proudly into the grounds' hallowed pitcher's box and began to throw at long last. Just then Carroll crept up behind him with a garden hose and shocked him with a cold blast, as his teammates exploded with laughter. Sopping wet, Murphy said nothing and simply turned and walked away, to the echoes of his tormentors' guffaws.

But he did not go far. While the Grays were beating the Phillies 8–4 that afternoon, Murphy stood just outside, near the gate of the Messer Street Grounds, quietly nursing his wrath, determined to show that he was not a man to be trifled with. Not long after the game, when a group of Providence players emerged in their street clothes, Murphy jerked out a pistol, aimed it at Carroll, and pulled the trigger, giving off an ear-splitting bang. In his excitement, the would-be assassin missed his soaker, but the bullet skimmed along the shoulder of Joe Mulvey, a twenty-four-year-old rookie utility shortstop, inflicting a painful though not mortal wound.

As Mulvey staggered in astonishment, his assailant turned and ran, hotly pursued by Jack Farrell and a number of other shouting witnesses, including a police detective. After a chase through the West End toward downtown, police found the madman trembling at home, foolishly trying to hide. At his court arraignment two days later, Murphy was still livid—growling and threatening like a half-crazed beast. Jailed until his trial on the charge of assault with a pistol, Murphy was being led out of court when he spotted Carroll in the crowd. "I will get even with you yet!" he screamed. "I'll break your head if I ever get out again!"

Most people, fortunately, confined their fanaticism to full-throated cheer-

Cliff Carroll

ing. On this opening day 1884, a deep crowd of men and women thronged the park's two ticket offices and poured through its two turnstiles to enter the grounds, a six-acre site enclosed by a twelve-foot-high board fence. Fifty cents was the standard price of admission. An additional 25¢ bought one access to the grandstand, which seated twelve hundred people under an overhanging roof. No self-respecting man who brought a lady to the park would fail to secure her a grandstand seat. Those who did not want to pay extra for the luxury of shade could find a seat on the bleaching boards.

Since clubs were not keen about paying men for nothing, managers assigned players left off the starting lineup to work as ticket takers, reducing the expense of hiring part-time staff. Given the character of ballplayers, this could be risky business. Before one game, Grays manager Harry Wright noticed that the open seats at the Messer Street Grounds were filling up with black men—improbably, since the 50¢ price of admission tended to make baseball a white, upper-middle-class attraction. Suspicious, he went to the gate to find out what in the world was going on. He discovered that the Grays' resident troublemaker, Cliff Carroll, had conspired with a Chicago player in a plot to obtain free food from the Narragansett, "one of the largest, grandest, best furnished and most satisfactorily kept hotels in the world." The Chicago man had invited all of the waiters at the 225-room downtown establishment to come out to the entrance he was tending at the grounds, promising to smuggle them in to watch a big-league game gratis. To avoid detection, he and Carroll admitted them only two at a time, but more kept arriving at the gate, and they tended to stand out in an otherwise all-white crowd. Fortunately for the conspirators, manager Wright was more amused than outraged, and the little scheme worked brilliantly. The ballplayers ate like kings the rest of their time in Providence, Chicago writer Byron E. Clarke recalled. "Every waiter in the place wanted to wait on them, and they missed nothing that the cook could make."

Most people came to the park via the horsecars or on foot, but well-to-do spectators who drove their expensive carriages to the games could, for a fee, pass straight through a large gate at the southeast corner of the grounds and park right in the deep outfield. The premier parking earned the Grays a few extra bucks, though carriages on the outskirts of the playing area could pose some interesting defensive challenges. In 1882, Chicago catcher Silver Flint drove a ball deep to center field, sending the Grays' Paul Hines on a long chase—until Hines saw it roll under a startled horse. Declining to risk a kick in his jaw, the center fielder froze in his tracks and frantically pleaded with the coachman to hurry up and fetch him the baseball. By the time Hines threw it back to the infield, Flint was crossing the plate with one of his four home runs for the year.

Once spectators passed through the turnstiles and walked inside a baseball park, they had to be careful, because light-fingered criminals often worked the crowd, deftly lifting wallets, gold watches, and other valuables. Mark Twain, attending a game in Hartford in 1875, lost his English-made brown silk umbrella when a boy snatched it away and disappeared in the crowd while the great writer was busy "hurrahing." Twain published a notice in the *Hartford Courant* offering a $5 reward for its return. "I do not want the boy (in an active state) but will pay two hundred dollars for his remains," he declared.

Meanwhile, slightly more honest boys strapped on sacks or bins and worked the stands, hawking sandwiches, cheap cigars, caramel candy, bags of roasted peanuts, a frozen concoction called Italian cream, and lemonade or beer that was poured from a pitcher into a communal glass or mug. (Coca-Cola was not invented until 1886, and even then was marketed as a tonic, with traces of cocaine in the formula.) The classic ballpark frank was still several years away, though the great American journalist H. L. Mencken distinctly remembered something like hot dogs being sold at home games of Baltimore's Orioles during the 1880s. "They contained precisely the same rubbery, indigestible pseudo-sausages that millions of Americans now eat, and they leaked the same flabby puerile mustard," Mencken wrote. "Their single point of difference lay in the fact that their covers were honest German Wecke made of wheat-flour baked to crispness, and not the soggy rolls prevailing today, of ground acorns, plaster-of-Paris, flecks of bath-sponge, and atmospheric air all compact." The busy vendors boosted ballpark profits but irritated baseball lovers. They perpetually drowned out the umpire with their shouts, making it impossible to figure out the count of balls and strikes on the batter; or blocked a spectator's view while waiting for a customer to swig his beverage and return the glass.

If spectators wished to tell the players apart, they were wise to buy one of Bancroft's scorecards, which listed the starting lineups of both clubs. It is true that an announcer equipped with a large megaphone stood in front of the stand and bellowed out the lineup before the game. But players wore no identification on their uniforms beyond team or city name—and sometimes not even that—so it was difficult to tell who was who, at least without a scorecard.

In an attempt to remove the mystery, the National League had experimented in 1882 with a truly bizarre scheme: it dressed the men in color-coded uniform shirts, depending on their position. All catchers wore light blue, all second basemen orange-yellow and black stripes, all pitchers dark blue and white, et cetera. The plan's flaws soon became glaringly evident. For one thing, players as well as spectators found it difficult to distinguish at a glance between the fielder and the runner when, say, a first baseman got a hit and ran to first, or a third baseman ran to third. In such cases, the fielder and runner, though on opposing teams, were wearing the same uniform—and neither, of course, wore a glove! And the whole point of the system broke down if players had to switch positions during the game. The men themselves felt ridiculous. When Joe Start first came to the plate in his outfit, "there was a great shout of laughter from the crowd. Joe looked like a great big overgrown school boy," the *Providence Evening Press* reported. "His jacket was red and black, and his knickerbockers with the broad white belt, appeared to come well up under his arms." Jack Farrell was so embarrassed he kept his old gray knit jacket over his uniform, but finally had to remove it when he got too hot. "Then the laugh was turned on him, for he bloomed out in a blouse of bright yellow and black, and as he danced about looked like a huge 'yellow jacket' wasp." Players despised the "clown" costumes, and the crackpot concept was abandoned long before the end of the season. Surprisingly, the infinitely simpler—and seemingly obvious—solution to the problem did not catch on until 1929, when the Cleveland Indians and New York Yankees put numbers on the back of players' uniforms, initially on the basis of place in the batting order (which is why Babe Ruth wore number 3 and Lou Gehrig number 4).

Even with an official scorecard in hand, a spectator had to pay close attention to follow the game. Hand-operated scoreboards posted only runs scored, not balls and strikes. The single umpire, his voice hoarse from overuse, did not yet employ hand signals, and people in the grandstand attempting to fathom the pitch count had to strain to hear what he called. Testy spectators often yelled, "Louder!"

At the Messer Street Grounds, Providence audiences looked out on an uncommonly smooth infield that was "as level as constant rolling by heavy stone and iron rollers can make it," the *Morning Star* noted. Good grass covered most of the field, with a wide dirt path linking home plate and the pitcher's box, and narrow dirt paths between the bases, not the sweeping, curving diamond of today. The press box stood in front of the raised grandstand, below the view of spectators; there, newspapermen kept score as they sat on a long sofa. Underneath the grandstand were a pair of twenty-foot-square dressing rooms, one for each club, sparing players the indignity of dressing at the hotel and riding to the grounds in uniform via public transportation, often an invitation to be assaulted by fanatics armed with rancid eggs and rotten tomatoes. There was even a washroom equipped with running water and a "closet"—presumably a toilet. Such amenities were rare, even in the top leagues, where a whole team typically got one pail of water to share in washing up after the game. In those early days of big-league baseball, "the request for an extra pail or a few more nails to hang clothes on would be greeted with derision," Sam Crane recalled, "while the thought of running water would have caused the owner to go daffy." As a further luxury, the park's dressing rooms were separated from the field by a fence, "thereby preventing the crowd from having any talk with the players." By the standards of 1870s and 1880s baseball, this was a state-of-the-art facility. "It is not too much to say that these elegant grounds are unexcelled in this country," the *Boston Globe* opined. "The fence which protects the enclosure is a piece of ornamental work, and the grand stand is good enough for royalty to occupy." Harry Wright said of the grounds, "They are beautiful."

And they were open again for a new season.

Sweeney was in his element, feeling strong and sure as he warmed up. Loosening up for the Blues of Cleveland was their ace, Jim McCormick, a genial twenty-seven-year-old born in Glasgow, Scotland, and raised in Paterson, New Jersey. Though hampered by injuries in 1883, the tall, heavy, hard-throwing McCormick had won a remarkable 135 games over his previous four seasons, and if anyone could beat Sweeney at this point, he was a top candidate. Ominously, Radbourn, who had battled many times against McCormick, was sitting this one out completely. A good hitter, he usually played in the field when he was not pitching. But Radbourn was of no use today, his pain evidently flaring up again after the thin ray of hope in New Bedford.

In the grandstand, decorated with opening-day bunting, sat invited guests—Mayor Thomas A. Doyle, judges, bigwigs of all sorts who could get away with skipping work. "Nearly the entire city government were present," the *Evening Telegram* noted. But plenty of less prominent spectators poured in, too, eager for the new season. "The butcher, the baker, the candlestick maker, they all went to the game together." Women turned out in large numbers—some of them ardent admirers of the sport, some merely admirers "of the lithe forms of the athletic-looking ball players." They wore long dresses that buttoned at the chin, with bustles in back, large hats, and gloves, but "their costumes were a mixture of winter and spring" that afternoon, with coats on top, given the cool breezes that were piercing through the sun's warmth.

Cleveland won the coin toss, choosing to send Providence to bat first. The crowd of 2,395 settled in to watch the two superb pitchers do battle, and a pitchers' duel is exactly what they got, with help from a brilliant little fielder. In the fourth inning, Cleveland runner "Gentle Willie" Murphy was taking a lead at second base, when Mike Muldoon teed off on a Sweeney pitch, driving the ball to deep right-center field, far over the head of the Grays' Paul Hines, for what looked like a sure inside-the-park homer. Racing across the field, a blur from nowhere, Shorty Radford caught the ball on a dead run and, Willie Mays–like, spun and fired it sharply to second baseman Moose Farrell, doubling up Murphy, who was as stunned as anyone at the improbable catch. Radford made two more dashing barehanded catches in the fifth inning, one off his shoestring. His spectacular sprinting catches were "the brilliant feature of the game," according to the *Journal*, underscoring Bancroft's wisdom in signing the Boston castoff.

As the scoreless innings passed, the afternoon grew colder, and the "sea of pinched faces and blue, chattering lips" in the stands suffered under "the chilling zephyrs that Old Boreas occasionally puffed across the field," the *Evening Telegram* noted operatically. A flock of wild geese honked and beat their wings over the park, their triangular formation breaking up when they reached center field—an aerial ballet that the *Telegram* reporter read as a bad omen. The game was still scoreless in the bottom of the seventh inning when Gentle Willie got his third scratch hit of the day. Muldoon then shot a "daisy cutter" past Farrell into center field, while Murphy tore for third base. Hines gobbled up the ball and heaved it to third, trying to cut down the runner. Instead, the ball soared over the head of third baseman Jerry Denny, and Murphy scored the first run. In the eighth inning, Cleveland added another.

The Grays were down 2–0 with only one inning left to play. It was nearing five o'clock, getting darker and colder. Providence had scratched out only one hit all day against the mighty McCormick. Then the Grays came to life. Catcher Barney Gilligan led off with a single, reaching second when Murphy muffed Radford's fly ball to center field. Hines fouled out, but Farrell slapped a single to right field, driving home Gilligan and halving Cleveland's lead to 2–1. On the play, right fielder "Bloody Jake" Evans, a fine fielder with a strong arm, tried to cut down Radford at third, but the little fellow slid in safely when Mike Muldoon dropped the ball. The tying run was now just ninety feet away, with only one out.

The crowd was into the game at last, roaring with excitement when Joe Start slammed a grounder to first, sending Radford tearing for home. Cleveland's Phillips scooped up the ball and fired it to catcher Fatty Briody. In a cloud of dust, "Radford slid under Briody, and touched the plate," the *Boston Globe* correspondent noted, "but he was declared out." The *Sporting Life*, the *Journal*, and the crowd all agreed with the *Globe* on this point: the umpire had robbed the Grays. Instead of tying the game with only one out, the Grays were still behind, and down to their final out. Joe Start stood on first base, the mean Moose Farrell on third. Then, in a daring if foolhardy play: Start tore for second base, drawing a throw from Briody, as Farrell broke for home. Rookie second baseman Joe Ardner ignored Start and fired a strike back to Briody, who tagged out Farrell at the plate. Game over!

The *Journal* reporter fumed over the opening-day defeat, complaining bitterly in the next morning's paper about the "infantile batting and careless base-running of the home nine," as well as the Grays' "nervous play at critical points." But the real culprit was the flustered umpire, working his first National League game—John S. Burns of New Britain, Connecticut, the brother of Chicago shortstop Tom Burns.

Umpires of the time were among the most hated figures in America, and not all of the contempt was earned. The National League did a poor job training them. They worked alone, making it virtually impossible to see everything that was going on in the field and thus to render absolutely just rulings. Moreover, they were subject to such a degree of abuse from the players, the newspapers, and the grandstand—up to and including life-threatening violence—that it was difficult for the League to find good men willing to take the job. It was little wonder that their work was uneven. Wearing the National League's regulation gray suit and straw hat, Burns proved in his very first game to be "a lamentable failure, his judgment on balls and strikes being decidedly wretched," the *Journal* groused, complaining that most of his calls went against the Grays. "He has lots to learn," the *Telegram* agreed, though it thought the ruffians in the bleachers along first base were out of line in directing ear-scorching vulgarities at him. Both catchers tried to take Burns's maddening inconsistency in stride, and Fatty Briody could be heard muttering sotto voce, "Well, he *is* a daisy," after an egregious call. "The way he dodged away from the ball and failed to see it when it crossed squarely over the plate was enough to make a stone statue weep," the *Providence Evening Press* lamented. Providence was far from alone in questioning Burns's fitness to be a major-league umpire. For weeks to come, there would be constant complaints about Burns's ignorance and incompetence, leading to his firing in the middle of the season. At one point, Burns allegedly protested idiotically to a pitcher who complained about his judgment of balls and strikes: "If you wouldn't curve 'em so much I'd give you more strikes." Later that spring, when someone presented Burns with a bouquet of flowers on the field, the *Sunday Morning Telegram* expressed astonishment, observing: "It isn't possible he has any admirers outside of deaf and dumb and blind asylums."

The *Daily Evening News*, which served the nearby factory town of Fall River, Massachusetts, and blatantly favored Boston over Providence, had no sympathy for the bellyachers. It dubbed the *Journal*'s baseball reporter "Sir

Misery," in tribute to his habit of carping about the home team and whining over unfair umpires. A loss in the season opener was sure to make him cry and kick in the next day's paper. "There were many here last night," the paper sneered, "who predicted he would play his baby act in the morning."

An opening-day defeat is always tough to take, but most ballplayers learn quickly that it's a good idea to roll with the punches of a long season. There were still 111 left to play. The big question now was whether the Grays had a functioning two-man pitching rotation anymore. Radbourn had endured an April of waiting and hoping, jealously watching Sweeney steal his glory. He could wait no longer. After a fair, cool opening day, Friday afternoon was damp and downright cold, hardly ideal conditions for a man with a sore arm. But Radbourn told Bancroft he was ready. Just to be safe, the manager posted Sweeney in right field, ready to trade places. After his brilliant opener in right field, Radford earned his salary in the second game by working the turnstiles, collecting tickets.

To Bancroft's immense relief, no switch proved necessary. Charlie was not flawless, but he could throw, he had good motion, he had control of his pitches, and he managed to work his way out of tight spots. In an economical one hour and twenty-five minutes, Radbourn dispatched Cleveland, 5–2, allowing only five hits. "Radbourn's return to the points seemed to give his team new inspiration, and any doubts as to his ability to curve or drop the sphere with his consummate skill and shrewd judgment, from lameness, were speedily expelled," the *Journal* enthused. After a long spring on the shelf, Radbourn was back—perhaps not in top form, but able to throw, and eager to resume his place as the Grays' star pitcher. The fight for the role of club ace was on.

On Saturday, some four hundred children, laughing, spinning, and tugging, passed through the turnstiles with their parents and friends, handing over the 10¢ admission for Children's Day. Their high-pitched cheers rang out over the crowd of fifteen hundred as their new hero, the dashing young Sweeney, strolled to the pitcher's box to face the Buffalo club, one of the hardest-hitting teams in the game. Aggravated by his loss on opening day and Radbourn's victory on Friday, the twenty-one-year-old threw one of the masterpieces of his career. Sweeney came painfully close to a perfect game: no walks, no errors, no runs, and one lousy hit—a feeble tap by Dan Brouthers between the pitcher and first baseman. Joe Start ran in to grab it and raced Brouthers neck and neck for the bag; he just barely lost. Still, the 3–0 win was sweet, Sweeney's first of the year. After the requisite Sunday break, Radbourn got his turn, and on Monday recorded his second straight 5–2 victory. The two teammates had begun a season-long battle to one-up each other.

Cleveland returned to town on Wednesday, a dark, windy, and rainy afternoon, like so many others that spring. Only about a hundred fanatics turned out for a game that most sane people thought would be canceled. But the contest went on, and Sweeney, following up on his near-perfect performance four days earlier, poured it on again. He was dominating his opponents, 7–0, in the fourth, when the Cleveland men—who were certain to lose unless they could get the game to be called before it became official—pleaded with the umpire, the irritatingly incompetent John Burns, to end this insanity before five innings could be played. To the Grays' utter exasperation, mere outs before the game could go into the books as a Providence victory, Burns called time. Manager Charlie Hackett, hoping to prod Burns to call the game, hurried his Cleveland men to pack up their bats and run off the grounds before he changed his mind. Not bothering to stop by the dressing room, they were outside the park's carriage gate in no time. Rain pouring off his derby hat, Bancroft furiously demanded that Burns declare a forfeit, since the umpire had merely called time, not the game itself, and the other team was no longer here to play. Catching some of this conversation, Hackett ran through the left field gate, splashed onto Messer Street, and hollered at his men to come back. The Cleveland players hurried back and waited just inside the gate, water dripping from their caps and soaking their woolen uniforms. During the twenty-five-minute delay, several "amused themselves in playing hop, skip, and jump, seemingly oblivious of the rain," the *Journal* reported, while Cleveland shortstop Jack Glasscock repeatedly badgered the umpire to call it. "I am running this game, Glasscock; shut up," Burns shot back.

The *Journal* reporter insisted the precipitation was a mere trifle: enough to moisten the infield grass, but certainly not enough to send home the intrepid band of spectators. Indeed, local diehards went out on the field and dramatically stood there in the drizzle with their closed umbrellas under their arms, pointing to the portion of the umpire's guidelines that read, "The game shall not be postponed while patrons do not seek shelter." No matter. With Sweeney sitting atop another shutout, only one inning shy of a regulation game, it began raining hard again. The hated umpire Burns waved his arms, and that was that—the game was called, and Providence was robbed of a sure victory. It was a travesty, the *Journal* complained, arguing the Grays had played in much worse weather: "Patrons remembered a game last season which was completed when it was found necessary to dig holes to drain off the water and to fill the base lines with sawdust." The *Fall River Daily Evening News* scoffed that the *Journal* would only be satisfied when the National League installed an utterly biased umpire incapable of heeding the other team at all: "It's no use; some one has got to secure a statue of [Rhode Island founder] Roger Williams, wheel him onto the Providence grounds, and insist that he shall turn his deaf ear to the visiting nine, and treat them with a heart of stone."

Cleveland left town without playing another game on the spongy, muddy grounds. It was another two days before the rain let up enough for baseball to resume. On Friday, May 9, another cool and dismal day—more "pneumonia weather," the *Providence Evening Press* lamented—Bancroft found his men in a crippled condition. Radbourn had a lame arm "and could get no speed on the sphere." Sweeney "could not raise his arm, owing to a troublesome stitch in his back." Sandy Nava was injured, Jack Farrell "had a very severe attack of apparent pneumonia," and Arthur Irwin had a terrible cold. Bancroft made hasty plans to pitch a twenty-one-year-old rookie named John Cattanach. A tall, strong, and graceful athlete who was raised on Providence's East Side, and a champion rower with the Narragansett Boat Club, Cattanach had been training all spring under Bancroft's tutelage to make the difficult leap to professional baseball. With his muscular arms and thick upper torso, he could throw the ball impressively hard, but like many novices he had serious trouble finding the plate, and Bancroft did not entirely trust him yet to win at the major-league level. Fortunately, just before the game, Radbourn rallied and—perhaps fortified with some medicinal whiskey—declared he would try to pitch after all. He strode onto a slippery field and threw his third straight five-hit victory, beating Buffalo's Bisons 3–1 in front of a stalwart crowd of 747.

To say the least, this was not the kind of weather that helped the muscles and tendons of pitchers. Buffalo's "Pud" Galvin made a decision that afternoon he would soon regret: he worked the game without his flannel sweatshirt beneath his uniform, unwittingly letting his muscles tighten up. The following morning, while riding the rumbling elevator in the plush Narragansett Hotel, the twenty-seven-year-old reached down for his heavy valise. A searing pain stabbed through his right side, making it hard for him to move or breathe. Galvin—who was an incredible workhorse,

Pud Galvin

having pitched seventy-two complete games in 1883—was nearly paralyzed with pain. He staggered home to Buffalo to rest up under the care of his family physician, Dr. Stockton, hoping to be ready for the home opener there on May 21. Galvin was soon throwing again. Still, under the tough conditions of 1880s baseball, when physical therapy was nonexistent, the episode was a reminder that injuries could strike down anyone at any time, even one of baseball's iron men.

With Buffalo and Cleveland out of the way, it was time for Providence to confront a much scarier adversary. And Radbourn had a particular reason—one from the heart—for wanting to defeat that big, domineering bunch.

CHAPTER 8

She's Yours, Rad

In her well-appointed parlor, the visitors beheld in the glow of gaslight a beautiful twenty-eight-year-old woman, fashionably attired in a long dress that accentuated her shapely body while keeping most of it hidden, from her plunging neckline to the toes of her high-heeled shoes. With sparkling eyes, a bright smile, and a sweet, warm voice, she rose from her seat to welcome the men who had come to visit her at her boardinghouse at the corner of Washington Street and Union Street in downtown Providence, just down the busy street from Union Depot and City Hall.

On the strength of these fetching personal attributes and her wit and ambition, this former shopgirl had become what one newspaper called a "prominent figure in town"—prominent, certainly, with traveling men who were frequent guests at her house in the evening, enjoying drinks, good conversation and other forms of hospitality. Carrie Stanhope "was attractive and a fashionable dresser," the *Boston Globe* observed, "and her admirers were numerous among the baseball fraternity and the theatrical profession." Actors and ballplayers, vagabonds who roamed far from home and family to perform before a demanding public, had much in common, and they often made fast friends. During a stop in Detroit that September, Grays third baseman Jerry Denny presented the comedian and minstrel star Billy Baxter with a fashionable walking cane stamped with the names of all the Providence players. "Billy looks upon it as a relic of friendship and favor," the *Sporting Life* reported. The players may well have formed their friendship with the hard-drinking star at Carrie's house, enjoying his banjo picking and southern songs crooned in a comical parody of black dialect. Certainly, members of the eight National League clubs that played in Providence were well acquainted with the attractive lady and her establishment. "She personally knew every man of the league teams, and many of them used to make their headquarters here at her big boarding house in lower Washington St." Since each of the teams carried about 14 players, that was 112 men to personally know.

She introduced herself to newcomers as Mrs. Stanhope, and told everyone she was a widow, but Carrie was no widow. Unbeknownst to her visitors, she was still married to a man named Charles Stanhope, who worked as a marine engineer thirty miles south in Newport. A sleepy city cooled by ocean breezes, and one of colonial America's major ports, it was now the summer playground of America's fabulously rich, who were building vast mansions they called "cottages" along the rocky Atlantic coastline. Carrie had been left to fend for herself in the much bigger, busier, smokier city of Providence, caring for her widowed mother, her teenage sister, and her young son, Charles, whose future meant everything to her. An astute businesswoman who capitalized on her assets, she made a good enough living from her house to support her family.

But, about to pass the zenith of her beauty, she was not without dreams of finding a man who would sweep her away from this place to live a different life, a man who would love her and take care of her and her child. It was said that she was deeply in love with a

Fashionably dressed woman
Detail of *The Love Letter* (1883), by
Auguste Toulmouche

member of Chicago's White Stockings, who were passing through Providence in mid-May 1884 for a series of games. Which player, it was not known. Among her many fervent admirers was another man, said to be of less interest to her, a quiet but intense member of the local team named Charles Radbourn—one more Charles, like her husband and her son. This Charles was wont to gaze at her, surely, with the watchful eyes of a hunter long accustomed to patience in stalking wild creatures. Jealous and fiercely competitive, Radbourn had reason to hate the White Stockings. They had not only repeatedly thwarted his pennant ambitions; they also counted in their ranks, it seems, the man who had stolen the heart of the girl he needed to be his own.

The White Stockings—known today as the Chicago Cubs—ate weaker clubs for breakfast, and for most of that decade had lorded it over their inferiors, the rest of the National League. They had won pennants in 1880, 1881, and 1882, and had nearly come from behind to win in 1883. There was every reason to believe the White Stockings would bounce back in 1884.

People stood in awe of this club, and many in that generation would go to their graves believing it was the best that ever took the field. The White Stockings of the early 1880s "played ball with more grace and knowledge of the game than any team before or since," former major leaguer Tim Murnane wrote in 1904, when he was the longtime baseball editor of the *Boston Globe*. The American public certainly thought these players were something special, and they drew bigger and more excited crowds—home and away— than any other team in the league. They were a jaw-dropping sight when they marched onto the field, their six-foot-tall players—muscular, mean, mustachioed men—out in front, the whole lot dressed in the best uniforms money could buy, with white silk stockings and crisp black knickers and jerseys, CHICAGO stitched in bold white letters on the front. "They look like murderers," one Worcester man gasped when the Chicago players arrived in his city. Their smaller, more shabbily attired opponents could not help feeling intimidated. "We had most of 'em whipped before we even threw a ball," Chicago star Mike Kelly boasted. "We had 'em scared ter death." It's no wonder men—and women—were impressed.

The White Stockings dominated baseball for one overriding reason: their great captain, Adrian Anson, had schooled them to play baseball the Chicago way, using brains, brawn, bravery, and bluster. A gruff, muscular, six-foot-tall leader, and a brilliant and unyielding hitter, surely the greatest of the nineteenth century, Cap Anson drilled his men hard in what came to be known as fundamentals, training them to coordinate their efforts, to back each other up, and to hit the cutoff man on a throw from the outfield. He taught them the hit-and-run play, the suicide squeeze, and how to move a runner along by hitting to the right side of the diamond. He taught them the newfangled hook slide, whereby players threw their bodies away from the bag, tapping the base's edge with a hard-to-tag hand or foot—a play that, for decades to come, sportswriters called "the Chicago slide." He taught them how to poke an outside pitch for a

Cap Anson

hit to the opposite field, instead of swinging with all their might and trying to pull the ball. Connie Mack called him the game's consummate general, "the Napoleon of the diamond."

Forever spoiling for a fight, Anson bulldozed umpires who dared rule against Chicago, so readily screaming that sportswriters dubbed him "Baby" Anson, while cartoonists depicted him as an infant, tears streaming down his red, bawling face. When a call went against his team, he typically "let out a war whoop that could have been heard above the roar of Niagara," and burst from the bench to jaw at the umpire, spewing spittle and industrial-strength profanity in the face of a man who was usually shorter and weaker. Hostile crowds jeered at his rages, but Anson did not care. "I have got used to being hauled over the coals, and rather like it, because it is a good 'ad' for me," he declared. "If the public can stand it, I'm sure I can." One of his teammates confirmed that boast: "I've been on the ball fields with him, and heard five thousand people shouting, howling and hissing him, but he only smiled. He liked it."

Most of all, Anson inculcated in his men the moral code of Gilded Age politicians and industrial moguls: a savage zeal to win by any means, fair or foul. "And if anything stood in the way of his ambitions, be it friend or foe, it had to get out of his way or go to the mat," recalled Hardie Richardson, second baseman for the Buffalo club. Anson despised rally-killing double plays, for example, and ordered his men to maul the infielders, if need be, to break them up. He showed the way in one game, thundering straight at Richardson, who tagged second and tried to throw the ball toward first— only to clobber the captain in the head instead. "The ball didn't hit him fair on the cranium, or there might not have been any more Cap," Richardson said. "It glanced off his skull to the stands without doing any more damage than 'raising an egg.'" If the brush with brain damage or death frightened Anson, he did not let on. As he jogged back to the bench, his head throbbing beneath his cloth cap, the captain laughed and called to his men, "I say, you white-livered boobies, I stopped that one, anyhow." Such examples inspired his White Stockings to threaten umpires, bang into infielders and block their view, grab the jerseys of enemy base runners, and heckle and insult opposing batters and pitchers, sometimes bellowing at them so ferociously that they could not focus on the task at hand.

The greatest of this bunch was Mike Kelly, who usually worked in right field or behind the plate but was so clever and athletically gifted that he could, and did, play any position, including pitcher. And while he adopted Anson's credo of intimidating and outwitting opponents, he did something more. He cheated—frequently, outrageously, and almost unbelievably. As a catcher, he threw his clunky mask in front of runners trying to score, hoping to make them stumble before they reached the plate. As a runner, he readily blocked fielders from making plays; as a fielder, he shoved and tripped men racing past him. Most notoriously, he recklessly cut bases, dashing from first to third without bothering to touch second base, or from second base to home without touching third, counting on the lone umpire to be preoccupied with following the flight of the ball. The press called it "the Kelly trick."

Providence had particular reason to resent Kelly and his wiles. In mid-September 1882, in the pivotal game of the season's most important series, the Grays were about to shut down a Chicago rally with a double play when Kelly veered out of the baseline and barreled into shortstop George

Wright, punching him in the shoulder just as he was throwing. The ball flew off wildly and rolled under the grandstand as the tying run scored, and the resulting rally tilted the game—and ultimately the pennant—to Chicago. George, one of the most graceful shortstops in history, suffered the ignominy of being charged with the biggest error of the season, the umpire having missed Kelly's brazen interference. Throwing aside his mild manner for once, Providence manager Harry Wright, George's older brother, blasted Kelly in the press for the dirty trick. Mike later tried to calm the waters: "Mr. Wright, I have played ball for a number of years; I will do everything in the world to win a championship game of ball. That is what I am paid for. . . . I play ball to win, and if I have to employ a few subterfuges to win I cannot help it. I wouldn't willfully hurt George Wright, or any man in your club. But self-preservation is the law of nature. When I saw George raise his arm, I knew that if something didn't occur we would be defeated. I didn't think of George nor myself. I simply thought of the Chicago club." Harry, a lifelong advocate of fair play, ruefully told a reporter about the incident: "It's a cold day [in hell] when Kelly doesn't work some racket or other."

If there was any threat to the White Stockings' continued dominance of baseball, it was their propensity to drink as fervently as they played. Chicago's star players were notorious for their all-night benders, and some were accused of appearing on the field at times still inebriated, unfit to compete. It seemed only a matter of time until the men began to lose their edge. Until they did, though, the big, bad White Stockings would be regarded as one of the best teams in the league, expected to fight hard against Boston and Providence. If the Grays wanted to go all the way, they would have to beat Anson's talented thugs, starting here and now.

Mike Kelly

* * *

Umpire Billy McLean strode onto the grass of the Messer Street Grounds, trying to close his ears to the usual catcalls popping out of the half-filled grandstand and bleachers. It was a Saturday afternoon, May 10, and a decent crowd of 1,478 had turned out to watch the hometown boys battle Chicago. Carrie Stanhope, eager to see her favorite in action, might well have been among them, since she frequently climbed aboard the horsecars a few blocks from her house and rode down Westminster Street to the ballpark. "If there was one thing that Carrie Stanhope loved better than anything else," the *Boston Globe* noted, "it was a stubbornly fought game of baseball." A fashionable woman was an ornament to any crowd, and owners encouraged their attendance, since the presence of females tended to temper males' proclivity for profanity and violence.

Umpire McLean, a pugnacious and short-tempered man, was relieved to hear a smattering of polite applause quickly drown out the bellowed insults. He was well known in this town, and the real baseball fanatics were happy to see him taking over the umpiring duties from his dubious colleague, John Burns, who could not call the game because of a glaring conflict: his brother played shortstop for the White Stockings. Unlike the flustered Burns, McLean brought battle-hardened experience onto the ball field, having umpired big-league contests for years. Nor was he easily intimidated. A former professional pugilist, he angrily turned on anyone who challenged him, and kept in shape with prodigious feats of walking. In 1879, he had reportedly trooped all forty-two miles from Boston to Providence to umpire a game, having stepped out of his doorway at 4:00 a.m. to make it on time.

All the same, like most of his umpiring peers, McLean was far from perfect. Just two weeks before this May afternoon, infuriated by one fan's taunts at Philadelphia's Recreation Park, he had grabbed a bat and flung it viciously into the grandstand, braining an innocent bystander and nearly inciting a riot. Handcuffed and hauled off for summary justice, McLean escaped a prison sentence by paying a $500 fine, a sizeable chunk of his annual income. In a public letter, he apologized and pleaded for understanding, but for all that did not sound terribly contrite: "Goaded by uncalled-for, as well as unexpected taunts, I, for a moment, and but for a moment, forgot my position as an umpire and did what any man's nature would prompt if placed in a similar situation." Nineteenth-century American males were not bred to turn the other cheek; their sense of manhood compelled them to answer insults with violence, and McLean urged club owners to "enforce the strictest order on their grounds," warning that "otherwise the death of an honest and manly game is in the near future," since no red-blooded American would stand for the kind of abuse that had been showered on him.

Bancroft assigned Charlie Sweeney to work the game on that Saturday afternoon, though the kid was starting to feel the effects of more than a month of hard pitching in cool, clammy weather. He faced off against Chicago's scrawny ace, five-foot-three, 127-pound Larry Corcoran. Like Cleveland's much taller and stronger Jim McCormick, Larry had won an impressive 135 games over the previous four years; unlike McCormick, he had pitched his club to three pennants. He was a rugged little pony, not easily rattled, and intense: a reporter noted he "is very clever and sociable off the field, but gets cranky and crabbed when playing ball and never smiles until he gets his uniform off." The Grays, always persistent foes, failed to improve his mood that day. After a scoreless first, Providence plated a run in the second, and added another in the third. Then the White Stockings bench, fearing the game might slip away, went to work. Kelly and his cronies, well aware of Sweeney's short fuse, began bellowing insults and complaining to McLean that the pitcher was cheating, and for a time Charlie seemed distracted. But he soon settled down with the help of his San Francisco buddy at third base, Jerry Denny, who brilliantly speared a low line drive barehanded and doubled a runner off first.

In the fourth inning, Providence broke it open, taking a 5–0 lead. Anson's men attempted a comeback in the bottom of the fourth, as George Gore blasted a drive over Paul Hines's head for a double, and Kelly slapped him home with a single. But, aided by what the *Journal* called Chicago's uncharacteristically "amateur fielding," the Grays added four more runs in the final three innings to walk away with a 9–1 victory before the amazed and delighted home crowd. Providence's manhandling of the mighty White Stockings—every Grays batter clubbed at least one hit off Corcoran, eleven all told—certainly surprised the *Journal* reporter, who noted that Anson's men "seemed to be demoralized and in poor playing form." Maybe they had stayed up too late the night before, celebrating their return to Providence with liquor and women. In any event, the big Saturday crowd, in the words of the *Providence Evening Press*, "watched the Providence nine do the Chicagos to a nice brown and turn them over."

Impressively, Sweeney had kept his emotions in check, zeroed in on Chicago's fearsome hitters, and allowed only six hits while striking out five. Two weeks into the season, Providence's starting duo, despite recurring arm pain, were performing beautifully. "Radbourne and Sweeney are using their 'lame' arms to good advantage; they had better not let them get well," the *Fall River Daily Evening News* quipped.

After a Sunday off, Anson's men seemed in better shape to do battle on Monday, May 12. Radbourn, itching to beat Chicago, got the start. But however much he hoped to impress Carrie and put his rival in his place, he simply could not muster the strength or control to keep Providence in the game. Chicago's Mike Kelly, playing shortstop that afternoon, stirred things up, as usual. When Paul Revere Radford tried to sprint to third base, Kelly—whom the *Journal* described as "the conspicuous sneak of the white-legged ex-champions"—jumped into his path and blocked him, earning the crowd's hisses and maledictions. This time, though, the umpire saw the whole thing. McLean waved the runner to third base and sternly reprimanded Kelly. All the same, Chicago hurler Fred Goldsmith cruised to a 5–0, four-hit shutout, a loss the *Journal*'s morose reporter attributed to the Grays' "useless air agitation and loose, spiritless fielding."

Chicago went to Boston for a couple of games, giving Providence a crack at a much weaker Detroit team. Sweeney set the Grays back on the winning track on May 13, beating Detroit 4–1 on a five-hitter. On the following afternoon, Radbourn sought to do the same. Before a tiny but enthusiastic crowd of 420, the Grays batters came to life, smashing the ball all over the park and treating Detroit's exhausted fielders "to some of the liveliest leather chasing that they will experience this season," while Radbourn flummoxed the Wolverines with his usual mélange of curves and fastballs. Indeed, he would have posted a shutout, but to spare his arm some, he deliberately put the ball directly over the plate in the waning innings, counting on his nimble fielders to do the work of finishing the game. Providence ended up thumping Detroit, 25–3, the Grays' biggest pasting of an opponent since their legendary 28–0 rout of the Phillies the previous August. Radbourn, happy to rebound from his dismal showing against Chicago, won the game both in the pitcher's box and at the plate, slamming as many hits that afternoon (five) as he allowed. All in all, it was a good tune-up for the return of the White Stockings, who had dropped two close games in Boston.

Some 1,450 people attended the battle on Thursday, May 15, a fine crowd for another gray, somber afternoon that prophesied rain. Sweeney took the box. The Grays were in a weakened condition: their stalwart captain, Joe Start, was sick with malaria, a mosquito-borne disease that prostrated the patient with recurring bouts of chills and sweats, and still struck Americans in the nineteenth century, particularly if they had been down south. Radbourn took Joe's place at first base, happy to be able to fight Chicago with his bat and hands, if not his pitching arm. Kelly, again playing shortstop, was in top form: he quite deliberately collided with Cliff Carroll, slowing the speedy runner, and earned a $5 fine for sassing umpire McLean. He also hooted at Sandy Nava so vociferously that the catcher dropped a foul pop-up. The White Stockings, displaying their old power, sent nine men to the plate in the third inning and jumped to a 5–0 lead—but from then on, Providence steadily chipped away at the enemy's lead, while a focused Sweeney silenced Chicago's big hitters. Providence scored two in the third, one in the fourth, one in the sixth, and one in the seventh, until it became a new game at 5–5.

By then, great gray clouds of mist were sweeping over the little park, making it difficult for the spectators and even players to see what was transpiring on the field. Chicago's fleet Billy Sunday—later to gain renown as America's most famous evangelist—took first base, and Sweeney tried to hold him there. But when Sweeney rushed an attempted pickoff throw to Radbourn, the ball sailed right past the first baseman, letting Sunday scoot to second. Radbourn "made a great 'kick,'" informing the umpire that it was too damn dark to see the mud-stained ball, but McLean told him to shut up and play. After one more pitch, the heavens opened, and the umpire called time. For eighteen minutes it rained, but the second it let up, Cap Anson, always the competitor, ran out onto the field and insisted that the game continue, persuading McLean to restart the action. Sweeney, dealing with a wet ball, uncorked a wild pitch, and Sunday scooted to third base as Anson and his men yelled lustily. The run that might secure Chicago the victory was a scant ninety feet away, with no one out. But Sweeney now had fire in his eyes, and the kid thrilled the home crowd by striking out the next three White Stockings hitters to escape the seventh inning unscathed.

In the eighth inning, the rain started blowing again, and McLean again halted the game. That looked like the end of it, and about two-thirds of the audience abandoned the stands for their warm, dry homes. McLean tried to get the contest restarted, but before the ninth inning could commence, the heavens opened again, necessitating a further delay. The shower drowned the field and made the ball so slippery that it was almost impossible to clutch and throw, and night was starting to descend over the misted, dark park. But the game resumed at 6:00 p.m. Shorty Radford got things going in the ninth with the help of the elements. He swung at and missed a third strike, but the catcher fumbled it, and the ball rolled toward the pitcher, who would have to throw him out at first. As Radford sprinted down the baseline, Corcoran grabbed the slick ball and whipped it to Anson. It popped out of his hands, and Radford was on. Exploiting the opening, Shorty hastily stole second, then got to third on an error by shortstop Kelly, the man who had arrogantly blocked him a few days before. When Jack Farrell ripped the rolling, spitting ball past Kelly into the outfield, Radford scored the go-ahead run. Paul Hines followed closely on his heels across the plate when left fielder Abner Dalrymple had trouble picking up the ball.

The game went to the bottom of the ninth, with Anson's men suddenly behind 7–5. Pitcher Larry Corcoran started things off auspiciously with a single and stole second and third, while Kelly got to second base. With two men out, one hit would tie the game—and Chicago's best and fiercest hitter, Cap Anson, was striding to the plate. Anson spat on his hands, grasped the bat, thumped the plate twice, and stared at the pitcher. Sweeney heaved the ball, and Anson took a vicious swing, pounding it toward second base. Anything could happen with a wet ball and barehanded fielders. But Farrell clutched the spinning sphere, flipped to Radbourn at first, and the rain-drenched game was over. Providence had roared from behind to beat Chicago, 7–5. "Water never did agree with Kelly's complexion," the *Fall River Daily Evening News* quipped; he preferred whiskey.

Providence had now won two out of three against the murderers from Chicago. It was Radbourn's turn to start the final game of the series the following day, but with his arm still weak and sore and Start still suffering in bed, Bancroft thought it made better sense to return Rad to first base. That meant Sweeney had to go back to the pitcher's box—without even a day's rest. That was risky, to be sure; even a young, resilient pitcher could strain his arm if he worked too hard when he was tired. But White Stockings pitcher Fred Goldsmith seemed to be the one whose arm had given out, surrendering eleven hits before the afternoon was through. Radbourn, who went 2 for 4 with a double that day, suffered a spike wound in his left hand while trying to score from third. The painful cut made it impossible for him to stay at first, where his hands would have to take a pounding from the ball on almost every play, and he traded places with center fielder Paul Hines. Later in the game, Goldsmith knocked a fly ball over Radbourn's head for a double, and Gore drove Goldy home with a single. But that was all the run getting against Sweeney, who threw a five-hit gem and won, 4–1, his third victory in the series against Chicago. "His Curves Puzzle Anson's Children," the *Evening Telegram* headlined. The crowd of 962 entertained itself by scoreboard watching, as a running tally of the ongoing Boston game was posted on the board. Cheers erupted when Detroit's Wolverines improbably beat the Red Stockings, lifting Providence to just one game behind the second-place champions and two games behind first-place New York.

The White Stockings, meanwhile, reeled into a death spiral of eight straight defeats, and even their usual cheating and intimidation did not seem to help. " 'Baby' Anson's pets are up to their old tricks. It won't do this season, Anson," the *Sunday Morning Telegram* exulted. "The days of bulldozing the Providence nine out of ten games is past and the sooner you come to this conclusion the better." Back home in Chicago, club president Albert G. Spalding could barely contain his rage. On May 20, Anson received a letter from his boss demanding a crackdown on the men's notorious drinking, authorizing Anson to hire private detectives to trail players who failed to stay in bed after the 11:00 p.m. check. The owner fumed that he was "thoroughly disgusted with the miserable exhibition made by the club on its trip and that players must be made to understand that they must render some equivalent for the high salaries they receive" and that "I am tired of apologizing for the shortcomings of some of our men." After reading the letter, Anson tore it up and threw it into a spittoon. But some enterprising reporter fished it out of the revolting muck and got it into print.

Shaking off the pain of his spiked hand, Radbourn beat Detroit handily, 5–2, on Saturday, May 17. When the men went to bed the following night, prepared for another week of work after a Sunday off, all seemed well, but the Grays' pennant aspirations very nearly perished with them in the dark. At 3:45 a.m., Bridget Sullivan, one of the live-in servant girls at the four-story City Hotel downtown, at 148–150 Broad Street, awoke in her room on the top floor to "the crackling and flash of flames" as a sheet of fire burned through the thin wall of the adjourning room, where a kerosene lamp had been left unattended. She screamed as the flames roared through the roof. The $2-a-night hotel, located downtown a few blocks from Carrie Stanhope's boardinghouse, was an old building, expanded from a mansion. Twenty-four years earlier, Stephen A. Douglas, battling Abraham Lincoln for the presidency, had spoken from one of its second-floor balconies to a crowd estimated at ten thousand people. Like most hotels, it was little better than a highly combustible wooden deathtrap, with no sprinklers to beat back a fire. Bridget owned some beautiful dresses and had "several valuable presents" in her room, but she wisely consigned her worldly goods to the hungry flames, "barely escaping in her nightdress."

Up on the top floor were the rooms where "the greater proportion of the Providence Club" lived during the season. Luckily, Miss Sullivan's screams awoke the hotel's bellboys and waiters, who sounded an alarm. Frank Bancroft, clutching the club's records and perhaps its money, ran out of his room and, "on being assured that all the boys were aroused," fled down the stairs, followed by Charlie Sweeney. Sweeney's pitching mate displayed greater heroism. "Charlie Radbourn was next seen, and, after assisting in waking everyone on the floor, he went to the room of Jack Farrell, who could sleep while a national salute was being fired, and, after repeated attempts, succeeded in arousing him." Farrell piled his clothes in the arms of a friend, who did not dare return to get his own, grabbed his trunk, and started down a long flight of stairs. Barefoot, he stepped on a shard of broken glass and badly cut his heel, but he and his teammates "managed to make their escape in their night clothes, although they were nearly suffocated by the smoke." The fire brigade arrived quickly and doused the flames, confining most of the damage to the fourth floor, though water seeped through all the way to the first. "Men, women and children rushed to the street in their night-clothes, carrying with them their trunks, valises, canes, umbrellas, and having as a rule their most valuable property," the *Telegram* reported. "Fortunately the hotel is well supplied with exits, else a terrible catastrophe would have taken place, as all the hallways and rooms were filled with smoke."

Since no one died, a *Journal* reporter found himself free to laugh at one incident: "A guest who had not felt well enough, he said, to carry up a pitcher of water when he retired, came rushing downstairs soon after the alarm was sounded, with a 150-pound trunk on his shoulder, and carried it with ease—such is the inspiration of a crisis!" Still, the Grays players had come "altogether too near to a sudden and awful death" to feel the experience was any too pleasant, the *Boston Herald* noted. In fact, "the settlement of the ownership of the League pennant . . . was nearly effected"—and not in Providence's favor. The proverbially lucky manager, Frank Bancroft, had dodged another disaster.

If Radbourn and his singed teammates were rattled by the near-death experience and a night of little sleep, they did not show it that afternoon. Rad threw a three-hitter, beating woeful Detroit, 4–2, to close out the Grays' first homestand of thirteen games. Nearly three weeks of baseball at the Messer Street Grounds had made something clear: as serviceable a pitcher as Radbourn was, Bancroft had been wise indeed to give Sweeney an equal share of the work. The young pitcher was, if anything, shaping up to be the better man. Though Radbourn had easily beaten Detroit and had thus far been beaten only by the hated Chicagos, he continued to feel the pain that had downed him in April, a telltale sign that his overused body was aging, slow to recover from hard work. "The old players who have for so long had the entire monopoly of the diamond field are beginning to find out that it is possible to fill their places by younger players," the *Sunday Morning Telegram* observed. Even if Sweeney was passing him by, Radbourn remained a useful part of Bancroft's two-pitcher rotation, of course. Thanks to the duo's work, the Grays found themselves in the thick of a three-team race as they gathered at Union Depot and boarded a train for New York City to take on the first-place Gothams.

	W	L	PCT.	GB
New York	13	1	.929	—
Boston	13	2	.867	½
PROVIDENCE	11	2	.846	1½
Philadelphia	7	7	.500	6
Chicago	4	10	.286	9
Buffalo	4	11	.267	9½
Cleveland	3	10	.231	9½
Detroit	1	13	.071	12

*   *   *

A legend long circulated in Providence about the love triangle involving Carrie Stanhope, her Chicago beau, and Radbourn. As the tale was told, the two ballplayers finally decided to settle the matter with a public duel for her favors. The knights of old would have done it in a jousting match, but Radbourn and his adversary did battle at the Messer Street Grounds in a National League game sometime in the early 1880s. The player whose team won the game would have a clear path to seek Carrie's affections. "That game," the *Globe* noted, was "one of the fiercest ever played."

Seated in the grandstand "among the frenzied crowd that shouted themselves hoarse yelling for 'Rad' was a handsome, well-dressed woman," the *Globe* recounted. "Intently she watched every play, and those nearby noticed a deadly pallor on her face as the deciding run was made." The silent, moody Radbourn, not her Chicago man, was the victor. After the game, as the story went, the player handed her over to Radbourn at home plate. "She's yours, 'Rad,' for you won her and the game," he said.

This hackneyed ending was undoubtedly the invention of some writer, who does not bother to tell us when, exactly, the game was played—if there really was one. But, curiously, many of the biographical details in the story do, in fact, check out, and reveal a detailed knowledge of Carrie's life, which makes one wonder: did the description of her "deadly pallor" contain a kernel of truth, a hint that she only reluctantly accepted the advances of the brooding, sullen Radbourn? And more intriguing: did he fight for her heart, not by winning one game but by taking on a much bigger challenge, a task that would require unparalleled courage and determination, in the months ahead?

Did he try to win the National League pennant itself to prove his worth to her?

9
CHAPTER

Red Fire

Radbourn sat morosely in the clubhouse awaiting the second game of the Memorial Day doubleheader. He was sore and exhausted, suffering from what the *Journal* called "rheumatism in the leg." In truth, the pain was so bad that he could barely hobble around, and his arm was not much better. He had pitched in unseasonable cold that morning. Now his muscles were tightening up, and Bancroft had failed to improve his mood any by informing him he had to go out and pitch all over again that afternoon, since the great Charlie Sweeney was tired.

The clubhouse—really, nothing more than a Spartan dressing room—was a bare, cold wooden chamber under the grandstand with some benches, hooks for clothes, and running water, but no electricity. A window let in light from outdoors, while a fence blocked prying eyes. But no one thought of installing any facilities that might actually help athletes get their muscles in better shape for hard competition. Indeed, the room's most prominent ornament was a horseshoe on a string, hung on a nail in a corner, and it served little purpose for Radbourn, who did not seem to be getting much luck out of it. Some of his teammates, though, could swear that this iron amulet was showering its happy influence over the Providence club during the first month of the 1884 season.

The talismanic object had come to the Grays as a bonus for signing Paul Revere Radford, who had discovered it and its extraordinary powers a year earlier, in 1883, when he was a rookie outfielder for Boston's Red Stockings.

RADFORD, R. F., Clevelands

OLD JUDGE
CIGARETTE FACTORY.
GOODWIN & CO., New York.

Paul Radford

On the May morning that it turned up, Boston had lost eight straight games and was mired in next-to-last place, its season almost over before it began. Radford, who had been benched for four games running and faced the threat of losing his place on the roster, was sitting with several dispirited teammates outside the Brunswick Hotel in Detroit, wasting some time before their afternoon game, watching girls walk by. Suddenly, something caught Radford's eye—not an hourglass-shaped beauty but the backside of a plodding horse pulling a hack. And the old hoss had thrown a shoe. Shorty raced into the crowded street, dodging carts and carriages, ignoring the curses of teamsters, to fetch the symbol of good fortune from the dust. When the twenty-one-year-old returned to his teammates and brushed it off to look at the manufacturer's name stamped on the bottom, he knew he had come across an extraordinary omen. *O. Winn*, the horseshoe read, as if exhorting Radford and his mates to go forth and collect victories.

Ballplayers tend to be intensely superstitious men, and the 1883 Red Stockings were no exception. Radford held up Owen Winn's shoe and studied it, turning it over and over. Then he passed it to his teammates, who touched the lettering, laughing. Within a few hours, Radford's luck had changed. He found himself back in the lineup, and this time the rookie made some beautiful catches in center field as the Red Stockings snapped their eight-game losing streak with a 10–4 victory.

Paul carried the lucky horseshoe back to Boston and then took care to bring it everywhere he went. Under its magic, the Red Stockings won twenty-six of their next thirty-three games, and then went on to capture the National League pennant. When he decamped to Providence for the 1884 season, he brought the shoe with him, hoping to repeat the pennant trick with the Grays. During every home game at the Messer Street Grounds, he faithfully hung it on its nail. Early in the season, Paul Hines began disappearing just before going to bat, and one day someone followed him to see what he was doing. Hines, he discovered, had been sneaking into the clubhouse, going to the corner, and turning around the horseshoe for luck before returning to the field. Whether or not it made the difference, Hines would end up leading the club in batting.

The horseshoe had not done Radbourn much apparent good, though. The frightening ache that had plagued him in April had come back, and Sweeney's boastfulness and the public's adulation for him appeared to mount in direct proportion to Radbourn's misery. The Grays, on the other hand, seemed blessed, and kept on winning in spite of the pitcher's struggles. On May 20, they had invaded brassy, pulsing New York City—"the Imperial City of the American continent," as Daniel Webster called it—and taken on the first-place Gothams in front of a big, noisy crowd at the Polo Grounds on 110th Street, between Fifth and Sixth avenues. The Gothams—who would soon assume another nickname, one that stuck: the Giants—had exploded out of the gate with twelve straight victories, leading the front-running New York press to impulsively dub them "the Invincibles." But Sweeney quickly put a lie to the nickname, edging them 2–1, and Radbourn utterly dominated the Invincibles, pitching a 3–0 shutout. "The manner in which he fooled the New Yorkers by his deceptive curves was anything but pleasing to the home club," the *New York Times* sighed. After taking a side trip to Philadelphia to whip the Phillies twice, the Grays hustled back to Manhattan and, behind Sweeney, throttled the Gothams 19–5 before more than six thousand disappointed spectators, who "saw the New Yorks wilt away like hot-house plants in the broiling sun." Some special guests in the Polo Grounds gallery—the ambassador of Siam and his staff—watched this inscrutable American game for a time and then left, probably never realizing they caught the home club on a particularly bad day.

Back in New England, accolades were flowing for the Grays' young pitcher, who was now steadily pushing Radbourn ever deeper into the shadows. Sweeney's name was on the lips of every Providence fanatic. "And do ye know that the howlers in Providence thought he was n.g. last year when he made his advent in Cove City?" the *Fall River Daily Evening News* asked scornfully.

On May 26, the Grays, behind Radbourn, completed their destruction of New York, "who showed up in their usual chicken-hearted style," a correspondent bitterly reported. The Grays clubbed the Gothams 10–4 to win their twelfth straight game. By the time the Grays left the big city, the Not-So-Invincibles had collapsed into third place, two and a half games behind Providence. Then something happened to Sweeney. In Philadelphia, he blew a 3–2 lead in the eighth inning to lose 4–3, breaking the winning streak. The Grays rushed back home to Providence to start a new homestand at the Messer Street Grounds the next day, on an afternoon so unseasonably frigid that spectators wore heavy overcoats and wrapped carriage robes around their legs. But a more ominous chill seemed to be developing between the team's two top pitchers. Radbourn was supposed to start, giving Sweeney a well-deserved rest, but "owing to . . . rheumatic difficulty"—a painful leg— he had bowed out at the last minute, dumping the burden onto his sore-armed teammate. Sweeney, none too happy about it, pitched lifelessly, losing 10–8 against New York and sending the Grays toppling out of first place. "The impression the spectators got was that he was either mad or sick," the *Evening Press* noted, adding: "It is to be hoped the latter."

In truth, it may have been both. Sweeney—overworked in April and used hard in May—had a dead arm. He needed a rest, and he was not one to be silent about it, playing the role of the deferential youngster to the proven veteran. As far as Sweeney was concerned, Radbourn was going to have to step it up and earn his big salary, however much his $3,000-a-year carcass hurt.

May 30 brought one of the big days on the baseball calendar—Memorial Day, when people by the thousands, finally getting a break from work and pressure, packed themselves onto trains, horsecars, and omnibuses and headed for America's ballparks. Club owners were only too happy to accommodate them by scheduling separate-admission doubleheaders that day. For the 10:40 a.m. game, some four thousand fanatics swarmed into the Messer Street Grounds, overflowing the stands, despite a sharp morning chill, to see Radbourn take on the old hometown favorite John M. Ward, now making big money playing for the Gothams. Ward had pitched Providence to its 1879 pennant, and he "showed traces of his old strategic pitching and sent in some puzzlers" that Memorial Day, but in general "the Grays took very kindly to his delivery" and hit him hard, as players tried to catch the ball with the morning sun in their faces. Radbourn was better, but not by much. In the slugfest that ensued, Providence plugged away to a 12–9 victory over New York, as Radbourn won his tenth game.

By the 3:30 p.m. starting time of game two, Radbourn "was so lame," the *Sporting Life* reported, "that he could hardly hobble from one base to another." But with Sweeney claiming arm pain, Radbourn had to drag himself off the bench in the Grays' dressing room and limp back onto the field to pitch again. A wave of appreciative applause rippled through the grandstand as he finally showed himself, walking nonchalantly across the damp grass to the dirt pitcher's box to face the Phillies, who had come down from Boston on the early afternoon train after losing the morning game there. The sore-armed Sweeney trotted out to right field. Bancroft wanted him there in case Radbourn's lameness proved just too much. Another monster crowd was on hand—3,883 this time—and it warmly greeted former manager Harry Wright on his first trip back to Providence since taking over the helm of the Phillies. During his two-year run as the Grays' manager, Harry had become a Providence icon. "A tall, energetic figure, he became 'hail fellow well-met,' and was on speaking terms with every fan in the city. He wore a full beard and was always dressed in a silk hat and long Prince Albert coat. The small boy looked up to him as little removed from a god," William D. Perrin recalled. Now, Radbourn, bad leg and all, would do his best to spoil noble Harry's homecoming. By ignoring the pain, mixing the locations of his pitches, and strictly reserving his fastball for when it was most needed, the veteran got through the game, capturing his eleventh victory as the Grays thrashed Philadelphia, 9–2. Behind the distinctly shaky pitcher, Providence had won both ends of a Memorial Day doubleheader for the first time in franchise history.

With a torrid winning percentage of .826, the Grays clung to first place, just ahead of Boston. But they were already showing definite signs of wear. Shortstop Arthur Irwin had wrenched his back during the first game of the doubleheader, and catcher Sandy Nava had been forced to fill in at the vital position. Second baseman Jack Farrell had fallen ill, too, and was woozy and feverish, though Bancroft had to deny him the day off "for prudential reasons"—namely, the lack of a replacement. Sweeney's arm still ached, and

Radbourn was walking with a pronounced limp. "The Providences need to go in the dry dock," the *Fall River Daily Evening News* observed. "Radbourne has the 'roomatiz'; Sweeney is lame; Irwin 'dropped a stitch' in his back."

When Sweeney and Radbourn went to bed that night, both men felt too lame to work, and it looked as if Bancroft would have to find another pitcher by the morning. But Radbourn returned on May 31, somehow finding the grit to pitch his third complete game in two days. Taking on the usually weak-hitting Phillies in front of a meager crowd of 902 on yet another cold, dreary day—a miserable turnout for a Saturday—the weakened Radbourn "was of necessity batted very freely." Fortunately, his fielders grabbed a number of hard-hit shots to keep Providence in the game, while Rad struggled grimly to make it through. As if he had not suffered enough, the ninth ended with a 5–5 tie, and he had to toil on into extra innings. The Grays finally scratched out a run in the tenth to go ahead 6–5, leaving Radbourn the task of holding the lead. With virtually no juice left, he surrendered two singles to open the bottom of the tenth. But his pal Cliff Carroll managed to chase down two fly balls in left field, and the runners were stranded when a pop fly to third baseman Jerry Denny ended the agony.

Radbourn staggered off the field with his twelfth victory of the season, against only one loss. Given his arm troubles, he had turned in a magnificent month of work. Radbourn even led the Grays in hitting, with a .333 average. But there was no telling how long he could hold out.

True to his nature, Frank Bancroft was working hard to wring every last penny out of his connection with the Grays. The June 10 issue of the *Sporting Life* noted one typical scheme: a ten-by-twelve-inch group picture of the team, which the paper described as "elegant," could be obtained for 50¢ from F. C. Bancroft, at the Providence Hotel. A surviving shot does show them elegantly attired in dark business suits, sitting on chairs placed on the grass. Another distinctly *inelegant* photo, taken at the Messer Street Grounds in late May or early June, shows a group of gritty and mean-looking men in rumpled uniforms, along with their skinny leader, Bancroft, all of them posing between the pitcher's box and second base, with the grandstand looming behind them. The grouping captures a bored Radbourn holding a bat—and not this time raising a middle finger—at the far left, farthest from Bancroft. Next to Radbourn, closer to the manager, stands young Sweeney, a half sneer on his defiant face. He holds the baseball in clear view—a common symbol in early team pictures of the ace pitcher.

The *Sporting Life*'s report from Providence conveyed other gossip: that the Grays were finding the Phillies surprisingly tough opponents now that Harry Wright had taken the helm; and that the boys considered their new drab uniform, manufactured in Brooklyn, to be a "Jonah," guaranteed to cost them the game whenever they wore it. Buried amid such fluff was more consequential, and ominous, fare: that Charlie Radbourn was "still suffering with a lame arm" and that someone would have to take over for him.

Radbourn's heroic efforts at the end of May—pitching, while in pain, three complete games in two days, and winning them all—had given Sweeney a desperately needed respite. After three days blessedly free from throwing, the young pitcher strutted back to the box on Monday, June 2, to strike out twelve New York batters en route to a 9–3 victory. Now Radbourn was the one in trouble. Obviously suffering, he returned on Tuesday and pitched horribly, surrendering fifteen hits in a 12–7 drubbing by the Gothams. To further spoil his day, umpire McLean insisted on squeezing him, shrinking the strike zone, making it harder for Radbourn to use his junk, and when Rad ventured to complain about it, the former pugilist slugged him with a $10 fine, no pittance to a frugal man who saved every penny. The next day, Sweeney returned with an impressive six-hit, 4–0 shutout of the Phillies. "KALSOMINED," the *Evening Telegram* crowed in the headline, using an amusingly high-toned word for whitewashed.

Something had to be done to give Radbourn's aging, aching arm a break. On Thursday, Bancroft finally sat him down. He had little choice but to send to the box his not-yet-ripe spring project, the champion rower John Cattanach—risky business, because the twenty-one-year-old was still suffering control problems. Sure enough, before a slender crowd of four hundred at Messer, the tall, barrel-chested rookie proved nervous and wild, surrendering seven runs to the Phillies in little more than four innings. Sweeney, whom Bancroft had prudently stowed in right field, traded places with the flustered rower. But even banished to the outfield, Cattanach proved a detriment, contributing a costly error to the Grays' 9–8 defeat. "Cattanach needs practice, but it ought to be with a semi-professional nine," the *Evening Press* jabbed. He was no substitute, even temporarily, for the once-mighty Radbourn.

It was a terrible time for the Grays to be without Rad, because now they faced their bitter enemies, the first-place Boston club, defending champions of the National League. The Grays–Red Stockings rivalry was a classic regional grudge fest—a forerunner of the celebrated Red Sox–Yankees war, in both cases pitting a smaller city with a chip on its shoulder against its bigger, brasher neighbor, whose team owned the most championship flags in history. "These clubs may be justly termed the giants of the league," the *Journal* noted on June 7, "and so intense is the rivalry that when they are pitted against each other it has been a 'fight to the death.' " For years to come, those who watched and played in the Providence-Boston clashes of the early 1880s remembered them as some of baseball's most stirring and bitterly fought games. "It was scrap from start to finish," captain Joe Start recalled.

The games drew hundreds of fanatics who readily traveled the forty-plus miles between the two cities, a mass migration the clubs encouraged. When the Red Stockings sold round-trip tickets for a special excursion train to Providence for the June 29, 1883, game, for example, Bostonians snapped up enough, at $1 a pop, to pack fifteen passenger cars with seven hundred boisterous Massachusetts rooters. They joined up in Providence with another three hundred Bostonians who traveled on their own. Giving way to the excitement stirred by the bitter rivalry, the yelling, taunting crowds at the Messer Street Grounds failed at times to exhibit the decorum that middle-class sportswriters thought proper. "The treatment of the Boston club at Providence yesterday by a band of hoodlums—they could not have been anything else—was simply outrageous and insulting in the extreme," a *Boston Globe* correspondent fumed after a July 1883 game. When Boston's pitcher at one point sprinted for a foul ball, the barbarians of Rhode Island howled at him—and when the player dropped it, they yelled derisively, with unseemly relish. "They did all they could to break up the players, hooting every man who attempted to catch a ball and acting like a set of fiends." In Boston, the reporter stewed, such jeering would never be condoned. In the Athens of America, "every man has a fair chance to capture the ball, and no demonstration is made until the play is finished. Probably no city ever treated its visitors with so little decency" as shabby, low-class Providence.

The Red Stockings—who were just as often called the Beaneaters those days, in honor of the popular local dish of steaming hot baked beans steeped in pork fat and molasses—had stunned the baseball world in 1883 when they fought their way back from seventh place and shoved aside favored Chicago, Cleveland, and Providence to capture the flag. Some considered the Cinderella victory pure luck, and on opening day 1884, when the Red Stockings raised their unexpected pennant at the South End Grounds, Bostonians' ringing cheers turned to roars of laughter when the flag unfurled upside down—a dark omen for the coming year. But Boston quickly proved that 1883 was no fluke. A superb blend of youth and experience, with strong defense and first-rate pitching, the Red Stockings shot out of the gate in 1884, winning eleven of their first twelve games and fifteen of their first seventeen. By late May, they had passed the Grays and taken over first place.

Boston's ace was one "Grasshopper Jim" Whitney, who had earned his memorable nickname with his bounding gait and spindly limbs. Standing well over six feet tall, he seemed a freakish specimen of manhood, with uncommonly long arms and legs, a craning neck, a sleepy expression, and ears that stuck out prominently from his smallish skull. "He has a head about the size of a wart," the *Detroit Evening News* observed, "with a forehead slanting at an angle of 45 degrees, and bears an extraordinary facial resemblance to the Aztec children, Tom and Hattie, of the dime museum," a reference to one of P. T. Barnum's exhibits featuring deformed people—in this case, what were called "pin-heads." Beauty is in the eye of the beholder, but no one disputed that Whitney, thanks to his long, whiplike arms, could throw a baseball incredibly hard. He was "the fastest pitcher that ever lived," asserted Boston shortstop Sam Wise.

In 1883, rookie Mike Hines earned the unenviable duty of catching Whitney's bullets, day after day, with little more protection than a face mask and a pair of fingerless hand gloves. In taking on the job, the nineteen-year-old Irish immigrant condemned himself to a season of misery, split palms, and jarred fingers. "There is no pitcher in the league that is nearly as hard to handle as Whitney, and all the clubs in the country acknowledge it," the

Globe observed. "It really makes one's head spin to hear the crack of the boards in the reporter's stand" when Whitney's pitches got past the catcher and banged into the planks. One man, carefully studying the movement of Whitney's pitches from behind home plate, was "amazed to see his wonderful 'in' and 'out,' and up and down sweeps of the ball, and singularly enough it was while the ball was under great momentum." Fortunately, Hines was "as full of pluck as an egg is full of meat." He stood up against "the hottest fire unflinchingly."

Like many players in the 1880s, Whitney was not content to make do with skill. He used cheating and outright violence to gain an edge. He threw overhand long before the rules legitimized the motion, daring umpires to call him on it. More ominously, he kept batters in a state of terror by hitting them repeatedly. Since the rules did not yet automatically award first base to a man struck by a pitch, the worst punishment a pitcher faced was a fine. Even that minimal penalty was rarely imposed, though, because umpires had to deem that the assault had been intentional, and many did not want to deal with the violent argument that would inevitably ensue after such a judgment call. Whitney exploited that opening. Indeed, some observers argued that his wild pitches—horribly painful if they smacked flesh, certainly capable of dealing death—were key to his effectiveness. "After a player has faced him once and had several ribs staved in by one of his chain lightning shots, he comes to the bat the second time and strikes at balls he couldn't reach with a ten-foot pole, in order to get out of the way of another shot," the *Cincinnati Enquirer* observed. Wearing only cloth caps to protect their vulnerable heads, batters were doubly unnerved by the way the Grasshopper took a hop, step, and jump to the forward line of the box before hurling the ball toward them.

Jim Whitney

Whitney had established his reputation as a dirty player early, bruising batters in the ballparks around San Francisco Bay. In May 1881, when he moved on to the National League, the *Buffalo Commercial Advertiser* branded the rookie "the hoodlum from the Far West," and complained that, in a shutout victory over the hometown Bisons, two-thirds of his pitches were illegal overhand throws. "Whitney's rugged nature and hoodlum instincts were exemplified when he hit [Jim] O'Rourke with the ball and made no apology. We are not surprised that the Buffalos were nervous when they faced this semi-barbarian for the first time, and we wonder that they did so well." Years later, O'Rourke—who actually played into the twentieth century with Christy Mathewson and Joe McGinnity, and faced some of the greatest pitchers in baseball history, including Cy Young and Amos Rusie—recalled that Whitney would "double up like a jackknife" and "let the ball go at terrific speed. It was a wonder that anybody was ever able to hit him at all. He was the swiftest pitcher I ever saw."

On a soggy afternoon in Boston in June 1883, a scrawny pitcher for Detroit's Wolverines named Dick Burns learned the grave danger of crossing such a man, even by mistake. When Whitney was up at the plate, Burns, who had been struggling to keep the wet ball under control, slipped and stung Whitney on the leg with an inside pitch. Whitney flew into a rage and warned the little pitcher there would be retribution. Sure enough, when poor Burns next came to the plate, Whitney took a running start from the pitcher's box, hurled with all his might, and nailed the batter in the head with a fastball. The missile instantly sliced open Burns's scalp, knocked him unconscious, and bounded high up in the air. Even ardent Beaneaters fanatics among the 850 sitting in the rain that afternoon were horrified, and hissed Whitney. "As can be imagined, to be struck by one of Whitney's pacers is no joke," the *Boston Globe* sympathized, "and the plucky little fellow bore the severe pain bravely." The newspaper assured readers, however, that the hometown hero meant no harm: "No one regretted the misfortune more than our pitcher himself," and the umpire apparently agreed the attack was unintentional; in any case, he declined to issue a fine. The *National Police Gazette*, for one, wasn't buying it. "Whitney . . . is so notorious for 'accidentally' hitting the batsman with the ball that he has been dubbed the 'man-hitter' throughout the league."

The leader of the Bostons was player-
manager and first baseman "Honest
John" Morrill, a cool, highly intelligent
protégé of Harry Wright, who shared
Harry's faith in rigorous training and
fair play. But other players—including,
notably, "Black Jack" Burdock, the team's
profane, irritable, hard-hitting, and hard-
drinking second baseman—would have
fit right in with Cap Anson's Chicago
menagerie. The Brooklyn-born Burdock
was an ill-educated, battle-scarred veteran of twelve seasons in the National
Association and National League. He
played with abandon, often displaying a
hair-trigger temper that may have been
linked to brain damage brought on by
three serious blows to his head. In 1881,

Jack Burdock

he was standing on the rear platform of a streetcar en route to the ballpark
when the vehicle rocked against a stone, jolting him off his feet. Burdock's
skull struck the pavement hard, and he was in and out of a coma for hours.
In 1882, he twice suffered collisions with other players, losing consciousness
both times. Fearless on the field, Burdock prided himself on standing his
ground and completing double plays while enemy runners tried to knock
him flat or dig their spikes into his legs. "Sometimes the runner downs me;
more times he don't and I get him," he boasted. Though team captain Honest John Morrill was a scrupulous gentleman and urged the men to win
through excellence, Black Jack Burdock's penchant for cheating by grabbing
enemy runners and "kicking" at umpires' calls colored the public's percep-
tion of this rather schizophrenic team. When the *Providence Morning Star* denounced the Red Stockings as "the red-legged kickers from Kickersville,"
the pro-Boston *Fall River Daily Evening News* retorted that the insult was "as
apropos as an umbrella for a frog."

*   *   *

Early Friday afternoon, June 6, they began arriving at Union Depot, first a few, then dozens, then hundreds. All told, between a thousand and fifteen hundred people poured in from Boston, and more came from New Bedford, Fall River, and Worcester. They swarmed over the downtown, some grabbing a quick bite to eat and draining a few glasses of beer, before stuffing themselves into the horsecars bound for the Messer Street Grounds. By the time the game started, 4,414 paying customers filled every available seat and stood along the foul lines, the biggest crowd at Providence all season. What they got to witness for their 50¢ or 75¢ was a game that they would tell their grandchildren about—"the finest exhibition of ball playing ever seen in this city," in the words of the *Boston Globe.*

The Grasshopper, of course, got the nod to pitch for Boston. But, given Radbourn's arm troubles, Frank Bancroft had a tough decision about his starter. He had slated the intrepid Sweeney to pitch the game, even though the Californian had worked the last two games, including the day before. But Radbourn was aching, and Bancroft could hardly afford to send out young Cattanach, who had been cannon fodder for the Phillies; there was no telling what Boston's heavy hitters might do to him. Before the game, Bancroft rethought his plan. Joe Start turned up sick again, forcing the manager to juggle the lineup. He put Hines at first, moved Sweeney to center field, and asked "old Radbourne" to pitch, a concession to hard necessity that made the Boston delegation smile. Many in the crowd "suspected that his right arm had forgotten its cunning," and given his pain, there was no reason to believe "badly lamed" Radbourn would do anything but badly lose. But what the veteran pitcher achieved that afternoon and evening would become Providence baseball lore.

As the game got under way, he actually seemed to have perfect control over his pitches, at least until the bottom of the fourth. Up until then, the teams had matched scoreless innings, but Black Jack Burdock led off the inning by dumping a double into left field. Always aggressive, and realizing not many more hits might come Boston's way, he immediately attempted to steal third base. Providence seemed up to the challenge: catcher Barney Gilligan cleanly caught the pitch and fired the ball to third baseman Jerry Denny, who tagged Burdock—before he reached the base, in "the opinion of gentlemen from Boston, as well as local patrons." But, to the amazement and rage of the Providence crowd, umpire John Burns—incompetent as usual, from the Grays' perspective—declared Burdock safe. When Grays shortstop Arthur Irwin fumbled a grounder, Burdock scored, giving Boston a 1–0 lead.

In the seventh, Providence came back, with a run manufactured entirely by the brains and spark of little Paul Revere Radford. With two strikes against him, Radford cleverly swung at a wild pitch by Whitney, reaching first before the catcher could retrieve the ball. Radford stole second to reach scoring position, and when Sweeney blasted a ground ball down the third-base line, he tore for third. To the amazement of almost everyone in the park, the veteran Ezra Sutton managed to fling himself to the ground and snare the speeding ball, trapping Shorty between second and third. Caught in a rundown, Radford fought for his life until Burdock lost his cool and heaved the ball over Sutton's head, letting Shorty speed around third and touch home, tying the score 1–1.

From then on, Radbourn and Whitney engaged in a gritty tug-of-war. Whitney was spectacular, and his speed and "deceptive drop ball" kept Providence batters at bay most of the afternoon, as he struck out thirteen men. Old Hoss, meanwhile, showed "wonderful control of the ball in the execution of drops, curves, etc.," the *Journal* noted, as the innings ticked by: eighth, ninth, tenth, eleventh. How much longer these men could go without tiring out completely was anyone's guess. "Whitney is a mere skeleton," the next morning's *Star* noted, "but oh! what a ball he pitches." Morrill finally got a piece of Radbourn, blasting a pitch to deep left field, over Cliff Carroll's head. At the crack of the bat, Radbourn's pal ran full tilt, leapt in the air, stretched his arm half out of its socket, and somehow plucked the ball from the sky, saving a triple or home run. The grandstand and bleachers erupted, compelling Carroll to doff his cap.

Finally, after sixteen full innings of intense competition, with darkness descending on Providence, umpire Burns pulled the plug. Though the game ended in a 1–1 tie, no one seemed to feel cheated as, emotionally drained, they boarded the horsecars for the journey back downtown and, for some, a nighttime train trip home and explanations to their skeptical wives about how a baseball game could possibly have lasted so long. "It would be impossible to describe in detail the many fine points of this phenomenal game, the like of which will probably never be seen again," the *Journal* enthused. "Suffice it to say that the patrons quietly acquiesced in the decision of the umpire in declaring the game a 'draw,' for their nerves had been strained to their fullest tension in their spirited partisanship and they had had abundant evidence that the teams were evenly matched and the game bade fair to be lengthened indefinitely." Radbourn had been nothing less than stunning. With only two days of rest between starts, he had pitched sixteen innings in one afternoon—almost two complete games—without allowing an earned run. And over the last twelve of those innings, he had surrendered only one base hit. "There is a rumor that Radbourne's days as a pitcher are not over," the *Star* observed wryly.

Aching arm or not, Radbourn was fighting, without boasting or fanfare, to regain his prestige as the Grays' top man. He may have been especially driven to impress the woman he loved, baseball-savvy Carrie Stanhope, who might not have been interested in a washed-up player out of a job. But Sweeney was not about to hand over top billing. The following day, in Boston, the young hurler trumped even that remarkable sixteen-inning performance.

June 7 was a perfect New England day, sunny, warm, and breezy, and that afternoon brought the glorious feeling of freedom that arrived every Saturday when businesses shut down after half a day of work, in advance of the day of rest. There was no better place to be on such a day than out at the ball yard, watching a great game, and a giant crowd of 7,387 descended on the South End Grounds, the Beaneaters' dumpy old ballpark crammed in between Columbus Avenue and the Boston and Albany railroad tracks. Surprisingly, Boston's captain, Morrill, started Whitney again, despite his sixteen innings of hard work the day before. Almost incredibly, the Grasshopper rose to the challenge, allowing only two runs and six hits. But Sweeney was even better.

From the very start, it was obvious that the kid was dead-on. "Outs and ins, drops and rises seemed to be all the same to Sweeney," the *Boston Globe* reported. "He could give them all, and pitched some of the most deceptive curves imaginable." Sweeney was "in magnificent form," the *Journal* asserted, "and he pitched with such remarkable strategy and speed that Boston's heavy hitters were forced to go down before him one after another."

Goaded on by Radbourn's masterpiece the day before, Sweeney struck out five of the first six batters he faced. Of the first nine outs he recorded, eight were strikeouts. By the end of the sixth, he had struck out fourteen men—all without the modern benefit of foul balls being called strikes.

Providence finally broke the scoreless tie in the fifth. With Arthur Irwin dancing off third base, Cliff Carroll lofted a high fly ball to center field. As Irwin tagged, Boston's Jack Manning got under it. But in his haste to throw out the runner at the plate, he took his eye off the ball for a split second and dropped it. Irwin breezed home, giving the Grays a 1–0 lead. The Boston center fielder quickly redeemed himself, however. Sandy Nava stroked the ball to right center for an apparent hit, but Manning caught the line drive in full sprint and gunned the sphere to first, doubling up the runner there. Without pausing, first baseman John Morrill smartly fired it across the diamond to catch Jerry Denny, who had tagged up at second, sliding into third. A triple play! "Immediately there was the wildest excitement and confusion," the *Globe* reported. The crowd leapt to its feet and cheered for several minutes as men threw their hats in the air and laughing women waved handkerchiefs.

The Grays added another run in the sixth, to edge ahead 2–0. In the seventh inning, umpire John Burns stuck it to the Grays again. Sweeney surrendered a walk to Whitney, though it might have been yet another strikeout, since Charlie split the plate five times, "which Burns did not seem to see," the *Journal* moaned. Morrill singled, sending Whitney to second base. Whitney then broke for third "and was thrown out fairly by [catcher] Nava to [third baseman] Denny. Even the spectators who were partial to Boston declared it so." But the one spectator who counted, Mr. Burns, declared him safe. Whitney then scored on an error by second baseman Jack Farrell to cut the lead to a nerve-racking 2–1.

In the ninth inning, the crowd came alive, urging the Beaneaters to erase the tiny deficit. But another story was playing out that afternoon. Sweeney, with his extraordinary fastball and biting curve, was smashing the major-league record for strikeouts. First up was Morrill, whom Sweeney whiffed. Next up, Jack Manning swung "at the sphere as if he would lift it over the

Scorecard of Sweeney's 19-strikeout game. Note the scorer counted only 18.

centre-field fence, but only empty air met the willow, and he, too, retired on strikes." When Sweeney struck out Crowley to the end the game, the great crowd, which had been silent for most of the day, erupted in cheers for the visiting pitcher, recognizing that Sweeney, at twenty-one, had performed a remarkable feat. "NINETEEN STRUCK OUT," read the *Globe*'s headline the next day. "Sweeney's Mysterious Curves Baffle Boston's Batters." It was an astounding total, "a record," the *Journal* predicted, "which will not be broken in many a day." It wasn't—until nearly 102 years later, on April 29, 1986, in another game in Boston, this one a twenty-strikeout masterpiece by another arrogant young fastball pitcher named Roger Clemens.

Back in Providence, alerted by telegraph of Sweeney's record-smashing achievement, civic leaders scrambled to prepare a suitable welcome home for the city's new baseball god, whose historic performance had propelled the Grays into first place. "Sweeney proved himself a jewel of the first water," the Boston correspondent of the *Sunday Morning Telegram* wired to Providence. Someone made certain to secure a large heap of pyrotechnics, including flares that would light up the dark downtown with glowing colored flames, called red fire.

When the train bearing the club pulled into Union Depot at 7:45 p.m., horse-drawn carriages and Herrick's Providence Brigade Band were waiting for them. As a grinning and waving Sweeney set foot on the platform, the brass band struck up "Hail to the Chief," soon drowned out by the sustained roar of the crowd. Sweeney was mobbed, snatched up, and carried on the shoulders of men to a waiting hack. His teammates followed him into the carriages, and the boys were given a triumphal ride through the principal streets of the city, right past Carrie Stanhope's boardinghouse, where she may well have watched from her second-floor wrought-iron balcony, smiling and trading waves with the men below, while the brass band played "Marching Through Georgia." Along the way, people cheered and shouted praise at the players, particularly Sweeney. The "streets were one vast blaze of red fire and the crowd packed the sidewalks thicker than sardines," the *Sporting Life* reported.

Sweeney was the focus of every accolade, the man of the hour, the toast of Providence. After years of brilliance, Radbourn found himself pushed off the stage by this obnoxious, self-infatuated kid. Fiercely jealous, he could do little more than brood silently amid the cheers, the red light thrown by the flames pulsing across his face.

That night of wild celebration was not the end of the Sweeney cult. For weeks to come, crowds at the Messer Street Grounds kept picking on Radbourn, "nagging him to 'break the record'" that Sweeney had set, a development that, not surprisingly, was said to bother the veteran pitcher "exceedingly."

A Working Girl

Carrie Stanhope's mansion on Washington Street in downtown Providence was a fine one, and though the decaying neighborhood was no longer fashionable, or even particularly safe after dark, she could feel proud of herself for having secured the house, while others in her predicament had ended up in the gutter. However low her position in life might seem to the pious businessmen who owned the soaring new Victorian mansions on Broadway or stately brick homes along Westminster Street, or to their snobbish wives, she had worked hard to create this business and to make her house a welcoming place for young men far from home. It had become a favorite spot in Providence for rootless, ambitious people who, like Carrie, were considered beneath the notice of decent society, especially the actors and ballplayers who entertained both rich and poor, easing the daily stress of America's hypercompetitive society. The dazzling impression she made on males as she swept into a room in a fashionable dress and sparkling baubles belied her poor upbringing and her desperate struggle to survive and care for those she loved.

Carrie came from solid, hardworking stock, people better acquainted with muddy boots and livestock than chandeliers and ballrooms. Her great-grandfather Josiah Allen owned a farm on Allen Avenue in Attleboro, Massachusetts, not far from the Rhode Island border. Swept up in the revolutionary fervor of his time, determined to live or die a free man, Allen enlisted as a member of the local militia—called Minutemen for their rapid-response strategy—and answered the alarm on April 19, 1775, when the battles of Lexington and Concord erupted. After serving with the Continental forces in Massachusetts and Rhode Island, he worked as a Bristol County sheriff and died a well-esteemed man. His son, Carrie's maternal grandfather, Pardon Allen, was born at the Attleboro farm in 1793, and married a girl from nearby Cumberland, Rhode Island, in 1813. Carrie's mother, Harriet W. Allen, entered the world in 1821, the fourth of their seven children. The Allen farm passed to Josiah's eldest son, Josiah Junior, and at some point in the late 1820s or early 1830s Pardon pulled up stakes, leaving the farm for work in the factory town of East Pawtucket, then part of Massachusetts, where he toiled as a machinist and served as a deacon at the High Baptist Church.

Carrie's father, Henry A. Clark, was born in 1814 in Petersham, in Central Massachusetts. The little town's only real claim to fame was that it had served, on February 4, 1787, as the place where officials finally quashed Shays's Rebellion, an armed uprising of struggling farmers who, in defeating the British several years earlier, never dreamed they would end up in an America of crushing debt and brutal taxes. Decades later, times were still tough for the region's farmers, Henry among them. He worked a farm eight miles to the south in the town of Hardwick, straining to raise livestock and earn his living from New England's rocky soil and short growing season. In 1838, when he was twenty-four, he married Freelove Carpenter, a Massachusetts woman who was one year his senior. Their life together was cruelly severed twelve years later when Freelove, only thirty-seven, died of dropsy, a swelling of the tissues that could have been related to heart failure. The wrenching misfortune left Henry with three young children to care for, ages twelve, seven, and one.

The widower sought better times in Pawtucket, where he met and wooed Carrie's mother, Harriet Allen. She was about thirty-one, perilously close to becoming an old maid, though seven years younger than Henry, when they married. She was willing to accept three children in the bargain. The former farmer had a hard time of it in his new home, working first as a drover—moving sheep and cattle, perhaps between his old haunts in central Massachusetts and Rhode Island—and later in the lowly occupation of unskilled laborer, while the burgeoning family he tried to raise with Harriet was haunted by tragedy.

Their first daughter, Harriet, was born in 1854. The precocious, head-strong Carrie—Caroline S. Clark—arrived two years later, on May 18, 1856. Carrie was followed by Elizabeth, in 1857; Charles, in 1858; and Julia, in 1863. But four of Henry's children died in childhood: his eldest son, Charles, born of his first brood, at 15; Harriet at 13; Elizabeth at 3; a second son named Charles at seven months. Poor housing, damp basements, overflowing cesspools, and contaminated water made deadly illness common, and hunger made children more susceptible to a wide array of diseases: typhus, typhoid fever, diphtheria, rickets, tuberculosis, and scarlet fever. However frequent childhood death was in those times, the heartbreak the parents endured was agonizing, and Carrie learned from an early age that life is often cruel and capricious, and that God does not always answer one's most fervent prayers.

The pretty girl yearned to escape from the sorrow and struggle of her family's life in Pawtucket. Unlike her middle-aged mother, she was willful and rebellious, hard for Henry or Harriet to keep in line. In her early teens, she fixed on a scheme for breaking free—through a romantic attachment with a promising young man from Newport, one Charles Lewis Stanhope Jr., a marine engineer from a sturdy family that was a few rungs up the social ladder from the Clarks. Charles's maternal grandfather was a sea captain in New Bedford. Charles's father, born in 1824, went to sea as a teenager, serving on one of the great whaling vessels that plowed the oceans and inspired such works as Herman Melville's *Moby-Dick* before the industry sharply declined in the late 1840s.

The elder Stanhope spent much of his adult life in less expansive waters, as a clerk aboard the steamship *Perry*, which transported people back and forth, at 50¢ a head, between Newport and booming Providence to the north. A lawsuit detailing the events of one trip in August 1862 preserves something of his stern, no-nonsense nature. An argumentative passenger, unhappy that Stanhope refused to make change for a dollar, tried to ride for free, tempting fate and the clerk's resolve. Finding the freeloader in the steamship's saloon as the vessel loudly chugged its way up Narragansett Bay, Stanhope seized him by the collar, yanked him violently off a settee, pushed him into a companionway, and shoved him down a flight of steps to the main deck and then down to the lower cabin, where he threw him onto a bench near the berths "and left him without any explanation." When the passenger stubbornly returned to the saloon, Stanhope handled him even more roughly. "Evidence was introduced by the plaintiff tending to show that he was seriously injured in his back and other parts of his body, and that the injuries were of a permanent character," a judge's ruling against Stanhope's employers stated. That did not seem to affect the clerk's standing in the community. Stanhope was a respected man, a city marshal, and he served as the Newport correspondent for the *Providence Journal*, filing colorful accounts of low and high life in the historic community.

We do not know if his sons, Charles Junior and Clarence, inherited his penchant for settling problems with anger and muscle. Both seemed to be less impressive figures, but loyal, hardworking, and upstanding men—Charles toiling diligently as an engineer, Clarence as an accountant for a local casino, spending many off-hours volunteering for the Newport Historical Society, and contributing to it fifty bound volumes of newspaper clippings.

By the time he was twenty-one, Charles, working in Providence, had made a fateful and life-changing decision, impulsively falling for a pretty and vivacious teen, six years his junior, from nearby Pawtucket. They were married in Providence on September 6, 1871, in a ceremony presided over by an Episcopal rector. Though Carrie S. Clark was a mere child of fifteen, she stated that she was eighteen for the marriage certificate. Just whom the teenager was trying to deceive—the state, Charles's parents, or Charles himself—is not clear. What did the parents think of all this? Why did Stanhope rush to wed a girl so young? Did she trap him into marriage in some way, perhaps by claiming she was pregnant?

In any event, something went terribly wrong. Within two years—possibly in a matter of months—a vast chasm had opened between them, and they were living on opposite sides of it, Charles with his father in Newport and Carrie on her own in Providence, using her maiden name. The crisis may have been provoked by disease, because Charles, who never married again, at some point contracted the fearful malady of syphilis, dying of its complications in 1898. Did he discover the sores one day and realize he could have gotten them only from his teenage wife, Carrie, precipitating an angry separation, followed by a cold refusal to ever see her again? (Some girls, desperate for money or affection, sold their bodies as early as the age of twelve, risking venereal disease in the bargain.) Did she get it from him, prompting her, in anger and disgust, to break free and try to make her own way in life? We are left in the realm of pure speculation. A reference to the marriage in the *Boston Globe* notes only that "she had been married in extreme youth to an engineer" from Newport, "but there was a disagreement and then she made Providence her home."

In its preliminary stage, syphilis shows up as telltale venereal chancres. But these quickly fade, and the victim might go through months or years—even decades—without noticing anything wrong. He might consider himself cured, and might indeed *be* cured, the disease never reappearing. But in other cases sores return, and, left untreated, syphilis can cause fevers and headaches, even grandiose delusions or bizarre insights into the world, and then begin to do truly horrible damage. It can turn bones brittle, bring on deafness or blindness, damage the heart and other internal organs, and, at its worst, inflict tabes dorsalis—agonizing pain in the spine, accompanied by insanity—and ultimately death. Treatment before the discovery of penicillin was primitive at best. Doctors dispensed pills of mercury, a potent poison that might well prove deadlier to the patient than to the bacterium. Abraham Lincoln, according to his longtime partner William Herndon, was infected with syphilis during his twenties, when he "went to Beardstown and during a devilish passion had connection with a girl and caught the disease"—a personal disaster that might help explain his searing depression and thoughts of suicide later, around the time he contemplated marriage to Mary Todd. For much of his life, Lincoln took mercury pills, called "blue mass," three times a day.

The ferocious spread of the disease was, like so much else in the nineteenth century, linked to the rampant commercialization of everyday life. Bribing police to look the other way, enterprising men and women were reaping a windfall from the sex trade all over the country, and a preponderance of whiskey-soaked dancing halls, brothels disguised as boardinghouses, and aggressive street-corner whores made it all too easy for fallible men to contract the syphilis bacterium and share it with their unsuspecting lovers, then or much later. While the horror of any public discussion of sex in Victorian America kept such matters shameful secrets, newspaper advertisements touting dubious cures offered compelling evidence that sexually transmitted diseases were rampant. In the Providence *Evening Bulletin*, one Dr. C. J. Lewis promoted his services under the italicized headline "*THE GLORY OF A MAN IS IN HIS STRENGTH.*" The doctor had discovered, "after intense study and deep research," a "new, extraordinary, quick, certain and inexpensive cure for the diseases of the Brain and Spinal Cord, Spermatorrhoea, Seminal Weakness, Fluid Escapes, Impotency and Deranged Functions of the Nervous and Generative Systems." In short, Providence men who suffered from sexual diseases and dysfunction—and there were obviously many members of that woeful fraternity—could seek help from the "Always Successful" doctor at his 129 Friendship Street office. Even men who had given up on sex would be wise to consult Dr. Lewis, the ad advised, for "he will restore the disappointed one to all the duties of life, whether they be physical or mental, pertaining to married life or 'single blessedness.'"

In any event, Carrie was on her own at the age of seventeen, her life as an "unspoiled" virgin over. She had to fend for herself in a vibrant, growing city with its full share of lures and dangers. Going by her maiden name, she lived in a boardinghouse on the East Side, then a rough section of town, at 34 Randall Street, and walked a mile each morning down a hill, along the sewage-filled Providence River, and past sooty brick buildings, then crossing a bridge to Westminster Street, where she worked long hours in a store called the Japan Switch Company. "Patronized by the best people in the city and surrounding country," according to an 1892 business directory, the house manufactured and sold ladies' and gentlemen's wigs, half wigs, and toupees made of human hair, "and they also have a large assortment of character wigs, beards, etc. for sale or to let"—which may have led to Carrie's first acquaintance with actors passing through the city. The store also ran a busy hairdressing salon, with rooms for cutting and styling the hair of Providence's rich and pampered ladies. Such jobs were hard to come by, and amiable and good-looking girls had the edge on the competition.

Providence was bursting with stores in the 1870s: bookstores, jewelry stores, confectioners, furniture stores, boot and shoe stores, hardware stores, cotton and wool stores, wooden and willow ware stores, millinery goods stores, and, by one 1878 count, 204 liquor stores. Westminster Street was the city's shopping mecca. One of America's first indoor malls, the three-story Arcade, built in 1828, watched over the street in the form of a graceful Greek temple, welcoming consumers up its great granite steps and through its massive Ionic columns. Plate glass windows, giving off a warm glow in the early evening, displayed the latest Paris fashions in hats and silk dresses, expensive jewelry and timepieces, men's suits and beautiful furniture, all symbols of Rhode Island's rising wealth and booming consumer economy. Criminals eyed the goods, sometimes returning at night with crowbars and lock picks to break in. The street was a place where residents, old and young, convened to gossip over the latest news.

In the early 1870s, it had also become a gathering ground for single young women who, freer than ladies in their mothers' generation, scandalously walked the streets, openly flirting with young men. Many were obviously prostitutes; some, perhaps, were just young ladies out to smile and blush with their friends. In any event, it had gotten so bad, and created such a public stir, that the authorities, including Mayor Thomas A. Doyle, were forced to take notice. "The number of young girls, from twelve years of age and upwards, allowed to promenade our principal thoroughfares in the evening has increased to such an extent as to be alarming to the thinking portion of the community," the mayor complained in his 1871 inaugural address. The girls' behavior was "not absolutely lewd," but it was "rapidly approaching it," he warned. "The conduct of these young promenaders on Westminster Street became so bad on Sunday evenings the last autumn that a very large detail of police was required to preserve even decent order on the streets." In spite of the police, amiable women continued to meet up with pleasant beaus on Westminster Street, and some got to know each other very well indeed.

In 1874, well after her break from Charles, Carrie discovered, surely to her horror, that she was pregnant. Eighteen years old and without a husband at her side, she worked at the store for as long as she could, then returned to Pawtucket, presumably to her parents' home, where she gave birth to a son she named Charles—perhaps after her husband, perhaps after her sweet brother who had died in infancy. It is not clear whether Charles L. Stanhope Jr., who had separated from her a year earlier and was living many miles away, was in fact the father, or whether Carrie had begun seeing other

men. The latter is a distinct possibility, since it was almost proverbial that
unattached shopgirls in Victorian America were freelance prostitutes on the
side. Girls who still lived with their parents could, of course, avoid tempta-
tion easily enough, but young women who had to fend for themselves found
it next to impossible on a salary of $4, $5, or $6 a week to cover the cost of
food, rent, washing, and coal, never mind buying and maintaining a sufficient number of the attractive outfits that they needed if they were to look
presentable to the public behind a store counter. By "hustling" a few nights
a week, as they called it even then, they could earn enough to get by. Public
investigators looking into prostitution in Chicago interviewed an attractive
young sales clerk who explained why she began selling her body. "She enumerated different articles of clothing which she was wearing, and gave the
prices of each, including her hat. The total came to over $200.00. Her eyes
had been opened to her earning capacity in the 'sporting' life by a man who
laughed at her for wasting her good looks and physical charms behind a
counter for a boss who was growing rich from her services, and the services
of others like her." Carrie, like this young woman, found some means to
become a fashionable dresser without wealth of her own.

Many people scorned women for taking the path of selling sexual favors.

Looking down Westminster Street, c. 1880

But others felt a pang of sympathy for girls who worked themselves to exhaustion for a pittance and then returned to a lonely room in a cold and shabby boardinghouse, hungry not only for sustenance but also to be touched and treasured by someone. Charlton Edholm, a deeply religious young woman who had embarked on a mission of helping prostitutes, pointed out that no one could survive on a shopgirl's salary. "Is it any wonder these girls in sheer desperation are forced into a life of shame?" she asked in an 1881 address. "And then we moan and talk of the alarming increase of prostitution. Well do these girls know that the men who will not pay them living wages for their most faithful work will give them a life of ease and luxury for their womanhood, and that, too, under the guise of tenderest love, for which every human heart longs so intensely; and we little know how barren, how desolate of the sunlight of love are the lives of these girls." While many churchgoers felt certain such young women had condemned themselves to eternal damnation, Mrs. Edholm wondered if, on Judgment Day, God would also weigh in the balance "these respectable Christian employers, who drove them into that terrible life by their starvation wages. Their blood will be upon their skirts."

Married women, as well, took to prostitution, particularly in times of acute financial want, sometimes at the urging of their husbands. In 1884, one Terence Comiskey went to the boardinghouse on Providence's Paine Street where his wife had gone to live and, in a rage, fired a pistol at her window from the street. When she declined to open the door, he battered it down and entered the building with his revolver still smoking. Finding his wife cowering, he drew a bead on her and shot her three times—once just behind her left ear, once in her forehead, and once in her left breast. Comiskey's quarrel with his wife grew out of his attempts to force her into a house of prostitution to help earn money. "She resisted all his persuasion," wrote one reporter, "which so infuriated him that he determined upon her murder."

Prostitution was a dangerous profession, in Providence and elsewhere, and not only for the diseases often caught and spread by the women. Jealousies and passions were almost inevitably part of a business involving the act of love. On a Saturday night in April 1876, Merchant H. Weeden, a married twenty-five-year-old carpenter, burst into a well-known house of prostitution at Providence's 24 A Street and fired several bullets into the head and breast of a beautiful young woman named Sarah Lillian Waverly, who worked under the assumed name of Josie Revere. A girl who found work in such a house, even with the intention of making some money or finding a husband and then getting out quickly, had to be careful.

Providence police were supposed to keep an eye on suspected houses of ill repute, and it is reasonable to assume that, as in other cities, they collected protection money from the houses to look the other way. Streetwalkers ran a greater risk. Early one morning, a white-bearded sergeant named Benjamin T. White made a visit to the notoriously rowdy India Street neighborhood, near the docks on Providence's East Side, to arrest a woman on a warrant charging her with being a "lewd and lascivious person." When she heard the officer coming up her stairs, she stripped naked and jumped into bed. From the adjoining room, the policeman pleaded with her to put on clothes and come with him, "but she only taunted him by daring him to lay a finger on her." The officer decided to call for an express wagon and wait her out. When the conveyance arrived, White sprang into her room, "and grabbing the bed-clothes, quickly rolled the astonished woman up in them, and telling the expressman, now on the spot, to take her wearing apparel, he carried her bodily down the stairs and deposited her in the bottom of the express wagon." She remained there quietly until they reached the police station.

The real money was in running a house. A madam typically took 50 percent of the payment for sex, and made more selling drinks at inflated prices. Though she had to pay a hefty bribe to police and politicians to turn a blind eye to it all—something they were perfectly willing to do as long as the madam generally kept the peace—the profits could be substantial. The Chicago inquiry found one madam had not only provided for her family by running a house but had also banked a small fortune of $7,000. Young ladies hired to work in such houses might undertake prodigious feats of service. At one low house in Chicago that charged a dirt-cheap 50¢ per visit, six women working over a four-day period served some 394 men, which would mean an average of about sixteen men per day each. At other houses charging much higher prices, stocked with younger and more beautiful women, a worker might tend to just one man all night.

Young women had various reasons for choosing this line of work. In 1884, the Massachusetts Bureau of Labor Statistics interviewed 170 inmates of Boston brothels. Twenty-two declined to give a cause; seventeen cited ill-treatment at home; twenty-six said they were motivated by poor pay and hard work; forty-six said they had been seduced and forced into the life. But, interestingly, the single cause most frequently cited, by more than one-third of the women, was "love of easy life and love of dress." Many of them thought that, given the harsh alternatives in their world, sex with strangers was not so terrible a price to pay. Indeed, it was a relatively easy way to earn enough money for the fashionable clothes they craved without slaving in a shop or a factory, or ruining their eyes and their health bent over piecemeal sewing work for starvation wages.

Carrie's father, Henry, died the same year her child was born, and suddenly the weight of the family began to bear down hard on the shopgirl's shoulders. She would need tremendous grit to keep them all alive and safe, and to set her son onto a path for a successful life. Her husband, far away, seemed indifferent to their plight, and Carrie later testified that he gave her no financial support after their separation. Perhaps he did not recognize Carrie's child as his own. Though still technically married to Carrie, he lived a very separate and seemingly lonely life, toiling away in the machine shop of the Old Colony Steamship Company in Newport. We catch a glimpse of him in December 1876, when he was working on board the steamer *Providence*. The local newspaper reported that a coworker swinging a sledgehammer accidentally slammed it down on Charles's hand, badly splitting one of his fingers.

Carrie still worked at the store as Carrie S. Clarke for a few years, perhaps leaving the baby with her mother. But at some point—probably to fend off raised eyebrows about the child—Carrie stopped using her maiden name and started instead calling herself Mrs. Stanhope. When anyone inquired about her husband, she lied that he was dead. Her shopgirl days ended, she was no longer identified as working in 1879, merely as residing at a Broad Street boardinghouse as a "widow"—earning her living in a manner she chose not to share with the city directory. By 1880, she was running her own boardinghouse downtown, at 1 Beverly Street, just off Washington Street, in a neighborhood that was known for harboring brothels. In the directory, and for much of the rest of her life, she continued to call herself a widow, though in the U.S. Census, with its air of officialdom, she admitted she was married.

We do not know for a fact that "Charming Carrie Stanhope," as the *Globe* called her, was a prostitute or a madam. But we do know that, with seemingly no other means of support than her boardinghouse, this alluring and ambitious woman in her early twenties provided for herself, her mother, her little son, Charles, and her kid sister, Julia, by then a teenager. In the 1880 census, twenty-four-year-old Carrie was listed as the head of the household, not her widowed fifty-eight-year-old mother, Harriet. The only two boarders named were, rather suspiciously, young women living apart from men: Anna McMann, who was married, and Susan Greene, who was widowed or divorced. Both were thirty, and both cited their occupation as servant.

At the best boardinghouses run as brothels, "quiet, order and taste abound," a contemporary writer noted. "The lady boarders at these houses never walk the streets nor solicit company." A woman who ran such a house welcomed men into her parlor, charming them with her wit and grace. Gradually, her lady boarders dropped in to chat with the visitors, over drinks. "As the evening wanes and wine flows, the talk becomes bolder. Home, early days, childhood, mother, the school of girlish hours, the Sabbath, the Sunday school, the home pastor, their style of life, what the world thinks of them, how absolutely they are cut off from society, and barred out as if lepers,—are themes of conversation." The lady of the house kept a sharp eye on her boarders. "She knows who comes and goes, the sum that is paid, and exacts of all her tribute," the writer added. Since the young women had to pay board and dues "for the privilege of the house," purchase costly dresses and baubles, visit the hairdresser, buy cosmetics, and hire a coach at times, they found it hard to save much, if anything. A young boarder, if she was savvy and charming enough, might move on to run a house herself, or entice a man to marry her and give her a new life. Otherwise, the prospects were grim. As her charms faded, a woman moved down to "poorer houses, meaner dresses, coarser fare, rougher company, and stronger drinks." Below that, the dangers of streetwalking beckoned.

After three years on Beverly Street, Carrie had turned a big enough profit to reinvest in a bigger operation just a few blocks away. She rented a mansion at 51 Washington Street, in former times one of the fine houses of Providence. Under her management, it became associated in the public's mind with the entertainment of large numbers of young men. It was there, it seems, that Carrie captivated the veteran pitcher of the Grays.

She did not love the butcher's son at first. A sullen man who threw an occasional sarcastic jab, he slugged down whiskey like water and seemed wrapped in his own thoughts much of the time. But in time she would come to see Charlie Radbourn's finer qualities: his ambition, his bravery, his stubborn determination, and his fierce loyalty. He would offer her an escape from life in the boardinghouse—marriage, respectability, and a more normal home for her son—as Charles Stanhope had once offered her a means of escape from Pawtucket.

As for Radbourn, smitten by Carrie's beauty, charm, and courage, he would try to mend her and make her whole—just as he had the quail with the broken wing, who, safe in her cage, forever fluttered to him when she heard his call.

An Ugly Disposition

"**T**ime out!" umpire John Burns bellowed.

Radbourn, rising from a crouch at first base as applause began to ripple through the Messer Park crowd, watched the little ceremony unfold. Sweeney was standing in the pitcher's box, holding on to the ball, as the smiling Burns approached him, clutching a big basket brimming with fresh flowers, the latest offering sent onto the field by Providence's baseball lovers. All of the unabashed idolatry of Saturday night—the red fire, the speeches and backslapping, the brass band, the blazing and exploding fireworks—had failed to satisfy the pitcher's votaries, evidently, because less than forty-eight hours later they were still keen on worshipping Sweeney's magnificence. Radbourn watched sullenly as the dirty cop's son accepted the floral gift. Looking up to the grandstand, Sweeney beamed and waved, bathing in the adulation, while the crowd of 2,131—a big showing for a Monday, out to watch the third Boston–Providence matchup—burst into "enthusiastic applause," the *Journal* reported, "in tribute to the skill and ability of the young pitcher."

Radbourn had displayed his own skill and ability in perhaps even more heroic fashion by pitching sixteen near-perfect innings on Friday, and he had received only a dead arm in tribute to *his* magnificence. It wasn't the fawning, though, that gnawed at him. It was that Sweeney, with that killer fastball and curve of his, was pushing him aside as the team's best pitcher, no matter how hard Radbourn tried. The Hoss had no appetite for taking second place to anyone, especially this insufferable braggart. Playing first base again, in place of the still-feverish Joe Start, Rad seemed distracted by it all, his head not quite in the game. In the first inning, as if in a daze, he failed to make any attempt to block a wild throw, which scooted past him and skittered along the fence in right-field foul territory, while Boston's Joe Hornung scampered home with the first run. On the next play, a scorching grounder bounced right off Radbourn to second baseman Farrell, who threw it back to first in time to retire the batter— while the runner on third, Ezra Sutton, scored. Those two runs, both perhaps preventable by Radbourn, proved decisive—because while Sweeney was brilliant all afternoon, "sending in a swift, puzzling ball which it was impossible to gauge successfully," the Beaneaters' young pitcher, Charlie Buffinton, was even better. The Grays could muster only three hits and lost, 2–0. "Too Much Red Fire Maketh the Heart Sink," the next morning's *Star* quipped in a headline.

The bitter adversaries were back in Boston on Tuesday, June 10, playing before another big crowd at the South End Grounds. Sweeney, pumped up by all the attention he had been receiving, took the box for the third straight game, while Radbourn still struggled to lift his arm. Both clubs were out for blood, as Paul Hines amply demonstrated when, stealing second, he slammed into the base with such fury that he flattened Boston's brain-damaged Jack Burdock, knocking him out cold. As the frightened crowd fell into respectful silence, his teammates gathered around Black Jack's motionless body and tried to revive him. Finally the second baseman came to, slowly sat upright, and regained his senses. After the fifteen-minute delay, and more applause when Jack struggled to his feet, Boston gained a swift revenge. Hines ventured one step too far from second, and Jim Whitney spun around and picked him off. "The 2306 people rose like one person, and for some minutes there was a perfect babel of sound, while many threw their hats into the air and yelled until they were hoarse," the *Globe* reported. Burdock's lumps aside, it was a banner day for the Beaneaters, who won, 3–1. "The Providence club did not find a band of music and carriages awaiting their return last evening, and neither was the town 'painted red,' but the walking was good from the depot to the homes of the players," the *Boston Herald* gloated.

After four full days off from pitching, a rare luxury, Radbourn finally returned to the box on Wednesday afternoon, in Providence. However eager he was to restore his dominance over Sweeney, "Radbourn was in no condition to pitch," the *Globe* observed, "owing to rheumatism"—the pain that had plagued him all year. His "lameness," the *Evening Press* reported, "has now extended to his shoulder and back," and while he "pitched pluckily," it was "apparent that every ball hurt him." As the game went on, Radbourn found himself unable to throw curves anymore, and began firing the ball underhand, letting Boston batters swing away, hoping his outfielders were up to the task of chasing down the line drives. "They responded nobly and saved several runs and made great catches, particularly Carroll, who did a great tumbling act in far left field," the *Evening Press* reported. But their circus catches weren't enough. Radbourn got hammered for ten hits in a 4–1 loss, the third straight defeat of the Grays. On the final play of the game, Denny blasted a long, hard line drive that smacked the bare hand of Boston left fielder Joe Hornung so hard that the outfielder "was groaning lustily" as he trotted to the dressing room. But it was worth the sting. Providence was fading before the Red Stockings' superiority. "Radbourn is lame and does not pitch in his old form," the *Fall River Daily Evening News* observed. Providence's only hope was that "warm weather will help him out."

More, and worse, followed on Friday the thirteenth. Boston whipped Sweeney and Providence, 4–0. "There are times when we weep. This is one of them," the *Evening Press* lamented. "Excuse us while we weep. * * * * We have wept. The Bostons have been here and have gone away the victors." The *Journal* got on its high horse about it, denouncing the Providence batters' "fruitless wind agitation, in which they have of late become so expert" in clutch situations, and complaining that "a more disheartening and even disgusting exhibition of professional ball playing has seldom been seen on the home grounds." Clearly, something was amiss. The *Journal* suspected excessive drinking, noting, "It has been found necessary to discipline one or two of the players who have not been keeping to the terms of their contracts." Don't be surprised, the writer warned, if those players were suspended in the near future, a punishment he thought the offenders richly deserved. "If it is the intention of the management to make even a respectable fight for the pennant, it would seem that the most vigorous methods should at once be adopted," the *Journal* urged, making a case that, it soon became apparent, resonated with the club's prickly directors. After soaring in May, Providence had suddenly dropped six of their last eight decisions, and trailed Boston by four games.

Having demonstrated to the satisfaction of many observers that they were not the Red Stockings' equals this year, the Grays headed back to Boston to conclude the series. Radbourn, by now pain-ridden, overshadowed, and undervalued, had to take his turn in the box, whether he was suffering rheumatism or not. He faced the Grasshopper, Jim Whitney, in front of another festive Saturday crowd of 5,424 at the South End Grounds. This time Radbourn somehow found his groove, keeping the game within reach until Providence tied it 3–3 in the eighth inning. The contest then marched on into extra innings, turning into a rematch of the memorable battle eight days earlier, as Whitney and Radbourn kept throwing, inning after inning, while the afternoon shadows lengthened. In the fourteenth inning, a Boston batter finally smashed a long drive to left field, and a sprinting Cliff Carroll leapt into the air for it. The ball bounced off his hands, but as he fell to the ground he reached out for the ricochet, making a miracle catch that robbed Boston of a triple or worse. Boston's baseball-educated fanatics were nothing if not appreciative of a brilliant play, even one made by a Providence man, and the crowd "yelled and applauded until it became tired," the *Globe* reported. The mighty struggle continued.

With two outs in the fifteenth inning, Paul Revere Radford clubbed his second double of the game. The crowd held its breath as the fleet kid, eager to beat his former teammates, edged off second base, in scoring position. Whitney, needing just one out, unleashed a pitch that Cliff Carroll, fresh from his fielding heroics, smacked into the outfield, sending Shorty sprinting home and putting Providence up 4–3. Though the Beaneaters were down to their last three outs, their supporters stayed on, refusing to give up— clinging to the hope that Radbourn, sore to begin with, would collapse, since he was now into his fifteenth inning of pitching. With the last of his strength, Radbourn fed the Boston batters an array of bamboozling junk, coaxing Bill Crowley to pop out, Sam Wise to slam "a nasty grounder" that Jerry Denny managed to smother, and slugger Joe Hornung to tip a fly ball into center field, where Paul Hines "took tender care of it" to end the game. Radbourn had staunched Providence's bleeding with a beautiful seven-hit victory over the defending champions. An *Evening Telegram* reporter overheard a lisping ten-year-old on the streets of Providence, analyzing the Bostons' season-long offensive problems: "Yeth, but you thee, the whole trouble ith, the Bothtenth don't bunch their hith."

After the severe strain of pitching fifteen innings Saturday, and forty over his last three starts, Radbourn was back at the Messer Street Grounds the following Monday, June 16. Weary or not, he whipped the Philadelphia club 13–1 on a five-hitter, a performance so good it persuaded Frank Bancroft that it was safe to release his failed project, the still hopelessly wild John Cattanach. But if Radbourn thought he had finally shown Sweeney who was boss, he had another thing coming to him. His success only inspired the younger man to pitch harder. On June 17, Sweeney threw his second near-perfect game of the season, beating New York 9–0 on a one-hitter. A double play quickly erased that sole hit, and from then on, Sweeney, in an amazing show of dominance, retired every man in succession. It was almost impossible to pitch better.

But Radbourn tried. On Wednesday, *he* threw a one-hitter, shutting out New York 15–0, as his teammates brutalized "Smiling Mickey" Welch, hammering him for twenty-three hits, including a home run and triple by the horseshoe-blessed Paul Hines. "Welch good-naturedly submitted to the slugging, and the patrons took solid comfort in watching the leather hunting," the *Journal* exulted.

The Grays played their final home game for three weeks on Thursday, June 19. Under threatening skies, Ladies' Day brought out 631 paying male customers and an equal number of women admitted for free, Carrie Stanhope surely among them. The ladies, fashionably attired in high-heeled boots, full-length dresses with bustles, lacy gloves, and sweeping hats, and clutching parasols to ward off any latent sun, watched Sweeney get hit hard, but the Grays managed to drive home three runs in the sixth inning to take a 6–5 lead. By then, the sky was growing blacker and the air was becoming moist, with great clouds of dust whipping across the field. Umpire Billy McLean hustled the players along, trying to get in as much of the game as possible. After the Phillies went down in order in the seventh, a tremendous thunderstorm exploded, and rain fell in torrents. Fortunately for the ladies, anxious about their expensive clothing, "the roof of the grand stand was pretty nearly water-tight, and not many of them had their apparel spoiled," the *Evening Press* noted. By then, the grounds were so thoroughly waterlogged that McLean called the game, giving Providence the narrow victory. The Grays and Phillies, short on time, hustled into the dressing room, stripped off their wet uniforms, donned business suits, and splashed through the streets to the horsecars, heading for the station downtown, where they caught the 5:40 p.m. train to Union Station in Worcester. From there, they would board a train bound for the expansive West. Providence had to be in faraway Detroit to play ball in only two days.

Nineteenth-century travel—with its ubiquitous bedbugs, mosquitoes, bad food, and bacteria-laden, cramp-inducing water—took a harsh physical toll on ballplayers. In 1884, the most distant outpost in the National League was Chicago (major-league teams could not practically play on the West Coast until the advent of jet passenger planes in the late 1950s). But even the Windy City was a wearying, three-day railroad journey from the East. Beyond the boredom, eased mainly by chatter and marathon card games, players sometimes had to deal with the discomfort of sleeping upright or slumped over their seats. They nodded off to the narcotic chugging of the engine, jostled by the swaying cars, feeling the incessant click over the rail joints, and were awoken repeatedly by the wail of the whistle or a conductor shouting out stops. The cars tended to be stifling on summer nights, but if a man opened a window for air, he ended up breathing ash and getting singed by hot cinders belched out by the engine.

Team owners, who hated spending money on railroad tickets and hotel rooms, strung together road games, and sent their teams out west (or east) only twice a season. That made for astonishingly long trips, sometimes grinding on for more than a month. Hotel rooms were liable to be roasting hot, and many of them lacked window screens, leaving guests to be tormented by long nights of whining pests and itchy bites. The responsibility of keeping heavy flannel uniforms clean was another burden of life on the road. A player might find a Chinese laundry with quick turnaround service, or soak his uniform himself in a hotel tub, then hang it out the window to dry. More likely, he would simply let the sweat in the flannel evaporate, apply a stiff brush to the dried dirt, and put the uniform back on again before the next game, pungent and unwashed. Richer clubs carted around uniforms in a communal trunk, but that could cause headaches, too. On July 14, the Gothams arrived in Philadelphia without their trunk, which had somehow separated itself from them, and were forced to scrounge up suits. The Phillies' road uniforms, which the Gothams otherwise might have borrowed, were in the wash. New York finally managed to cadge the olive-colored togs of the Union Association's Cincinnati Outlaw Reds, who were in town to play the Philadelphia Keystones. Outfielder Danny Richardson made do with a spare Phillies home outfit, while Roger Connor put together a "mixed uniform."

There was a psychological toll as well. Far from the constraints of home, bored and lonely players often got roaring drunk, gambled away their earnings, and spent large sums on prostitutes. Naturally, trouble followed them around. One August evening in 1883, St. Louis Browns left fielder Tom Mansell celebrated a big victory over the archrival Reds with a night on the town. He returned to Cincinnati's Grand Hotel, staggered across its handsome lobby, and strode straight through the open door of an elevator—without noticing the absence of a car, somehow. Mansell plunged ten feet down the dark shaft, gruesomely gashing his right knee, an injury that arguably cost the Browns the American Association pennant. Other players entertained themselves with public brawls in saloons or on sidewalks, at times getting hauled away by local constables and thrown in jail. After a game on June 28, 1884, the Metropolitans of New York were enjoying their evening sitting in front of the very same Cincinnati hotel when pitcher Jack Lynch and outfielder Chief Roseman got into a playful sparring match. Lynch's temper began to flare when Roseman got the better of him, and a full-fledged fistfight broke out, while their fellow Mets, instead of breaking up the tussle, joyfully egged the two on. Finally, a saloonkeeper ran across the street and halted the brawl. "Both men were bleeding profusely and one of them sat in front of the hotel half an hour after the fight was over spitting claret," the *Sporting Life* reported. "The fight was disgraceful and carried on in a manner common to bar-room loafers." But the Grand Hotel found traveling ballplayers such lucrative trade that it was willing to put up with the occasional escapade.

It all worked to wear down travelers, giving home teams a mighty advantage over their frazzled visitors. And it ratcheted up tensions in clubs, doing little to improve the temperament of players who were already at each other's throats. Given teams' tiny rosters and the regular beating players' bodies took, the spring-to-fall season was always a harsh test of the skill and endurance of every man. Providence faced such a test now, with sixteen scheduled games on the road.

The Grays headed out in decent shape, at least, thanks to a run of five straight victories that had significantly cut into Boston's lead. On the morning of June 20, the standings revealed three eastern clubs bunched at the top, and the once mighty Chicago club mired in mediocrity:

	W	L	PCT.	GB
Boston	30	10	.750	—
PROVIDENCE	28	10	.737	1
New York	25	16	.610	5½
Buffalo	20	18	.526	9
Chicago	16	22	.421	13
Cleveland	14	23	.378	14½
Philadelphia	13	28	.317	17½
Detroit	10	29	.256	19½

Arriving safely in Detroit, the Grays went straight to work before thin crowds at Recreation Park. Radbourn, though surely tired by his long journey, opened the series with his fourth straight beauty, a 10–0 shutout. "The Detroits were as helpless as so many school boys before Radbourne," the *Detroit News* reported. After Sweeney won 4–3, Radbourn returned with another astounding performance, doggedly pitching a fourteen-inning shutout, allowing only three hits as the Grays won 1–0. Sweeney, keeping pace, threw a two-hit shutout, leading the Grays to a 3–0 win and a sweep of the series. Having shut out the last-place Wolverines in three of four games, the Grays headed farther west, for Chicago. "Sweeney is surely doing the most effective pitching in the League up to the present time," the *Fall River Daily Evening News* noted, "and with Radbourne, makes the best showing of any brace of pitchers in the country." But while Sweeney was getting most of the attention, Radbourn was on a red-hot streak. He had won his last five games, having edged Boston in a big, fifteen-inning contest; pitched a one-hitter; thrown a two-hit shutout; and fought his way to a fourteen-inning shutout victory—surely enough to shut up any critics who thought he was washed up.

Cap Anson was in a foul mood about the miserable performance of his White Stockings, spoiling for a fight by the time the Eastern teams arrived. He quickly started one. In the second inning of Boston's opener at Chicago on June 21, Beaneaters outfielder Jack Manning turned his ankle sliding into second base. Hobbling and in pain, Manning tried to play on bravely. But before the fourth inning began, the joint had become so badly swollen, and the pain so intense, that he collapsed on the bench, letting Charlie Buffinton trot out to center field in his place. The moment Anson saw that, he raced over to umpire Billy McLean and began his trademark bellowing.

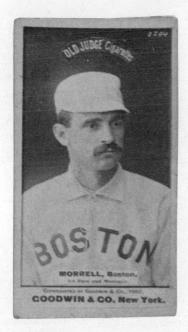

John Morrill

The rules permitted substitutions only in case of injuries that disabled a player. A man could play with a wobbly ankle, he insisted.

For some reason, McLean agreed with Anson's absurdly rigid construction of the rules and ordered that Buffinton be removed and Manning restored. John Morrill heatedly refused, insisting that the starter's bad sprain made it impossible for him to put weight on the ankle and that he was obviously unfit to play. The stubborn ex-pugilist tugged out his pocket watch and informed the Boston captain he had precisely five minutes to get Buffinton off the field or he would end the game then and there and declare a forfeit to Chicago. At the last second,

Morrill pulled his center fielder and, unwilling to exacerbate Manning's injuries, played with only eight men. Not surprisingly, Boston lost, 11–7.

Beaneaters fanatics were livid, claiming that Anson had, once again, managed to intimidate a gutless umpire into favoring Chicago. Open threats of violence followed. "If you step your foot upon the Boston base ball grounds again you do so at your peril," a Bostonian named J. M. Allen warned McLean. "I write this for friends who mean business." Since there was no return address, the red-blooded McLean answered in the newspaper. "Sir, you are a coward. If you are not, write and inform me where you can be found, for in that case I shall certainly find you when I go to Boston again." He signed his letter "WILLIAM MCLEAN, Gentleman, and not Monkey." The umpire also held his ground about the ruling on Manning's ankle. "I expect abuse and am prepared for it. I do not court popularity at the expense of justice of fair play," he declared in an interview with the *Chicago Herald.* Asked why, when the rules stipulate nine men to a side, he let Boston play with only eight, he answered, "Anson did not protest." But shouldn't the umpire, acting on his own, have *ordered* Manning to hobble about on the field and take his turn at the plate? "Perhaps so. It was overlooked anyway," McLean said.

Meanwhile, Anson was out to gain another dubious edge. He had turned up with a new kind of bat, costing a pricey $5, made of strips of ash glued together lengthwise around a central, one-inch-square rod of twelve pieces of rattan—an early version of a corked bat, designed to provide "more spring" to any baseball that was hit off it. Players who tried it testified that it propelled the ball 25 percent farther than the standard item. Anson insisted that it was legal since the rules said only that bats be made "wholly of wood." (In his view, the glue apparently did not count.) In the two games he used it, both against Boston, Anson slammed six hits in seven at-bats, including two doubles and a home run. For some reason, though—probably because opponents persuaded the league that it was rankly illegal—the bat never caught on.

After Chicago beat Boston in two out of three games, Anson looked forward to administering similar punishment to Providence. The Grays arrived in a city that was a favorite escape for many young men, drawn to its salacious late-night delights of dancing halls and accommodating women who catered to every taste. They stayed in the bustling downtown, at the Clifton House at the corner of Monroe Street and Wabash Avenue, a quick stroll from the ballpark and not a long walk from the red-light district. The Clifton was a busy place, popular with actors and boisterous ballplayers, though one might not know it from the way it advertised itself: "Here everything is quiet, genteel, and aristocratic, and the proprietors pride themselves upon the high character of the people who make the Clifton their stopping place." As in most hotels, tobacco-chewing businessmen thronged the public rooms, talking boisterously, spitting streams of black saliva at shiny spittoons, even in polite company, and often hitting the carpet instead. A block away, at the corner of State and Monroe streets, was the even fancier Palmer House, where the visiting ballplayers could feast on an impressive array of appetizers, fish courses, main courses, and desserts: Blue Points on shell; mallard, teal, or tame duck with applesauce; antelope; prairie chicken; calf's liver, fried, with salt pork; fried parsnips; steamed plum pudding in cognac sauce or Neapolitan ice cream; Malaga grapes or Florida oranges; Roquefort or Stilton cheese; coffee or buttermilk. All this was consumed in sumptuous dining rooms "lighted by the Edison System" of electricity, while people in the poor neighborhoods ringing the downtown often went hungry.

Rudyard Kipling, the fastidious British writer who harbored little affection for America's elbow-throwing citizens, described the Chicago hotel as "overmuch gilded and mirrored, and there I found a huge hall of tessellated marble crammed with people talking about money and spitting about everywhere. Other barbarians charged in and out of this inferno with letters and telegrams in their hands, and yet others shouted at each other. A man who had drunk quite as much as was good for him told me that this was 'the finest hotel in the finest city on God Almighty's earth.'" Built at a staggering cost by department-store mogul Potter Palmer—one of the investors in Chicago's White Stockings—the Palmer advertised itself as "the only thoroughly fireproof hotel in the United States." That was a comfort to travelers who knew only too well the dangers of sleeping in crowded wooden hotels illuminated by flaming gas—especially those who remembered the great Chicago Fire a decade earlier, which in the course of killing three thousand people had swept through twenty-eight miles of streets and more than two thousand acres, consuming the original Palmer and Clifton in its path.

After lunch, the players strode outside the hotel and along a crowded sidewalk toward Lake Michigan. The traffic hummed in the early afternoon. The sweetish stench of sewage from the Chicago River, a quarter of a mile north, wafted over the neighborhood at times, blending with the acrid smoke belching out of factories and the stacks of engines chuffing in the Illinois Central rail yard nearby. The massive grain elevators along the river towered in the distance.

The ball yard quickly loomed into view. A long whitewashed fence along Michigan Avenue advertised its formal name in huge block letters: *Chicago Base Ball Park*. Crossing Michigan Avenue, the athletes had to step lively to reach the other side unscathed, dodging the oncoming wagons and carriages while avoiding any heaps of manure not yet stomped down and pulverized into a wind-whipped dust. Though it had to be crammed in between Michigan Avenue, Randolph Street, and the rail yard, Lake Front Park, as it was popularly known, was ideally situated for attracting large numbers of middle-class males, a mere stroll away for the harried, bewhiskered, cigar-chomping clerks and executives in the five- and six-story ornate brick and stone office buildings of the city's central business district. The main grandstand accommodated two thousand people in relative comfort, while upper-crust Chicagoans who disdained mixing with their social inferiors could sit, literally, above them, in the exclusive luxury boxes of the small upper deck. There they stretched out pleasantly with wives or consorts on comfortable chairs and sofas, watching the game unfold while drinking in the view of expensive yachts tacking gently out on Lake Michigan beyond the outfield walls. Nestled among his wealthy peers, White Stockings president Albert G. Spalding had equipped his own private box with the latest in business technology, a telephone, only eight years after its inventor, Alexander Graham Bell, had placed the first successful call, famously telling his assistant, "Mr. Watson—come here—I want to see you." By shouting into the receiver, communicating with the muffled, distant voice on the other end, Spalding could employ this modern marvel to conduct business instantly with his assistants at the ball club's headquarters or his own sporting-goods firm, A. G. Spalding & Bros., at 108 Madison Street, several blocks away.

One of the park's distinctive quirks was its absurdly close right-field fence. It sloped from deep center field to just 196 feet from home plate down the foul line, easily reachable by even the weakest hitter. A tall canvas extension atop the wall managed to trap some baseballs inside the park, keeping them in play. All the same, unimpressive fly balls—outs in other parks—could readily clear it. For years, the Chicago owners had dealt with these comical dimensions by maintaining a sensible ground rule: balls hit over the stretch of fence closest to home plate were doubles. But in 1884, the owners had changed the rule to render such flies home runs, on the theory that Chicago's big hitters would clear the fence more often than their rivals, giving the home club an edge over the long season. Sure enough, the team's home-run total ballooned from 13 in 1883 to an unheard-of 142 in 1884. On May 30, Chicago's Ned Williamson, a left-handed hitter whose quick, powerful stroke was ideal for the short fence, became the first man in major-league history to club three home runs in a game, and his teammate Cap Anson duplicated the feat on August 6. At season's end, seven of the league's top ten home-run hitters were Chicago players, including the champion Williamson, whose twenty-seven round-trippers stood as the major-league record until Babe Ruth broke it with twenty-nine in 1919. The *Evening Telegram* called the wall a "potent home run machine." Batters loved it, but the "home-run fence" gave pitchers nightmares.

Radbourn took the box on Thursday, June 26, before a big crowd of 2,067, drawn to watch the fine club that had served as Chicago's foil for years. Radbourn quickly discovered that the White Stockings would not lie down as Detroit had. Chicago jumped to a 3–0 lead. But the Grays began chipping away against White Stockings pitcher Fred Goldsmith, a former ace who was in his sad final months as a major-league pitcher, his arm ruined by overuse. A tall, slender, twenty-eight-year-old right-hander from New Haven, Connecticut, the "very cool and witty" Goldsmith was said to greet a hot liner scorched past his ear by softly humming a bar of the sentimental hit song "We Never Speak as We Pass By." He somehow retained a sense of humor as well about the new Lake Front ground rule. "He has a habit of taking home runs over the right field fence made off him very good-naturedly, and never fails to whistle 'Over the Garden Wall' as the ball clears the fence," the *Sporting Life* noted. That month, when Goldsmith had been forced to take a seat on the bench midgame, supposedly because of illness, he found himself hounded by a spectator. "What makes you sick,

Goldsmith?" the man bellowed from the stands near first base. "You do," Goldsmith shouted back, to derisive laughter from the Chicago crowd. On June 26 he seemed little improved. "He has all the curve he ever had and used his head as well as ever, but he is no longer able to impart speed to the ball, and it is only a question of a few innings when his medium pace will be heavily batted," the *Chicago Tribune* lamented. Though "Anson got his $5 bat squarely on the ball and drove it over [the] centre-field fence," Radbourn seemed to get stronger as Goldsmith faded on that hot afternoon, and Providence roared back to win, 8–6.

Sweeney pitched the next day, June 27—a date, the *Chicago Herald* asserted, that the Grays would remember for as long as they played baseball. They faced "a small, quiet player in a brown cap, named Lawrence J. Corcoran," who mowed them down, one after another, to record the unprecedented third no-hitter of his distinguished career—a record that would hold until September 9, 1965, when Sandy Koufax of the Los Angeles Dodgers threw a fourth one. Even Paul Hines, "the headlight of the Providence team, was scarcely a rushlight yesterday," the *Tribune* gloated, "and his companions were extinguished like glow-worms."

But that was not the worst of it for Providence that afternoon. Sweeney had actually been matching Corcoran, goose egg for goose egg, through six innings, when disaster struck. He had pitched hard all season, throwing his fiery fastballs since early April, when there was snow on the ground. And now, on a muggy summer's afternoon in Chicago, it caught up with him. On one agonizing pitch, he felt something pop in his arm. "A cord in his arm above his elbow has given way," the *Cleveland Herald* reported—an injury that Bancroft described as "exactly similar" to the one that had felled Jim McCormick a year before, dooming Cleveland's pennant hopes. Expected to finish any game he started, Sweeney kept on pitching, despite the pain and weakness, and surrendered six runs in the seventh and eighth innings, to lose, 6–0.

But that was all the pitching Sweeney could do for a while. The kid faced the prospect of being shelved for weeks. Obviously, Sweeney had been critical to the club's success thus far, and his loss robbed the Grays of one of their two starters. More than that, though, the layoff seemed to infuriate Radbourn, who, after all, wasn't letting a little thing like pain stop him.

Though Radbourn by then possessed a sparkling 18–3 record, he had endured months of a condition that the papers called rheumatism, an agonizing ache in his arm and shoulder, and he had kept on throwing in spite of it, perhaps risking career-ending complications. Now his club wanted him to do double duty while Sweeney rested up.

If Radbourn was going to do that, he would at least have to be paid for it. At some point, he confronted Bancroft, probably in the manager's hotel room. The pitcher insisted in his quiet, businesslike manner, always carrying an edge of warning, that he expected to be paid extra to take over Sweeney's duties as well as his own. The bushy-mustached manager, who owed his own job to his penny-pinching ways, flatly told Radbourn no— the same answer he had given Cleveland's surly One Arm Daily in the same situation a year earlier. Never one to take no well, Radbourn began "to show an ugly disposition" and "kicked" at the way the club was treating him, the *New York Times* reported. He was not pleased with Bancroft, Providence, or the precious Sweeney, and he wanted out.

For his part, Sweeney insisted he was blameless. He had done at least as much for the club in 1884 as Radbourn, and earned far less money for his efforts. He could not help it if the people of Providence thought he was the better pitcher. He, and not Radbourn, had struck out nineteen men in one game, and pitched two near-perfect games. Now that he was hurt, he had to protect his arm, his meal ticket. No one else in this heartless business would put his interests first. In any case, Sweeney could hardly pitch in excruciating pain. Let Radbourn, with his big salary, take over. "What work I did, from the opening of the championship season the public knows," Sweeney recalled thirteen years later. "Suffice it to say I was always ready and willing to pitch or play whenever called upon up to the time of snapping a cord in my arm, in Chicago."

As if the Grays did not have enough problems, Joe Start, Providence's stalwart captain and first baseman—who had already missed a fair number of games because of the recurring agonies of malaria—tried to catch a ball bare-handed and "got a finger knocked out," as the *Chicago Tribune* put it. The Grays peered into the abyss.

Given the troubles he now faced, manager Bancroft was in no mood for bad umpiring, and Billy McLean's shaky performance that week only stoked his anger. "Providence has no use for McLean," Bancroft told the *Chicago Herald.* "His eyesight is poor, he cannot read without spectacles, and he does not take a position which enables him to fairly judge balls and strikes. I have never seen worse decisions than McLean has made since we have been in Chicago." The spectacles jab was no joke. During a game that month, Boston's Joe Horning had advised McLean to get some eyeglasses—a suggestion that cost him a $20 fine. "Billy has since got the specs, though," the *Sporting Life* added.

Relying now solely on Radbourn, the Grays took the field at Lake Front on June 28 in front of a Saturday crowd of 3,241 against twenty-two-year-old pitcher Tom Lee, who had been promoted from Chicago's "reserve" team— essentially its farm club—in hopes he might replace the fading Fred Goldsmith. But Lee was worse than useless. "He delivered a slow drop," the *Journal's* correspondent noted, "and after one inning the visitors had little difficulty in hitting him and placing the ball over the right field fence." With thirteen hits, including three home runs, Providence battered Chicago 13–4.

The series ended on Monday, June 30, with the sore and bitter Radbourn pitching again. He contributed a home run but got hammered hard, surrendering ten hits. With two outs in the ninth, the tiring Radbourn tried to sneak a pitch past the always dangerous Mike Kelly, who cranked it over the right-field fence for the game-winning home run, handing Chicago the 5–4 victory. The Grays left town in a sour mood, having dropped two out of four to the White Stockings, who were way behind in the standings but still playing with stubborn pride. "Chicago may be sick but it is a dangerous foe for all that," the *Sporting Life* noted. "Neither Boston nor Providence could win a majority of the games on the Chicago dunghill."

A wearing seventeen-hour train journey brought the Grays to Cleveland, where the usually quiet and dependable Radbourn began to rebel openly against pitching every day. He was still smoldering, furious at Bancroft for refusing to pay him extra to take Sweeney's starts, after the club had paid Sweeney extra to pitch alone in April. "When the club reached Cleveland, I wasn't able to pitch," Sweeney recalled with some bitterness, "yet when Radbourne was asked to go in, he said he wasn't earning anybody's salary for them." Since the Providence club had no chance of winning without Radbourn, Bancroft was compelled to order the rebellious veteran to go in. Radbourn obeyed, under protest, but over the next several games he pitched so poorly that some questioned whether the famous pitcher, long regarded as a loyal and stalwart warrior, was even trying his hardest anymore. He seemed jealous of Sweeney, angry to be stuck in Providence, resentful over working extra for no money.

The *Sporting Life*, for one, thought Radbourn was double-crossing his employer. The Radbourn-Sweeney rivalry, it argued, was a prime example of the "cliqueism" that had infested professional baseball. Radbourn and his catcher Barney Gilligan, the writer insinuated, were the ringleaders of a gang of teammates who detested Sweeney and worked together to make him look bad. "Here is a pitcher . . . who, not satisfied with legitimately earning the handsome salary paid him, wants to control the entire team, leaving the manager to be a mere figure-head in his position, or limiting him to attend only to the outside business of the club. Such a pitcher goes to work to get a clique of heelers among the players who will help him in his little game, and the result is that each battery in the club have their special supporters in the team, and each clique works for the advantage of their pet battery, at the cost of the general interests of the team as a whole."

On July 1, Cleveland hammered Radbourn for ten hits, including a towering shot by Bill Phillips over the fence to straightaway center field—the longest hit anyone had ever seen on the grounds. Luckily for Providence, Cleveland's wretched fielding and the wildness of starter John Harkins, a big, tall right-hander who had played college ball and studied chemistry at Rutgers University, more than made up for Radbourn's dismal showing, as the enemy handed the Grays a 10–3 victory. Radbourn walked off the field that afternoon with his twentieth win of the season—not bad, given all that he had endured. Grays shortstop Arthur Irwin, meanwhile, annoyed the local press to no end by behaving like "a pestiferous little varmint" when he got on base, keeping up "an incessant howl" at Harkins, in behalf of every Grays batter, to "let him hit it!" "Such tactics belong to the loafer, and not to the ball player," the *Cleveland Herald* chided.

On July 2, Cleveland hitters battered Radbourn "until he looked hurt and surprised," dealing him his fifth defeat of the season. Cleveland ace Jim McCormick made the day no more pleasant for the Grays when he squelched a ninth-inning Providence rally by slugging Cliff Carroll in the face with a fastball. Then Radbourn confronted the nightmare of Independence Day. The prospect of pitching both ends of another separate-admission doubleheader, as he had on Memorial Day, was daunting, to say the least. Fortunately for his arm, the plumes of Krakatoa still hung over the continental United States, and drenching rains washed out the morning contest. The reprieve was only temporary, however, because the rain let up by afternoon, forcing Radbourn back to the box. Sweeney had thrown some practice pitches, hoping to work, but quickly had to give up, turning over the job to his disgruntled teammate. Some seven thousand Cleveland fanatics, said to be the biggest crowd ever at League Park, braved the dampness, filled the stands to capacity, swarmed over the field, crowded into the outfield, "climbed on the roofs and roosted on the fences," the *Cleveland Leader* reported. They cheered as they watched their hometown boys rattle the sore-armed veteran for ten hits. But Radbourn hung on stubbornly as the Grays collected eleven, including five doubles and a triple, salvaging a 4–2 victory.

By the time the Grays reached Buffalo, the final stop of their western road trip, Radbourn simply couldn't, or wouldn't, pitch. According to the *Evening Telegram*, he had become so embittered that "he refuses to associate to any extent with his own nine," and had even begun using the opposing team's dressing room. Moreover, he had surrendered thirty-two hits in his last three games, a clear sign that something was seriously amiss. In the Buffalo opener, manager Bancroft was forced to send to the box right fielder Paul Revere Radford, who had not pitched in more than two months. Before the game, Bancroft visited with reporters at Olympic Park's press stand and glumly confessed "he had no expectation of winning" because he had "no confidence" in scrawny Radford's amateur-caliber pitching. The murderous Buffalo lineup quickly demonstrated why, clubbing fourteen hits—Big Dan Brouthers alone went 4 for 5, with three doubles—as Buffalo throttled Providence, 9–1. Obviously, Radford offered little relief.

Radbourn returned on July 7, after the relative indulgence of two days off, and for six innings did a reasonably good job of restraining Buffalo's hitters, while his men built up an 11–3 lead. But in the seventh inning, the *Journal* reported, "his arm partially gave out," and Charlie gave up six runs during the last three innings. Though Radbourn ended up surrendering twelve hits—forty-four in four games, now—he managed to scrap his way to a 14–9 victory. But he was in pain, and growing more irascible by the hour about Sweeney's extended sick leave.

The younger pitcher had been absent for only ten days, and he risked exacerbating his injury if he tried to pitch again before he had healed. But, eager to shut up Radbourn, Sweeney attempted his comeback on July 8. For five innings, he seemed solid, shutting out Buffalo. Then—as he had feared—his arm began aching badly. The Bisons' hitters unloaded on him, scoring three runs in the sixth inning, and two more in the eighth. With the score locked 5–5 after nine innings, Bancroft called Sweeney over to the grandstand.

"Had you not better let Radbourn go in, Charlie? Your arm is pretty sore yet," the manager asked tenderly.

"All right, if he wants to," Sweeney replied, throwing in the towel, a rare concession for those days, when pitchers were expected to finish what they started.

Radbourn, who was playing in right field, accordingly traded places, saving the game for Sweeney when the Grays plated the winning run in the tenth inning.

With Sweeney claiming arm pain again, Radbourn had to drag himself back out to start yet another game, an increasingly dicey proposition for the Grays. In the final game of a road trip that had turned into a painful slog, Radbourn took a 1–1 tie into the seventh inning, then fell apart, losing 5–1. The weary Grays dusted themselves off and caught a train for home.

Radbourn departed in a cold fury, nursing a bitter resentment against his employers, who were too cheap to pay him for the extra work he was doing at the risk of his arm and his career. Worse, his character was under attack. Critics who could not have retired a professional hitter to save their lives began to ask if he was dogging it, deliberately pitching poorly to punish his bosses, as if all that extra throwing had not inevitably weakened him and eroded his effectiveness. Radbourn could not have been faulted for wondering if it was time for him to leave Providence and try his luck with another club, one that would pay him the money he deserved, and show him the respect he had earned. A rage was building inside the moody warrior, threatening to erupt at any time. In the meantime, at least, the long trip was ending, and he was returning to the home he had made in Providence, perhaps to the arms of the woman who had captured his heart.

Rendezvous of the Wayward

The men arrived, weary from their journey, at busy Union Depot, a massive Norman-Gothic pile of smoke-stained redbrick, split into two wings— an east and west side, each attached to three of the six railroad lines converging there—and in the middle, a large two-story structure with immense windows, high-ceilinged waiting rooms (one reserved for ladies), and two enormous towers. Visitors could not help being impressed—even the great naturalist and writer Henry David Thoreau, a man given to intense observation. "Was struck by the Providence depot, its towers and great length of brick," Thoreau jotted down after one visit. The station went on and on, stretching out in a slight semicircle for a remarkable 625 feet, and when it was built in 1848, city fathers pointed to it proudly as the longest building in America. Its back curved along the circle of the Cove, a decorative basin of water about a mile in diameter in the heart of the city; its similarly curving breast thrust out into one of the city's great gathering spaces, windswept Exchange Place, where scores of hacks and cabs lined up on the cobblestone pavement, waiting day and night, ready to transport passengers and their baggage to their destinations.

From the depot, the Grays dispersed for their homes, some on foot, some climbing into a cab or one of the horsecars, whose tracks ran right in front of the station. If Radbourn was headed for Carrie Stanhope's boarding-house, he would have grabbed his bag and walked. Passing through one of the eleven arches of the depot's eastern wing, Radbourn would have stepped down from the platform and turned sharply to his right, strolling along the front of the station, dodging rushing travelers and heavy traffic, in the direction of the new city hall at the western end of Exchange Place. Built in the French Second Empire style, the edifice had been completed six years earlier at the staggering cost to taxpayers of $1 million, a price surely larded with patronage and kickbacks. Out in front of city hall stood the Soldiers' and Sailors' Monument, erected in memory of the thousands of Rhode Island boys killed in the Civil War. A ten-foot-tall statue of *America Militant* stood on a pedestal thirty-two feet off the ground, extending a wreath of laurels in her right hand, symbol of postwar peace, her sword at her side. Below, on projecting abutments at each corner, were statues representing the slaughtered heroes from the infantry, cavalry, artillery, and navy.

To the left, across Exchange Place, loomed one of the city's tallest and proudest structures, the six-story Butler Exchange, a behemoth constructed on a grid of iron beams, graced by four magnificent towers, and designed, like city hall, with mansard roofs in gaudy Second Empire style. Among its many tenants, it housed the main offices of the Providence Telephone Company, which was creating a rapidly expanding network of customers linked together through Alexander Graham Bell's miracle invention. The company boasted over a thousand miles of wire and more than twenty-one hundred connections, including four public telephones: one there at the Butler Exchange, one each at apothecary stores on Westminster and on Eddy streets, and one at the baseball grounds, way out on Messer Street—a phone heavily used, no doubt, by reporters who quickly conveyed game results to newspapers or gambling interests. Users paid 15¢ per call within city limits and 25¢ per call outside the city, within the company's still small network.

On a stormy April night in 1877, the thirty-year-old Bell himself had demonstrated the magic of his telephone right in Providence, before a spellbound crowd of three thousand at the Music Hall, with the help of his obliging twenty-three-year-old assistant, Thomas A. Watson, who was stationed in the professor's laboratory in Boston, forty miles away. "It is snowing here," Bell informed his distant helper. At Professor Bell's suggestion, a cornet player in Boston shrilled the popular sentimental ballad "When Other Lips and Other Hearts," from Michael Balfe's 1843 opera *The Bohemian Girl*, followed by "Yankee Doodle," sending over a scratchy, tinny din that the attentive Rhode Island crowd somehow heard and applauded. (A large megaphone must have amplified the sound.) Someone in the music hall requested the "Woodhull Quickstep," and the trumpeter in Boston complied, "much to the delight of Providence." Watson followed by singing "Auld Lang Syne" and the Christian hymn "Hold the Fort," both of which were plainly heard in the Providence hall. These were truly miraculous times.

Leaving behind Exchange Place, Radbourn would have walked onto Washington Street, just north of city hall, passing the Aldrich House, a handsome four-story brick hotel, followed by a pungent stable where neighbors boarded their horses and garaged their carriages. Next stood the three-story Shattuck's Exchange, a shabby wooden tavern that had seen better days and served as the waiting and drinking place for passengers who still wished to avail themselves of one of the city's last surviving stagecoach runs. In 1829, before the railroads had changed everything, there had been 328 stages running each week from Providence to Boston. Now the longest coach route from Providence was a bumpy twenty-five-mile jaunt to Danielsonville, Connecticut, leaving each morning at eleven from Shattuck's.

Across the street from Shattuck's, there on the corner of Washington

In the Bowery, across Washington Street from Carrie Stanhope's house

Street and Union Avenue, stood Carrie Stanhope's boardinghouse. It was hardly a quiet retreat for a tired ballplayer. The neighborhood was packed with hotels, shops, factories, stables, barrooms, apartments, and even a small brewery, all housed in a jumble of buildings, from sturdy modern brick structures to sagging, grimy clapboard houses of an earlier era. Just beyond Carrie's house, sharing her block, was a nondescript saloon, followed by the Wah Shung laundry, where Radbourn could have taken his filthy Grays uniform, and C. A. Cook's grocery store. Across the street were more stores and the Ladies and Gents Dining Room, advertising its bill of fare on a big sign next to the door, beside garish posters for shows in local theaters. Chugging, squealing trains running to and from the Union Depot on tracks just north of the block added to the constant cacophony. People called the neighborhood "the Bowery," perhaps after the famously rowdy section of New York City.

Carrie's towering house—with a shop on the ground floor, a wrought-iron balcony protruding from the second floor, and dormers on the fourth floor—had seen better days. When it was built several decades earlier, lower Washington Street was a pleasant residential area, safely across the river from Providence's bustling and sometimes dangerous East Side. One of its selling points then was its close proximity to the air-freshening, crystal-blue water of the charming Cove, encircled by a splendid twenty-foot-wide promenade that was well used by strolling lovers. "It is adorned by fine shade-trees, provided with comfortable seats, and in the evening is well-lighted by numerous gas-lamps," a city guidebook noted.

Around 1850, a cheery, flamboyant former sailor and stagecoach driver named William Ross purchased the estate at the corner of Union and Washington, and he and his wife raised their four children there. Colonel Ross, as he liked to be called, had made his fortune by figuring out how to trim the time between Providence and Boston, operating the swiftest stagecoach runs between the two cities, carrying business express packages as well as passengers. Later he shrewdly invested his growing fortune in railroads. A boisterous man, and "one of the most eccentric characters of Providence," according to the *Providence Press*, the transportation mogul was a distinctive sight as he trooped about town in his peak-toed, square-heeled boots, his hats with enormous rolling brims, and his bright vests of striking colors and textures. But if William Ross is remembered at all today, it is not for his quirky sartorial tastes but because his name was forever linked to P. T. Barnum's famous project of bringing the "Swedish Nightingale," Jenny Lind, to America. Barnum signed her to 150 concerts at the unheard-of fee of $1,000 per show and, with his uncanny knack for generating publicity, quickly whipped up an outright mania for her in the American public. Some thirty thousand people greeted Miss Lind at the dock in New York City when she arrived in 1850, and Barnum found he could auction off seats to her concerts, making vastly more than the sums he was paying Jenny. Colonel Ross, always a show-off, grabbed national attention and wound up in the history books by bidding more than anybody in America—$653, roughly $16,700 in modern money—for first choice of a seat at her Providence show. Rather than attend the concert, Colonel Ross asked Barnum and Lind to autograph his record-breaking ticket, and visitors could see it, "well-framed and hanging on the inner walls of the old estate on Washington street," the *Press* reported. He was a strange man, in short, but beloved all the same. "With all his eccentricities and oddities, not many can say that he ever did him wrong, but many of the needy ones of the city can and will testify to his kindness and the open-handed way with which he scattered about the gifts of plenty Dame Fortune favored him with."

The needy ones of the city were crowding up awfully close to him by the time he died in his mansion in 1879, and the family chose to rent out the house rather than live in a neighborhood that was getting a little bit scary. Businesses had sprung up on the first floor of former homes, painted ladies in bright dresses roamed the sidewalks, shabby boardinghouses with missing shutters and torn blinds in the windows had proliferated, and buildings had become dirty and long destitute of a fresh coat of paint. The Cove, meanwhile, once "the apple of the eye of Providence," had begun to fill up each day with untreated sewage and industrial waste carried from upriver by the two tributaries that flowed into it, breeding a plague of flies and mosquitoes while blanketing part of the downtown in a stomach-churning odor before sluggishly expelling the putrid brown "mud" with each tide into the Providence River and Narragansett Bay, leaving behind repulsive "filth heaps." Its stench wafted over Washington Street. ' "The Cove, the Cove, the beautiful Cove' stinketh to Heaven," the *Sunday Morning Journal* noted tartly. Yet Car-

Carrie Stanhope's house (with dormers on roof). To its left, a saloon, the Wah Shung laundry, and C.A. Cook's grocery store

rie was happy to rent the place, seeing it as a move up from her cramped quarters around the corner on Beverly Street.

Still, it was a dodgy area, particularly at night. A mere stone's throw from the Ross mansion was a dark alley named Westminster Place, "a rendezvous of the scum of the city," according to one police reporter, "the habitual resort of thieves, cut-throats, lewd women, and offenders of every description. It was folly for any respectable citizen to attempt to pass through the locality after dark." Muggings were common, and sneak thieves worked Washington Street. Even police were not safe, as Sergeant Frank A. Mathews discovered in June 1882. Leading a thug toward the police station, the sergeant found himself jumped by a gang bent on the prisoner's release. Mathews, while being punched and kicked in the ribs, beat them back somehow and held on to his handcuffed man, though "the encounter caused him prolonged suffering." In June 1884, two toughs throttled a man on nearby Eddy Street and proceeded to terrorize the neighborhood. "They pushed every person they met in the street, slapped ladies' faces, threw men's hats into the street, upset boxes and barrels and smashed windows," the *Evening Telegram* reported.

There was always something or other happening in the Bowery. One day, a jealous wife spent hours skulking around the Union Depot, waiting in growing anger and despair for her husband to return on a train. Her suspicions were confirmed when he stepped down from the passenger car with another woman on his arm and strolled through Exchange Place toward Washington Street. Sneaking ahead of the couple and secreting herself in the shop door of Carrie's mansion, the betrayed spouse leapt out when they reached the corner of Union Street. Producing a horsewhip, she flogged her astonished husband until he finally managed to stop her by twisting the lash away, spraining her wrist. It was a lively neighborhood.

A hot-tempered, Irish-born officer named Thomas McCusker patrolled the Bowery in 1884, and quite possibly was involved in taking protection money from some of its businesses. "Addicted to drink," he was eventually drummed out of the force for violating department rules. By 1892, his wife, Catherine, had left him and was working as a housekeeper in the 712 Westminster Street home of one Hattie Ellis, who refused to let McCusker in to see her. On the night of December 13, Mrs. Ellis again turned him away, but McCusker wedged his foot in the door and forced his way into the hallway. Hattie screamed a warning to Catherine, who hid in her bedroom and bolted the door. McCusker pulled out a pistol and fired two shots through the panel, wounding her in the left arm and the right hip. Later that night, after visiting Donley's saloon, he turned himself in. Police officers in 1880s Providence could be a mixed bag.

A couple of blocks away from Carrie's boardinghouse was 24 Chapel Street, a whorehouse frequented by both blacks and whites, "and several white girls of youthful age were seen going in and out of the place daily," the *Evening Telegram* noted. On Memorial Day night, after Radbourn won both ends of a doubleheader, police raided the place and hauled away ladies of the evening named Annie Mack, Mary White, Grace Howard, Mary Foster, and Gertrude Wright. Within two days, all five "girls" were "run out of town." Three short blocks away from Carrie's house was Weybosset Street, where mixed-race parties regularly took place at a dance hall, inevitably igniting the racial hatreds that pervaded nineteenth-century America. "The place did not bear a Queen Victoria reputation," a police reporter dryly recounted, and though two police were detailed to keep order at the dances, an all-out donnybrook erupted one night. A sergeant hastening to the scene "found men cursing, and women shrieking, while razors flashed, and blood was flowing freely." The officer fought his way through the crowd to a man named William Jackson, who was standing on a chair, "flourishing an open razor in his right hand, and threatening anyone who approached him." He had "begun the row by claiming to be an escort of a white woman, the latter preferring another companion."

But the Bowery was not the only neighborhood contributing to Providence's reputation as a haven for lawlessness and illicit enjoyments. Far smaller than New York and Boston, Rhode Island's capital functioned as a jumping-off place for railroad travelers between the bigger cities. Because of that, one contemporary newspaper correspondent noted, the city served as a "rendezvous of the wayward," including men and women who were not exactly married to each other. Those "who seek facile pleasures," the writer observed, "never go by this burg" without stopping for a while. "Scandals of high and low life generally develop here," and while Providence was geographically a part of prim and puritanical New England, it had somehow taken on the flavor of the Wild West. "The sporting fraternity predominates here, and for a 'quiet New England town' it harbors the best confidence men, card players, adventuresses and base ball enthusiasts to be found east of the shambling territory of world-known Leadville," the rip-roaring Colorado mining town, notorious for its plentiful prostitutes and for a legendary sign posted in one saloon: "Please do not shoot the pianist. He is doing his best." As the reporter observed: "You may go to New York, Boston or Philadelphia, but if you wish to see full fledged, simon pure dudes and dudines you must come to the edge of the Narragansett."

Little Rhode Island made a big impact in other ways as well. Its humming economy was built on the rivers and factories of the industrial revolution, which traced its American origins to the eighteenth-century Slater Mill, in Pawtucket, constructed with technology smuggled out of England. In the 1880s, people were still flocking to Rhode Island for the work, many of them French Canadians or immigrants from Ireland, Britain, and, increasingly, Italy. Newcomers were drawn, in particular, by the jobs and money spun off by the state's cutting-edge companies, each employing thousands of workers: Brown and Sharpe, Gorham Manufacturing, Nicholson File, American Screw Works, and the Corliss Steam Engine Company, whose gigantic 1,500-horsepower double steam engine had been the very symbol of American ingenuity and might at the 1876 Centennial Exhibition in Philadelphia, powering thirteen acres of machines in the great hall.

All those factories meant Providence was shrouded in smoke, winter and summer. Everything was fired by coal, from home heating to kitchen ovens to industrial forges. Not that many people complained about it. Air pollution was a nineteenth-century symbol of prosperity, and artists who prepared lithographs of Providence factories made certain to depict smoke billowing out their stacks. Whatever effect it might have on local lungs—and no doubt it hastened many citizens to an early grave—a thick haze over a city meant that there was work to be found and money to be made there. And that meant a roof overhead, shelter from the cold, and food on the table.

Providence's prosperity made it a noisy place, too. Vehicles with iron-rimmed wheels scraped and clattered along cobblestone streets. Horses clip-clopped, metal on the carts jangled, drivers shouted at each other, and police bellowed and blew whistles as they tried to untangle the traffic at crowded intersections. Like most Americans, Providence men were fiercely addicted to tobacco, though only a minority of them smoked. Many more chewed, and spat streams of sticky brown tobacco juice everywhere—in hotel lobbies, church pews, theaters, out on the street. Their spitting markedly increased the danger of tuberculosis, a rampant health threat. Baths were a once-a-week phenomenon at best, and laundering was expensive and time-consuming. Sweating men gave off a strong aroma in their dirty clothes.

At night, Providence was gloomy and decidedly dangerous. The Rhode Island Electric Light Company, chartered in 1882, was advertising that it could install lights in offices and mill buildings, and ten arc lights had been installed as an "experiment" on Westminster Street and near Market Square, the financial center of the city. But electricity remained a rare luxury, and Edison's incandescent bulb had yet to conquer the night. The city, which burned forty million cubic feet of gas a year in its street lamps and city hall, employed sixty-two lamplighters, who made their rounds igniting the gas

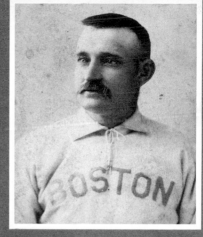

Charlie Radborne, circa 1887
(Robert Edward Auctions)

Charlie Sweeney, 1886
(Transcendental Graphics)

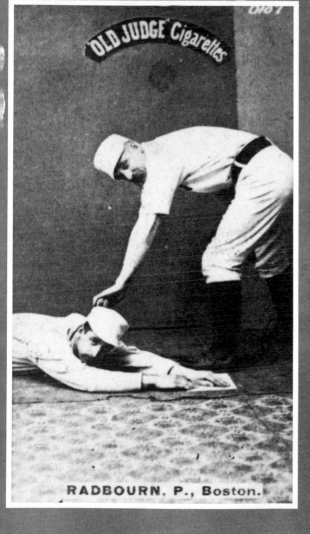

'OLD JUDGE' Cigarettes

RADBOURN, P., Boston.

Radbourn applies the tag
in an 1887 baseball card.
(Library of Congress)

Exchange Place, the pulsing heart of Providence, circa 1880. Taxis and wagons line up in front of Union Depot on the right, the new City Hall is rear center, and the Butler Exchange (with its fancy roof) is on the left. Carrie Stanhope's boardinghouse (not visible) is located beyond the railroad station on Washington Street, to the right of City Hall. (Rhode Island State Archives)

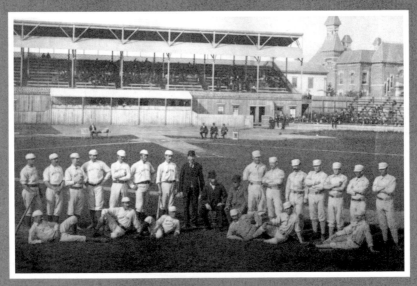

The Boston and Providence teams pose in a classic shot of the Messer Street Grounds, in 1879. Harry Wright is the bearded, seated gentleman with a top hat and cane; his brother, George, is sprawled on the ground to the right, in the middle of three Providence players. The building on the right beyond the park, then the Willow Street School, still stands. (National Baseball Hall of Fame Library, Cooperstown, New York)

Radbourn, standing far left, deviously flashes his middle finger as the Boston and New York teams pose at the Polo Grounds on opening day, April 29, 1886. That's Jim Mutrie (center) wearing his Sunday best and high hat. The meticulous photographer, according to the *New York Times*, "was compelled to take several plates, and the delay was annoying to the spectators, and they gave evidence of their feelings by shouting at the gentleman in charge of the camera." Radbourn certainly ruined this shot. (Transcendental Graphics)

Radbourn, here identified as "Radburn," adorns the front of a gorgeous 1884 Providence scorecard. (Don O'Hanley)

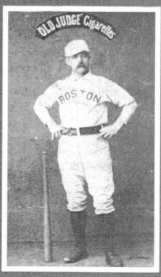

Radbourn flashes his middle finger again, this time on a baseball card. (Robert Edward Auctions)

Radbourn pitches against the New York Giants at the Polo Grounds in a wonderful early action shot. It's the bottom of the fourth inning, on April 29, 1886. Dude Esterbook takes a long lead off first base, kicking up dust, Mickey Welch swings the bat, Con Daily catches, and John M. Ward stands on deck. (Collection of the New-York Historical Society, negative no. 32485)

The grubby Grays of Providence pose at second base at Messer Street Grounds in 1884. Standing, from left: Radbourn, Sweeney, Murray, Denny, Hines, Bancroft,

The 1883 Boston Beaneaters, defending champions of the National League in 1884. Standing, from left: Hornung, Sutton, Wise, Burdock. Sitting, from left: Buffinton, Radford, Whitney, Morrill, Hines, Hackett, Smith. (National Baseball Hall of Fame Library, Cooperstown, New York)

Stat, Bassett, Cattanach, Carroll, Irwin, Farrell. Sitting, from left: Gilligan, Radford, Nava. (Transcendental Graphics)

An "elegant" team photo (National Baseball Hall of Fame Library, Cooperstown, New York)

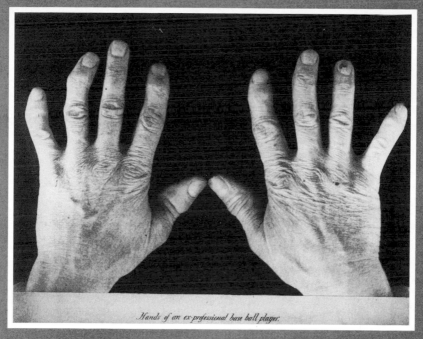

Hands of an ex-professional base ball player.

These 1889 photos of the hands of retired catcher Doug Allison pow-
erfully convey the agonies endured by early professional backstops.
(Courtesy of the National Museum of Health and Medicine, Armed
Forces Institutes of Pathology)

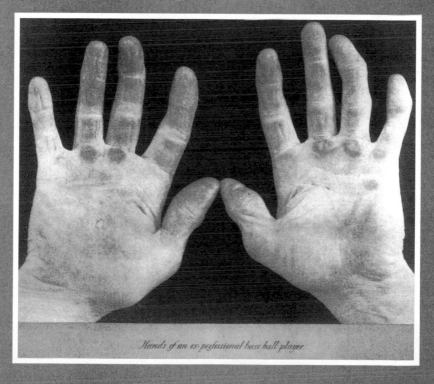

Hands of an ex-professional base ball player

THE SPORTS OF THE SEASON.—BASEBALL AND ITS PLEASURES.
SEE PAGE 203.

The May 19, 1883, edition of *Frank Leslie's Illustrated Newspaper* captures the varied joys of attending a ball game in Radbourn's day. (Author's collection)

when night fell. Even so, the lamps gave off a feeble light and some areas of the city had none at all. This was still a dark world.

Providence, naturally, stank to high heaven. Steam-powered railroads and ships connected the city with the outside. But virtually all travel *inside* the city involved the use of legs. There were no gasoline-powered cars or electric trolleys. Residents either set off on their own two feet or rode in horse-drawn vehicles. All those horses sprayed the streets with urine and covered them with droppings, contributing to Providence's powerful odor. Outhouses were still in common use. Some parts of the city had yet to be equipped with sewers, and in poor neighborhoods raw sewage seeped along alleys piled high with rotting garbage. Even the sewers merely flushed into the rivers the untreated waste, which notably ended up in the Cove before making its way to Narragansett Bay. City fathers were talking about covering over the water with roads and railroad tracks, trapping the odor, though it hadn't happened yet.

Still, nineteenth-century Americans could stand just about anything but boredom, and Providence's many amusements afforded welcome diversions. The city had a good number of theaters and auditoriums—Low's Opera House, the Music Hall, the Providence Opera House, the Theatre Comique—that drew thousands each night during the fall-through-spring season. In the summers, Park Garden on Broad Street beckoned with its acres of lawns, lakes, and paths, as well as a pavilion for stage shows. Illuminated by gaslight, electric lights, and fireworks displays, the park gave men and women welcome relief, long into the evening, from the close smells and suffocating heat of their tenement apartments and houses. Residents similarly flocked on summer nights to the Sans-Souci Garden on Broadway, enjoying its flowers, fountains, and colored lights as well as its shooting gallery and twelve-hundred-seat theater, used for comic operas and light comedies. People interested in playful exercise could choose between two indoor roller-skating rinks, and poorer residents could avail themselves of one of Providence's two floating bathing houses, where swimming was permitted for free, though the city charged for towels. Diving into Providence's water could be fraught with danger, though, particularly if any of it entered through the mouth or nose. The city's bathing house at the Point Street Bridge had to be moved to South Providence in 1882, "on account of the filthiness of the water," polluted with chemicals and raw sewage. For those who could afford to go sailing or take a steamboat excursion, Providence's greatest playground was Narragansett Bay, which widened out south of the city. As *King's Pocket-Book of Providence, R.I.* (1882) noted: "In summer, when the bay is filled with sailing-craft of every description, from the staunch and handsome steamers down to dingy but suggestive fishing-dories and oyster-boats, a sail between its green banks, adorned on every hand with pictur-esque cottages and villas, pavilions, and hotels, is an enjoyment not to be forgotten." Less nautical citizens who sought the excitement of gambling on horse racing could repair to the Narragansett Trotting Park, in the nearby town of Cranston. Finally, there was the local ballpark on Messer Street, "considered the finest in the country," a mecca for baseball fanatics from April to October.

King's did not venture into the city's plentiful illicit amusements—its sleazier saloons, dancing halls, gambling dens, and brothels, run by hard-nosed businesspeople who were protected by the police and local politi-cians. Nor did it mention Carrie Stanhope's boardinghouse. But it seems clear that Radbourn made his way there at some point and fell hard for the lovely woman who ran it.

One imagines he sought relief from the pressures of his high-profile profession in the faded glory of the old Ross mansion—some kind words, a sympathetic ear over his troubles with Sweeney, a stiff drink or two, a small cool hand on his raging-hot forehead, a bathtub filled with steaming water heated on the stove, a massage for his aching arm and shoulder, and maybe something more. The record shows Radbourn loved Mrs. Stanhope for the rest of his life, with the dogged commitment and unshakable loyalty that were his hallmarks. Here he found the family that he had missed so much since leaving Bloomington. And Carrie, a determined personality herself, may have been the one who got him through the next few weeks, when his career threatened to crash and burn.

Crackup

Radbourn had failed to pry one dollar out of the Grays for the work they now required of him, handling Sweeney's starts as well as his own. That was a snub he found hard to forgive, but he had persuaded management to make one concession. At Radbourn's urgent request, the club had provided him a stove—probably from team president Henry T. Root's kitchen appliance store—for the Grays' dressing room. It was a new model that employed coal oil, a highly flammable liquid much like kerosene. Such stoves heated up rapidly and threw off a lot of warmth. They were, admittedly, known to explode on rare occasions, even burning their users to death, but that was a risk nineteenth-century Americans seemed willing to take in exchange for the convenience. Even on the most sweltering summer afternoons, Radbourn could now get a hot stove going quickly after games to boil water and steam his aching arm, on the theory that heat would loosen and soothe his muscles.

Modern sports medicine suggests that was exactly the wrong approach—that Radbourn would have been better off icing down his arm and shoulder, shrinking the inflammation in his muscles. But who knew? The treatment available for lame arms and painful joints was primitive at best—no arthroscopic surgery, no whirlpool baths, no sophisticated physical therapy. For a sore arm, the *Sporting Life* recommended a "crude petroleum remedy," or this: "Rub with a mixture of a dime's worth each of sweet oil, liquid ammonia and rye whiskey." When Boston's Ezra Sutton was suffering a sore arm a few years later, the third baseman dropped nickels several times a day into the "electric machine" at Baltimore's Eutaw House, clutching the handles and receiving a sharp shock—a newfangled therapy believed to cure all sorts of ailments. Sutton concluded that the painful jolts had "done him lots of good, and that his arm feels better." But none of these treatments was likely to make a pitcher feel much better toiling day after day.

The art of treating sore arms was becoming an urgent matter in 1884, and Radbourn and Sweeney were not the only duo who required attention. The National League's expanded regular-season schedule—with fourteen additional games, almost one more per week—was proving to be more punishing than many of its hard-throwing, two-man rotations could bear. "One thing is evident. The National league is playing too many games per week; the batteries cannot stand it," the *Fall River Daily Evening News* warned. By midseason, it had become an open question whether the extra games were even worth it, given sagging attendance and the increased risk of injury to pitchers and catchers. "Base ball can be run into the ground; the people are called upon to attend too many games and they may, after a year or two more, count the draw on the pocketbook and stay home," the *News* argued. "Already businessmen in Providence say too much time is absorbed. Four games per week is enough. Will managers be wise in time?"

Overexposure was only one reason for dwindling attendance, though. A sharp recession loomed, and men were beginning to worry about the time and money they spent at the ballpark. That year's unseasonably cool and wet weather had not helped, either. And then there was the competition from the new, outlaw Union Association, vying to become a third major league. Though its level of play was markedly inferior, it offered baseball lovers a bargain admission charge of 25¢—half that of the National League's.

All the same, large numbers of New England fanatics were willing to spend top dollar for the luxury of a midsummer dustup between the Grays and Beaneaters. On the Friday afternoon of July 11, thousands descended on the Messer Street Grounds, many arriving on trains from Boston and Worcester. Halfway into the season, Boston and Providence were the only two teams still left near the top of the standings, battling for supremacy, though both were already bruised and tired, like boxers who had swung fiercely from the opening bell and were punch-drunk by the middle rounds.

Sweeney had failed under the strain, but Radbourn had somehow sustained the Grays in the pennant fight, keeping them in sight of the Beaneaters, only two games back. Boston had suffered its own reeling blow during its western trip. Fastball ace Jim Whitney had been sent home with a lame arm, forcing Charlie Buffinton to take up the slack.

The gawky, six-foot-one-inch, rail-thin Buffinton, who had just turned twenty-three on June 14, hailed from Fall River, Massachusetts, a mere eighteen miles east of Providence. Smart, modest, and hardworking, he was a different sort of pitcher than the Grasshopper. Charlie specialized in strategy rather than power, and his perplexing curves and mixture of speeds had been flummoxing batters all year, to the point that some experts now regarded Buffinton as the greatest pitcher in the country. His brilliant sinkerball had become something of a national sensation, drawing fanatics from all over to take a look. Buffinton's "slow drops," as the *Sporting Life* described them, "are apparently slow moving balls till they do drop and then they dart like lightning." Batters were amazed to be swinging past a pitch that had already exploded in the dirt. The one-two punch of Whitney's fire and Buffinton's finesse tended to keep hitters badly off balance during a series, and the duo had provided sixty-two of Boston's sixty-three wins during their championship season of 1883. Whether one could make it alone was an open question.

The question haunted Providence as much as Boston, and Bancroft was not eager to risk his club's chances on the answer. Though reluctant to give Radbourn extra money to pitch Sweeney's games, he was trying desperately to get him some help. On the way home from Buffalo, the Grays had stopped in Springfield, Massachusetts, for one of Bancroft's annoying exhibition games, and the manager had loaned a Grays uniform to twenty-eight-year-old, Irish-born Tommy Bond to see what he could do. Bond had once been baseball's premier pitcher, blessed with remarkable speed, control, and savvy—"foxey to a finish," as his contemporary Tim Murnane put it. He led the Red Stockings to the 1877 and 1878 National League pennants while winning more than forty games in three straight seasons. Not surprisingly, he had ruined his arm doing so. Though Bond had spent years on the shelf, Boston's Union Association club offered him a job in 1884, recognizing that he remained a local hero and a strong gate attraction. Bond even managed to win thirteen games before the club expelled him on the grounds of "insubordination and neglect of duties," though sympathetic friends claimed he quit only because the club refused to pay him the $208 it owed him. On July 10, certainly, Bond was in fine fettle, beating the minor-league Springfield club 6–3 on an impressive three-hitter.

Unfortunately, the pitcher had seemingly neglected to inform Bancroft that he had already agreed to play for the American Association's Indianapolis club. Getting wind of his Providence debut, Indianapolis frantically shot off a series of telegrams, warning Bancroft to keep his hands off, while ordering the pitcher to report for duty in Indiana immediately. Bancroft was happy to steal players from the faithless Union Association, but the American Association was quite another matter. It had become a loyal ally of the League and could demand harsh penalties. Bancroft was back to square one.

Both Boston and Providence, then, had no practical choice of starting pitchers for the big homecoming on Messer Street. They had to go with Buffinton and Radbourn, even though both had pitched two days earlier, with a wearying train trip wedged in between. The fickle baseball gods quickly hurled their thunderbolts at Boston. In the first inning, a thrown ball sheared off a fingernail of second baseman Jack Burdock, and while the infielder was trying to shake off the agony of that, a fierce shot off Radbourn's bat in the next inning sliced open the same finger, putting even that tenacious veteran out of commission. The Beaneaters could have used him, the *Boston Globe* noted, since "there were many tight boxes when a hit from Burdock would have been most acceptable." Instead, Radbourn and Buffinton got locked into one of their great pitchers' duels, scoreless through six innings.

The lanky Boston pitcher seemed particularly good. One Providence fan, watching one Grays batter after another flail away, blurted out: "Just see that Buffinton—awkward as a cow, but spry as a cat." Providence finally scratched out a run in the top of the seventh, but only by virtue of two Boston errors. When Buffinton walked to the batter's box to take his turn in the bottom of that inning, the umpire called time, and a group of Fall River admirers stepped onto the field to present Buff with an overflowing basket of flowers. (The florists of Providence were having a pretty good summer at the Messer Street Grounds.) The grateful recipient hoped to answer the gesture with a timely hit but only managed to foul out, "greatly to his disgust," the *Journal* reported. Providence added another run, and that was that. Radbourn, pitching a sparkling four-hitter, rode the 2–0 edge to victory, dealing Boston its first shutout all season. After his shaky performances out west, this was a very good sign.

While Radbourn was working that afternoon, the real world intruded via the park's scoreboard, with news posted by hand in big letters: New York governor Grover Cleveland had been nominated for president at the Democratic convention that afternoon in Chicago. The report was "received with an icy coldness. Not half a dozen in that large crowd cheered," the *Fall River Daily Evening News* reported. Rhode Island was a rock-ribbed Republican state, and its voters strongly favored Senator James G. Blaine of Maine, nominated by the GOP at Chicago a month earlier. During the next several months, one of the closest and nastiest presidential races in U.S. history would unfold alongside the 1884 pennant fight. In July, the Grays' own Paul Hines received a memorable telegram from one Republican, seemingly a baseball fanatic: "If Blaine is elected I am promised the position of Consul at Cork. Will want you as Irish secretary." The *Sporting Life* dismissed the message as "apparently from some crank." Meanwhile, according to a story making the rounds in Louisville, someone asked the notoriously ill-read slugger Pete Browning whether Cleveland would win. "Certainly not," he replied learnedly. "Neither Cleveland nor Chicago has any chance to win. The fight is between Boston and Providence."

Indeed it was. With the Beaneaters' lead down to one game, 6,137 paying customers mobbed the South End Grounds on Saturday, July 12, as the Boston boys played their first home game in three weeks. Buffinton was the man of the hour, receiving prolonged cheers when he came to bat for the first time. He was on his game, as was his catcher Mert Hackett, notwithstanding that a foul tip blasted through Hackett's mask in the third inning, driving its jagged wires into his face. The gritty young catcher wiped off the blood and kept on playing.

Sweeney was still protesting that he could not pitch. There was no pain in his arm, he admitted, but "it is weak and refuses to obey him," the *Sporting Life* reported. Radbourn, who most certainly had considerable pain and had burned up his strength in his four-hit shutout the day before, warned his manager that he was in no condition to pitch again on Saturday, risking permanent injury (for no extra compensation) by doing the work of another man—one who, for some reason, was being pampered, petted, and, presumably, paid. Growing tired of Radbourn's bitter lament, Bancroft sharply ordered the surly veteran to go back out. Providence could ill afford to fall too far behind Boston. Radbourn set his jaw and strode to the box, but he was not happy about it.

The dismal performance that followed may or may not have been a metaphorical middle finger to his boss. "Radbourn acted careless and indifferent," the *Journal* complained, adding that most of his teammates followed suit and "apparently didn't seem to care much whether or not they won." Charlie got walloped, as Boston batters smashed three doubles, a triple, and even a home run over the left-field fence. The Beaneaters ended up drubbing the Grays, 7–1. After the game, according to Providence's *Evening Telegram*, the angry pitcher informed management that, from then on, he was going "to pitch ball for Charlie Radbourne, and not for the nine."

His dismal performance fueled darker suspicions: that he was trying to lose, to force Providence to release him. "Radbourn seemed to find it very agreeable to pitch the ball just where the batsmen could hit it safely and effectively. Whatever may be the reason for this wretched showing by the Providence nine, it is certain that such exhibitions can but lessen the interest in the game by those who are disposed to patronize it," warned the *Sunday Morning Telegram*. "It is hinted that Radbourne was cranky and did not want to pitch," the *Fall River Daily Evening News* added. "It is too bad to have too much to do; still, when a club is disabled, each player ought to do his best, especially if he is used rightly by management." Bancroft, taking his Sunday break in his hometown of New Bedford, gave Radbourn the benefit of the doubt, at least publicly, telling a reporter there that he attributed the defeat Saturday to the pitcher's "tired" arm. Frank deftly changed the subject by boasting that the Providence club had cleared $15,000 already that year, "which surprises no one who knows its manager," the reporter noted. "We have no doubt," he added wryly, "but Mr. Bancroft could make a league nine pay on Cuttyhunk," the small, sparsely inhabited island in the Atlantic twelve miles south of New Bedford.

At the same time, there were well-founded rumors that Radbourn was drinking, drowning his pain and anger. While not an open drunkard, at least on the field, Radbourn was known to imbibe straight through the season. His own brother revealed that Charlie downed a quart of whiskey every day at the height of his career. It might seem far-fetched that a top professional athlete, especially one as dedicated to his craft as Charlie was, would abuse his body that much, but Radbourn stood in great need of something to take the edge off his agonizing arm and shoulder pain, and reports of his heavy drinking stretch all the way from one of his first newspaper clippings to the coverage of his death.

His fellow players knew all about his habits and hardly relished facing a surly Radbourn after he'd had a pop or two. Grays second baseman Jack Farrell made it a practice to visit the enemy team's bench from time to time to issue a friendly warning. "It is best for none of you fellows to say anything to Rad today, as he has been hitting the bottle and is ugly," Farrell told them. "He is as liable to hit one of you with the ball as not." They believed him, especially when Radbourn underscored the threat by sending his first pitch whistling past the batter's chin. Before the frazzled hitter got settled in, he was back on the bench, having struck out.

Meanwhile, rumors swirled through Providence that an agent of the Union Association's St. Louis club was lurking in the shadows, trying to lure Radbourn away from the Grays, providing him a safe haven where he could earn his handsome salary without being compelled to pitch every day and destroy his arm. Years later, Bancroft posited that Radbourn was "dissatisfied" pitching for Providence at that point and "as a result he was not exerting himself." It would be a serious matter if the resentful veteran was in fact failing to give his best effort in every game. If the club's directors had solid evidence of that—or even strong suspicions—they might suspend him, perhaps expel and blacklist him.

For the moment, however, they felt compelled to use him, game after game. Making his third start in four days, Radbourn squared off on July 14 against Grasshopper Whitney, back for the first time since *his* arm had gone out. Unlike the cautious Sweeney, Whitney was rushing his return, "and he plainly showed the effects of his indisposition," walking four men and allowing eight hits. The game turned into a "muffing, fumbling and wild-throwing exhibition on both sides" that "would have made amateurs blush," the *Boston Globe* observed. When the dust settled, Providence had won, 9–6, trimming Boston's lead back to one game. But it was far from a glorious performance, and everyone knew it. Radbourn needed help.

Manager Bancroft was frantically searching for it, his experiments with Paul Radford, John Cattanach, and Tommy Bond having bombed. Major league teams of the time had no armies of scouts patrolling the fields of America and no organized minor-league feeder system. Relatively untested players were often given a shot in a major-league game on the strength of one solid performance, strong word of mouth, or a mere recommendation in a letter. Bancroft now set his sights on one Joseph "Cyclone" Miller, a five-foot-nine-and-a-half-inch twenty-four-year-old from Springfield, Massachusetts, a rare left-hander who had won twenty-two of twenty-eight games for Worcester's team in the semipro Massachusetts State League.

He was not the only manager watching. The Union Association's Chicago club actually beat Bancroft to Miller, hiring him to pitch on July 11, at Boston. Cyclone threw impressively, beating Boston's Unions soundly, 10–2, striking out thirteen men and allowing only four hits. While the Union Association was dismally inferior to the National League, that performance was all Bancroft needed to see. He brazenly stole Miller away from the new league, getting his signature onto a Providence contract. Trying to make it all nice and legal, Bancroft paid $150 for Miller's release to Worcester, which had expelled its star from organized baseball after he skipped out on his contract. Without further ado, Bancroft handed Miller a Grays uniform and sent him out to pitch against Boston's Beaneaters, only four days after his Union Association debut.

Boston captain John Morrill, unhappy to see Providence make a move toward solving its pitching dilemma, played the game under protest, insisting that Miller was still technically under contract to Worcester, since the club had not formally reinstated him before releasing him to the Grays. (No one cared about any promises Miller might have made to the Union Association.) For all the bickering, few people imagined this raw rookie would be any match for the champions, and the "vast crowd, almost to a man, expected to see the Bostons bat him out of his position," the *Globe* reported. Yet Cyclone proved to be superb, whipping the ball past some of the best hitters alive, matching Buffinton goose egg for goose egg through seven innings, and even carrying a 3–1 lead into the bottom of the ninth inning. The Grays were three outs away from tying Boston for first place.

At that moment, the rookie's frayed nerves—or frazzled arm—began to tell. To the joy of the big Boston crowd, which had been waiting all day to cheer, Miller surrendered three straight singles, loading the bases. The battle-scarred Mert Hackett, no great hitter, then dumped a little flare into center field, bringing home two runners to tie the game, "while hats went into the air amidst wild confusion," the *Globe* reported. Luckily for Providence, Paul Hines threw out a runner on the play, and Miller managed to coax a ground ball for out number two. If Miller could just get slugger Joe Hornung out, the Grays would have a chance to win in extra innings. The southpaw snuck two strikes past Hornung, but when Cyclone tried to punch him out, the slugger blasted a line shot to deep left field past the outstretched arm of the speeding Cliff Carroll, giving Boston a 4–3 victory—capping a stirring ninth-inning comeback that the *Globe* hyperbolically called "the most exciting ever seen in the city." Instead of dropping into a tie for first place, Boston had built up a two-game lead over Providence. Still, the day was not a total loss for Bancroft. He now knew he had found a pitcher who could compete on the National League level, at least until the late innings of a game, giving Radbourn something of a break.

Miller's arrival did little to cheer up the testy veteran, though. Hurting in body and soul, furious at his manager, miffed that the public was clamoring for Sweeney, and well aware that he could make more money with less risk to his arm in the Union Association, Radbourn seemed to be on the edge of a nervous breakdown. Now, on Wednesday, July 16, he faced the unpleasant duty of pitching in his twelfth game in nineteen days. In sending Radbourn out to pitch yet again, Bancroft was willfully ignoring the loud warning signals that the veteran had endured more than enough and was heading for a collapse, or maybe something worse—right on the field, in front of more than a thousand people.

The contest was the official replay of the famous sixteen-inning tie on June 6, when Radbourn had kept his cool while performing brilliantly. This time his arm throbbed and his emotions were on a knife-edge. He entered the sequel "in no condition, physically or mentally, to pitch," according to the *Globe*.

"His nerves were unstrung, which rendered him irritable," the *Providence Evening Press* noted. Like most Boston-Providence games, this one bristled with bitter disputes and high emotion. Bancroft complained repeatedly that Boston ace Buffinton was illegally stepping out of the pitcher's box, while Boston players retaliated with the same charge against Radbourn. After seven innings, with the score tied 2–2, umpire Stewart M. Decker issued a warning to both pitchers to knock it off. Radbourn, who thought he was blameless, began to get angry.

Decker, a frustrating amalgam of courage, arrogance, and jaw-dropping incompetence, was not someone who responded well to edgy ballplayers. A former bookkeeper at the banking house of Huff Bros. & Co., in Bradford, Pennsylvania, he was studying law in the winter, using his salary as an umpire to help cover his tuition while supporting his mother and sister. As an umpire, he performed with insensate fortitude, braving vicious criticism from the newspapers that in many cases seems to have been entirely just. In 1883, his rookie season as an umpire, the *Providence Press* complained that the young man's bum judgment on balls and strikes "was almost enough to make an angel weep." And his mindless stubbornness was worse. In a bitterly fought game against the Beaneaters that year, the Grays had runners on second and third when Radbourn whiffed at three pitches. But Decker refused to ring him up. "The scorers were consulted, who testified that Radbourn had struck three times at the ball; then the official scorer was called for, who corroborated the fact, but it made no difference to Decker," the *Boston Globe* griped. Boston police felt compelled to offer Decker protection after the game. He proudly declined, but on the following afternoon in Providence, he had little choice but to accept. A gang of Rhode Island thugs threatened to break Decker's skull, and a squad of police escorted him from the Messer Street Grounds after the last out, to a chorus of jeers and hisses.

All during that first summer on the job, he suffered similar complaints. In Philadelphia, the crowd hooted and booed at Decker for calling a man out at home plate, when the ball was reportedly five feet away from the runner. When he returned to New York City in July, cries of "Shoot him!" and "Hang him!" greeted his work. "If there is an incompetent man on the league staff," the *New York Herald* mused, "his name is Decker." In Cleveland, one reporter protested the "bare-faced robbery of that burlesque of umpires, Decker." The *Cleveland Leader* noted, "He is not a bad umpire; oh, no—he is just miserable, that's all, . . . Decker ought to write a book about what he knows about umpiring—it would only take him a second—and then go and jump into the lake." The *Chicago Tribune* reported acerbically, "Decker, the alleged umpire, has not been killed yet." Decker toughed it out—and was, in fact, the only of the National League's four umpires to retain his job into 1884.

Now Decker was facing a surly Radbourn in a tense 2–2 game between two pennant contenders. Warning both pitchers that they risked balk calls, the umpire called time at the end of seven innings and drew a line of sawdust where he thought the front of the box should be. Never one to take criticism well, Radbourn told his teammates as he stood up to pitch in the eighth inning "that he was going to see how far out of the box he could go," and he took the field looking for trouble. Blinded by anger, Radbourn proceeded to break an unwritten code of conduct among players by pitching with such unbridled fury that he threatened his own catcher, Barney Gilligan.

Radbourn "took the sphere," the *Evening Telegram* reported, "and gave an exhibition of ball tossing seldom seen on a ball field. He changed his style of delivery, and his only object seemed to be to knock Gilligan out, in which he proved successful. He would go to the rear part of the box, and then jumping forward, would shoot the ball wildly across the plate at a terrific speed." As the *Journal* put it, "Radbourn became vexed and slammed the ball in over the plate," endangering everyone standing behind it—not only Gilligan but also the umpire. Decker, growing vexed himself, refused to call any of Radbourn's pitches strikes, and awarded Boston's Ezra Sutton a base on balls. "Then Radbourne gave Gilligan the wrong sign, and the result was that the plucky little catcher did not get a grip on the ball, but recovered it in time to save an error, though it terribly hurt his hand, and he was forced to take a short rest." Like some pitchers in the 1880s, Radbourn flashed the signals for his coming pitches to his catcher, rather than let the catcher call the game (the universal modern practice), and to cross up a catcher could be deadly, given the meager equipment protecting the man's hands and body.

Beaneater Bill Crowley began to shout to the umpire about Radbourn's delivery, but his captain told him to hush up: this tantrum was playing into Boston's hands. "Again Gilligan went in and faced the cannon ball delivery, and was again knocked out." Radbourn's fury only raged hotter when Sutton attempted to steal second base, and Gilligan, "who was dazed," heaved the ball wildly into the outfield, sending Sutton scampering home with the go-ahead run. Radbourn's mood did not improve any when third baseman Jerry Denny fumbled a ground ball that should have been yet another out, and Jack Manning got a feeble base hit. "At this point Radbourne again gave Gilligan the wrong sign and the ball struck his left

Barney Gilligan

hand with great force. The little fellow did not know what to do, and first looked at the umpire and then at John Morrill, who shook his head and walked away," the *Telegram* reported. Gilligan "would have been justified in refusing to hold Radbourne any longer," the reporter opined, but he gritted his teeth and played on. Radbourn, it seemed, was at least still trying to win. He bore down to strike out Buffinton. When he did the same to Crowley, umpire Decker declared the third strike a balk and gave the Boston batter his base.

That was it; Radbourn came unglued. Thwarted by a hostile umpire and the fumbling of his teammates Gilligan and Denny, forced to pitch while the pampered Sweeney sat out the game, Radbourn continued to throw "with reckless haste and wildness, giving Gilligan false signs, and seemingly striving to 'break up' the little fellow," the *Journal* reported. "Morrill felt as bad as anyone over the misconduct of Radbourne, and though he wanted his men to score, he made no attempt to coach them in," the *Telegram* added. Two more Boston runners crossed home plate to ice the game, 5–2. The loss dropped Providence a game further behind the pennant leaders and did a number on the poor catcher. At the end of the game, Gilligan "exhibited his hands to some of those present and showed that his fingers were pounded almost to jelly."

The Grays and their supporters were "greatly exercised" about Radbourn's "ungentlemanly and unprofessional conduct" as the pitcher stomped off to the dressing room in a fury. "To say that the 1254 patrons of the Boston-Providence game at Messer Park, yesterday afternoon, retired with feelings of utter disgust at the exhibition of puerile peevishness by Charles Radbourn, the heavily-salaried pitcher of the Providence nine, in the eighth inning, would but faintly describe the bitter feeling that prevailed," the *Journal* fumed. In the heat of the moment, Radbourn uncharacteristically blasted his teammates for their floundering on the field. When asked what was the matter with him, he spat out that "it had got so bad that he was forced to strike out twenty-seven men in a game, as his men would not back him up." The crowd, on the other hand, put the blame squarely on Radbourn. Many thought he had deliberately thrown the game, "and the general verdict is that the management should let him go, as he will be of no more good to them," the *Telegram* reported.

Manager Bancroft had put up with a lot of grief this year—Radbourn's sitting out April, his constant carping about carrying Sweeney's load in June and July, and that 7–1 loss when he seemed to put in little effort. But this behavior—his blowing the game in a fit of pique, or worse—was intolerable. The club's board of directors could have cut him some slack, perhaps, in light of his hard labor, his sore arm, the questionable work of the umpire and his teammates, and his brilliant record for the year (he had already won twenty-four games, against only eight losses, with half of the season to go). Instead, the directors resolved to teach the great pitcher a hard lesson.

They met immediately after the game and voted unanimously to suspend Radbourn without pay pending an investigation. "He has been served with a summons to appear before them today and answer certain pungent conundrums touching his 'peculiar' conduct for the past three weeks," the *Journal* reported. There were rumors, specifically, that his "sudden lameness, which was set down as rheumatism," had all been an act and that, in truth, he was "anxious to leave the League and join the St. Louis [Union Association club], which would be nearer his home, which is in Bloomington, Ill.," the *Telegram* reported. Considering the "dark insinuations afloat" about Radbourn's intentions, the *Journal* thought management had shown extraordinary patience, but "when every inducement, financial and otherwise, has been offered him to play ball to his best ability, and he had been coaxed and petted beyond all reason to seek to carry the nine to victory, it is high time that more compulsory measures be undertaken." A punning *Telegram* editorial hinted that drinking might explain Radbourn's behavior: "A 'pitcher' that goes to the well too often is liable to get broken— or suspended." He went home, perhaps to Carrie, to nurse his wrath and plot his next move in professional baseball. "He is one of the most brilliant pitchers in the country, but is cursed with a bad temper," the *Evening Press* explained.

It certainly looked like the end of Radbourn's career in Rhode Island. After the crackup, "Radbourn's popularity with the Providence people is ruined," the *Boston Globe* reported. Even so, the *Fall River Daily Evening News* thought Providence was crazy to risk losing the great pitcher. "If Radbourne leaves Providence good-bye any hope for the pennant in that city," the paper noted shrewdly. If the Grays "lose Radbourne they have 'broken the main belt.'"

It was no idle fear that Radbourn would bolt. Wads of cash were being waved in his face to leave Providence, where he was now officially unloved, unappreciated—and unpaid.

Drunk Enough to Be Stupid

For weeks, representatives of the Union Association's Chicago, St. Louis, and Boston clubs had been trailing the Providence players, conspiratorially meeting them in dark corners and hangouts, trying to bribe them to leave. Well-financed ball clubs were spending thousands of dollars in pursuit of a limited pool of players, and poorer teams were being left in the lurch. "It looks as though the base ball craze of 1884 has developed into an epidemic of insanity against which the quarantine of sound judgment would be ineffectual," the *Sporting Life* lamented. "The trouble is, there is too much professional base ball; the country has gone crazy on the subject." Men were being offered vast sums to jump to the Union Association, ruining club morale in the older leagues. "The skillful player is constantly dwelling upon the possibility of a larger salary with some other club. He loses his zeal in behalf of the club he is engaged with," the *Chicago Herald* pointed out. "Dissatisfaction, jealousies and poor play result." The writer could have been describing the Grays in mid-1884.

Jack Farrell had turned down a $1,000 offer to jump to the Chicago Union club, and Sandy Nava, known as "the Spaniard" for his dark skin and Hispanic origins, had been approached. Nava was a highly skilled catcher, and a reporter who studied his unclothed body noted that he "strips splendidly, showing a well-proportioned physique and a finely knitted muscular system"—though he may not have had the healthiest habits, since another paper described him as a "cigarette fiend." By mid-July, club director Ned

Allen was alarmed enough to write in confidence to league president Abraham G. Mills, seeking his advice about using the pretext of Nava's heavy drinking to blacklist him for life, should he jump. "It does seem to me that there can be no possible objection to your suspending or expelling him for drunkenness, as soon as you find he has left your club," Mills advised. Expulsion would mean the Grays could never get him back, of course, should the Union Association fold. Still, "the moral influence upon the other players would undoubtedly be better if you take the course you suggest"—if, that is, Nava went ahead and "actually deserted your club."

The UA was a new league, founded the previous September by a group of wealthy men who wanted a foothold in the suddenly profitable industry of professional baseball but lacked the patience to wait their turn for admission into the established major leagues. Its driving force was a bold, rather reckless twenty-six-year-old millionaire named Henry V. Lucas, whose family had made its fortune in St. Louis real estate, and who owned the Mound City Transportation Company. A true baseball nut who loved male camaraderie, Lucas installed a beautiful ball field at his estate, Normandy, and had friends over to play and enjoy refreshments. Determined to run a professional team in St. Louis, he had discovered he could not crack the American Association or the National League, which conspired to give the existing St. Louis Browns franchise a monopoly in the city. Refusing to accept defeat, he went to the extraordinary length of creating his own league, with some impressive associates: Baltimore mattress manufacturer A. H. Henderson, who backed the Baltimore and Chicago clubs; Ellis Wainwright of the Wainwright Brewery Company and Adolphus Busch of Anheuser-Busch fame, who helped to fund Lucas's Maroons; and George Wright, the retired star and owner of the Wright and Ditson sporting goods company, who supported the Boston Unions. The upstart went head-to-head with the National League and American Association in a host of big-league cities—not only Baltimore, Chicago, St. Louis, and Boston but also Cincinnati, Philadelphia, and Washington.

As an outlaw league, the Union Association refused to respect the existing practices of the top professional leagues—including the notorious reserve clause, which bound a player to his team, season after season, even after his contract expired. In junking the reserve clause, Union Association owners hoped they might entice large numbers of players into their ranks.

But most top professionals kept their distance, fearful of being blacklisted for life by the older and more financially sound National League and American Association. Who knew whether the new organization might flop, leaving them unemployable?

Most of those who did take the plunge simply could not resist the big dollars that Lucas was offering. "A rich man like Lucas runs a base ball club as a hobby and not for the money there may be in it. It is a luxury and money is no object," the *Sporting Life* asserted. With his spending power, the millionaire relieved his baseball itch by signing a bevy of well-known professionals to his St. Louis Maroons: Cleveland's star second baseman Fred Dunlap, who would lead the UA with a .412 batting average; Louisville third baseman Jack Gleason, who would hit .324; and veteran outfielders Buttercup Dickerson (.365), Dave Rowe (.293), and Orator Shafer (.360). Lucas spread so much money around, in fact, that his club thoroughly outclassed the rest of the league, ruining any chance of a competitive pennant race that would have generated bigger crowds. The Maroons set a killing pace right out of the gate by reeling off twenty straight victories. By July, the pennant was a foregone conclusion. Some in the press took to calling the league the "Onion" Association because most of its other teams, frankly, stank. Still, Lucas was not satisfied. He lusted after the one remaining part that would make his team his masterpiece: a top major-league pitcher, perhaps the best pitcher in baseball.

Maybe Charles Radbourn.

Nava, it turned out, was scared away from jumping, something league president A. G. Mills was "very glad indeed" to learn, as he noted in a July 18 letter to Ned Allen, adding: "Trust you will be equally successful with Radbourne."

Far from feeling any twinges of remorse about blowing up the economics of the game, Lucas boasted to reporters that he was about to make an acquisition that would really jolt the lords of baseball. "I'll not only go into the business of breaking contracts, but I'll break up the League and American Association, too, if I am pushed to do my utmost," he declared, in remarks published in early July in *Sporting Life*. "I have come to the conclusion that everything is fair in baseball as in war and I want my share of the fun while it is going on. Wait for a few days and you will hear a howl all through base-balldom that will make your hair stand on end."

Sure enough, on July 20, the *Boston Herald* reported some hair-raising news "on perfectly reliable authority": the great Charles Radbourn had agreed to sign a contract with St. Louis's Maroons and would journey west within days, abandoning Providence—and breaking a contract that was still in effect, even though the Grays were no longer paying his salary. Lucas had offered Radbourn a whopping $5,000, covering the rest of the 1884 season and all of 1885, with $1,000 of it in advance.

However shocking this development was to the baseball world, it came as no surprise to some who had watched Radbourn closely during the previous series. Now he stood on the brink, preparing to cross the Rubicon into an outlaw league. "Radbourn is an old player, and a good pitcher, when he has a mind to be," the *Herald* noted, "and, if he joins the ranks of contract break-ers, he does it with his eyes wide open and knowing well the consequences." The consequences were banishment from professional baseball after the Union Association's likely collapse. "The end of the Unions cannot be far distant, and it is then that the jumpers will discover what a fatal misstep they have made," one unnamed League team official told the *Evening Telegram*.

Not everyone was down on Radbourn. The *Fall River Daily Evening News* expressed sympathy for the long-suffering veteran while blasting the club's high-handed management and hectoring followers. The editor recalled that the great John Ward had been driven away from the Grays in a similar man-ner. "If a player is to be reprimanded don't make it disgracefully public," the editor advised. "We claim that nearly all players have their whims. A manager who understands human nature can generally overcome those freaks."

Radbourn, the writer added, had special cause to be frustrated. He had been "overworked last year. He was assured he would not be this year. Were the managers keeping their promise?" To be sure, the paper faulted Rad-bourn "for not finishing his game like a man after he had begun one." But he had a right to expect management to live up to its agreement and relieve his workload. "The management have everything in their own hands, and some of them are tyrants. We know what we are talking about, and will repeat that we have much sympathy for the player who has to play in Provi-dence."

*   *   *

While these plots and counterplots unfolded, there was a relentless schedule of games to be played, including one on July 17 in Boston that the Grays sorely needed to win if they wanted to keep the champions within range. Manager Bancroft assigned Cyclone Miller to start against the Beaneaters, though he took care to station the recovering Charlie Sweeney in right field in case of emergency. The southpaw went to work and pitched impressively, carrying a 2–0 lead into the sixth inning. Then, once again, he lost his nerve or his strength, falling apart in the late innings. Boston chipped away to tie the game, then took a 4–2 edge into the ninth. With a costly defeat staring Providence in the face, the club's bats finally came to life. Cliff Carroll cleared two men off the bases by blasting a triple to tie the game, 4–4, and Denny drove home Carroll with the go-ahead run.

Clinging to a 5–4 lead in the bottom of the ninth, Frank Bancroft removed his starter from the box and waved in Sweeney from right field. Late-inning relief was an almost shocking breach of custom in 1884, when a pitcher was expected to finish the game he started and was considered something less than a real man if he failed to do so. The Boston crowd of 3,722 booed lustily, reading the switch as an unjust slight against Miller, a public declaration of Bancroft's lack of faith in the young pitcher. "If Miller had been weakening the crowd would have expected the change, but as it was it seemed hard on him," the *Globe* explained. Bancroft, though, saw only that the well-rested Sweeney, his arm finally mending, stood a better chance of sealing the victory than the shaky rookie. That's just what Sweeney did, retiring the side without another run. Rather than dropping four games behind, close to tumbling out of the pennant race, Providence had slashed Boston's lead to two. "Miller's splendid work in the pitcher's position will cure Radbourne's perversity quicker than suspension," the *Telegram*'s editorial writer quipped.

Life without Radbourn continued the next day, when the Gothams of New York came to Providence. Once again Bancroft sent out Miller to pitch, not yet certain that Sweeney was ready to start. When the rookie confessed after only one inning that *his* arm now hurt from overwork, the manager was compelled to bring in Charlie from right field, ready or not. The California kid "pitched with old-time skill," the *Journal* reported, getting through the rest of the game with aplomb. Sweeney was back, and Providence won, 5–2.

Still, the search for a replacement for Radbourn continued, no easy task midseason when every half-decent pitcher in America was already signed. Bancroft came up with one of his novel ideas for the Grays' game against the Phillies on Saturday, July 19: for that day only, he would lend Paul Radford to a semipro team in Woonsocket, a burgeoning mill town fifteen miles north of Providence, in exchange for the use of that team's skinny, baby-faced hurler, twenty-year-old Holy Cross College student Ed Conley, who hailed from the Rhode Island factory village of Lonsdale, just north of Providence. Standing five foot eight and weighing 142 pounds, Conley hardly cut a striking figure; the *Providence Evening Press* described him as "an undersized youth" who "looks more as if he were studying for holy orders than like a professional athlete." But, as unimpressive as he was physically, he had been pitching brilliantly for Woonsocket against the best teams in the Massachusetts State League, exhibiting perfect control and striking out batters by the bucketful, including twenty-one of the Stars of Bristol on July 1. Conley "twirls the sphere with swiftness and accuracy," the *Journal* reported, "having it under excellent control, and displaying coolness and self-possession when occasion requires." He proved stunningly effective in his National League debut against Philadelphia, holding the Phillies to only two hits—both of them by the South Providence boy Joe Mulvey—and winning, 6–1.

That was a promising start, to be sure, and Harry Wright offered to sign him then and there and take him with the Phillies to Boston. But Conley seemed afraid to make that leap, saying he "couldn't stand the strain." And there was reason to doubt that the slender college boy was ready for the big time. When the Grays played an exhibition game two days later, on Monday, July 21, at Woonsocket's Island Park, Conley was back with his old team. Pitching this time against a top major-league lineup—his erstwhile teammates, the Grays, who were no Phillies—the Rhode Island boy flopped dismally, surrendering thirteen hits, three for extra bases, in an 11–2 rout. He was no Radbourn.

To avoid putting any strain on Sweeney in a meaningless exhibition contest on an ill-kempt amateur field, Bancroft wisely divided the Grays' pitching duties that day between Miller, Radford, and Nava. Sweeney did play in center field, however, and went 3 for 5 against Conley, evidently trying to impress one particular guest among the nine hundred on hand. He had appeared on the Woonsocket grounds with a woman, gallantly leading her to a seat in the little grandstand. When he wasn't preening, or perhaps giving his lady a wink, Sweeney spent much of his time between innings stealing into a dressing room and fortifying himself with whiskey, according to the *Evening Telegram*. After the game, when Bancroft ordered Sweeney to pack up and come home on the train to Providence with the rest of the boys, the half-drunk player arrogantly refused to do so, insisting on remaining behind, no doubt enjoying a night with his female companion.

Frustrated to be tending to another prima donna in his ranks, only days after Radbourn's ouster, Bancroft clenched his jaw and left without his star pitcher. Fate was preparing another explosion in the Grays' ranks.

Charlie Sweeney woke up on Tuesday morning, July 22, with a howling headache. A glance at his pocket watch told him he had missed the Grays' mandatory morning practice, and if he did not get a move on, he would miss his scheduled start against the Phillies that afternoon in Providence. The unpleasant prospect of fines and hectoring lectures confronted him. Staggering, stinking of drink—apparently still drunk—he got up and got dressed.

When he arrived at the Messer Street Grounds that afternoon, Charlie was showing the influence of liquor, Bancroft recalled. The pitcher found his frowning manager in a side room off the clubhouse. "If you want to know why I was not here this morning, I will tell you. I was drunk last night and did not get home," Sweeney confessed. That was a violation of his temperance pledge, certainly, and an admission of reckless disregard of managerial authority, but Sweeney had at least conceded the truth, and he wanted to make up for his lapse by pitching. Bereft of Radbourn, Bancroft felt he had little choice but to cut his ace some slack and send him out to the box. Bancroft posted Miller in right field, planning to bring him in during the later innings if Sweeney faltered.

Sweeney worked effectively for five innings, finding the plate in spite of his woozy condition. He was ahead, 6–2, when Bancroft, worried that the pitcher was beginning to get hit hard, and not wishing to risk Sweeney's recently healed arm, asked his field captain, Joe Start, to make the pitching switch. But when the first baseman went to the box and relayed the order, the pitcher barked at him to go away. Sweeney wanted to win, and he knew he had the stuff to do it. He may have also been "evincing jealousy of young Miller who is a promising pitcher," the *New York Times* speculated. In any case, "Sweeney was a bull-headed fellow, and had made up his mind to pitch the game. He curtly refused to give way," Bancroft recalled. For two more innings, the manager let him get away with this flagrant insubordination, but in the seventh, Bancroft called Sweeney over to the scorer's stand behind home plate and instructed him to let Miller pitch for a while. As Sweeney recounted, Bancroft, who had spoken nicely to him when he made a similar switch in Buffalo, addressed Charlie this time in a disrespectfully "surly tone." Worn out by Radbourn's antics, Bancroft had dwindling patience for Sweeney's defiance, "and there came nearly a fight on the field," the manager recalled.

"You go out to right field and let Miller come in and pitch the game out," Bancroft told Sweeney.

Charlie had no intention of giving way, in front of a worshipful home crowd, to a young southpaw who was not nearly his equal—and who might indeed blow the game, given his recent late-inning troubles. If Bancroft had no better sense, Sweeney surely did.

"As long as I've got my game won, I'll finish it," Sweeney replied.

Bancroft was through negotiating. "You go out in right field or I will fine you $50."

Sweeney, his anger rising, asked Bancroft if he meant it.

"You will find out that I do," the manager replied icily.

"All I have asked you to do is to let me finish this game and you want to fine me $50 for it," Sweeney complained. "You can take that $50 along with the rest of my salary"—and, he surely added, shove it somewhere.

The *Evening Telegram* reported that Sweeney told Bancroft: "I give you a tip. I finish all the games I start, or I don't play ball." When Bancroft told him to stop that foolishness, the pitcher declared, "I guess I'll quit," and stomped off.

Harry Wright, Providence's previous manager and now the Phillies' leader, turned to the local reporters. "Gentlemen, you now see what I went through last season," he said. "I have no trouble with the gentlemen now under me." In the next inning, only eight men left the bench and jogged into the field. Sweeney was nowhere to be seen. Bancroft trotted down the grandstand stairs and found him in the dressing room, already in his street clothes. When he ordered Sweeney to put on his uniform again and go out and play, the twenty-one-year-old "most villainously abused" him. "It is true I called him names," the pitcher later admitted, "but I think at the time and under the circumstances that I had sufficient provocation, and when you take into consideration the work I had done in keeping the club in the lead and the little wish I wanted Bancroft to grant me, that of finishing my own game, I think he could have reasonably complied with it without injury to his managerial dignity, were he so inclined." Club director Allen, rushing to the dressing room, warned Sweeney he would be laid off without pay unless he obeyed Bancroft's orders. Sweeney replied that he did not care, saying that "he had a place to go, and could make a living away from Providence," the *Evening Telegram* reported. "He was just drunk enough to be stupid, and one could not reason with him." As Bancroft recalled, Sweeney added the threat that he would "thrash the directors" if they got in his way. He walked out of the dressing room in street clothes and actually stood there on the field, arrogantly watching his teammates flounder while the crowd of 450 hissed him.

Since the Grays could only make a replacement in case of injury, they were forced to play on with just eight fielders. Providence got through the eighth without damage. But, as luck would have it, the Phillies lit into Miller in the ninth inning and repeatedly drove the ball between the two outfielders, who were unable to cover the ground that three would have. Harry Wright's "face brightened up like a luminous match safe in the dark" as the rally went on, the *Fall River Daily Evening News* gleefully reported. The Phillies made up the deficit and more, scoring eight runs in the inning to win, 10–6. The Grays had plucked defeat from the jaws of victory, sending the Providence crowd home disgusted.

Sweeney felt he had made his point. "At the conclusion of the game," the *Sporting Life* reported, "the foolish pitcher left the grounds in the company of two women"—prostitutes, described as "very bad company," whom he had escorted to the grounds in his half-drunk state—"and an hour later could have been seen staggering up the principal street of the city," bustling Westminster.

Allen, meanwhile, raced downtown after the game and pulled the club's directors together for an emergency meeting, probably at Root's office at 144 Westminster. As evening came on, Bancroft glumly told the group he knew Sweeney's nature so well that he was convinced he would keep his promise never to pitch for him again. Sweeney left them no choice. That night, "in order to retain the respect of the base-ball public," as the *Chicago Tribune* put it, they voted to expel their brilliant young star, and contacted National League secretary Nick Young to secure Sweeney's immediate blacklisting from organized baseball. The *Sunday Morning Journal* heartily approved of the dire punishment, arguing that Sweeney's act of insubordination "was one of the most disgraceful exhibitions ever witnessed on a ball field."

The *Fall River Evening Daily News*, on the other hand, thought the Grays had blundered badly in turning Sweeney into a "criminal" for refusing to decamp to right field and "chase the balls that the Phillies knocked around like corn in a popper." Bancroft's decision to take out Sweeney for the floundering Miller looked utterly ridiculous in hindsight, and the *News* predicted another team would be happy to snap up the extraordinarily gifted pitcher. Sweeney had reason to feel he had been treated unfairly all season, the paper added, since he had been paid far less than Radbourn for work that was as good or better. "These unequal salaries have much more to do with the players' tempers than outsiders are aware. For instance, Radbourne gets $3,000. Sweeney did not approach it, neither had he a right to expect it. But he was worth more than he did get."

Suddenly the Grays, who had been blessed only a week earlier with arguably the two best pitchers in baseball, now had neither, with little prospect of finding replacements. Rumors swept the city that the directors intended to parcel out among the stockholders the $17,000 left in the coffers and close the business down. The rumors were true. "The club was going to disband, for pitchers were scarce and things looked bad," Bancroft recalled. "The directors were about to toss up the sponge." Miller, who could barely get through a game without collapsing, could hardly pitch the rest of the way alone, and Conley was no major leaguer. "There are no pitchers to be had, and, with the present feeling on the team, the pennant cannot possibly be won," the *New York Times* reported. This was about more than pride. Without competent pitchers to make games competitive, paying customers would abandon the club in droves. Expenses would quickly outstrip income, saddling the stockholders with debt. The directors had a fiduciary responsibility to prevent that, even if it meant boarding up shop.

League president Mills was stunned to receive word from Providence that the club was folding. Certain that Providence's disbandment would provide a tremendous propaganda boost to the Union Association, disclosing the League's vulnerability and perhaps freeing up scores of players to jump, Mills pleaded frantically with President Root to reconsider. "Disbandment would be crowning triumph of scoundrels who have corrupted your players," he telegraphed on the morning of July 23. This was no longer only about Providence's chances of winning. "To win championship is a laudable object but more important objects of League will be promoted and your courage vindicated by carrying the club successfully through this difficulty." Mills called on Root to instead convene a meeting with his remaining players and lay down the law. "I believe they are honorable men but if any more have been corrupted they should be expelled and thus forever debarred from playing in any respectable club." In a telegram to Allen, he was more terse: "Don't give up the ship."

Allen and Root were apparently of the same stubborn mind, and they set to work that morning persuading their fellow directors to rethink disbandment. In the end, the directors committed to finish out the season with whatever players they could scrape together, no matter how miserable, praying that customers would still buy tickets. Allen telegraphed Mills the good news: "Will run a nine [even] if we put amateurs in the field"—or, as the *Boston Globe* expressed it tartly, "if they have to put in wooden cigar-store Indians to represent the club." Meanwhile, Providence would now clamp down on the halfhearted play and prima donna behavior. "A watch is to be kept on 'funny players,' and on the slightest provocation they will be blacklisted," the *Chicago Herald* reported. Mills gave a long sigh of relief. "I am proud of the Providence club as I always have been and am confident your action will reflect credit upon Providence and the League," he wired back.

The sports editor of the *Fall River Daily Evening News*, less enamored of the Grays, found the whole soap opera deliciously amusing. "There seems to be something cyclonic in the Providence air. First, Radbourne tears around at a great rate, dashes fond hopes in pieces, and calms down thoroughly exhausted. Then Sweeney, the wizard twirler of the national pleasure-giving sphere, whirls and twirls . . . and is decapitated. Some new sun spots must have burst over the little plantation." And Sweeney, decapitated only meta- phorically, was still staggering about town with his two painted ladies. "The conduct of the fellow is shameful," the *Sporting Life* opined, "and he will regret it when he fully wakes up to its enormity."

The post-mortems began. "If reports are true, rum killed Sweeney's chances," the *News*'s baseball editor noted later that week. "The ballplayer that can score the winning run, when having rum for an opponent, has not yet been born." Still, the editor thought the right leader might have kept Sweeney in line. "Mr. Sweeney! It's a great pity that [Boston's John] Morrill was not your manager. Under his guidance you would have been in the league to-day." The editor further speculated that the mighty swelling of Sweeney's head after the night of red fire, coupled with Radbourn's insane jealousy, had caused the crackup. "There are just two sides to each story and Sweeney couldn't stand the brass band. It made a discord," the editor punned.

There was no time to rest and regroup. On the day after Sweeney's ex- pulsion, the Grays faced a game against third-place New York. Would Miller pitch, with his sore arm, after his horrible performance against the Phillies? Or would the Grays send in the baby-faced, overmatched Conley? Or had some other equivalent of a wooden cigar-store Indian been found? As the game was about to begin, the startled crowd at the Messer Street Grounds saw a familiar figure stroll to the box in his nonchalant, businesslike fash- ion, as a smattering of applause built to a crescendo of cheers.

He was not leaving for St. Louis, after all. Charlie Radbourn was back in a Grays uniform, and he was going to pitch.

Hauled before the board of directors, Radbourn firmly declared that the charges against him were false. "He claimed that in Boston his arm was lame, and that he could not get control of the ball," the *Evening Telegram* re- ported. As for his temper tantrum in the July 16 game, "he had no intention of hurting Gilligan, or of giving the game to the Bostons. He simply became angered at Decker's actions, and tried to keep the Bostons from scoring, but was unfortunate enough to not get the ball in the right place." The directors listened to his plea and put him on the shelf, partly to "give him a rest, which he claims he needs."

And now, almost a week later, here the great man was, rested and refreshed, pitching well again, "with uncommon speed," the *Journal* noted. Moreover, he was keeping his cool, even though umpire Decker, obviously bearing a grudge, was squeezing the life out of him, "determined to make him send the ball squarely over the plate to a fraction of an inch." Radbourn had decided, whether on his own or after consultation with Carrie, to behave this time like a consummate professional. He backed up his teammates swiftly and shrewdly, and he kept enemy runners glued to their bases. "It was a gratifying exhibition to the spectators, who believed that his 'odd' turn has permanently disappeared, and that he is determined to be independent of 'outside' influence, and abide by the terms of his contract."

Much had been going on behind the scenes over those last several hours. Hard on the heels of Sweeney's suspension, when disbandment seemed imminent, Bancroft had concocted a scheme to save the franchise, and his own job. It came down to courting Rad, the sour and disgruntled complainer. The directors would have to swallow their pride and accept whatever deal Bancroft could strike.

The problem, of course, was that the pitcher detested Providence and wanted out. "Radbourn had been pitching great ball, but I happened to know that he was not very happy in Providence and was anxious to get away," Bancroft recalled. Knowing that the board of directors desperately wanted a pennant—there might never be a better opportunity than this year—he brought Allen and Root a plan. The club would give Radbourn Sweeney's salary as well as his own—exactly what old Charlie had wanted for doing the work of two men. But the pot had to be sweetened even more. Since Radbourn wanted out, they would give him that as well—at the end of the year, *if* he made an all-out effort to win the pennant. "If you will strike out the reserve clause in Radbourn's contract and leave him free to go where he likes next year, I think he can be persuaded to pitch out the rest of the season by himself," Bancroft said. All of this was highly irregular. The Grays would, in effect, be throwing away rights to their most valuable player. What the team would get in return was a shot at the championship—a long shot, to be sure, with Radbourn pitching alone, but a shot.

Allen and Root, by all accounts wise and generous men who wanted to keep baseball alive in Providence, strongly supported the notion and sold the scheme to the directors. Providence would in all likelihood lose Radbourn after the season and would have to pay him two men's salaries, but for this year, at least, the club might achieve glory. Allen and Bancroft then met with the suspended pitcher and delivered the proposal.

This was not a bad deal. Though $5,000 awaited him in the Union Association, Radbourn knew full well that he risked lifetime expulsion from organized baseball if he violated his contract. It was true that he could escape immediately from Providence if he jumped, and avoid toiling all season for owners who, in his view, had betrayed him. But he feared that the outlaw league would not last. "I can jump a contract with the league and join the [Union] association, but I can never get back into the league," he pointed out at the end of the season. This hard profession gave his life meaning, and he did not feel good about placing all his chips on the fate of the Unions. There was only one safe passage out: a release from his contract and freedom from the reserve clause.

And here, Bancroft and Allen were finally offering him what he had sought for so long: to receive extra pay for doing extra work, to prove that he was the slave of no man, to break the chains of the reserve clause, to escape to a bigger market and a bigger payday, to make himself the master of his own life—and, just maybe, to impress Carrie Stanhope with his savvy and greatness. All he had to do was endure the agony of pitching with a sore arm, day after day, for months to come, and to win the pennant in spite of that. He had almost done it in 1883. Maybe he could somehow summon the strength to do it in 1884. He always could sit back and rest his aching arm and shoulder *after* he won the pennant.

"I can win the flag all right," he said quietly, matter-of-factly.

It seemed a preposterous promise. "Nobody believed 'Rad' could make good," sportswriter William D. Perrin recounted. But Radbourn took the deal and firmly resolved to keep his word. As Bancroft recalled: "He said he'd pitch his arm off to win the flag." With a handshake, Radbourn was back with Providence's Grays.

From the start, and for years to come, Sweeney believed that he had been the victim of a conspiracy. He claimed that Ned Allen even divulged the dirty secret to Lucas in 1885—that Radbourn, jealous of Sweeney, had engaged in an underhanded plot to force the young pitcher off the team. Radbourn supposedly had complained to Bancroft that "Sweeney was getting all the credit for everything," and had promised to stop slacking off and start working hard if the club would just dump his competition. Sweeney also disputed the charge that he had shown up drunk in the fateful game against Philadelphia, arguing it was unlikely he could have pitched seven strong innings while intoxicated. "At any rate," he added mischievously, "wouldn't it have been better to let the drunken man stay in" than to take him out and lose the game? His teammates, though, showed little sympathy for Sweeney's position. "All the boys are down on him," the *Evening Telegram* reported several days after the incident. "'Served him right,' seems to be the unanimous verdict of the base ball public on the Sweeney expulsion," the *Evening Press* reported, congratulating the management for "purging . . . the club of such a bad egg." As shortstop Arthur Irwin recalled years later, "Charley Sweeney's temper throttled his good judgment and twisted his mental trolley." The superb pitcher arrogantly "thought that the management would have to flop at his shoe latches and beg him to return. But there never was a man, be he ever so talented, whose equal doesn't exist, as Sweeney discovered to his sorrow."

Sweeney was gone. And Radbourn, refreshed by six days without pitching, returned in fine form. He struck out the first two New York batters he faced, Buck Ewing and John Ward, and toiled on to beat the Gothams 11–5 on a nine-hitter. "Radbourn is himself again," the *Evening Press* reported with relief. "I candidly believe he never had any intention of skipping the nine," Bancroft said after the game. "I know he has been suffering with a nervous bilious complaint, rendering a person unfit for work, physically or mentally." But Radbourn's work against New York "satisfies me that he means business in the future." The *Telegram* headlined its story the next day, "THE CRISIS OVER." The dire gloom of the past week lifted suddenly as the Grays packed their bags for another road trip.

The greatest sustained pitching performance in baseball history had begun.

The Severe Wrenching

The big story exploded over the wires on Saturday, July 26. As Radbourn was working in Philadelphia, methodically sweeping aside the Phillies, 16–3, to lead the Grays to within half a game of Boston, news came that his former pitching mate had crawled out of the gutter—perhaps literally—and staggered down Eddy and Point streets to the Port of Providence, to catch a boat for New York City, whence he had taken a train out west. The young millionaire Henry Lucas had stolen a great Providence pitcher for his St. Louis club after all—just not the one everyone had expected. Charlie Sweeney was his. "There is . . . great pleasure in going into the enemy's camp, capturing their guns and using them on your own side," Lucas crowed. Some argued the Grays had it coming to them for stealing Cyclone Miller from the Chicago Unions, an act that set the millionaire owner to seek revenge. But Frank Bancroft, still sore over Sweeney's truculence and insults, said Lucas was more than welcome to the pitcher. "All the harm I can wish the Unions is to get a few such characters on their teams," he said.

The *Missouri Republican* spun the tale entirely in Sweeney's favor, evidently taking his account as the truth. It reported that the Providence directors begged Charlie Sweeney to stay, but that, as a man of honor, he was forced to refuse. He had done his team "splendid service in the early part of the season" but had aroused jealousy with "the famous Boston-Providence game in which he struck out nineteen men," the paper reported. After his glorious, record-breaking performance, "he was made a little god of at home. These things angered Radbourne and others in the club, and a clique was formed for the purpose of making things unpleasant for Sweeney." Bancroft's haughty command that Sweeney leave the box "was another insult to other indignities previously heaped upon him, and it was only then that he refused to obey orders. His expulsion followed, and this is what the clique had worked for." This highly colored version of events, which conveniently left out the booze, the whores, and the failure to report for practice, was ridiculous on its face, but the little god stuck to it.

On July 28, the Grays beat the Phillies 11–4, a game most notable for igniting a controversy a century later among baseball historians and statistics freaks. Cyclone Miller, who started it, was once again found wanting, and when he was through pitching after five innings, the Grays were behind 4–3. In the top of the sixth, the Grays' bats finally came to life, giving Providence a 7–4 lead. After the Grays had gone ahead, Radbourn took over pitching in the bottom of that inning, and no-hit the Phillies for the rest of the game. Who deserved the victory? The Macmillan *Baseball Encyclopedia*, and many others, gave it to Charlie; others say that a reasonably consistent standard of scoring games would give the win to Miller. (I reluctantly side with the latter, though that subtracts one win from Radbourn's victory column.) In the final analysis, though, all of this is something like the disputations between medieval clerics over the number of angels that could dance on the head of a pin, since the statistic of pitching wins, counted many different ways over baseball's long history, was virtually unknown in 1884. It is doubtful, in fact, that Radbourn himself had any clear idea how many games he was winning; he just knew he was pitching his *team* to victory.

As Providence sidestepped Boston into first place, the month ended with yet another controversy involving a Grays pitcher. July 31 was a rainy Thursday in New York, the afternoon so miserable that only about five hundred diehards, a fair number of them seedy gamblers, paid their way into Manhattan's Polo Grounds. The umpire assigned to work the game was Eugene Van Court, a dapper little man with a blond mustache who was known for dancing around the field in his bluish gray umpire's suit and amusing the crowd with his theatrical calls. At game time, Van Court was still nowhere to be found, a sign, it appeared, of his rapidly waning interest in his job. The rookie umpire had certainly had his fill of Polo Grounds crowds by then, having been forced to flee for his life in a speeding carriage after an earlier game, barely eluding the enraged mob by cutting through Central Park. And the crowds were only part of it. On July 19, when Van Court was working in Boston, a foul tip blasted through his wire mask, knocking him senseless to the ground with blood spouting out of him, delaying the game for several minutes until he could regain his wits and the deep cut above his left cheek could be covered with court plaster. He could hardly be blamed for entertaining second thoughts. Within days, he would lose his job and go home to San Francisco, where he emerged the following spring as "the champion roller skater of the Pacific coast," having also taken up boxing and "all 'round athletics"—anything but the mortal danger of umpiring. When Van Court failed to show on July 31, the clubs agreed to let Cyclone Miller serve in his stead—since Radbourn was working once again in the box and Miller had nothing in particular to do—trusting in the impartiality of the increasingly extraneous Providence pitcher.

The trust was sorely misplaced, as far as the New York crowd was concerned. "His decisions were wretched, and he evidently tried to throw the game to Providence," one wire correspondent scathingly observed. As the muggy, drizzly afternoon wore on, the "highly indignant" mob hooted and hissed at what they saw as Miller's blatant favoritism, and when the Grays appeared to be in danger of losing the game in the ninth inning, the *New York Times* charged, "their umpire came to the rescue." Miller awarded a base on balls to his teammate Charlie Bassett, and after Bassett came around to score, leaving the game deadlocked 3–3 after nine innings, the umpire abruptly shut it down on account of darkness, before Providence could fall behind again. By then, the rowdies in the stands had become so angry that Miller, fearing he might not escape the Polo Grounds alive, wisely sought police protection. The *Fall River Daily Evening News*, per usual, found the uproar delightful. While many players who served as umpires bent over backward to be fair, Miller "looked out for 'number one,'" the paper opined. "It's a poor miller that won't grind his own corn."

By August, most major-league hurlers were struggling to get by one day at a time, fighting off pain and exhaustion. "All the pitchers are now showing the effects of the hard, muscular strain of the arm required of them," the

Sporting Life observed that month. "It is a wonder that the arm can stand the severe wrenching it receives." It would be a bigger wonder if Radbourn's arm could endure pitching almost every game. On August 1, he won his twenty ninth game, but the season stretched out for another two and a half grueling months, and he faced the prospect of working in agony the rest of the way.

If he had any hope of getting through, he would need plenty of help from his largely unheralded catcher, handsome, twenty-eight-year-old Andrew Bernard "Barney" Gilligan. Raised in Cambridge, Massachusetts, the son of poor Irish immigrants—his father a laborer, his brother a bakery worker—Gilligan stood only five feet six inches and weighed a mere 130 pounds; a stiff wind might have blown him over were it not for an unyielding determination that kept him rooted to his post, come what may. Barney was too small to match the strength and reach of the National League's elite catchers, perhaps, but he was quick and resourceful, tough as nails, and as brave as any man in baseball. Moreover, he knew how to handle the touchy Radbourn, coaxing the best out of him. Barney had caught him for three years now, shepherding his 1883 no-hitter, smoothing over his eccentricities, channeling his intensity into his work, and snatching his junk pitches from the air before they could spin off to the backstop and let runners advance. Though he had been seriously endangered by Radbourn's tirade of two weeks earlier, Gilligan had risen above it, moving quickly to rebuild a bond of trust with a man he knew was a stalwart friend and brilliant competitor when he was in his right mind. They made a good team, and Radbourn surely admired and drew confidence from the little Irishman's steadiness and professionalism.

It did not seem to matter much to anyone that Gilligan was a weak hitter. His work behind the plate was what was important. In the 1880s, a good catcher—one blessed with savvy, stamina, leadership instincts, quick reflexes, and a strong and accurate throwing arm—was as highly prized, and almost as highly paid, as a star pitcher. Habituated to Rad's tricks and traits, Barney admirably performed his most important task: *catching* the ball, preventing it from skipping past him, and keeping runners honest, all of which could easily decide a game—an emotionally draining effort, since it was possible, on every pitch, for a foul tip to blast into him, inflicting agonizing injury. Pain simply went with the job, and no catcher had the least hope of ultimately

Barney Gilligan, 1884 Grays scorecard

avoiding it. The most important trait of any man who filled that position, therefore, was dauntless courage—something Gilligan possessed in abundance.

In the early 1880s, before the dawn of the padded mitt, Gilligan and his fellow catchers wore leather hand gloves with the fingers sheared off, so that they could easily grasp and throw the ball. They tried to protect themselves by shaping their fingers to form what they called a "spring-box," endeavoring to make their two cupped hands absorb the shock of a pitch, thus preventing the ball from slamming straight into, and splitting open, their rough palms or fingers. It didn't work very well. Though constant practice made a catcher's fingers tough and gnarly, swift pitches or foul balls could easily shatter them. In August 1883, for example, a foul tip smashed into the left hand of Will Salkfeld, catcher of the aptly named Painsville Club of Ohio, dislocating his middle finger, thrusting the end of the bone through the flesh, and tearing off the tendon. The finger had to be amputated at the first joint.

No matter how much Gilligan tried to blunt the impact, the constant pounding of pitches often left him with sore, raw palms and jammed fingers that made his work untold agony. In hopes of helping the catcher, pitchers deliberately let up a little, getting fewer crowd-pleasing strikeouts. But they could not afford to go easy on professional hitters too often—not if they wanted to win. Base runners, meanwhile, could smell blood in the water when a catcher was playing in pain. They were ready to steal on a weakened man, poised to pounce for an extra base if he allowed a passed ball. A game could quickly careen out of control if a catcher let his misery or his fears get the better of him.

To reduce the threat of serious injury, catchers at times backed up ten feet behind home plate, and gingerly caught the pitch on a bounce. That spared their hands to some degree. But catchers did not dare back off when there were runners on base, since they needed to be right behind the plate to prevent a stolen base, or when there were two strikes in the count, since the rules required them to catch the third strike on the fly to register an out. Much of the time, therefore, the "battered, bruised, crippled and blood besmeared catcher" of 1884 crouched exactly where his modern counterpart does—without a modern catcher's protection. Doing such a thing was so dangerous that it is almost a wonder anyone had the nerve to take on the job.

With ghastly frequency, catchers' thumbs and fingers were knocked out of joint and bones splintered or driven through the skin, splattering blood around home plate. Everyday work did incredible damage to the hands. "On a hot day, when the blood circulated freely, the catcher's hands would swell about the third inning," recalled Jim O'Rourke, who caught 227 big-league games, including 33 for Buffalo in 1883. "When swelling started the pain caused by the impact with the ball decreased, because the swollen flesh made sort of a cushion.

Charlie Bennett

But on a cold day, when the blood did not come freely, the pain was intense. I have seen catchers hold a piece of soft rubber in their mouths, and whenever the ball was pitched they would screw up their faces and bite on the rubber as hard as they could to offset the pain." On warm days, he recalled, a catcher might tell his teammates, "Oh, I am getting along fine—my hands are swelling up in great shape."

Detroit's Charlie Bennett, regarded by many of his contemporaries as the game's top defensive catcher, entered the 1883 campaign with severely chapped hands—the result, he said, of working too long in frigid air in his off-season job. Unfortunately, when he started catching that spring, his hard hands cracked open, and the cracks, pounded daily by fastballs, refused to mend. Bennett, who had a mother and sisters to support back home in New Castle, Pennsylvania, and could not afford to go without a pay packet, "caught many a game" that season "with blood dripping from his fingers' ends." That August, when he could stand the pain no more, he finally sat out and gave his split palms time to heal.

Bennett usually kept on working, though, even in "the most intense agony," recalled Lon Knight, a teammate for four seasons. In one game, a ball split open Bennett's thumb from the base to the tip, clear to the bone. A doctor ordered him to sit out until he had healed, warning Bennett that he was liable to contract blood poisoning that might well force the amputation of the thumb, or even his arm. But the catcher stubbornly played on, game after game. "Between each inning he would have to sponge the gash in his thumb with cotton soaked in antiseptic which he carried with him in his pocket, in order to remove the corruption which was continually flowing from the wound," Knight recalled. Eventually, it healed over, but his hands permanently bore the scars of his trade. The *Sporting News* surveyed the damage in 1887: "His fingers have been battered almost to pieces . . . until he has not a whole or straight finger in the lot. Every joint is swollen and misshapen." That was typical of veteran catchers.

By 1884, catchers were experimenting with a new form of protective gear, a heavy cork chest protector—an idea soon adopted by umpires as well. (When Chicago's Mike Kelly wore an oversized one that year, a kid in the stands yelled out: "Oh! get a bed!") Face masks, meanwhile, were still a relatively new phenomenon, having been pioneered seven years earlier by the Harvard College team's baseball manager, Fred Thayer. But the masks of the 1880s were far from perfect, as umpire Van Court could have attested. They shielded the face with what the players called a "bird cage" of thick wire, rather than solid metal bars impervious to baseballs. They could be staved in, and foul tips sometimes snapped the wire, driving razor-sharp metal into the face. It took many decades before catchers got adequate protection from better masks, throat protectors, chest pads, padded mitts, and the shatterproof protective helmet. Until such blessings as shin guards came along, catchers suffered the kind of misery that Kelly endured in May 1883, when he caught a fastball on his kneecap and, according to the *Chicago Inter-Ocean*, "wriggled over about 10 square feet of grass before he could control his language."

Clubs typically carried two starting pitchers, and each would team up with one of the club's two catchers in what was called a battery, named after an artillery unit, well remembered from the late Civil War. Charlie Sweeney had formed a battery with Sandy Nava, Radbourn with Gilligan. When Sweeney departed and Radbourn took on all the pitching duties, Gilligan's workload thus increased dramatically. Now he was being called on to catch as many games and endure as many bruises as the league's bull catchers, Buck Ewing and Charlie Bennett, each of whom was several inches taller and had at least fifty pounds on Barney. If Radbourn was going to endure the severe wrenching of his arm for the rest of the season, the bantam Gilligan would have to be right there, suffering with him. Like Radbourn, he was known to get through the pain with a stiff jolt or two of whiskey.

On paper, the Gothams of New York were a great team. Their starting nine numbered some of the game's biggest and best-paid stars. The men got along beautifully and took orders well. The biggest crowds in baseball now thronged their games. And yet, for some reason, the Grays had beaten them like a rented mule all season, frustrating local fanatics to no end. "There is something radically wrong with the New York team," the *New York World* complained on August 6. "Why is it that Welch and Ewing cannot pitch and catch three games like Radbourne and Gilligan? . . . There is no reason Welch should be sore when Radbourne, Galvin, McCormick and others have pitched more games and innings and are still able to keep their end up." Some attributed New York's problems to the "glorious uncertainty of the game," the paper noted. "But is it the 'glorious uncertainty' that enables the Providence team to defeat the New Yorks at nearly every meeting?"

The sharp words may have done some good, because the Gothams roused themselves to beat Radbourn, 2–1, in eleven innings that afternoon. Ward was the star, displaying what the *New York Times* called "the agility of a cat and the fleetness of a deer" in rounding the bases and eluding Gilligan in a rundown to score what proved to be the winning run. "The spectators, young and old, jumped to their feet, yelled 'Ward! Ward!' and shouted like wild men," the *Times* reported. Ward tried to take his seat on the bench without further fuss, but finally had to acknowledge the mayhem by turning to the grandstand and doffing his cap.

It was Radbourn's ninth defeat, but it would be the last one for a long time. On August 7, Radbourn and Gilligan got their revenge, beating New York, 4–2, for the Grays' thirteenth victory in sixteen decisions against the Gothams, and the start of a historic streak.

If the Grays games could have been subtracted, the Gothams would have had a sizzling winning percentage of .691. But the games did count, and they were enough to thrust New York out of the pennant race, nine and a half games back. New Yorkers, boiling angry by now, were ready to erupt when the Gothams hosted Boston on August 8. When the wayward Van Court failed to show up yet again, the clubs deputized the Beaneaters' twenty-two-year-old backup catcher, Tom Gunning. The New York crowd, it turned out, liked Gunning no better than they had Cyclone Miller.

All might have turned out well had Boston's quiet, resolute, and fair-minded captain been on hand, but John Morrill had left town for his father's funeral. Taking his place for the day as captain was the hotheaded Black Jack Burdock, and he quickly went to work in his inimitable fashion, stirring the pot. "This gentleman was in the worst humor possible, and he pranced about the field and yelled in a manner that would lead one to believe he was a fit subject for a lunatic asylum," the *New York Times* complained. Gunning, who had been with the club for only two weeks and stood "in mortal fear" of crossing up his captain, began shading his calls for Boston, the paper claimed. The *Sporting Life* gave Gunning slightly more credit, saying he initially "umpired fairly and impartially, if anything, giving the New Yorks the best of it"—but, by the end, he let himself be "bulldozed" by Burdock. After the Beaneaters had managed to rally from behind to tie the game, 8–8, Burdock—worried that his pitcher was finished for the day—gave the kid an order: "Call the game. What can they do?" And so, after eight innings— when, though it was cloudy, there was still light enough to play for another hour, according to New York reporters—Gunning ended the game on account of darkness.

An audible "growl of indignation" spread ominously through the crowd. A "wild and uncontrollable rabble," as the *Sporting Life*'s correspondent put it, jumped the fence and rushed onto the field. While well-dressed gentle-men and handsome women "forgot themselves" and joined the mob, shout-ing spectators surrounded the umpire, accusing him of throwing the game. Suddenly, one man launched his fist into Gunning's face—"a stunning blow," the *Times* said—and in a flash, several others seized the umpire, eager to finish the job. Policemen raced onto the patchy grass and beat back the thugs with their batons, forcing them to release Gunning. They hustled him to the dressing room, while the rabble, still in a fury, stormed the door. "A regular pitched battle ensued, but the police eventually succeeded in driv-ing the howling mob into the street and the gates were closed," the *Sport-ing Life* reported. Nonetheless, the feral crowd lingered at the entrance of the Polo Grounds, waiting for Gunning. When he finally emerged, he was surrounded by three police officers, with another six lurking in the back-ground. They hustled him into a carriage and sped away for the elevated railroad station, to a chorus of jeers and shouts. Though not seriously in-jured, the young catcher was bruised and badly shaken by his debut as a major-league umpire. "Things have reached such a state in New York City that it is as much as a man's life is worth to umpire a game on the Polo Ground," the *Sporting Life* noted with disgust.

Maybe so, but New York players sided more with the crowds than the umpires. "We have been shabbily treated by the umpires, even the official ones," one unidentified player complained bitterly to the *Times*. "One or two of the clubs rule the League, and I give you my word every umpire favors Boston and Chicago. New York somehow or other gets the worst of it in this respect, and it is about time it should be stopped." One Gotham star even-tually did more than grouse. On September 24, a dark, rainy afternoon in Buffalo, umpire John Gaffney called the game after seven innings, giving the Bisons a 6–0 victory over New York. That night, in the splendid rotunda of the Genesee House, while the hotel's well-dressed guests chattered po-litely, the Gothams' John M. Ward appeared in front of the umpire and began chiding him for stopping the contest when there was light enough to continue. Gaffney, refusing to be intimidated, coolly informed the musta-chioed, muscular athlete that if he really meant that, he was the only man on the field who thought so. The player denounced Gaffney's umpiring, an insult the umpire returned in full about Ward's playing. Roused to a fury, Ward then struck Gaffney in the cheek, knocking him into a chair. Before

Gaffney could struggle to his feet, Ward blasted him again, this time clipping the ump with his ring, opening a deep cut over his left eye that gushed with blood. Coming to his senses at last, Ward apologized profusely and accompanied Gaffney to a doctor to have his wound treated. Gaffney was willing to let bygones be bygones, but when he tried to work the next day, his mask kept painfully reopening the cut. Finally, he went home to Worcester to recuperate. Gaffney had no intention of pressing charges against Ward, but the umpire thought the player should at least have the decency to cover his lost pay. It's not clear whether Ward ever did.

On the afternoon that Gunning was being surrounded and punched in New York, a quieter game unfolded in Philadelphia. Manager Bancroft finished up the road trip by giving Radbourn's aching arm a rest—though Radbourn still had to work out in right field. Ed Conley, the local kid who had owned the Phillies on July 19, had somehow been coaxed to make another start. Little Eddie was even better in his second big-league appearance, shutting out Philadelphia, 6–0, on a two-hitter. After the game, the men hustled to the station and boarded a night train for home.

Back in New England, they faced the most important series of the year: four straight games against Boston's Red Stockings, their last meetings of the regular season. The standings on the morning of August 9 showed that Providence and Boston had turned the National League race into a two-team affair:

	W	L	PCT.	GB
PROVIDENCE	51	20	.718	—
Boston	50	21	.704	1
Buffalo	43	28	.606	8
New York	41	30	.577	10
Chicago	37	35	.514	14½
Cleveland	26	46	.361	25½
Philadelphia	21	52	.288	31
Detroit	18	55	.247	34

For Radbourn, the next four games were especially momentous, a test of whether he could indeed make it alone, earning Sweeney's pay as well as his own. He wanted to win these games, pocket the money for pitching them, and set Providence on the path of capturing the pennant, rather than hand over the ball to the likes of Miller or Conley. After he returned to Providence, perhaps staring at the ceiling in the old Ross mansion while Carrie slept at his side, Radbourn brooded silently, lost in himself, pondering the task ahead: conjuring up the Boston lineup, playing out the pitches he would have to make, and steeling himself for the pain he knew was coming.

That week, a big, rugged-looking man arrived in a thick night fog at Providence's Union Depot. He came in on a train from Woonsocket, where his Wild West Show had performed that afternoon before a whooping audience of more than six thousand people. While the rest of his entourage was switched to a local train bound for the Narragansett Park racetrack nearby, which it would soon transform into a city of tents, Bill Cody left the station on foot for Rhode Island's most sumptuous hotel. "The conspicuous slouch hat was not necessary to attract the attention of passers-by on Westminster Street to a tall, broad-shouldered man who was making his way to the Narragansett Hotel, and the familiar face of Buffalo Bill was readily recognized," the *Journal* reported. At the hotel, "Buffalo Bill" Cody showed the reporter a telegram he had just received from the filthy rich James Gordon Bennett, publisher of the *New York Herald* and the owner of a stunning mansion on Bellevue Avenue in Newport. Bennett planned to visit the show, bringing with him several English noblemen who wanted to see what the American West was really like. Another famous visitor to the 1884 show asserted that Cody had got it exactly right. "Down to its smallest details, the show is genuine—cowboys, vaqueros, Indians, stage coach, costumes and all; it is wholly free from sham and insincerity, and the effects produced upon me by its spectacles were identical with those wrought upon me long ago by the same spectacles on the frontier," the old Western prospector Samuel Clemens—better known as Mark Twain—wrote in a letter to Cody the following month. "Your pony expressman was as tremendous an interest to me yesterday as he was twenty-three years ago, when he used to come whizzing by from over the desert with the war news: and your bucking horses even painfully real to me, as I rode one of those outrages once for nearly a quarter of a minute." The show featured the original Deadwood stagecoach, used on the Cheyenne and Black Hills line. "Everyone rides in that coach. I've had noblemen and lords and mayors of cities and a lot of big personages in that coach," Cody boasted to the *Journal*.

But a bigger show—at least to baseball fanatics—was taking place in Boston on Saturday, when New England baseball fanatics by the thousands descended on the South End Grounds. The little park—its hallowed soil occupied today by the Ruggles Street Station, a subway stop on the Massachusetts Bay Transportation Authority's Orange Line, near Northeastern University—was a veritable temple to baseball. It had flown more pennants than any yard in the country, having served as the home of the game's greatest team in 1872, 1873, 1874, 1875, 1877, 1878, and 1883. The 1884 Beaneaters had continued the winning tradition, making their grounds one of Boston's most popular summer destinations once again. Still, the shrine had its share of detractors, people who happened to notice that the sagging wooden park had become little better than a dump. In 1883, the *Boston Globe* complained about the grounds' "sadly dilapidated" seats and fences, griping that reporters had a poor view, and that the wooden outfield fence, decayed and riddled with holes, was "a disgrace to the city and the club." That was not purely a local opinion. The *New York Clipper* reported that the South End Grounds were widely considered "the poorest and most shabbily fitted-up in the country."

Boston's adolescent boys contributed to the damage, poking holes through the rotting fences in their zeal to see games for free. Eventually, the club's frugal president, Arthur H. Soden, hit on the idea of installing a second barrier, so that when the boys drilled or cut peep holes, all they could see was the back of another fence, beyond the reach of their busy pocket knives. Soden was forced to fight back against more serious freeloaders as well: enterprising landlords in the neighborhood had taken to installing stands on their roofs, and charging a bargain fee of 10¢, one-fifth the price of admission to Soden's grounds. This was no minor threat. In May 1882, some three hundred people had watched a game from outside, compared with only eight hundred inside. Soden struck back that summer by installing a tall picket fence on top of the right-field fence, and he followed through with more "screen work" in 1883. Not to be denied, a number of men and boys began shinnying up the telegraph poles surrounding the ballpark in 1884. They received their comeuppance on July 19. While they were on top, enjoying the game against New York, somebody came along and painted the poles with a slow-drying brand of sticky black paint. When exhaustion, thirst, or hunger finally drove the freeloaders down, they had to slide through the wet black goop, ruining their clothes.

Soden's tactics worked, and on August 9, more than six thousand people shelled out full price—50¢ apiece, and another 25¢ to sit in the grandstand—to see the start of the last big series between the great antagonists, the two best teams in baseball. For that afternoon's opener, both clubs sent out their aces—Radbourn for the Grays, Charlie Buffinton for the Beaneaters—and, though both men had been worked hard in recent days, a gripping pitchers' duel ensued. "It was one of those games for which the Bostons and Providences have become famous this year," the *Boston Globe* marveled. "A stubborn contest, marked by wonderful exhibitions of pitchers' skill on both sides, and containing plays in every inning which produced long and loud applause." The *Providence Journal* called it "the great game of the season."

Paul Hines started it off by smashing a ferocious shot past Buffinton's head—"so close that he must have heard it sing," the *Globe* quipped—into center field. But Buffinton quickly picked off Hines at first base, and that was that. In their half of the inning, the Beaneaters put men on second and third with one out, but Radbourn bravely struck out Burdock and Morrill to get out of the jam. Inning after scoreless inning followed, as both pitchers stubbornly refused to relinquish a run.

Unable to crack Buffinton by swinging away, Providence's Cliff Carroll tried something radically different. He led off the eighth by squaring off with his bat and tapping a bunt down the first-base line—such a rarity that "the great gathering roared with laughter" when Carroll beat it out to first base for a hit. Years later, Arthur Irwin recalled that when Carroll tried out that first bunt, "the entire Boston team simply stood and looked at it and then looked at Carroll who could have made two bases if he had tried." The crowd may have laughed, but not everybody appreciated the play. "A vigorous striking out is preferable to a baby blow with the bat," one reporter griped.

With speedy Carroll taking a lead off first, Irwin then drove a long fly to right, seemingly good for extra bases. But Boston's Bill Crowley dashed for the sphere and, somehow, caught it on the fly—as Carroll, oblivious to the notion it might be caught, was tearing around the bases. Crowley pegged the ball to first to catch him easily in a double play, ending that threat, to an explosion of cheers and a rising chant of "Crowley! Crowley!" Through nine innings, Buffinton had pitched a near-perfect game, retiring twenty-seven men in twenty-seven at-bats. Through ten, the score remained 0–0.

Buffinton struck out Carroll to open the eleventh, and Grays shortstop Arthur Irwin, who was 0 for 3 on the day and had struck out twice, dug in at the plate. A scrawny man who had thinning light hair, pale beady eyes and stick-out ears, Irwin was far from a slugger. He would end his big-league career with only five home runs in 3,871 at bats. But he was a fighter who refused to be distracted from the business at hand. (On June 16, after his wife gave birth to their eleven-pound boy in the morning, Irwin took the field that afternoon, going 3 for 6 with no errors.) This time, he got the sweet spot of his bat on the ball and drove it deep to right field, toward the rotting fence with the slatwork on top. There was a hole in the shabby old wall where it connected with the addition, six feet above the ground, an opening not much bigger than a baseball, and when Irwin "came to bat he set his eye on that hole, and aimed for it," Bancroft claimed. The Boston outfielders scooted to take the rebound, hoping to throw out Irwin at second, or at least hold him to a double. But the carom never came. "Without taking even a splinter off the board the ball shot through the hole and disappeared," Bancroft marveled. Irwin sprinted around the bases and stomped on home plate while the Grays hollered and jumped for joy, and the Boston men stared, shocked, or shook their heads in disbelief, foiled by an act of God. In the bottom of the eleventh, Radbourn, who had thrown a two-hitter, retired three men in succession, for an extraordinary 1–0 shutout.

The loser had pitched no less brilliantly, leading one columnist to muse over how dominant a team might be if it could obtain *both* Buffinton and Radbourn. "Now that would depend," the *Fall River Daily Evening News* responded with its usual sneer. "It would not do for the band to be called out when Buff. got a victory, for Rad. would start the horn of discord to blow-

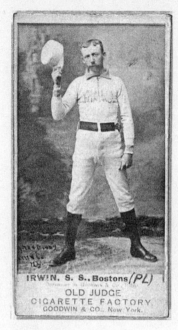

IRWIN, S. S., Bostons *(PL)*
OLD JUDGE
CIGARETTE FACTORY
GOODWIN & CO., New York.

Arthur Irwin

ing." In any event, Irwin's hole-in-one had given Providence a two-game lead now, putting Boston under intense pressure to gain back ground. "But is it not about time for Providence's annual 'go to pieces' to take place?" the *Evening News* asked. Not a bad question, since the Grays had blown late-season leads in 1882 and 1883.

Unfortunately for Boston, Buffinton needed a break after his eleven innings of hard work. For the rematch two days later at the Messer Street Grounds, the Red Stockings brought out their former ace Jim Whitney, still struggling with a sore arm. "With Whitney in the 'box,'" the *Boston Globe* noted, "a stubborn fight was looked for, as he appeared to be in good trim." Tired or not, Radbourn, meanwhile, insisted on starting again, warming up slowly and bracing himself for more pain. The day brought out 2,895 fanatics.

Boston drew first blood, in the bottom of the first, when Radbourn uncharacteristically had a hard time finding the plate. He walked Ezra Sutton, who stole second base. Radbourn's wild pitch sent him to third, and a *second* errant pitch sent him home, prompting the visiting fanatics from Boston and Fall River to howl with delight. "But while they were in ecstasy in this inning, they were simply wild in the second," when the Grays failed to score after putting men on second and third with no one out. In the third inning, the Grays had better luck. Providence's Paul Hines and Jack Farrell led off with singles, then pulled off a daring double steal. Bearing down, Whitney coaxed Joe Start to pop out to third and struck out Radbourn, but Cliff Carroll slapped a sharp grounder up the middle to drive in both runners and give Providence a 2–1 lead. In a game featuring such superb pitching and fielding, the *Boston Globe* observed ruefully, "the scoring of one run meant fully as much mischief as a half dozen would in a game between any other two clubs in the League." The Grays added more mischief in the sixth, when

Carroll slapped a single, and reached third on Irwin's double. With one out, Gilligan could produce only a slow grounder to Whitney, who tossed him out at first base, but Carroll "girded up his loins, dashed for the plate, and scored the third earned tally amid great enthusiasm over his fleetness of foot," the *Journal* reported. Providence had a 3–1 lead going into the ninth.

Radbourn, meanwhile, had settled down and reasserted his famous control, displaying what the *Journal* called "his thorough mastery of the sphere and intimate knowledge of the weaknesses of the opposing batsmen." Radbourn retired the side to win, 3–1, dropping the Beaneaters to three back in the pennant race. In two games of this critical series, against the Grays' toughest opponent, he had pitched twenty innings without allowing an earned run. The *Journal* was ecstatic, claiming that Radbourn's performance was "unparalleled in the history of the national game."

And he was only getting warmed up.

The following afternoon, in Boston, the betting ran 2 to 1 against Providence, as the gamblers figured Radbourn would be too weak to pitch again, and the newspapers had announced Conley would start the game. One man who had bet a whopping $6,000 on Providence actually approached the bench and begged Charlie to start the game instead, Grays shortstop Arthur Irwin recalled. "Sure," Radbourn responded. "I'm all right . . . I'll pitch for you." He informed Bancroft that he would start rather than Conley, "as he believes he can hold out against any and all League teams with the superb field support he is receiving," the *Evening Telegram* reported. He strode to the box for his third game in four days, facing a slightly more rested Charlie Buffinton before a crowd of 4,754. For six innings, the game was scoreless, both pitchers superb. Then Boston's luck cracked, as Providence scored four runs on scratch hits and errors. Though Buffinton surrendered three fewer hits than Radbourn's seven, Hoss held on to win, 4–0. He had now pitched twenty-nine innings in the series without allowing an earned run. And the Grays held a four-game lead in the standings over the Beaneaters. "There is a tradition among the oldest inhabitants that Boston once had a baseball team that could win a game," the *Boston Post* observed with bitter sarcasm.

After a rainout on Wednesday, the two clubs met Thursday in Providence for the final time in the regular season. If Boston hoped to get back into the pennant fight, it would have to begin this day. A three-game deficit could be overcome, but five games would be a much steeper climb.

Some three thousand people, a big Thursday crowd, packed the Messer Street Grounds for what turned out to be another nail-biter. Amazingly, Radbourn answered the call to pitch in his fourth straight, while Boston passed over the risky Whitney and sent out the tired Buffinton. Buffinton drew a big crowd of cheering supporters from nearby Fall River, including the tart-tongued sports editor of the *Evening News*. Not to be outshone in their idol worship, Providence fanatics arranged for the surprise presentation of a lavish bouquet to Paul Hines when he stepped to the plate in the first inning.

Hines was a notorious character. Vain, competitive, and poorly educated, he was so deaf that he needed to hold a brass trumpet to his ear to hear what others were saying, and he often talked out loud to himself, as if such a conversation were as natural as any other. At one point that season, when umpire Billy McLean warned him that he would be fined if he kept sassing umpires in his audible monologues, Hines grumbled to himself, "If me was out of debt, me would not play ball another day." He liked to boast to his teammates that he had been raised in an affluent Washington family, but when one actually looked up Hines's "good Hibernian parents" one day, he was shocked to learn they lived in a shanty.

His honesty was suspect in other ways, too. Once he stole another man's prized buckskin baseball shoes, and when the man asked Hines if he had seen them, he got no answer. "Paul is very deaf when he wants to be, and the shoes were carried off," a *Cleveland Herald* reporter recounted. The next time Hines played against the man's team, he did not dare to wear the stolen shoes, and went out on the field in his street shoes. Hines cost his team the game by slipping, trying to field a fly ball that soared over his head, prompting his manager to fine him for his poor performance— more than the stolen shoes were worth. On another occasion, a reporter had deposited at a hotel front desk his official score of a game, for use by a fellow newspaperman. Upon returning, "I found Paul at work on it, with a carpenter's pencil as thick as a club, changing his single hit into two. He was at once so deaf as to be unable to hear my admonition against any future trick of the kind." Even without the benefit of fraudulent scoring, he was a great hitter, and had twice led the National League in batting. Later statisticians would credit him with winning the first triple crown in baseball history, leading his league in 1878 in batting average (.358), home runs (4), and runs batted in (50).

Since he could not hear, someone that August 14 afternoon had to grab his arm, wave to him, or tap his shoulder to present the bouquet. The Grays star grinned and doffed his cap, but "while Paul was admiring the gift," captain Morrill stepped up and insisted on inspecting Hines's bat. Finding that it "was inclined to be a spring bat"—perhaps the kind of rattan-loaded weapon that Anson had used earlier in the season—Morrill persuaded the umpire to appropriate it from the duplicitous ballplayer. Hines seemed unruffled. He handed off the flowers, got his old bat, and then drove a single into center field. But he could not score, and just as in the first three games, another pitchers' battle ensued.

Through seven innings, the game was scoreless. In the eighth, Gilligan got a walk. Paul Revere Radford tried to bunt him over to second, only to see Buffinton pounce on the slow-moving ball and gun out Gilligan at second. But Radford managed to advance to scoring position nonetheless, scampering to second on a passed ball. The bouquet man, Hines, then drove the ball into left field, as Radford raced for home, barely beating the throw by Joe Hornung to break the scoreless game, giving Providence a 1–0 lead. Hines recklessly sprinted for second base on the play and would have been out on Hackett's perfect throw had Burdock not dropped the ball. When Farrell drove another single to left field, Jerry Denny—coaching at third—noticed Hornung was taking his time to get to it, and frantically waved home Hines. But Hornung, it turned out, "was playing Fox on Hines," the *Globe* observed,

Jack Farrell "tags out" Paul Hines

and he gunned him down at the plate. Thanks to Radbourn, Providence was able to take its precious 1–0 lead all the way into the ninth inning, needing only three more outs to sweep the series. "Radbourn now began to put on steam," the *Globe* observed.

It was a fair question how much steam he might have left after four straight games of brilliant work against Boston. Mert Hackett threw a scare into the Providence crowd when he led off the ninth inning with a line shot to right field, but the speeding Radford captured it in his bare hands. Ezra Sutton hit a grounder to second that Jack Farrell deftly scooped up, retiring him at first. Boston was down to its last out when the fireworks began. "John Morrill stepped to the plate, waited for a good ball, got one where he wanted it and sent it away for a single," the *Journal* reported. Whitney spit on his hands, stood in, and followed Morrill's example, driving him to third with a single. Whitney quickly stole second, and Hornung, the club's slugging left fielder, came to the plate with two runners in scoring position and two men out. A hit could win the game. Cries of "Now, Joe!" erupted from the Boston faithful. Hornung got his pitch and slammed the ball down the first-base line. As Joe Start raced for it, the ball took a vicious hop and soared over his head. Start leapt up, plucked it from the air, and came down on the bag to end the game, the series, and quite possibly Boston's season. "A shout went out from those Providence throats that was never heard before," the *News* reported.

Next to capturing the pennant, there was nothing Grays fanatics loved more than New England bragging rights for winning the season's series against the hated Beaneaters, nine games to seven. The *Providence Star* was giddy and eager to gloat. "Good-by, Fall River delegation, your presence has been the means of urging on Buffinton to 'knock us out,' and as he has not done it, we will shake hands over the 'bloody chasm,' thank you for your attendance, dollars and kindly cheers, that availed not a whit in the long run, and will be pleased to see you next year. Ta-ta! Ta-ta, Mr. *News*." The *News* editor responded in kind: "Mr. *Star* seems happy. And it is refreshing to note the contrast between this happiness and his usual sniveling, snarling and snapping peevishness when the Providences lost a game." The editor seemed especially irritated by the praise being heaped on Arthur Irwin for his hole-in-one homer. "The Providence scribes are lubricating Irwin all over with taffy," he noted, but given the fickleness of Providence crowds, he warned Irwin not to suffer a slump, "for you'll be lashed with a salted thong if you do."

The Fall River writer complained that Providence's low-class fanatics had unduly influenced the outcome by screaming at the Beaneaters and pressuring the umpire to punish the visiting pitcher for stepping out of the box. Hub crowds, by contrast, had comported themselves with dignity and expressed just appreciation of good baseball. "Boston audiences are behind the times," he noted sarcastically. "They can't begin to sustain their club with Comanche yells and low bred jockeying, as can the Providence audiences." Equally annoying as their loutish jockeying, the writer thought, was their excessive praise of the hometown heroes for the most absurdly unimpressive achievements. "Even if Gilligan throws back a ball high to Radbourne which is stopped, it is rapturously applauded, even when no one is on the bases and the ball might have been allowed to go by." When, that month, the writer got wind that audiences in Boston, the self-styled "Athens of America," were beginning to follow the example of Providence's "howlers," he burst out, "Too bad! It were better that they enter the big sewer, float down to Moon Island [in Boston Harbor] and drown themselves, for Providence has had an exclusive right to abuse visiting clubs for years, and it ought not to be taken away by the Athenians."

The columnist at the *Boston Globe*, by contrast, felt no bitterness over the sweep, "for a better-played string of games has never been witnessed in the history of the National League." The *Sporting Life* concurred, noting that all sixteen games between the New England clubs had been gems, "magnificent contests, and fortunate indeed were the people who witnessed them. They have had the cream of the season."

Radbourn was the cream of the cream. In one of the game's legendary pitching performances, Old Hoss had thrown every inning of all four games of a critical series against his toughest adversary. In those thirty-eight innings of ball, he had won four games, surrendered no earned runs, and collected three shutouts. The great workhorse, tortured by arm and shoulder pain for much of the season, simply could not have been more dominant. Boston was now five laps behind, perilously close to dropping out of the pennant race. The *Telegram* did not even resent the raider Lucas anymore.

"Providence people have great cause to thank him for relieving us of such a great noodle as Sweeney," it laughed.

But could the Grays keep it up with one pitcher? "On Radbourn will fall the brunt of the battle for the Providences," the *News* noted. "It will be wonderful if he can stand the strain." Should his arm give out, or Boston's luck turn a little bit, the pennant could be wrested from the Grays, as usual. "Will the Providences go through the season without a grand and lofty tumble?" the writer asked. "Manager Bancroft has never yet seen that pennant fly proudly over his domains. Now or never, Frank!"

No one knew what the future held, but what Radbourn had achieved already was astonishing: thirty-three victories by mid-August, with two months of baseball left to play. And though Sweeney had begun to dazzle Union Association crowds, Radbourn had won back Providence's affection. Now he faced an agonizing ordeal: eight final weeks of work, a last hard drive to win his release, position himself for big money as a free agent, and show everyone, Carrie included, that he was a great man—maybe the greatest pitcher there ever was.

CHAPTER 16

Inward Laughs

The work was relentless. After beating Boston four straight times, Radbourn was back out at the Messer Street Grounds the very next afternoon, straining his arm against Cleveland's Blue Stockings. Admittedly, Cleveland was not nearly as good a team as the Beaneaters, even at full strength, and in the past week it had been weakened considerably. The club had fallen victim to the prowling Union Association, which had stolen three of its biggest stars, all supposedly under contract with Cleveland through the rest of the 1884 season—ace pitcher Jim McCormick, catcher "Fatty" Briody, and "Pebbly Jack" Glasscock, perhaps baseball's best shortstop.

The three signed new contacts with the Union Association's Cincinnati club on August 8, and informed their poor manager, Charlie Hackett, of their betrayal a scant thirty minutes before the start of Cleveland's scheduled exhibition game in Grand Rapids, Michigan, as paying customers were already climbing up into the stands, part of that day's big crowd of twelve hundred. When Hackett begged the trio to remain through the afternoon, at least, noting they had left Cleveland with too few men to take the field, they had the nerve to demand an extra $25 apiece to play—and the manager, facing the loss of hundreds of dollars in gate receipts and travel expenses, had little choice but to dicker with them, finally agreeing to fork over $10 each. The faithless Briody reportedly caught the game with his $1,000 Union Association advance stuffed into his stocking. Cincinnati owner Justus Thorner, who had arranged the luxury of sleeping berths for his three new stars on the 4:00 p.m. train from Grand Rapids, got nervous, then angry, when the men failed to arrive at the appointed hour, fearing they had hoodwinked him. But, in time, the game ended and they showed up at the station, and all four chugged away happily to Cincinnati. Thorner had made a similar offer that day to Cleveland's broad-shouldered center fielder, Pete "Monkey" Hotaling, but Pete stubbornly refused, saying his team "had used him 'white' and he would not break his contract with the club for $5,000," the *Herald* reported. "Such rugged honesty is rare," the paper noted appreciatively, "and Pete will not be forgotten for it." The club soon promoted him to captain. Third baseman Mike Muldoon also held fast. "They wanted me to go, and Mac asked me to join the rest, but I told him that I would not break my contract."

Still, the loss of three stars was catastrophic enough. Few Clevelanders would pay to see a floundering team bereft of their favorite players. Facing runaway financial losses, the board, like Providence's several weeks earlier, moved to close down the operation. As all this transpired, National League president Abraham G. Mills was up in the White Mountains of New Hampshire, trying in vain to get away from it all. He had left behind the sweltering heat of Manhattan for his annual August retreat, staying at the well-appointed Plaisted House, in rural Jefferson, high up the slope of picturesque Mount Starr King, near clear mountain streams running with his beloved trout. Guests enjoyed the latest conveniences, including modern plumbing and gas lighting, and the hotel's prize attraction: a breezy piazza that commanded a spectacular vista of fifty miles. Yanked back into unpleasant baseball affairs, recognizing instantly that the rest of Cleveland's players would bolt to the Union Association unless he acted, Mills fired off a telegram from his mountain paradise, urging the Cleveland owners to soldier on: "Disbandment now would seriously injure League and gratify nobody but Wreckers"—or, as he called them in another letter, "the unscrupulous gang of thieves, known as the 'Union Association.'" At the same time, Mills coaxed National League clubs to provide an indirect subsidy by splitting the gate take of home games against Cleveland fifty-fifty, rather than tender it the usual visitor's share of three-tenths. Their backbones stiffened, the directors resolved to keep going, even though it meant bringing in far less talented players to "supply the places of the traitors." Cleveland caught a train from

Michigan to Providence for an August 15 makeup game against the Grays.

About fifteen hundred people turned out on an unseasonably cool, gloomy Ladies' Day for what was, in a way, a pity party for denuded Cleveland. When the notoriously pro-Providence crowd began applauding the visitors for every good play, "it was evident that the spectators accorded the Clevelands much sympathy in their present weakened condition, which had been brought about by players who had no respect for contracts and waited only the opportunity of securing more money to break their bonds, as well as their words," the *Journal* sermonized. But for all the crowd's pity, stripped-down Cleveland proved a worthy foe, making a dogged fight of it and forcing Radbourn to throw hard. Providence finally broke a 2–2 tie in the fifth inning in less than heroic fashion, when Gilligan hit a long fly to center field that one of Cleveland's new men, a raw minor leaguer named Gurdon Whiteley, promptly misplayed into a double. Gilligan scored on two wild pitches by John Harkins, the former Rutgers chemistry student. In the fifth, sixth, and ninth, Cleveland had men on the bases, but Radbourn clung on for a 3–2 victory.

The day was not entirely happy for the Grays, though. Early in the game, Arthur Irwin was "seized with a hemorrhage of the bladder," according to the *Boston Globe*, and had to leave the field. Irwin had been doing "the grandest short stopping in the League," the *Sporting Life* contended, grabbing hot grounders other men could not reach because his strong arm permitted him to play unusually deep. Now Providence would have to get by without him, at least for a few games.

His substitute was a green rookie, a tall, slender twenty-one-year-old named Charlie Bassett whose only significant baseball experience had been in playing for the Brown University team. Bassett was gifted enough to have been offered a big-league job by the Worcester club when he was a nineteen-year-old sophomore, but he had declined, explaining he had come to college for an education, not to work in professional baseball. Bancroft, for one, was willing to be patient, waiting until Bassett's graduation to take him on as a much-needed utility player at $1,000 for the remainder of the season. In moving up to the pros, Bassett brought along a cherished token of his college life: his favorite bat, into which he had proudly burned the number 448, representing his magnificent senior-year batting average. Sometime after that, a Providence teammate introduced him to the ways of major-league baseball when, miffed by an umpire's call, he grabbed the nearest object, which happened to be Bassett's prized bat, and angrily heaved it over the fence. That was the last anyone saw of it. "His new professional colleagues had little respect or sympathy for such college mementos," a reporter explained. Bassett's most urgent task in joining the Grays, he remembered decades later, "was not to make good on the field, but to grow a mustache to belie his [youth]," helping him fit in with his grizzled teammates. "The mustache, despite great attention and care, turned out to be the skimpy variety," the *Journal* quipped, though it looks fine in team photos.

Bassett got some practice the following day in an exhibition game in Lawrence, Massachusetts, about seventy-five miles north of Providence, another draining trip during the dog days of August, just so Bancroft could stuff a few more dollars into his employer's coffers. The overworked Radbourn got the day off, but most of the Grays had no choice but to suit up and play. Eddie Conley, who had whipped major-league competition, struggled against this unimpressive local team, barely escaping with a 5–4 victory. Two days later, the Grays trudged out to another exhibition game, this one at Presumpscot Park in Portland, Maine. Cyclone Miller fared better, pitching Providence to a 20–1 rout, but the men would have preferred a few hours of rest. "We do not like the idea of these exhibition games," the *Telegram* complained. "Take the Portland trip, for instance. It is a long, hard journey, constituted to tire the players."

Radbourn was back on the job at the Messer Street Grounds on August 19, when he struck out ten men to beat Detroit, 4–2. On the following afternoon, after starting the club's last six straight official games, he finally got a break from pitching, though not from playing. Bancroft, still unsure about Bassett, sent his ace out to play shortstop. But by the next day, August 21, Rad was back in the pitcher's box, where he would be stationed in every game, incredibly, for more than a month, winning one contest after another—one of the greatest feats, perhaps *the* greatest, in baseball's long history.

It seems clear that Radbourn had gotten this far in this agonizing season only because of his remarkably intuitive and strategic mind. Looking back a quarter of a century later, his teammate Arthur Irwin, by then a New York Yankees scout, said he considered Radbourn the "brainiest pitcher that ever delivered a ball across the plate." Every generation, of course, thinks that it invented baseball strategy, Ted Sullivan pointed out in 1909, well into the so-called modern era of baseball. "But Radbourne, as sure as you live, in his day had everything the very best pitchers of today could boast of." Radbourn flummoxed enemy batters by mixing up his pitches and points of release, and by coming at them from various parts of the pitcher's box. A good fastball that seemed to "jump" as it neared the plate was, of course, the most powerful weapon in his arsenal. But power alone was not enough; the key to using it effectively was mixing it with off-speed pitches and curveballs, keeping the batter guessing about which was coming next and where it would go.

That had certainly been proven in 1884. The National League's new rule legalizing overhand pitching brought out of the woodwork "hundreds of would-be pitchers," young bucks with fresh arms, contributing "little else than wild, swift overthrowing, in which everything has been sacrificed to speed," the *Sporting Life* noted. It didn't work, in part because fastballs inflated the number of passed balls and wild pitches, endangering and exhausting catchers in the process, and in part because pitchers ruined their arms doing it. But the biggest reason a steady diet of fastballs failed was because professional batters could catch up to even the speediest of them. Thus, while "overthrowers of the Whitney school" had failed, men such as Radbourn, Buffinton, and Pud Galvin remained highly effective, demonstrating "that there is but one kind of pitching that pays in the long run, and that is headwork in the box, or in other words, skillful strategic pitching." Mere speed, "without thorough command of the ball, is worse than useless."

Radbourn's thorough command—his pinpoint precision—was second to no one's. "This was the basic secret of his great success. He could always put the ball wherever he wanted to," Bancroft observed. Most often, he challenged a hitter to take a swing. "I want the men behind to have something to do," he said, "and so I pitch accordingly." He had a saying about pitching: "When you are in doubt, put it over." Contemporary observers seemed amazed at the kind of pitches Radbourn was able to sneak past batters. "Radbourne, in some games, deliberately tossed the ball to batsmen and they could not hit him, whereas if some other pitcher had done the same thing the ball would have been driven down into Connecticut," the *Fall River Daily Evening News* noted. A master of psychological warfare, he bamboozled enemy hitters by employing arts that kept them guessing.

Radbourn enjoyed lulling enemy batters into a false sense of security. He "would bear the most careful watching at those times," Sam Crane recalled, "for he could fairly 'make the ball talk,' even when he looked the least dangerous." He supplemented those sudden, explosive fastballs with curveballs that broke in different ways. Not all of them were strictly legal. He knew how to swish the ball against his spikes when no one was paying attention, cutting grooves that made his slow pitches buck and dive. One of his most devastating pitches was a "drop" ball, a knee-buckling curve that plunged to the shin level of left-handed batters. The ball confounded the experts because it spun rapidly but moved slowly. "It seemed impossible, because a ball that revolves rapidly usually has great speed, the greater the speed, the greater the revolution," Johnny Evers and Hugh S. Fullerton recounted in their book *Touching Second*. "But Radbourne, pitching for Providence, kept practicing until he found his slow ball. He had been a good pitcher before that, and after his discovery, he became one of the greatest the game has ever known." He imparted the secret pitch to his friend Clark Griffith, who taught it to Christy Mathewson, who turned it into his famous "fadeaway" pitch. Thus, both Griffith and Mathewson entered the Baseball Hall of Fame with Radbourn's help—as did, perhaps, generations of superb pitchers who learned from them.

Radbourn made full use of the rectangular pitcher's box, prowling around it and throwing from different locations within it. He "was liable to spring some new pitching wrinkle any old time, and he could get away with them, too," Crane recalled. "No batter could fathom what Radbourne was about to deliver. He changed his position in the box and his swing so suddenly and frequently in games that he was outguessing his opponents right along." Radbourn never used the same motion in two successive games, John Morrill contended. "They may get used to his delivery today, and tomorrow he will go in and fool them with an entirely different style." At other times, as incredible as it seems, he completely eliminated his windup. "Pitchers in his day had the privilege of taking a running jump in the box, and could have their backs turned to the batsman before making their cyclonic gyrations, but Radbourne often disdained to take that advantage of the rules, and would frequently face the batsman and deliver the ball with both feet on the ground in the most sang-froid manner," Crane noted. "He had no high overhand reach in preparation for his delivery, nor any weird conglomeration of crazy wind-up swings. In fact, his highest delivery was comparatively low . . . and he pitched nearly as many balls with an easy, frictionless underhand swing as he did from above his waist," straining his arm only against dangerous batters.

His greatest strategic advantage, though, might have been his peerless ability to calibrate exactly when to pour it on and when to let up, preserving something for the late innings and later games. He used "the least exertion possible to get the results he wanted," Crane recounted. Part of that involved throwing underhand at times, counting on the generally dead ball and his talented fielders to keep the enemy in check. By doing so, he willingly surrendered hits and runs, which naturally damaged his statistics. But he did not care, as long as Providence ended up with more runs than its opponent. "One secret of his success is that he does not pitch for record, but when he has the game well in hand he saves himself by easing up his delivery," the *Sporting Life* noted that season. "The best pitcher is the one who wins the most games for his club, and not the one who suffers the fewest base hits," Radbourn explained.

Though not a demonstrative man, Charlie obviously loved his work. "He would play with a weak batter like a cat with a mouse, and notwithstanding his stern, unsmiling face, he loved a joke, and to 'fan' a heavy hitter on his slow in or out curve was great fun for him," Crane remembered. "He would not give the discomfited batsman the outward guffaw and jeer, but his inward laughs must have been immense."

Radbourn beat Anson's White Stockings, 5–3, on August 21, with the help of a rowdy Providence crowd, which unnerved Chicago's pitcher, Larry Corcoran, by bellowing "Keep in the box!" at him with unsportsmanlike persistence and ferocity, while ignoring Radbourn's own transgressions. "It shows a contemptibly mean spirit to say the least," the *Fall River Daily Evening News* complained. After the tiring contest, Bancroft hauled the Grays away to

Hartford for another exhibition game, this one against the Gothams of New York, before fifteen hundred paying customers. On Saturday, August 23, Radbourn again whipped Chicago, this time 7–3, and he and his exhausted teammates set off once more for Portland—a 320-mile trip, about four and a half hours away by train—for another exhibition on Monday against Boston's Red Stockings. Some thirty-five hundred turned out, a huge crowd for such a small city, no doubt hoping to see a classic Providence-Boston struggle. What they got was a 9–0 shellacking of the uninspired Grays. The tired Radbourn had to suit up and play, in center field—and, worse, later in the game even had to waste his arm strength by pitching, taking over for the thoroughly whipped Conley, who was looking less and less like a professional pitcher.

Radbourn lugged his tired arm back into the box at the Messer Street Grounds on August 27, again facing his old enemies, the White Stockings. His third pitch drew horrified gasps, as it rocketed off the skull, just behind the right ear, of leadoff batter George Gore, who was apparently in no condition to lean out of the way. Gore went on the field "so drunk," the *Fall River Daily Evening News* charged, "that he could not catch a ball or dodge one that hit him in the head when it was pitched for him to hit." Though the blow to the cranium seemed only to raise an egg, Anson wisely thought it best to let George ride the bench the rest of the afternoon. Larry Corcoran, who had not planned to play and did not have his uniform with him, ran into the dressing room, put on the Grays togs of little Sandy Nava and took over in center field. It was a rough day for Kelly, too, who was hit by foul tips no fewer than nine times, and was finally forced to trade places with third baseman Ned Williamson. At first, Ned, not terribly interested in getting pummeled by foul tips, argued with Anson about going in, warning that opponents might run on him. The captain was furious. "Go in, even if they make a thousand runs!" he screamed at the slugger, in earshot of the press box. Little Barney Gilligan suffered his own agonies, as a foul tip split his fingers in the eighth inning. In that same inning, a foul ball shot back and got stuck in the eaves of the grandstand's roof. Rather than cough up the money for a new ball, the ever-frugal Bancroft got some men and a ladder, and finally "sent a boy on the roof after the sphere," extracting the ball in a ten-minute operation.

That day, Chicago introduced a brilliant young pitcher who might have been Radbourn's 1884 partner in Providence. One of five sons of a prosperous Boston jeweler, John Gibson Clarkson was a thin and touchy twenty-three-year-old who had pitched a few unimpressive National League games for Worcester two years earlier, before getting in two years of minor-league seasoning with the Northwestern League franchise in Saginaw, Michigan. Frank Bancroft, who knew talent when he saw it, had avidly sought Clarkson's services for the Grays, willing to run the risk that another young star on the team would leave Radbourn sullen, jealous, and contentious. He reportedly offered Clarkson a cool $400 a month, which would have made him one of the league's best-paid players. But it wasn't enough. The pitcher went for even bigger money to play for Chicago—and proved he was worth every penny. A highly intelligent, baseball-savvy pitcher who, like Radbourn, relied on craft and strategy, Clarkson went on to win 328 major-league games. The *Journal* declared that his debut for Chicago that afternoon "showed him to be a player of much value. Though wild at times, his delivery is swift and effective, and the Grays found it no easy task to gauge his curves correctly." But he was not good enough to beat Radbourn and the Grays' fielders. Chicago loaded the bases with no outs in the fifth, but Radbourn doggedly got the side out without surrendering a run. Cliff Carroll made a marvelous running catch to the foul line in left field, while Paul Hines's magnificent one-handed grab averted a double to right center. The Grays won 5–3, their twelfth straight. Providence seemed unstoppable.

Not that Radbourn had much energy left. In the final game of the series, before a small but vocal crowd of 782, Chicago batted him hard for eleven hits. But Providence got under the skin of Larry Corcoran. In a daring double steal, Paul Revere Radford and Sandy Nava took off and got caught in rundowns. But catcher Mike Kelly, who, like Gore earlier in the series, seemed suspiciously woozy, "lost his head completely." When he ran up the line to tag Radford, "the Mascot" simply darted past him for home plate, beating Kelly's wild throw to Corcoran. Radford's proud dad, delighted that his son had helped beat mighty Chicago, 6–4, reportedly gave Paul a $5 reward for scoring the key run. The Grays had swept Anson's men.

Anson, who refused give up on the season, was fit to be tied by these cascading losses. One writer imagined him storming into the dressing room "with glaring eyes, pale countenance and froth dripping from his kisser," and laying into his men: "You are a fine set of stiffs, ain't you? You're the rottenest set of bum players in the country. I can pick a better nine out of the morgue than you are. A nice thing it is to be giving you all a President's salary and then to make such a sorry exhibitions of yourselves. Bah! From this date forward you will to a man retire to your couches at 7 o'clock in the evening chained together. Your food will be raw tripe until you win a game. Two detectives will constantly watch each man and the first unfavorable report he makes the culprit will be sent to Joliet. D'ye hear, you 'en, yes! you-you!"

Whiskey and women, it seemed to many, had destroyed baseball's greatest team. The White Stockings, who obviously enjoyed the hospitality of Providence, were so intoxicated during the four games that they "did not know whether they were muffing, catching or hitting the ball," one paper asserted. "Some of them were fined for their conduct and one of them told Anson to go to—a certain hot place." Club president Albert G. Spalding admitted that his players had run wild all season. "This year it has been impossible to discipline and control the men in their habits on account of the bad influence exerted by the Union Association," he complained. "If we rebuked or attempted to punish a player for dissipation we were met with the reply, 'Well, if you don't like it, I'll go elsewhere.' All of them had offers from Union Association clubs, and threats of blacklisting had no terrors for them."

The following season, Spalding gave each man a bonus of $100 "for having abstained from intoxicating drinks and orgies," the banes of 1884. Still, Spalding continued to hear well-founded rumors that his players were indulging in drunkenness and debauchery. At one point, he hired the famous Pinkerton detective agency (its slogan: "We Never Sleep") to trail his men after hours. The private eye returned with a scalding report that seven of the club's fifteen players had been found going up and down Clark Street and the saloons and shady haunts of Chicago's tenderloin district late at night. When the report was read aloud at a team meeting, Kelly strenuously objected to one passage—the one charging him with being at a saloon at 3:00 a.m., violating curfew, drinking lemonade. That was a bald-faced lie, Kelly protested. "It was a straight whiskey. I never drank a lemonade at that hour in my life."

After the inebriates of Chicago left, last-place Detroit came to Providence. Rain all but ruined Ladies' Day on August 29, and only four hundred people showed. Still, the drenched men played on, braving several heavy downpours that drove much of the small audience under the grand-stand. Though sopping wet and trying to control a slippery ball, "Radbourn did his work with old-time strategy and skill," the *Journal* asserted. Both teams collected six hits, but Radbourn struck out six of the Wolverines and triumphed, 7–1, for his fortieth victory. "Radbourn's easy delivery is what makes everyone laugh," the *Evening Telegram* observed. The overworked pitcher won an exhausting extra-inning battle the next day, beating Detroit 6–5 after Carroll dashed home on Radbourn's grounder in the bottom of the eleventh, eluding the tag. It was Rad's thirteenth straight pitching victory, tying Larry Corcoran's major-league record, set in 1880.

As September began, only Providence's nemesis Boston realistically remained in the hunt.

	W	L	PCT.	GB
PROVIDENCE	64	20	.762	—
Boston	58	26	.690	6
Buffalo	50	34	.595	14
New York	50	36	.581	15
Chicago	41	45	.477	24
Cleveland	31	55	.360	34
Philadelphia	27	58	.318	37½
Detroit	19	66	.224	45½

Grouchy over Providence's lead, the *Fall River Daily Evening News* contended that the Grays had leapt into first place only because they engaged in the sort of dirty tricks scorned by their moral superiors. Radbourn, he charged, picked off runners by committing balks that umpires failed to see. Arthur Irwin and Cliff Carroll, stymied by good pitching, had taken to making their bats go dead and dropping down bunts "to the disgust of all but admirers of 'baby' acts." (The strategy was so novel that sportswriters had not worked out what to call such attempts; some called them "punts.") Catcher Barney Gilligan, on two-strike counts, gobbled up any pitch close to the plate and fired it to the infielders before the umpire could make a call, pressuring him to sing out "strike three" for fear of receiving a chorus of boos and threats. Similarly, second baseman Jack Farrell swiped at any runner stealing a base and, with two outs, jogged off the field, intimidating the umpire into calling a third out. Paul Hines routinely "kicked" at umpires' calls he did not like.

The *Sporting Life* scoffed at the criticism. "These hints and innuendos are all wrong," the paper said. "This is good ball playing and the team should have credit for it." While other clubs seemed to have better individual players, the Grays worked in a remarkably steady, focused manner, refusing to lose their cool, even when they fell behind. "Those who watch the Providences play," the paper observed, "rarely see any evidence that they are the least rattled."

On September 2, Charlie Radbourn picked up his big bat and walked out to home plate, preparing to face his former teammate Pud Galvin, the squat and dogged ace of Buffalo's Bisons. This was the team Charlie enjoyed beating, repeatedly tormenting it for letting him go in 1880. It was a Tuesday afternoon, golden and warm, and 1,529 had paid their way in to enjoy baseball before this historic season faded out at the Messer Street Grounds. As Radbourn dug in at the plate, umpire John Gaffney waved his arm, calling a halt. A sputtering of applause built to sustained cheering as a pair of men dragged out a massive and elaborately detailed gold frame, embracing a life-sized crayon portrait of Radbourn. A few minutes later, his battery mate Barney Gilligan came to the plate, his hands red and tender from the pummeling he had received all season catching Radbourn's pitches. The umpire called time again. Somebody who understood how much Radbourn owed to his stalwart battery mate had commissioned a life-sized Gilligan, too. Both men raised their caps in gratitude to the crowd, and then went to work.

If any club was likely to slow the Grays at this point, the Bisons were. Their star hitters had been slamming the ball hard in recent games, propelling the club past New York into third place, and stimulating lively speculation over whether they could do a better job against Radbourn than Boston had a month earlier. The crowd soon got its answer. Radbourn "was a monument of skill and strategy," the *Journal* reported. For six innings, he toyed with the Buffalo batters, mixing heat and slow stuff, varying locations, throwing from different corners of the box, and retiring every man in succession. He eventually surrendered three scattered hits, but he struck out ten and secured another shutout, as his teammates gobbled up hard grounders and sped to catch drooping fly balls. "The Grays played without the semblance of an error, and with a spirit and unity of effort which made them superior to defeat," the *Journal* enthused. The brisk, hour-and-forty-minute game was over by 5:15 p.m., leaving the Grays with a 4–0 win, their sixteenth straight. Radbourn had now won fourteen in a row, something that had never been done at baseball's highest level. When it was over, a reporter tracked down Big Dan Brouthers, the Bison's six-foot-two, 207-pound behemoth, a man who could hit the ball as far and as hard as anyone in the game, winner of the league's last two batting titles. He told a reporter he would be happy to get out of Providence for the season. Why? "Because you have such demon pitchers here."

The following afternoon, before a slightly smaller crowed of 1,158, the demon was back at work, however much his arm was crying out in pain. Providence held a 2–0 lead in the fourth inning when Buffalo second baseman Hardie Richardson, Radbourn's hunting pal, caught one of his pitches over the inside half of the plate and launched it over the left-field fence for a home run. But that was it for Buffalo scoring, while Providence batters went to work, pummeling the Bisons' rookie right-hander Billy Serad. There was an unsettling note for Providence fanatics when, with two out in the ninth inning, a foul tip blasted Barney Gilligan's finger. The catcher was not injured severely enough to win the umpire's permission to leave the game, however, and traded places with third baseman Jerry Denny, who donned the mask, stomach pad, and gloves. After a passed ball, Denny settled down while Radbourn secured the third out on a grounder to second base. The 10–1 win was Radbourn's forty-third of the season, his twentieth win in his last twenty-one decisions, and his fifteenth straight victory.

By then, local fanatics were getting spoiled. Even with Radbourn's remarkable winning streak on the line, only 528 of them bothered to pay their way into the Messer Street Grounds to see the woeful Cleveland club on September 4, leaving wide stretches of empty seats in the grandstand and bleachers. The loyal troopers were treated to a hard-fought game, tied 1–1 until the top of the eighth inning, when Cliff Carroll reached first on an error, raced to second on a passed ball, stole third, and electrified the crowd by scoring on a wild pitch. The Grays added a more substantial insurance run when Joe Start clubbed what the *Journal* called "one of his old-fashioned three baggers to right centre field," and Radbourn drove him home with a single to right field. The 3–1 victory was the Grays' eighteenth straight.

On Friday, Radbourn seemed overmatched at last, his arm obviously weakening from overuse. He got hit hard, and feeble Cleveland took a 4–2 lead into the eighth inning behind the strong pitching of John Henry, a rookie from Springfield, Massachusetts, who had turned twenty-one just two days earlier. Rad's sixteen-game winning streak seemed destined to end. But the Grays scratched out another run, and Jerry Denny came to the plate. The hard-hitting, smooth-shaven, slightly potbellied third baseman "took up his little bat, spat upon his hands, pulled up his pantaloons," and then jumped on a pitch the rookie surely wanted back. Denny launched a drive "the like of which was never seen on the Messer Street Grounds," the *Providence Star* reported. "The ball sailed away like a hawk, rising and rising long after it had passed the left field fence and until it was far above the housetops, finally dropping in a garden near the street."

The tape-measure blast plated what would prove to be the tying and winning runs. The *Evening News* editor, never one to celebrate the Grays' good fortune, questioned the colorful account. "That garden, according to the description of the sailing powers of the ball, must have been several miles over the Connecticut boundary," he scoffed. With Denny's help, Radbourn had won seventeen in a row; Providence, nineteen straight.

Jerry Denny

Summer was passing, and though the season had more than a month to go, the Grays would soon leave the Messer Street Grounds behind. The club heavily promoted its final games, alongside *Journal* advertisements for late-summer excursions to Martha's Vineyard and Saratoga, New York, a playground of the rich that was home to world-class horse racing, casino gambling, and a horrible-tasting mineral water, served at ornate public fountains downtown, that was supposed to restore health. Closer to home was the Grand Republican Mass Meeting at Oakland Beach, touting the ticket of James G. Blaine and John A. Logan, to be capped by a "grand illumination" and torchlight procession. "LAST GAMES OF SEASON 1884. GRAND GALA WEEK," the Grays advertised. "Ladies Admitted Free to All Games This Week." After that week, the Grays would have to play their final eighteen games on the road, getting tired out traveling—a possible threat to their pennant hopes, since winning away from home was never easy.

On Friday, September 5, against Cleveland, little Gilligan demonstrated his "plucky support" for Radbourn yet again, blocking the plate to prevent a run, though the bigger runner crashed into Barney and brutally flattened him. "He put out his man, however, and when stretched upon the ground, everybody thought he had been disabled for the game; to their surprise he arose, and in a moment resumed his stance behind the plate," an action that the *Sunday Morning Telegram* deemed "heroic." The play was crucial in preserving a 5–4 Providence win.

On Saturday, Radbourn worked yet again, the eleventh straight time Bancroft had started him for the Grays, and his fifth start in five days. He was in pain and weak with exhaustion, but the proud pitcher was not deigning to show it. All that mattered to him now was fulfilling his pledge to win the pennant and securing his release from Providence's grip. "Radbourn pitched with his old-time effectiveness, giving no indication of weakening, as might be looked for after his continuous work in the points," the *Journal* reported with some amazement. He threw a six-hit shutout, beating Cleveland, 3–0, his eighteenth straight victory. He had now won an incredible twenty-three of his last twenty-four decisions, and the Grays had captured twenty in a row. "20TH STRAIGHT. Unparallelled Record of the Grays. An Unbroken Chain of Victories," the *Sunday Morning Telegram* bragged in its biggest and boldest front-page headline, with greater verve than spelling proficiency. "This has been accomplished by steady and united playing, and the strategetic [*sic*] pitching of Radbourn, who has bravely stood the continuous strain on him," the paper noted. "The giant hitters of the League have all fallen before the masterly and lightning curves of the incomparable Radbourn, while the players have attained a very high standard in fielding."

The victory left Providence with a seven-game lead over Boston, with twenty-three left to play. The *Boston Courier*, for the first time, contemplated the unthinkable: that Boston, though superior in size, influence, cultural attainments, and baseball achievements, might actually surrender the pennant to "the citylet" of Providence. "If Providence gets it, it will look like an infant in the tall hat of its father," the *Courier* mocked. There was much, in truth, to the charge that Providence was a pipsqueak major-league city. Turnout had been meager for such a historically great team—only about 60,000 for the season, compared with more than 140,000 for second-place Boston—and there were rumors the club might pick up and leave in 1885, possibly to Brooklyn. Boston, having made loads of money out of its fierce New England rivalry, wanted the Grays to stay right where they were. The Beaneaters would even "rather see the pennant go to Providence this year than to see no club in Providence next year," the *Sporting Life* asserted.

Still, many Boston fanatics were not prepared to give up. The *Boston Herald* argued that the defending champions actually held the edge over the upstart Rhode Islanders going down the stretch, simply because it had two superb pitchers "in prime form" to Providence's one, who was surely tired and susceptible to a total breakdown. Boston's Charlie Buffinton was turning in a spectacular season, en route to winning forty-eight games—a total that tied Radbourn's 1883 record, and stands to this day as the fifth-highest in major-league history. On September 2, Buffinton struck out seventeen Cleveland batters, just two shy of Sweeney's record, including eight in a row, and twelve of the last fifteen batters he faced. While Buffinton's pitching mate, Jim Whitney, had suffered arm troubles, and would never again match the greatness he had achieved in 1883, the Grasshopper was still among the National League's leading hurlers, and his midseason layoff seemed to have helped his arm recuperate some. Meanwhile, surely, no one man—not even Radbourn—could stand the strain of pitching virtually every game all the way to the end. "Radbourne might get disabled in the meantime; then, good-bye, pennant," the *Fall River Evening News* observed hopefully. The *Journal* would have none of it. "Radbourn is in splendid trim at present," and had the advantage of working with superb infielders and outfielders, plus the gritty Gilligan. "True it is that accidents may happen, but the Providence club has been playing a game which means to defeat her most formidable opponents, and that lead of seven games is a heavy obstacle to the final victory of the boastful champions."

By Tuesday, September 9, the Grays were feeling the pressure of reeling off twenty wins without a loss. "The whole country had been looking . . . to accomplish the defeat of Radbourn and the Grays," sportswriter William D. Perrin recalled. "The strain had become so violent that even the Providence players felt a defeat would be welcome." On that afternoon, Buffalo's Bisons returned to Messer Street, fresh from a 2–1 victory over Boston on Saturday. "It seemed in the air that something was going to happen," Perrin recounted.

What happened was a poor performance by umpire John Gaffney, the *Journal* bitterly complained. With one out in the fifth, Buffalo center fielder Dave Eggler hit a ball to right field that Paul Revere Radford, playing shallow, scooped up and threw to first, "putting Eggler out, as every person who witnessed the play thought"—every person except for Gaffney, who called him safe. Radbourn blew two strikes past Jim O'Rourke, one of the game's best hitters, and had just sent a third pitch straight over the plate when Eggler broke for second, distracting the umpire, who mistakenly ruled the pitch a ball. Given an extra life, O'Rourke blasted the next pitch for a double, driving home Eggler with the first run. O'Rourke got to third on a passed ball and scored on a hit by catcher Jack Rowe. Meanwhile, Buffalo workhorse James "Pud" Galvin kept the Grays scoreless, taking a 2–0 lead into the ninth inning.

Providence, as usual, refused to quit. With one out, the Grays put men on first and second base. Radbourn, in a position to save his eighteen-game winning streak, strode to the plate, glaring at Galvin, looking for a pitch he could hit. He got one and blasted a line drive to right-center field, sending his risk-taking friend Cliff Carroll tearing around third. Buffalo's fleet right fielder, Jim Lillie, sprinted hard for the ball, reaching out his long arms and fingers; he grabbed it in midair, then pegged it to Hardie Richardson at second. It was a jaw-dropping, game-ending double play. Carroll kicked the dust, and Radbourn's historic run of victories was over, as was the Grays'. The *Evening Telegram* tried to put a happy spin on the defeat. "This thing was getting monotonous," it claimed, "and base ball enthusiasts are indebted to James Galvin." At Boston's South End Grounds, where the crowd roared and cheered when the Providence score was posted, the Beaneaters edged Cleveland to trim the lead to six games.

Now that the great streak was over, it seemed a good time to sit down Radbourn and give his arm at least a day or two to rest and heal. But on the next afternoon, it was Radbourn, not Conley or Miller, who walked out to the box at the Messer Street Grounds to face the Cleveland club before a smallish crowd of about 930. Aggravated by the loss, he pledged that Providence would not lose again at home. At first, Radbourn was wild—a sign that exhaustion had set in—while even feeble Cleveland managed to hit him hard. In the end, nothing but Providence's sharp fielding kept Radbourn in the game, though third baseman Denny was out with malaria, the same ailment that had felled first baseman Joe Start earlier in the year. Still, he held on. Radbourn coughed up nine hits, including three doubles, but his fielders scooped up many other shots, and he escaped with a 5–3 victory. It was his forty-seventh win of the season, and if each one was getting harder, he was still showing no signs of relenting.

On September 11, Radbourn started for the Grays for the fourteenth straight time, his third game in three days, before another slim crowd of about nine hundred. Ominously, Cleveland's faithful Pete Hotaling smashed a home run over the left-field wall in the first inning, but from then on Radbourn shut down his opponents, striking out twelve and winning 9–1, to tie his own major-league record for games won in a season, set in 1883. Rad's "strong right arm," the *Journal* was pleased to report, "has not 'forgotten its cunning' despite the severe strain to which it has been subjected by continuous pitching." Behind Pud Galvin's superb pitching, meanwhile, Buffalo beat Boston, 1–0, to restore Providence's lead to seven games, prompting the *Journal* to burst out with an optimistic headline: "The Pennant will Fly at Messer Park in 1885."

Buffalo's star-studded lineup was a better draw than Cleveland's feeble array of castoffs, and on Friday afternoon, September 12, a fine crowd of 2,016 people thronged the Messer Street Grounds. Among them were several members of the Beaneaters—obsessed with the pennant race, even on their day off—who took the train down from Boston with a number of their supporters to root against the Grays. Radbourn, grim and quiet, took to the box for the fifteenth straight time, his arm somehow strong enough to pitch. The Boston men had something to cheer about in the first inning, as the Bisons hammered the tired Radbourn to take a 2–0 lead. But they fell silent from then on, and watched with grudging respect as the haggard veteran toiled on, throwing his incredible array of fast and slow stuff. Not another Buffalo runner crossed the plate, while Providence came back to win, 8–2. It was Radbourn's forty-ninth win, and though no one seemed to be counting, it established a new major-league record for victories in a single season.

By then, manager Bancroft was getting worried. This was risky. If Radbourn pushed himself too far—mortal pitchers did it all the time—and something snapped, Providence would be left without a hurler capable of delivering the pennant. It was clearly time for Radbourn to trade off with Cyclone Miller or Eddie Conley, conserving some of his strength for the final push. Bancroft broached the subject with his great pitcher. "I looked for him to give up the job every day, but he wouldn't," Bancroft recalled. "He said he wouldn't quit until we clinched the flag." Bancroft could always override Radbourn's judgment and insist that he sit down, of course, just as he had insisted earlier in the season that Rad take over when Sweeney was injured. But Bancroft preferred to let Radbourn work if that made him happy. Over the weeks since the pitcher's crackup, the manager had come to respect him enormously. So, against his better judgment, Bancroft let Old Hoss keep pursuing his extraordinary goal. One never knew: maybe his arm would hold up.

The Grays closed out their home season on the following day, September 13, with a duel between the league's two great iron-armed hurlers, Galvin and Radbourn. Local fanatics made it a gala event. Grateful for the glory that had unfolded before them, Rhode Islanders wanted to express their thanks before the Messer Street Grounds fell silent for the winter. In front of 3,019, umpire S. M. Decker—the man who had precipitated Radbourn's career-threatening temper tantrum in July—halted the game to present Old Hoss with a huge bouquet, courtesy of adoring Providence cranks, along with something the pitcher probably appreciated much more: "a bulky envelope containing lawful currency of the United States." Hard-bitten second baseman Jack Farrell received a requisite life-sized crayon portrait of his own, and an elegant gold watch, chain, and charm in the form of a $20 gold piece "prettily monogrammed," a tribute costing $185. "The spectators enthusiastically applauded the modest pair, and they proceeded to play with renewed energy and effectiveness," the *Journal* reported. In the second inning, Buffalo's Brouthers—such a fearsome hitter that he led the National League in slugging average every year from 1881 through 1886—hammered a Radbourn pitch over the head of right fielder Radford for a triple, and scored on a single to left field. Bancroft watched nervously. Was Radbourn's arm giving way at last? Unfazed, Charlie kept on throwing, and held the Bisons from then on. Providence won, 6–1.

Locking the gates of their grounds for the regular season, the Grays headed for Union Depot downtown, where they made their farewells to wives and girlfriends before boarding a 6:00 p.m. train, the beginning of their final road trip. They departed "in excellent spirits and fine physical trim," the *Journal* noted, "and confident of returning as champions of the country." At their connecting stop at Worcester's shimmering, ornate Union Station (modeled on a Russian basilica), they and the Buffalo team met up with the Boston and Cleveland teams, along with umpires Gaffney and Decker. The whole bunch—literally, half the National League—left for the West that Saturday night aboard the same Boston and Albany train, talking baseball, playing cards, and perhaps sneaking drinks to pass the time on the swaying cars.

The Grays held a significant lead as the trip got under way:

	W	L	PCT.	GB
PROVIDENCE	73	21	.777	—
Boston	65	28	.699	7½
New York	54	40	.574	19
Buffalo	53	40	.570	19½
Chicago	49	46	.516	24½
Cleveland	31	64	.326	42½
Philadelphia	31	64	.326	42½
Detroit	21	74	.221	52½

Though the *Boston Herald*, among others, had warned that Providence could not possibly win the pennant with only one pitcher, Radbourn was "not alarmed" to be working alone, the *Journal* reported, adding that it "will require something more substantial than newspaper encouragement to place the boastful champions at the top." Newspaper editors could predict all they wanted, but it was Radbourn's arm that would determine who won the pennant.

On that same Saturday night, five officers stealthily parked their horse-drawn "Black Maria," the popular term for a police van, in front of a boardinghouse kept by Mary Larvin, on Clemence Street, one block over from Carrie Stanhope's establishment. Police had "no difficulty in getting into the house," or arresting Mary, her boarders Mary Walker and Annie White, and the two men inside with them, who stubbornly refused to divulge their names. They were all "escorted to the carriage in waiting" and driven to the central police station, on the grounds that the place was a "house of ill-fame." The story appeared in Monday's paper next to the box score of the ball game. Life may have been hard for professional baseball pitchers in 1884, but it was no breeze for boardinghouse keepers, either.

A Promise Kept

As a sore and exhausted Radbourn strolled to the box on the gray Friday afternoon of September 26, the crowd of two thousand forming a half circle around him at Lake Front Park broke into a smattering of respectful applause. The baseball lovers of Chicago knew they were watching the best pitcher alive, and they hoped to see the home club thwart him one more time, spoiling Providence's hopes of wrapping up the pennant. There was little else at stake. The once-mighty White Stockings had squandered the 1884 season with their carousing and womanizing—and their somewhat shaky pitching. Nevertheless, under Anson's bulldog leadership, they remained proud and dangerous adversaries, refusing to lie down, even now. Indeed, they were in the midst of a furious burst of winning twenty-one of twenty-five games to close out the season.

Holding the ball, Charlie squinted at his catcher, Barney Gilligan. As soon as he threw a few pitches, both men realized that Radbourn had little power this afternoon. The big, muscular Chicago hitters, on a pace to lead the league in batting average, slugging average, and home runs, just might have a field day with him. As usual, he had undergone his lengthy preparation to get his stiff arm moving again, and the boys had declared that Old Hoss was ready, but that was no guarantee of anything. The right-field fence loomed ominously over his left shoulder.

It had been a grueling road trip for Radbourn. It started with a makeup game eleven days earlier at Cleveland's Kennard Street Park, two days after

Charlie had pitched in Providence. Making his seventeenth straight start, Radbourn surrendered nine hits to the weak-batting club, but his strategy of letting the enemy knock the ball to his fielders worked out, and he walked off the field with a 10–2 victory. After a tiring overnight boat trip across Lake Erie, Radbourn won again the following afternoon in Detroit, beating the cellar dwellers, 4–2, and he added 9–5 and 9–6 victories over the next two days. What Radbourn had achieved by then was nothing less than astounding. He had pitched on fourteen of the previous seventeen days, including five days in a row. He had won thirty of thirty-two decisions since his triumphal July 23 return from his weeklong suspension. He had fifty-four victories on the season—already more than anyone else in the long history of baseball would ever have.

But in doing so, he had all but wrecked his arm. On Monday, September 22, in front of six hundred diehard baseball lovers in Detroit, Radbourn could put nothing on the ball. He surrendered nine hits and three walks to the last-place team, and lost in embarrassing fashion, 7–1. That night, the suffering Radbourn and his teammates boarded a train for a four-game set at Chicago's Lake Front Park. Each bump and sway must have hurt.

A rainout on Tuesday gave him a blessed day of relief, but when he pitched on Wednesday, Charlie was little better. Chicago's Fred Pfeffer popped him for two home runs, including a three-run blast to give the White Stockings a 5–3 victory. Bancroft, recognizing that Radbourn's strength was gone after seeing him lose two in a row, insisted that Eddie Conley work the September 25 game at Lake Front Park. The Holy Cross kid held on in extra innings to win, 6–5.

By then, Boston stood on the brink of elimination. The hope that its two healthy pitchers would outshine Providence's one exhausted man had all but fizzled. The Beaneaters had opened in Chicago, well aware they would have to be nearly invincible over the next two weeks if they were to have any hope of retaining the pennant. When news of the game reached Boston by telegraph, their supporters were dumbfounded. Chicago's hitters had knocked the great Charlie Buffinton right out of the box, and John Morrill, taking his place, fared no better. With the help of four home runs, two of them by George Gore, the White Stockings slaughtered the Beaneaters 17–0, a staggering humiliation for the defending champions. "How about

Buffinton now, Mr. Boston *Herald*? What will the Fall River *News* man say of 'our darling pet'?" sneered Providence's *Evening Telegram*. Eight days earlier, in Fall River, Buffinton had joined with Miss Alice Thornley in holy wedlock, "Does that account for his weak pitching in the 17–0 game with Chicago?" the *Sporting Life* asked mischievously.

Maybe, but Boston's pitching was even weaker the next day, without the newlywed. Chicago drubbed the Beaneaters 18–9, this time hammering Jim Whitney, who also gave way to Morrill in relief. "The Providence Club may just as well order the pennant now," the *Sporting Life* remarked. Boston stayed alive, barely, by beating Chicago in the next two games. But it fell 7–2 in its Chicago finale, Boston's third loss in the five games against the White Stockings. Barring some miracle, it seemed only a matter of time now before the race was over officially.

Until his day off, Radbourn had started and completed twenty-two consecutive games—every Grays game from August 21 through September 22. Since July 23, he had pitched in all but three of the Grays' thirty-nine games. Now, on September 26, he stood poised to clinch the pennant.

The Grays staked him to a three-run lead in the top of the first— Radbourn himself drove in one, with a single—but Charlie's weak arm and the close right-field fence threatened to even things out. Sure enough, Radbourn ran into trouble quickly. Shortstop Arthur Irwin, usually spry and supple, fumbled a grounder, and Chicago's Abner Dalrymple and Cap Anson followed with sharp hits. By the time the rally was over, two runs had crossed the plate. One inning later, Radbourn fed Chicago catcher Silver Flint a pitch that he popped toward right field. Radbourn watched in dismay as the windblown ball disappeared over the canvas extension for a home run, tying the game 3–3. Well, that was the curse of playing here.

After suffering two straight losses, Radbourn faced the prospect of a third, with little strength left to do anything about it. But he had not given up all season, and he did not intend to start now. Since his fastball was off, he would have to employ art. As the innings passed, Radbourn worked like a magician, practicing his pitching sleight of hand, winding up to heave a ball that fluttered to the plate, hurling fast pitches when a slow one seemed certain, disrupting the timing of the Chicago hitters, making them look foolish.

FLINT, C., Chicago's
OLD JUDGE
CIGARETTE FACTORY.
COODWIN & CO., New York.

Silver Flint

In the third inning, the Grays wrested back the lead, thanks to a wild throw by Mike Kelly, who usually worked in the outfield or behind the plate but was filling in as a third baseman that afternoon. In the fourth, errors by Chicago first baseman Anson, second baseman Fred Pfeffer, and catcher Flint handed Providence a 5–3 edge. In the seventh inning, Providence's captain, Joe Start, delivered the coup de grâce. With two runners aboard, one on another Kelly error, Start popped the ball to right field. It vanished over the fickle fence, which had now turned against Chicago, for a three-run blast and an 8–3 lead.

After enduring a season of incredible frustration, Chicago reporters responded to the embarrassing series of miscues in this late September game with a stream of bitter invective. "The Chicago ball team is made up largely of cripples, bums and bigheads. There are perhaps four players who do not belong in either of these classifications, and there are some who belong in all three," the *Chicago Tribune* fumed. The *Chicago Herald*'s man agreed, complaining of the "disgraceful exhibition on the part of the local players, who seem to have degenerated into hopeless inefficiency" with their "vile misplays." As the afternoon darkened into dusk, Radbourn kept on throwing pitches that the Chicago batters hammered at his fielders, who were able to record precious outs, each one moving him closer to his great goal.

Though his body screamed for relief, Radbourn went out one more time in the ninth inning. Showing no emotion, he coaxed one out, then another, and finally faced Silver Flint, who had hit that miserable pop homer earlier in the afternoon. This time, Radbourn won the battle. As city workers prepared to ignite the gaslights along Michigan Avenue and ladies of the night strolled around the ballpark's perimeter, trolling for men who might want further entertainment after leaving the game, the great pitcher walked off the field with an 8–3 win, his fifty-fifth of the season. The reporters on the scene recounted no raised fists, no teammates rushing to Radbourn for a mass hug and pileup, no boyish jumping up and down, no show of generous applause from the supporters of the defeated club. They only told the facts of the game, which testified to one man's steady, dogged effort to the end.

At the same time, Boston was losing to last-place Detroit, 9–5. By late that afternoon, the race was over—officially. Radbourn collapsed, unable to throw anymore. But he had done it. Somehow, working virtually alone, confounding the experts, he had captured the flag.

The crowd gathering outside the plate-glass window of the *Providence Journal* bellowed cheers and waved their hats when the telegraphed report was posted. By Friday night, word had swept through town, possibly reaching the ears of a beaming Carrie Stanhope. "THE PENNANT WON," the *Journal* informed readers Saturday morning, while the *Morning Star*, almost literally crowing about the local team, ran a big rooster at the head of its baseball column, over the headline "W-H-O-O-P!" The Providence club "has earned in fair play the right to take the largest of the sporting banners to the smallest State in the Union," the *Sporting Life* cracked.

In their extensive postmortems, local reporters remembered the dire straits the club had confronted only two months earlier, when the "wreckers' association" engaged in the "contemptible trick" of trying to lure away the best players, notably Sweeney and Radbourn. At the time, the *Journal* recalled, Radbourn "apparently was suffering from a fit of 'temporary' hostility, but promptly recovered from the attack," when it became clear to him that Providence's management and supporters, and indeed baseball lovers all over the country, "looked to him to lead the nine to victory and supremacy"—in short, when he came to realize he was loved and admired. When Radbourn stiffened his spine and promised to pitch the rest of the way, his teammates "determined to stand together and make a vigorous and persistent effort to close at the top." Their twenty-game winning streak in August and September "commanded the surprise and admiration of the country," while in the Grays' now legendary battles against Boston, "Radbourn's unparalleled work in the points at critical moments in prolonged games placed him high among the galaxy of League pitchers in cool, effective and masterly manipulation of the sphere." In short, Radbourn "promised the management that he should face all the opposing teams until the pennant was surely won, and . . . he has nobly performed his obligation." His catcher Barney Gilligan received accolades for his "pluck and endurance" during Radbourn's remarkable run. "Not that he has escaped injuries from foul tips and collisions in base running and at the plate, but he has recovered with surprising activity and has never refused to receive the punishment which such swift and perplexing pitchers as Radbourn and Sweeney must necessarily inflict."

"This has been Radbourn's year," the *Boston Herald* said. "Undoubtedly the leading all-around pitcher in the country today, he threw into his work an amount of ambition, determination and energy that surprised his admirers and confounded his depreciators." The *Boston Globe* added its congratulations, noting that many local fanatics had waited patiently, "many with a knowing smile," for Radbourn to collapse under the brutal strain of pitching every game, but had waited in vain. "Radbourn has made a record which will probably never be equaled in the history of base ball. No man in the profession ever deserved [more] what is due him. He has fulfilled his promise and has the satisfaction of knowing that he has done what probably no other man in the world could do." The *Sporting Life* called him "the acknowledged king of the box."

At the same time, the sporting journal had high praise for manager Bancroft, now "the happiest man in the profession." The paper noted that while Bancroft had turned a remarkable profit yet again, this time in the range of $20,000, he "now adds to his reputation as the pilot of the League champions." More than an astute financial manager, he had finally become a "leader of men." For his part, Bancroft credited his players, then and for the rest of his life. "That club was certainly a hummer. Our boys were in the game up to their necks every minute," he declared. Outfielder Paul Revere Radford, celebrating his second straight National League championship, attributed both pennants to his "lucky horseshoe find." The question now, the *Sporting Life* quipped, was: "Which club will he select for the pennant next year?"

The *Boston Herald*, for one, found it difficult to extend the hand of congratulations, given Rhode Island's unpleasant crowds. "It is to be regretted

THE GRAYS TAKE THE PENNANT AND CONGRATULATE BOSTON
AND FALL RIVER.

Newspaper cartoon celebrates Grays' pennant victory. Date on flag signifies Providence will be reigning champions throughout the 1885 season.

that the championship is not to go to a more deserving city than Providence. The manner in which visiting clubs and umpires have been treated by the audience and press in that city has been simply outrageous," it grumbled. "Nearly every visiting player and umpire will attest to the truthfulness of this statement." The *Sporting Life* was of somewhat the same mind about the city's obnoxious citizens. Writing about the dominance of pitchers in 1884, the paper observed that "batting for the most part [was] as scarce as politeness among the Providence spectators."

No matter; the pennant was safely in Providence's hands. Back home, the club's board of directors voted to present each of the men, upon their return, with an elegant suit of winter clothes and an overcoat. Radbourn, meanwhile, got Bancroft's permission to dash from Chicago to his home in Bloomington, 135 miles downstate, for a brief vacation. On September 29, the manager informed his bosses by telegram that, with the pennant secure, he planned to rest his star players and work in his substitutes. First baseman Joe Start was still unable to shake the shivers and misery of malaria, and Bancroft shipped him back to Providence. The manager shifted third baseman Jerry Denny, suffering from a lame shoulder, over to first, where he would have to throw less. Charlie Bassett would play third. Miah Murray, a nineteen-year-old from Boston, was to take over catching duties for the well-pummeled Barney Gilligan. And the club's ace would get a blessed week off. "Radbourn is feeling the effects of his continuous pitching," the *Journal* reported.

That might have been the understatement of the year.

When Eddie Conley promptly lost three straight games, Bancroft thought it wise to revisit his plan to rest his tired stars. Even though the pennant was safely won, he could see that he risked poor attendance unless he played his best men—and his share of the gate was important to the club's profit margin. "Radbourne, Gilligan and Denny resume their regular positions to-day and will play in all important games [during the] balance of season," Bancroft telegraphed the *Sporting Life* on October 4 from Buffalo. That afternoon, before a big Saturday crowd, Radbourn reappeared, strengthened by eight luxurious days free from pitching. In the first inning, he grooved a pitch (intentionally?) to his pal Hardie Richardson, who blasted it for a triple, and Hardie quickly scored on a single by Jack Rowe. But Radbourn seemed to be toying with his adversary, because from then on he shut down Buffalo, winning 4–1 and pocketing his fifty-sixth victory. On the following Monday, Bancroft threw in some position players as pitchers—Paul Revere Radford, followed by Arthur Irwin and Paul Hines. They got drilled, 13–7, but Radbourn got to nurture his arm for the final burst of glory that would put his name in the record books next to unassailable numbers.

While in Buffalo, Bancroft, a confirmed roller-skating junkie, finally relaxed after months of tension and headed out for some fun at a local rink, taking Paul Hines for company. Bancroft was gliding along when his skate suddenly came apart. Instinctively, he grabbed Hines, and both came down on the hardwood floor, Hines with a crash. Hines lay on the ground, groaning in agony, gasping that he was "hurt bad." The crowd of skaters who gathered around the stricken man seemed sympathetic until Bancroft told them the victim was a professional ballplayer. He might as well have revealed that he was a drunkard and a thief. "They left him to get up and withdrew all sympathy," the *Sporting Life* recounted. Hines played all four Buffalo games, so his rink spill could not have hurt him as much as he thought initially.

All that remained on the official schedule was a four-game set against lowly Cleveland and a rainout makeup against the Phillies. Radbourn, returning to action on October 7, took it easy, letting Cleveland hammer him for ten hits. Fortunately, the porous fielding of that talent-stripped club handed Providence a 9–7 win. Radbourn now had fifty-seven victories, and Bancroft again gave him time off to rest his throbbing arm. Conley lost his fourth straight game two days later, as Cleveland blasted him 11–2. It was clear that Providence needed another pitcher for 1885, and there was even loose talk in the press about trying to lure back Charlie Sweeney, with the proviso that there would be no brass bands to puff up his ego (and threaten Radbourn's). "But that reminds us that 'Rad' must be consulted," the *Fall River Daily Evening News* scoffed, "for Sweeney's presence always makes Rad's arm lame, or at least strains the muscles of his happiness." In the third Cleveland game, the Grays tried out a new man, a twenty-nine-year-old journeyman named Harry Arundel, who won easily, 11–2. Radbourn returned on October 11, for the final game against Cleveland. Throwing a four-hit gem, he won his fifty-eighth, 8–1, aided by what the *Journal* correspondent called "the worst exhibition of thick-headed ball playing ever seen here" on the part of the Cleveland fielders. On the way back home, the Grays stopped for an exhibition game in Freedom, Pennsylvania, where Radbourn sat in the grandstand and "was regarded of more importance than the game, and was gazed at as a wonder." In Pittsburgh, the wonder took the box—Bancroft was apparently willing to abuse his exhausted hero, yet again, to lure more customers to an exhibition game—and shut out the American Association's Alleghenies, 9–0, before a crowd of about one thousand.

Three days later, at Philadelphia's Recreation Park, Radbourn returned to the box for the last game of the regular season. The Phillies were playing to win, shooting for forty victories on the season, "but Bancroft and Radbourn wouldn't have it." Radbourn could have turned the ball over to Conley, but he wanted to cross the finish line himself on that October 15, and with Bancroft's blessings, he did. No one on hand quite seemed to grasp that this was one of baseball's historic afternoons—a day for carving in stone a record to stand forever. "The weather was cold, and the crowd was small and unenthusiastic," the *Philadelphia Inquirer* reported. But Radbourn, indifferent as always to his audience, was ready to work, and poured out the last of his strength on his season-long masterpiece. He was simply brilliant, holding the Phillies to five scattered hits and winning 8–0, his eleventh shut-out of the season. After suffering untold agony for months, Radbourn had reached the plateau of fifty-nine victories in a single season against only twelve defeats, a towering achievement that has never been matched—and surely never will be.

By any measure, Radbourn had completed a season of unparalleled brilliance. Statistics derived with the help of computers a century later would show he won the pitching "triple crown"—leading the league in victories, earned run average (a microscopic 1.38), and strikeouts (441). He led the league in winning percentage (.831), games pitched (75), games started (73), complete games (73), innings pitched (678 2/3), and batters faced (2,672). Only one pitcher in major league history ever threw more innings in a single season: Will White, who barely edged him out with 680 innings, in 1879. But White, then a balding twenty-four-year-old who wore wire-rimmed glasses, had done it for a fifth-place team, the Cincinnati Reds, at a time when pitchers threw far fewer hard, arm-destroying curveballs. Radbourn did it, winning day after day. The final League standings were a testament to his grit:

	W	L	PCT.	GB
PROVIDENCE	84	28	.750	—
Boston	73	38	.658	10½
Buffalo	64	47	.577	19½
New York	62	50	.554	22
Chicago	62	50	.554	22
Philadelphia	39	73	.348	45
Cleveland	35	77	.313	49
Detroit	28	84	.250	56

By now, Providence fanatics were worrying about what would become of Radbourn the next season. Thus far, he had not indicated what he would do, but it seemed clear that, as a free agent who had just turned in the greatest season ever, he could sell his services at sky-high prices. Still, the *Journal* offered its readers hope: Radbourn had been treated well by the public and the management—at least after Sweeney's abrupt departure—and "a 'little bird' has whispered that he likes Providence better than any other city in the country."

The little bird may have known a secret: Carrie Stanhope loved him and wanted him to stay.

The Best on Earth

On Friday, October 17, some seven thousand citizens packed downtown Providence's Union Depot and the dusty open plaza next to it, Exchange Place, waiting for the headlight of a certain Shore Line train to pierce the cold night air. Small firecrackers popped and fizzed. Some of the revelers had been drinking all afternoon, starting the party early, and their laughter and songs carried over the buzz of conversation and the chuffing of trains pulling in and out of the station. Prostitutes, turning on the charm, wound their way through the crowd, finding men who wanted to take their arm for the night. Burly policemen with bright copper badges waved the good-natured throng back from the tracks, trying to keep a path clear. Inside the building, the ladies' waiting room was packed with excited women. Men and boys perched atop railroad cars, trucks, boxes, and barrels, and in a penned area in the center of the station, they clambered on top of the baggage, transforming it into a "pyramid of humanity."

As the one engine they were waiting for hove into sight at last, the crowd began to applaud. Chugging and huffing, belching gray smoke into the dark sky, passing through the downtown and past the rim of the Cove, the great locomotive shrieked and sighed as it slowed to a stop in the station, inching through the crowd. The throng roared with joy. The twenty musicians of White's Military Band, stationed in the gallery of the train station's great waiting room, broke into "Hail to the Chief." This time it wasn't Charlie Sweeney who was the little god of Providence, but rather a man who was determined to be regarded as the best but had scant interest in the fuss that came with it. "As Radbourne left the cars and began to walk through this long line of humanity, followed by the remainder of the club, the people set up a great shout," the *Brooklyn Eagle*'s correspondent reported. "Cheers followed cheers. The ladies waved their handkerchiefs and the small boys yelled like tigers." Men eagerly shook the players' hands and pounded them on the back. From the gallery, ladies dropped bouquets to the men. Many in the crowd spotted the cascading mustache on the skinny, pale face of Frank Bancroft, and rushed to shake the hand of the proverbially lucky man who had reached the summit of a brilliant baseball career. Unnamed "lady friends" presented him with a large basket of flowers. Students from Brown University broke into a roaring college cheer—"Rah-rah! Rah-rah! Bassett!"—for their onetime classmate who had done yeoman's work as a utility infielder, and then led three cheers for Radbourn. The Grays had to squeeze and push their way through the crowd, despite a police escort. No one had seen such an outpouring of emotion in Rhode Island since its boys returned in 1865, safe at long last from the horror and carnage of the Civil War.

The grinning players were led out of the depot to barouches in Exchange Place, lit brilliantly now with carmine-colored gas shoots. There, the reception committee thrust huge brooms into the players' hands, symbolizing their sweep of the opposition—notably Boston in Radbourn's glorious August series. Each player slung his broom over his shoulder, climbed into a horse-drawn carriage, and waited for the marching band to line up. A detachment of the Providence Marine Artillery made the crowd flinch by firing off eleven cannon rounds—symbolizing Providence's eleven-victory margin over second-place Boston.

Then the parade set out on a circuitous route for the Narragansett Hotel through the usually dark and forlorn streets of the smoky downtown, on this autumn night brilliantly alive and illuminated. Every twenty feet or so, the men marching in the "rocket brigade" set off an explosion of red fire, lighting up hundreds of excited faces. Wheezing fireworks exploded everywhere, spawning shrieks and laughter. Thousands marched in the wake of the parade, which passed right by Carrie Stanhope's boardinghouse. Proud residents packed the sidewalks, many of them discharging Roman candles, and pretty women leaned out of upper-floor windows, greeting the conquering heroes with applause and fluttering handkerchiefs. The players' faces, clearly visible as they rode by, revealed boyish surprise and joy. "Everybody was on the street; in fact, the quiet town seemed torn up by the roots," the *Sporting Life* noted. "Some men are born great, some achieve greatness, but if you are in a champion base ball club you have greatness thrust upon you and are nearly choked to death and smothered with red fire," the *Evening Telegram*'s editorial writer quipped.

At the Narragansett Hotel, another waiting crowd burst out and waved wildly as the men arrived. Brown students, obtaining choice spots, outscreamed the others with their college cheers: three cheers for each member of the club, and "three times three for Bassett and Radbourne." As the men entered, lady and gentlemen guests of the hotel applauded. Some of the state's most prominent men crowded the rotunda. The players, still clutching their satchels from their long road trip, made their way through the adoring mob in the lobby to the top of the grand staircase, where they basked in more cheers from the crowd below. All in all, the Grays enjoyed a greater reception "than would have been tendered either of the Presidential candidates, had they visited the city," the *Telegram* opined. Then their hosts led them to a private parlor for an elegant hot supper with local baseball writers and director Ned Allen. Their table was adorned with colorful bouquets, with a boutonniere on each plate. Over their meal, the players ribbed each other and traded baseball yarns. They seemed "in the best of health and spirits," thrilled to be home again, the *Journal* noted. At nine o'clock the dinner came to a close, and the exhausted but happy and well-fed players were permitted to go. They had more work to do the following afternoon.

The relentless Bancroft had arranged for two postseason exhibition games against Cincinnati's Reds, a strong American Association team that had posted an impressive .624 winning percentage even though it had finished a disappointing fifth. Though Saturday afternoon in Providence proved cloudy, damp, and cold, a thousand people turned out for the opener of the meaningless set—"at League prices," meaning a 50¢ admission, the *Sporting Life* marveled. Radbourn, who had gone through the agonizing ritual of warming up, strolled to the pitcher's box at the Messer Street Grounds for the last time in 1884. His goal, at this point, was to retain his value and sign the lucrative 1885 contract that a bidding war for his ser-

vices would undoubtedly precipitate. He was superb against the American
Association team, holding the Reds to two hits, winning 4–1.

On the following Monday, only six hundred people paid their way into
the Messer Street Grounds, a turnout that hardly seemed to justify Cincinnati's weekend hotel expenses. Still, other clubs had it worse: Cleveland attracted all of twenty-six paying customers to its final exhibition game, a
death rattle before the collapse of the franchise. Bancroft rested Radbourn
and Gilligan and started Eddie Conley, who was anxious to get back to Holy
Cross College that month and resume his studies. Conley proved sharp, surrendering only four hits, and the always dazzling Cliff Carroll made "three
phenomenal catches," but the Grays halfheartedly ran themselves out of
potentially big innings, and with darkness and cold approaching, the umpire called the game after nine innings, with the score locked 2–2. On that
unsatisfying note, baseball on Messer Street ended for 1884.

Barney Gilligan sat in the grandstand in his street clothes, his hands half
beaten to hamburger, happy to have the day off. But during the game, he
was called out onto the field and over to home plate to receive a $175 gift

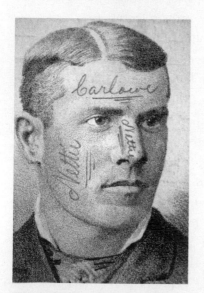

Barney Gilligan, 1884 scorecard.
Closeup shows name of Nettie B.
Carlowe (an admirer?) scrawled
across his face.

(worth about $4,100 in modern money):
a beautiful engraved Springfield watch,
with a charm attached in the form a
shield, featuring crossed bats on one
side and a monogram on the other. He
was also awarded cuff links in the form
of $5 gold pieces, monogrammed—"a
present from a lady friend," who presumably was in the crowd, smiling and waving as he opened the gift. The audience
applauded the plucky little catcher who
had done so much to help Radbourn
achieve baseball immortality. Smiling
broadly, Gilligan raised his derby hat to
the crowd in gratitude.

More celebrating followed at eleven
the next morning, when the Grays gathered at the Providence docks. Only one
player failed to join the party—the sul-

len Radbourn, curiously apart, even now. Rad tended to be embarrassed by hoopla, but what he was doing instead was not recorded. He may have spent the day enjoying his own festivities with Carrie Stanhope. Despite his absence, some 110 baseball-obsessed guests were happy to join the boys, including Congressman Henry J. Spooner, Grays president Henry T. Root and chairman Allen, Cincinnati star Pop Snyder, and Detroit outfielder George Wood. The party boarded the steamer *City of Newport* for a brief trip across Narragansett Bay to East Providence. Moments after the crowd disembarked onto the dock of the Vue de l'Eau Club, a popular pleasure resort, the fun began in the October sun. "Coats were thrown aside, and the ball-players and their friends entered with spirit and complete abandon into the pleasures of the hour," the *Journal* reported. On level ground to the east of the clubhouse, the professionals joined with the dazzled novices in playing a game of baseball, treating them as equals. Others played football, or even enjoyed a friendly bout with boxing gloves. Root and Allen worked the crowd, making sure everyone was having a good time. There was one troubling moment: Cyclone Miller, going out for a football pass, ran into some barbed wire and toppled over a stone wall, cutting his face and neck. But it did not seem to cast much of a pall over the celebration.

At 2:00 p.m., a clanging dinner bell summoned the men from their sports. They sat down, appetites sharpened by a morning of exercise in the open air, to the quintessential Rhode Island institution of the clambake, popular at the resorts along the bay. The clams were steamed on hot stones, blanketed with seaweed and covered with a tarpaulin. Rhode Islanders loved tugging the sweet meat from the shell, dipping it in warm, melted butter, and popping it into their mouths. Still, the "savory bivalve could hardly maintain its supremacy" among side dishes of sweet corn, lobster, fish, and sausage, all washed down with foaming mugs of beer and topped off with watermelon. "Pleasure ruled the hour, and to the cross-fire of wit and friendly badinage the merry laughter of the party played a fitting accompaniment," the *Journal* reported. After the dinner ended and blue cigar smoke curled up around the tables, the speeches began. Colonel John C. Wyman, a local politico, delivered the twenty-minute keynote address, and concluded by calling up the players, one at a time, cracking jokes about each of them—Barney Gilligan, Joe Start (now an ancient forty-two, having

celebrated his birthday a few days earlier), Jack Farrell, Jerry Denny, Arthur
Irwin, Cliff Carroll, Paul Hines, Paul Revere Radford, Miah Murray, Cyclone
Miller, Eddie Conley, and Charlie Bassett. Wyman pinned on the proud
chest of each a handsome gold badge with a blue bar, with *Champions 1884*
engraved on front; on the back were crossed bats and balls. "I would rather
wear that badge than be president of the United States," Denny proudly told
the gathering. The players (and Bancroft) also received handsome crayon
portraits of themselves in "massive gold frames" and gold watch charms
in the form of a rooster, symbol of the state's famous Rhode Island Red, a
notoriously tough bird, much like the members of the state's famous baseball team. More speeches followed, none recorded—by the congressman,
by Allen, and, finally, by manager Frank Bancroft. The group then went
outside for more play on the fields, until the steamer docked at five o'clock
to take them home.

The season was almost over. One piece of history making remained,
however, and this time Old Hoss Radbourn would be at the center of it.

Baseball's original World Series was set to begin two days later at the Polo
Grounds in New York City. Bancroft had been negotiating for weeks with an
old friend, adversary, and fellow showman, Jim "Smilin' Jeems" Mutrie, the
cigar-puffing thirty-three-year-old manager of New York's Metropolitans,
famous for his handlebar mustache, tall derby hat, striped pants, and Prince
Albert coat. The talks had dragged on for so long, in fact, that some wondered whether the Grays lacked the courage to face the strong American
Association champion. The truth was, baseball had not yet established its
classic best-of-seven World Series formula, and Mutrie and Bancroft had to
work out all the details, including how many games to play, where to play
them, under what rules, and, perhaps most important, how to divide up
the money. Even the name of the series was in flux. Bancroft wrote that the
teams were competing for the "Championship of America," but some reporters were already referring to the series as a battle for the "world's championship." So a version of "World Series" was present from the beginning.

Baseball men had already discovered that, without something meaning-
ful at stake, postseason exhibitions had a tendency to tumble into absurdity,

with players going through the motions as
the public's interest dwindled in bitterly
cold weather. Bancroft had an idea for inspiring the men to play their hearts out,
drawing big crowds until the series was
decided. He proposed that the players on
each team pool their money for a stake of
$1,000. With their own money at risk, and
the prospect of winning $1,000 more, the
men would fight ferociously. Mutrie proposed that each club put up $1,000 but gen-
erously give the proceeds to "the poor of
the city represented by the club winning"
the series.

It would never happen, sneered the
baseball editor of the *Fall River Daily Evening News*, who well remembered Mutrie
from his days as shortstop, captain, and

Jim Mutrie

manager of the Fall River club in 1876 and 1877, and as a shortstop for Bancroft's New Bedford team in 1878. The two managers, the writer charged,
were merely "getting up some free advertising" by talking about a $2,000
pot. "This blowing about what each club can do, and these bets—with the
mouth—remind us of those days when Bancroft used to arrange games
between the Fall Rivers and New Bedfords, and when announcements
were quite flaming." The son of a Scotsman, Mutrie—already nicknamed
"Truthful James" because he had a tendency to be less than so—could be
tight with the purse strings. "The Mets and Providences may play, but no
money will be put up. Mutrie don't put up."

Furthermore, the notion of players' wagering troubled some of baseball's
graybeards. Veteran sportswriter Henry Chadwick, a moralistic old-timer
who ranted about modern baseball's failings from his post at the *Brooklyn
Eagle*, alerted National League president Abraham G. Mills to the impropri-
ety of what was essentially a high-stakes bet on the outcome. Mills seemed
to share some of his worries. "But, while the project strikes me unfavorably,
and, as you say, looks like a lowering of the dignity of the League, and of the

game, yet I hardly think it would open the door of 'crookedness,' any form of which I am certainly as bitter a foe to as you can be," he wrote to Chadwick. Mills noted that Henry T. Root, the president of the Providence club, had "for many years been one of the pillars of the League, and that if this project has his sanction, he certainly has good reasons therefor[e]." Still, he wrote privately to Root on the same day, expressing his concern.

Bancroft responded defensively in a public letter. "I regret very much that any one would misinterpret our intentions and not understand the drift of the challenge," he stated. The stake would simply inspire the men to play harder, tending to make the games more competitive, and less like the halfhearted exhibitions that raised questions about players' motives. "As the players subscribe the funds themselves to make up the prize we think it a pretty sure guarantee that they intend playing the games in a manner to elevate instead of degrading it."

In the end, though, he dropped the idea, as apparently more trouble than it was worth, and agreed to a series played for a split of gate receipts. Mutrie, quite reasonably, proposed a best-of-five set, with two in New York, two in Providence, and the fifth, if needed, at a neutral site. Some believed a five-game series between the great champions might draw huge crowds, perhaps seventy-five thousand people. But Bancroft, unwilling to pour so much travel money into the affair and looking to maximize profits—not surprisingly, he never warmed to the suggestion of playing for charity—talked Mutrie instead into a three-game series at New York's Polo Grounds, where turnout would be biggest. Providence's loyal rooters would just have to live with being denied any home games. Bancroft was even willing to play the World Series under American Association rules, with an important caveat: National League pitching rules would be applied, giving Radbourn the freedom to throw exactly as he had during the season.

Mutrie believed his well-balanced Mets were poised to win, proving to the baseball world that the American Association, after three seasons, had become the National League's equal, if not its superior. He boasted to all who would listen about "how easily his Metropolitan crew could put the Providence gang on the blink," Bancroft recalled, "and he seemed very anxious to get a whack at us." For all of Mutrie's confidence, Bancroft felt good about the Grays' chances. The National League was clearly the better circuit, and Providence had easily outshone its opponents. Still, it did not escape Frank's notice that the battle would take place after his men had spent days off being wined and dined, growing sluggish, having "the time of their lives"; in baseball even a few days off can cost men their edge and their timing. "The boys were hardly in shape to play championship ball at the time," Bancroft recalled, "but, after a consultation, they decided to get together and try to trim Mutrie's aggregation." The fiercely competitive Radbourn was surely one of the men most intent on showing once and for all who was the best. The first World Series was on.

It is no surprise that both the American Association and National League had franchises in America's biggest market, New York City. But it is intriguing that the same men—primarily Mutrie and Manhattan tobacconist John Day—owned both clubs, operating them under the umbrella of their Metropolitan Exhibition Company, a situation rife with conflicts of interest. Mutrie and Day had treated their Mets like a less-loved child. To compete in the older and markedly superior National League, they steered their best players to the Gothams rather than the Metropolitans. And while the two teams shared the Polo Grounds, the owners gave the Gothams the better end of the deal. On days when both clubs had games scheduled, a canvas fence was drawn across the park's massive left field, creating playing space for two games. The Gothams roamed on the side with the park's handsome grandstand, charging 50¢ admission through the Fifth Avenue gate; the Mets, charging 25¢ through the Sixth Avenue gate, were shoved onto a portion with makeshift stands and a shabby field. Double-barreled games created some problems, of course: The playing area was cramped, and balls sometimes slipped over or under the canvas, interrupting play on the other side. Moreover, Mills was a stickler about the National League's ban on liquor in all parks, and forced Day and Mutrie to close down their lucrative saloon at the Polo Grounds, even on days when the Gothams were not playing there. That meant a significant loss of revenue, a high price for the Metropolitan Exhibition Company to pay to keep one foot in the League camp.

To get around such troubles, Day and Mutrie hastily built a new wooden park on the cheap for the Metropolitans to use on days when the Gothams were at the Polo Grounds. Unlovely Metropolitan Park, located on 108th Street, was built atop an old city dump, with a bumpy field and a rough-hewn wooden grandstand. Located near the East River, it was susceptible to whipping winds that shuttled fly balls in unpredictable directions, while wafting noxious fumes from nearby factories over the stands, making watching a game there highly unpleasant. As for the field, it was loaded with rotting waste not far below the surface. Mets player Jack Lynch joked that "you could go down for a grounder and come up with six months of malaria." The park was a flop, the main reason the Mets lost $8,000 in spite of their pennant triumph, and the club abandoned it after 1884.

The American Association had expanded that season from eight to an unwieldy twelve teams, and New York—after finishing a respectable fourth in 1883—suddenly found itself thrust into a seven-team pennant race with the Columbus, Louisville, St. Louis, Cincinnati, Baltimore, and the Athletics of Philadelphia. The Mets clinched the pennant on October 1, behind the solid pitching of Jack Lynch (37–15, 2.67 earned run average) and Tim Keefe (37–17, 2.25) and the hard hitting of first baseman Dave Orr (American Association batting champion, at .354), third baseman Dude Esterbrook (.314), and center fielder Chief Roseman (.298). Though they were series underdogs by virtue of the American Association's general inferiority, the Metropolitans were a fine professional club, with two superb pitchers and home-field advantage. They had every reason to believe that, with strong performances from their starters, a psychological boost from the hometown crowd, and a bit of luck, they could sneak away with the title of world champion.

The well-fed and feted Grays set out in good spirits for the big city. During the trip, Radbourn had time to mull over the weaknesses of Mets batters he had faced in the past. He had no intention of letting this opponent mar his reputation, and he quite evidently considered the series worth the strongest effort he could muster after months of torturing his arm. "These will probably be the greatest games ever played," the *Sporting Life* enthused, "and will be the first time in the history of the game that the champion teams of two associations have met in a formal series to decide superiority. If the weather is fine their meeting will be witnessed by larger crowds than have ever been seen on the Polo Grounds."

* * *

The weather was fine enough on Wednesday afternoon, the day before the series began, registering a balmy 76 degrees in Manhattan. But just before 6:00 p.m., as thousands of amateur ballplayers were lining up for a grand torchlight parade through the downtown celebrating the Mets' pennant victory, raindrops began to spit down. Over the next seven hours, a wind-driven storm deluged the city, washing out the parade.

The rain clouds cleared out before the World Series opener on Thursday, October 23, but by then the temperature in Manhattan had plummeted, with cutting winds that helped dry the field but made 51 degrees at game time feel more like 31. Some twenty-five hundred people huddled in the stands at the Polo Grounds, their eyes tearing up when gusts blasted them in the face and made the ballpark's flags snap like gunfire. "A cold, raw wind blew across the grounds with considerable force, and made even the players

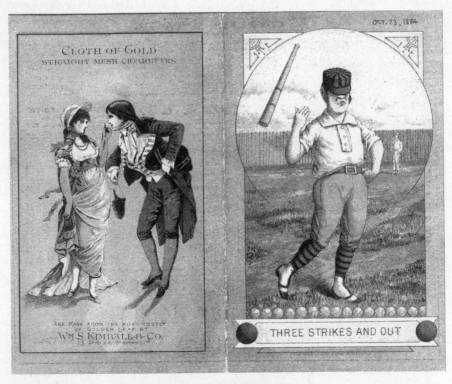

Back and front of scorecard, first game of 1884 World Series

shiver at times," the *Journal* reported. With better weather, the correspondent speculated, three times that crowd would have turned out for such a classic baseball spectacle.

Tim Keefe

Adding to the hometown gloom was a nagging wrist injury that sidelined Jack Lynch, the scheduled starter. The Mets sent out their tall, slender, red-haired ace, twenty-seven-year-old Tim Keefe. Like Barney Gilligan, Keefe was born in the 1850s in Cambridge, Massachusetts, the son of Irish immigrants: his mother, one Mary Leary, and his father, Patrick, a builder. Proud of his carefully waxed handlebar mustache, Keefe was nicknamed "Sir Timothy" for his native intelligence and gentlemanly deportment on and off the field, but he was also a fierce competitor who would win 342 major-league games, and as worthy a foe as Radbourn ever faced. Keefe had thrown 1,102 innings and won seventy-eight regular-season games over just the previous two seasons, including both ends of a memorable doubleheader against the Buckeyes of Columbus on July 4, 1883, when he pitched a one-hitter followed by a two-hitter. But he entered the series tired and aching himself. The opener was, in effect, a test of the resilience of two right-handed pitchers who had been worked excessively hard for two years and had every reason to feel exhausted.

As the Grays trotted onto the field, Radbourn strode to the box, hearing light applause ripple through the Polo Grounds stands, a show of grudging respect from fanatics who had watched him humble the hometown Gothams all season, beating them in five of six decisions here. Charlie blew two quick strikes past the Mets' leadoff man, shortstop Jack Nelson, putting him in a hole. But Nelson managed to slap a grounder to third, which Denny, prouder than the president, threw wide to first baseman Joe Start, and the batter reached first base safely. It was an inauspicious start for the

Grays, and perhaps an uncharacteristic sign of nerves. Providence quickly got its act together, though, as Mets right fielder Steve Brady skied a foul ball that Providence catcher Gilligan grabbed after it bounced once—an out under American Association rules. New York third baseman Dude Esterbrook then hit a sharp grounder to his counterpart Denny, who fired the ball to first, getting his man this time. Nelson, who had reached second on the play, scurried to third on a wild pitch by Radbourn and was ninety feet away from scoring the first run ever in a World Series; but he was stranded there when Old Hoss struck out center fielder Chief Roseman.

Now it was the Grays' turn. Keefe was working without his battery mate, Bill Holbert, who was banged up, and had to settle for Charlie Reipschlager, Lynch's partner. Reipschlager seemed out of his element, while Keefe quickly found it tough to grip the ball and control his pitches on that sharp and windy afternoon. His first pitch, against the Grays' leadoff man and sole .300 hitter, Paul Hines, was a strike. But then Keefe grazed him with a pitch—and, under American Association rules, the batter was allowed to take his base. Hines quickly got into scoring position on a wild pitch. Cliff Carroll then was hit by a pitch and took first. Radbourn came to the plate, and Keefe and Reipschlager continued having trouble meshing. A ball scooted past the catcher—ruled a passed ball—and Hines raced to third; on another, Carroll got to second, still with no one out. Radbourn, hoping to drive in some runs, dumped a ball toward shallow left field, but the whipping wind blew it back into the hands of shortstop Nelson for the first out. Joe Start, another good hitter who knew a thing or two about moving runners along, slapped a grounder to the right side of the diamond into the hands of second baseman Dasher Troy, who retired him at first. Still, that was good enough to bring home Hines with the first run in World Series history. When Keefe uncorked a wild pitch—no blaming the catcher this time—Carroll quickly broke for home. Keefe, whose head uncharacteristically seemed to be someplace else than in the game, hurt his own cause when he failed to hustle to the plate in time to catch the runner barreling in from third. The Grays led 2–0 after one frame.

In the third inning, the Mets started floundering again. Paul Hines rapped a single, and got to second on a passed ball. A Keefe wild pitch sent him to third, and *another* wild pitch brought him home, putting Providence up 3–0. "One may see, therefore, that Mets patterns are firmly imbedded in the fabric of tradition and that there really is nothing new in baseball," *New York Times* columnist Leonard Koppett quipped in 1965, writing about the first World Series at a time when the modern "Amazin' Mets" were engaging in similar feats of stumbling and bumbling—though the modern version, at least, was equipped with gloves.

Radbourn, meanwhile, had somehow found the strength to utterly bamboozle the Mets hitters. He struck out the side in the third, putting on a "masterly exhibition of strategic skill," even though he was not throwing the ball as swiftly as "half the pitchers of the American clubs," Henry Chadwick noted in his report for the *Brooklyn Eagle*. Throughout the game, Radbourn's well-disguised change of pace, his ability to confuse hitters, and his matchless control silenced the Mets.

The press described New York's struggle as a loss of nerve, almost a moral failing. "The Metropolitans plainly showed that they were afraid of Radbourn," the *Boston Globe* asserted. The *New York Times* was even more disparaging. "The curves of Radbourne struck terror to their hearts, and they fell easy victims to his skill. Some of the local players who have good batting records were like so many children in the hands of the pitcher of the Providence team. They made ineffectual plunges at balls that would reflect discredit on some of our third rate amateurs."

Although the odds were now running against them, the Mets were still within striking distance in the seventh inning, trailing 3–0. But the Grays began hammering the sore and tired Keefe. Farrell clubbed a double to left field, and Irwin drove a ball over the third baseman's head that left fielder Ed Kennedy sprinted for, in a desperate attempt to grab it on the fly, only to see it shoot by him for a triple. Gilligan drove Irwin home with a single, and Denny followed with another hit. By the time the inning was over, the game was out of New York's reach, 6–0. For the rest of the way, Radbourn elegantly shut down the Mets. When it was over, he had allowed no runs and only two hits, and had won the first game of the series. The shivering New York crowd, used to seeing the Mets triumph, went home disappointed in the whole spectacle. "AFRAID OF RADBOURN: Provincial Providence pummels the Metropolitans," the *Boston Globe* roared in its headline. If Radbourn could keep up this level of performance in the teeth of pain, no one could beat him.

Disappointed that the crowd had not been bigger, Day and Mutrie sus-

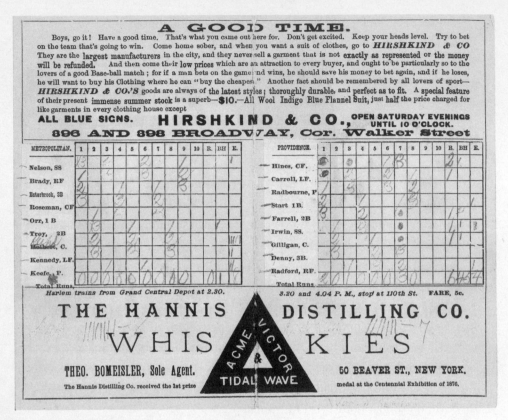

One attendee's scoring of first World Series game

pended their "free list" for game two, insisting that everyone pay the full half-dollar price to get into the Polo Grounds. Few did. Providence's blatant superiority—not to mention temperatures in the forties—slashed the turn-out on Friday, October 24, to only one thousand. The Metropolitans needed to win that afternoon to remain in the fight for the title of world champion. There was not much of a margin for error in a three-game series.

The Metropolitans seemed to realize that, and treated their followers to a far superior performance this time. "Both teams, especially the Mets, fielded grandly, and from start to finish the game was stubbornly contested," the *New York Times* reported. Sir Timothy and Old Hoss met again, and this time Keefe had his battery mate Bill Holbert, which seemed to help. Each pitcher was on his game, each dead set on winning, retiring every man—one, two, three—through the first four innings, and by the fifth, "the interest in the game was at a fever pitch," the *Times* noted. That's when Providence's big veteran, Jack Farrell, tried to light a spark. After he singled, Farrell made a dash for second, attempting a steal. Catcher Holbert "threw him out by about five feet," the *Times* asserted, but umpire Jack Remsen, center fielder for the American Association's Brooklyn club, declared Farrell safe, to the astonishment and disgust of the Polo Grounds denizens, who had never been shy about raging at umpires. After Irwin made the second out of the inning, Barney Gilligan rocketed a double, driving home Farrell with the first run. Then Jerry Denny, the club's top home run hitter during the regular season (with six), strode to the plate and stared keenly at Keefe. He got the pitch he wanted, and launched it over the picket fence in center field for a two-run homer, giving Providence a 3–0 lead, a strong edge with Radbourn in the box.

In the bottom of the inning, the Mets finally got on the scoreboard for the first time in the series. But it was not much of an achievement. Chief Roseman drizzled an infield grounder to short, got to third on Irwin's rushed, wild throw to first, and scored an unearned run when Jack Farrell, hurrying to throw him out at home on a subsequent grounder, muffed the ball. With Providence leading 3–1, the pitchers then held on, throwing scoreless ball in the sixth and seventh innings.

In the top of the eighth inning, the Grays poured on two more runs, but it was getting dark, and at 4:55 p.m. Remsen called the game, the score reverting to the 3–1 tally at the end of seven complete innings. By then, the crowd and the players were almost too cold to care, and everyone could see Providence was the better team, bound to win. The Metropolitans did not even bother to put up a fight about shortening the game—and with that, the Grays had captured baseball's first World Series.

In its analysis of the deciding game, the *Times* groused some more about the stolen base call. But there was really one reason the Mets had been beaten soundly in two games, and it wasn't umpiring. "Radbourne," the *Times* lamented, "was an insurmountable obstacle for the Metropolitans." He won both his starts, while surrendering a grand total of five hits, and pitching sixteen innings without allowing an earned run. In short, his unmatched brilliance in 1884 was emphatically carrying into the postseason.

Since the clubs had set aside Saturday, October 25, for baseball anyway, the Metropolitans decided to get in a third game, even if it counted for nothing but a few more dollars in receipts. Only five hundred people came out in blustery, 52-degree weather for the end of an extraordinary season. When the Grays saw all the empty seats, they "turned up their noses and said they would not play," the *Times* reported. The game meant nothing, and many of the men preferred getting their winter break under way to pocketing the few dollars per man such a thin crowd would produce. In their attempt to squirm out of another day's work, the Grays stubbornly rejected every umpire the Mets proposed, until New York pledged to accept any man Providence captain Joe Start might name—up to and including Frank Bancroft. Finally, Arthur Bell, the treasurer of the Metropolitan Exhibition Company, pointedly reminded the Grays that they had drawn poorly themselves in Providence, and insisted "he would not disappoint his patrons if [there] were only 10 persons within the enclosure." The impassioned little speech "brought Bancroft's pets to their senses," and they reluctantly played, though the late-October conditions were miserable. "A keen northwest wind swept across the field and thoroughly chilled the players as well as the spectators, and rendered the game a drag," the *Journal* reported.

After two straight days of pitching, Keefe gave his aching arm a break, turned over his pitching duties to twenty-five-year-old Buck Becannon, and served as umpire. But indomitable to the last, Old Hoss came out to work his exhausted arm one more time. Providence scored a run in the first and two in the second, while Radbourn, determined to prove something even now, methodically shut down the Mets. In the top of the fifth, the Grays broke it open, taking a 7–0 lead. While the New Yorkers eked out runs in the fifth and sixth, the Grays added four more, to hammer the home club 11–2. "The Metropolitans played most wretchedly both at the bat and in the field," the *Boston Globe* reported, "and proved mere children in the hands of the Providence men." After six innings of play, everyone had seen enough. Keefe called the game on account of darkness, and the 1884 season was over.

The Grays walked off the field with a silk pennant valued at $100, half of the gross receipts (about $75 per player, Bancroft recalled), and a new title, according to a *Sporting Life* headline: "CHAMPIONS OF THE WORLD," a name that has stuck to World Series winners to this day. (Or, as the *Fall River Daily*

Evening News put it, "They are the 'Champions of this Mundane Sphere.'") Over the three games, the Grays had walloped the Mets 20–3. Radbourn won all three, allowing zero earned runs, while holding Mutrie's team to a wretched .142 batting average. Shortstop Arthur Irwin never forgot the great pitcher's performance over those three remarkable days in Manhattan. "He was as strong in the third game as in the first, and could have easily worked four games in a row without a day's rest," Irwin said in a 1915 interview.

Jim Mutrie was devastated. "Well, the result of that series just about broke Mutrie's heart," Bancroft recalled. "The Providence men put it all over his men, knocked them silly and then tamped on them. It was a clean victory, and, as the New Yorkers failed to win one of the games, they could not even squeal." For the Grays, winning the first World Series was the perfect coda to an extraordinary season. "After beating up the Metropolitans," Bancroft noted, "no fields remained to be conquered, and we patted each other on the back and called ourselves the best on earth."

Before the team broke up, there was a little matter of Radbourn's free agency to settle. At some point, Ned Allen called Radbourn into his hotel room and pointed to a table. On it was the great pitcher's release, as promised; next to it was a blank contract, which Allen asked Radbourn to complete with any dollar amount he thought plausible. If Charlie picked up the release and walked out of the room, that meant his days with Providence were over, his dream fulfilled. Radbourn, a poor reader at best, looked at both documents for several minutes. Then, to Allen's amazement, he filled in a figure for the new season, and tore up the release. "Allen almost fell on his neck and wept for joy," sportswriter Jacob C. Morse recounted. Radbourn, who could not write, knew enough to scrawl in $4,000, making him one of baseball's best-paid pitchers. Still, it was far from an extravagant amount, given the year he had just had.

And so, after all that effort, all that pain, Radbourn was returning to the Grays. It was as if what had really mattered to him all that time, during months of acute pain, was simply proving that he could do it, or, as the *Brooklyn Eagle* put it, "to fulfill a boast of his prowess as a pitcher." Once he had proved himself the master of his fate and cracked the $4,000 plateau, he seemed to lose interest in leaving.

But there was another explanation for his decision to stay. The directors had always harbored the hope that Radbourn would sign up again, and for good reason. "They knew there was a girl in Providence who was pretty sweet on the pitcher, and they did not forget to tell him," Bancroft recalled. The attractive and fashionable Caroline Stanhope, it seems, had broken through this sullen man's tough hide to his vulnerable heart, inspiring him to stay on in 1885. Radbourn, the churlish loner who had fought with pure grit to win his freedom, in the end gave it up, and surrendered once again to the bondage of Providence and the reserve clause, for the love of a woman.

The Grays went their separate ways, catching trains out of New York. After his arm had recovered some, Charlie Radbourn was soon enjoying what he perhaps loved best, next to baseball and Carrie: wandering in the wilds of Illinois, away from humans and their incessant chatter and demands, taking the occasional swig of whiskey, screwing the top back on, and listening intently for the sound of stirring animals. When he saw a quail lift from the brush, he quickly raised his shotgun, followed it steadily, and pulled the trigger, feeling the recoil slam his sore shoulder as the shot echoed through the woods. The bird dropped to the tall grass.

He was the best, no doubt about it.

Called Out
by the Inexorable Umpire

> How swiftly grows the laurel in Fame's glades;
> But not as swiftly as the laurel fades;
> The World remembers while they rule—and then
> The World remembers some one else again;
> Sweeney and Radbourne . . .
> Or all the rest who one day ruled supreme
> Within the borders of a golden dream,
> Who held their day beneath the olive bough—
> Where are they now?
>
> —Grantland Rice, syndicated columnist, 1915

The Union Association, which had threatened to shake the foundations of the National League, collapsed after one season. But it did succeed in destroying the Cleveland franchise, opening up a slot for Henry Lucas's St. Louis club in 1885. Over Providence's fierce objections, Lucas the "Wrecker" got what he wanted all along: entrée into the National League. And Charlie Sweeney, Radbourn's nemesis, was his pitcher.

Sweeney had won twenty-four games for St. Louis in 1884, on top of seventeen in Providence, making forty-one on the year. That was a brilliant record, to be sure, but the numbers do not capture how his contemporaries

281

regarded his performance over that remarkable season. Sweeney was so overpowering in so many games that he struck many observers as one of the best pitchers of all time, if not *the* best. John M. Ward, for example, a highly intelligent man who knew his baseball, considered Sweeney that year "the greatest pitcher in the country, and his equal never existed before or since." Tim Keefe, Radbourn's formidable opponent in the World Series, argued that Sweeney's equal never existed and never would. Tim Murnane, writing for the *Boston Globe* in 1905, called Sweeney "the most difficult man to hit that ever tossed a ball, and this includes [Christy] Mathewson." Many others shared that view. "He was a man of great strength and power," sportswriter Alfred H. Spink recalled in 1911, "and one of the most skillful pitchers that ever lived." A glorious future seemed to be opening in front of the young flamethrower when he broke free from the orbit of Radbourn's bitter animosity.

But his future proved a blighted one. His 1884 heroics, it turned out, had effectively destroyed his arm, and he would never be the same again. Sweeney's baseball career followed a swift and ruthless downward trajectory marked by ugly squabbles with teammates, whom he liked no better than Radbourn. In 1885 he resumed drinking in earnest and spent much of the season needling journeyman outfielder Emmett Seery. At the end of the year, when the players were gathered in a saloon, Sweeney prepared to leave but stopped off first to say farewell to his supposed enemy, who was warming himself by the stove. "Well, Seery, old man, it isn't likely I will see you again this season, and we may as well part good friends as bad ones," Sweeney said. Seery shook his hand in friendship. "I will give you something to remember me, though," Sweeney added. With his left hand, the *New York Clipper* reported, Sweeney "hit Seery a terrific blow on the face between the eyes, which sent him over the back of his chair, with blood spurting from his nose and mouth." All of their teammates sided with Seery against their star pitcher, whom the *Sporting Life* branded a "whiskey-guzzling cowardly nincompoop."

In 1886, Sweeney obtained a gun permit—one of the last men in the world who should have been given one, considering his hair-trigger temper—after a pack of St. Louis hoodlums attacked him on the street. Sweeney began to "carry a small arsenal in his back pocket," and made it a point on several occasions to "flourish his weapon and threaten to let daylight out of those who happened to be in his way." After getting heaved out of a bar at 2:00 a.m., Sweeney pulled out his revolver and began methodically firing bullets into the front door. The men inside vaulted over the counter and hid among the pop bottles and kegs of beer, or tried to make themselves small behind posts and under tables. Some managed to escape through rear windows, since the doors were locked. Sweeney emptied his smoking revolver, reloaded it, and emptied it again. After he discharged fourteen shots, police appeared on the scene. Sweeney, "in the coolest manner possible, put his revolver in his pocket, laughed and walked away," the *Sporting News* reported. The police discreetly let him go. He was finally thrown off the team in late June after trading blows with another teammate, catcher Tom Dolan. A few years later, after dismal performances in the East, Sweeney headed home to San Francisco, where his psychopathic viciousness, mood swings, and heavy drinking showed few signs of abating.

In 1891, Sweeney was strolling through Golden Gate Park with a young woman named Maggie Kearns, described in one account as "a worthless girl of fifteen years of age," when the couple came across a man named Leek, conductor on the Haight streetcar line, and his buddy, a cable-car grip man named Finch. The two men commenced speaking to Sweeney's shabby doll "in a familiar manner," prompting the ex-athlete to tear off his coat and roll up his sleeves, preparing to fight one or both. Somehow, Leek managed to get Charlie aside, out of range of the girl's ears, to calm him down. But while Sweeney was distracted, Finch absconded with the teenager. The former pitcher exploded with fury and set upon the conductor, beating him over the head and finally knocking him down and jumping on him. The bloodied victim was carried to the aptly named Terminal Hotel at corner of Haight and Stanyan streets, where the newspapers reported he was barely clinging to life. Sweeney had beaten the conductor so savagely, the *Chicago Inter-Ocean* noted, "that Grim Death is likely to punch his ticket."

By July 1894, drunkenness and pain had finished off what was left of his once extraordinary baseball career, and Sweeney was reduced to taking odd jobs. For a time, he ran a saloon on Bryant Street, near Sixth. He tried his hand as a special police officer but, like his father, lost his badge. Eventually he was drawn into the sinister circle of San Francisco mobster Frank "King"

McManus, reportedly as one of his bodyguards as well as a bartender in Mc-Manus's raucous Grand Central Wine Rooms, at 16 Third Street, in the city's Potrero neighborhood. The Irish-born boss, who reached San Francisco via the dangerous trip around the horn of South America, had learned the ways of America as a "race-track habitué" and boardinghouse runner, a man paid by an establishment to bring back boarders by hook or by crook. "Naturally bright, and a leader among men," he quickly rose to become a powerful local figure, a political string puller of some renown and a two-fisted gangster famous for thrashing a prizefighter in front of his establishment. Hundreds of men employed at the Union Iron Works and Pacific Rolling Mills gave him their political allegiance for favors rendered, and regularly visited McManus's saloon, ordering drinks from Sweeney. The King was not a man to be trifled with.

Nor was the King's younger brother, Cornelius "Con" McManus, who two years earlier had been shot in the left breast in a bar brawl with another gangster whom he had stabbed in the side. Both were taken to the Receiving Hospital, and when Con's assailant was stretched out on the operating table, Frank burst in and attempted to beat out his brains with a club. In Frank's world, no one messed with his brother and got away with it. Both victims, improbably, survived.

Charlie and Cornelius were said to be good friends, but on July 15, 1894, both were drinking heavily and arguing while tending Frank's place. "I never knew him in such an ugly mood," Sweeney later said. Early that morning, Con had quarreled violently with the King, almost coming to blows with his ruthless brother. At about 10:00 a.m., Con asked Sweeney to tend bar while he went into a back room to sleep on a lounge. When Con woke up at noon, he "at once he began to abuse me," Sweeney recounted. "While I was serving drinks in the card room upstairs, he came up and struck me. He threw me on the floor and choked me. After that he broke a pitcher and some glasses and threw things around the room like a wild man." Sweeney claimed he begged Con to stop, but when Sweeney went downstairs, Con followed and cuffed him some more.

At some point, Sweeney claimed, McManus pulled out a gun, placed the muzzle against Sweeney's stomach, and held it there for at least a minute and a half, while he "called me all the names he could think of. I did not say a word because I knew he would kill me if I did." Sweeney claimed he fled to the card room, where McManus tackled him, struck him in the face, and drew his hand back to his hip pocket. Certain that McManus was going for his gun, Sweeney pulled out his own pistol and fired, hitting his attacker in the right arm. When McManus, in a rage, struggled to his feet to come after him, Sweeney fired two more shots, one hitting the bar and one passing through McManus's ribs to his liver. In agony and gasping for breath, Con was a threat no more. Sweeney fled the scene before the victim's brother could return. Police found him wandering on Sixth Street. When they disarmed him of his Smith & Wesson pistol and put him in handcuffs, Sweeney burst into tears and cried out, "I'm sorry for what I have done, but I was afraid of him," and he pointed to the marks of Con's fingers on his throat. That night, in his cell, Sweeney "had the appearance of a man on the verge of delirium tremens." His jailers medicated him, and he "sobbed and sniveled until he fell into a profound slumber."

When "King" McManus found his brother dead, he cried out in rage, vowing to kill Sweeney. The King then sought out the Reverend Peter J. Grey, the tough, Irish-born rector of St. Patrick's Church on Mission Street, demanding that he celebrate a requiem Mass in memory of his beloved sibling. When the fearless seventy-four-year-old Father Grey—said to be "an earnest and stern man of the old school"—staunchly refused to honor the unrepentant murderer, Frank smashed the windows of the priest's house and threatened to kill him.

Protected in his jail cell, Sweeney pleaded in the ensuing court trial that he had acted in self-defense. King McManus, he insisted, was using perjured testimony to frame him, and had intimidated and silenced witnesses who could have exonerated him. These were not outlandish arguments. McManus had been implicated the year before, along with state senator William J. Dunn, in reports that he bribed four jurors to secure an innocent verdict for a well-known actor, Maurice B. Curtis, who had shot a police officer to death outside the Mission Hill station. But Sweeney's arguments failed to sway the jury. When it returned with a verdict of guilty for manslaughter, Sweeney's wife fainted in the courtroom. The judged sentenced the famous pitcher to eight years at the state penitentiary at San Quentin, where if violence and hard labor failed to kill him, squalor and disease might well do the trick.

From his jail cell, Sweeney continued to protest his innocence, and when he learned that Frank McManus had died of dropsy in Oakland in October 1896, he redoubled his efforts to win his freedom. (He also wrote a rather eloquent letter from prison challenging Frank Bancroft's account of his final game with the Grays.) Heavyweight boxing champion and baseball fanatic John L. Sullivan, learning of the great pitcher's troubles, enlisted the services of influential Californians in his behalf, "and I know that he will be amply repaid for his kindness when he learns that his exertions are helping me to bring my case to a conclusion," Sweeney wrote to the *Sporting Life.* Many thought that Sweeney was unfairly jailed for defending himself against a worthless gangster. "By good rights," wrote Alfred M. Elias in *Baseball Magazine,* "he ought to have been rewarded for the killing."

The campaign to free Sweeney ultimately worked. California governor James Budd granted him a formal pardon, and in April 1898 the former pitcher walked into the sunlight after four years in the notorious hellhole. Four months later, he was working as an umpire in the California League. Incredibly, though, he had learned nothing about controlling his impulsive rages. When he got wind that Fresno's catcher, one "Midget" Mangerina, had disparaged his umpiring, Sweeney caught up with the young player and administered such a brutal beating that police quickly arrested the ex-con for assault. Two local men supplied his bail, whereupon Sweeney promptly skipped town. Police apprehended him on a San Francisco–bound train during a stop in the town of Newman, about ninety miles away, halfway to the big city. But the next day, when Fresno Deputy Constable Con Angel caught a train to Newman to get his man, he discovered on his arrival that the famous ballplayer had suspiciously managed to give the slip to officers there. Angel returned to Fresno, and Sweeney temporarily vanished from the public eye.

Four years later, Sweeney was reported to be poverty-stricken and deathly ill, suffering from tuberculosis he had contracted in prison. His friends chipped in to keep him from want. In February 1902, he was taken to the City and County Hospital to "await the final summons of death which is fast approaching," a San Francisco paper reported. In his prime, the writer recalled, "Sweeney was the greatest pitcher of the day and was known from Maine to California." A broken man, Radbourn's old adversary died on April 4, nine days short of his thirty-ninth birthday.

* * *

Radbourn had thrown a staggering 1,311 regular-season innings over the course of 1883 and 1884. "Next year will be the time when his arm will show whether it has been injured or not," the *Fall River Daily Evening News* predicted late in the '84 season. Sure enough, the new season proved disastrous both for Radbourn and for Providence. Old Hoss's record dropped to a mortal 28–21, his worst win total since his rookie season and his worst winning percentage yet. After struggling to stay in the pennant race during the first four months of the season, the defending champions simply gave up, nightmarishly losing thirty-three of thirty-eight games between August 7 and October 1. Paul Radford's horseshoe, having exuded all of its charm on the seasons of 1883 and 1884, had become a useless chunk of metal. Anson's White Stockings, turning their energies back to the field, captured the pennant.

On September 11, a *New York Times* reporter caught up with the thirty-nine-year-old Bancroft, who was placidly watching the Grays lose yet again to the Giants from the Polo Grounds grandstand, alongside his passionate seventeen-year-old wife. Bancroft had gotten remarried in New Bedford on March 28, taking as his bride Irene Fitch, a "handsome woman" and "pronounced brunette," according to a brief news story. "Mr. Bancroft seemed to regard the defeat of his nine in a matter-of-fact sort of way, but Mrs. Bancroft regarded it in another light," the reporter observed. "Every base hit gained by the Giants seemed to annoy her, and judging from the sighs that escaped her as she tallied the singles, doubles and triples on her scorecard, the game afforded her little amusement." Some of his players were drinking heavily, and there seemed little that Bancroft could do about it but look on with disgust. The writer asked him about reports that star third baseman Jerry Denny was hoping to join the Giants. "Denny is probably anxious to leave Providence," Bancroft replied blandly. "That is, I judge so from his conduct. He is down stairs now trying to consume the stock of whiskey sours."

Just as Providence fanatics had feared for years, the directors folded the club when the season ended, and sold off the best players, including Radbourn, to Boston's Red Stockings. "You have got the best pitcher in the world," Bancroft told Boston baseball lovers. "There isn't a man that can pitch—day in, day out—as can Charley Radbourne." The fire sale, which netted the Grays $6,600, finished off major league baseball in Providence forever. Bancroft thought it was a foolish move—"and this is not croaking, either"—because the fierce Boston-Providence rivalry had paid the salaries of all the players with ticket receipts from their face-to-face contests alone. In the decades that followed, Providence hosted a series of minor-league teams, including one in the International League, also called the Grays, whose most famous player was a boisterous nineteen-year-old pitcher about to join the Boston Red Sox—an overgrown kid named Babe Ruth. But the champagne had gone flat for many Rhode Islanders. Their vivid memories of the National League's Grays "deterred them from attending later games, which wholly lacked savor for those who had seen the stirring contests of the early 80s." One who did keep coming out was Henry T. Root, president of the 1884 Grays. Later elected to the city council and the state legislature, Root loved baseball so much that he attended games even after he went blind in his old age, counting on a helper, perhaps his daughter, to give him the play-by-play while he listened to the sound of a bat hitting the ball and the crowd cheering.

His colleague Ned Allen, who had done so much to keep the Grays on an even keel in 1884, had a somewhat more sensational ending. His name came up during a 1907 trial, a media spectacle that involved spiritualist Mary S. Pepper, wife of a Vanderbilt. A witness essentially accused Mrs. Vanderbilt, known as "Bright Eyes," of having an affair with Allen, then seventy, who was also married, and working then as treasurer of the National Electric Light and Battery Company in Providence. "I have kissed Mr. Allen hundreds of times," Mrs. Pepper-Vanderbilt testified at the packed New York trial, "but it was the kiss of spiritualism that I gave him. It is delivered on the cheek at parting and has no relation to any other kiss and no earthly significance." A lawyer peppered her with questions. "Did you ever go kiss Allen good night in his bed room?" he asked. "No sir, no sir!" she answered with intense indignation. Allen, deeply mortified, insisted he had done nothing but advise the woman on financial affairs. On the day the story about Mrs. Vanderbilt's kisses was splashed across the front pages of the local newspapers, Allen literally died of shock.

Bancroft moved on to a series of minor-league and major-league managing jobs, and the lucky man continued to skirt disaster. He withdrew at the last minute from an exhibition game in Johnstown, Pennsylvania, on May 31, 1889, the day the South Fork Dam broke and a wall of water slammed the city, killing over 2,200 people. "Every human being in the hotel where the team would have been quartered was swept to death," according to a newspaper account. Years later, Bancroft was aboard a ship bound for Honolulu for a series of exhibition games when a savage storm struck. At the height of the tempest, while the boat was tipping, groaning, and heaving, St. Louis Cardinals infielder Cozy Dolan reportedly threw himself at Bancroft's knees. "Please, Banny," he wailed, "when the ship goes down and you get home tell my folks my last thought was of them!" Bancroft stared at the begging player. "What's the matter with you, man? Do you think I'm a fish?" Fortunately, no one had to swim.

By 1892, Bancroft had bounced around baseball like a Ping-Pong ball, and an outsider could not help wondering if the man could hold a steady job. To this day, no one in major league and National League history has ever managed more teams (seven and six, respectively). But that year, he finally got a job he *did* hold steadily—for the next twenty-nine years, in fact—as business manager of the League's Cincinnati Reds, handling travel arrangements, arranging exhibition games, planning ceremonies, collecting money, issuing paychecks, and balancing the books. By 1917, Bancroft had handled the cash in more than four thousand ball games.

In 1907, the man who had taken a ball club to Cuba in 1879 did the same thing with the Reds, drawing huge crowds in Havana, where he was styled the "Father of Baseball in Cuba" because his earlier visit had dramatically spurred interest in the game. "No person on earth can appreciate the growth of baseball in Cuba more than I can," Bancroft told a reporter. "The advancement of the game since I came here in 1879 with the 'Hop Bitters' is simply astounding." Always a visionary, Bancroft saw an international future for baseball. "While I may not live to see it, I predict that it will not be many years before the world's championship will be between the two champions of America, Cuba and Japan and other foreign countries, where baseball is getting a firm hold." He warmly praised young Cuban players and advised major-league scouts to keep an eye on them. And in 1910, he even talked about taking the world champions to Japan, though he never got around to it. His innovative spirit and generous nature earned him admirers throughout baseball. "Frank C. Bancroft stands out as conspicuous as a full-bloom peach tree on a mountain's side," sportswriter Tim Murnane noted the year Bancroft revisited Cuba. "May his shadow never grow less." Syndicated sportswriter Grantland Rice, writing in 1915, called him "one of the most popular and one of the most competent men that baseball has ever known—a kid at 71."

The 1919 season was among the happiest of his career, as his beloved Reds defeated the heavily favored Chicago White Sox in the World Series— only to learn later that some of the Chicago players had conspired with gamblers to throw the series. Bancroft's fondest baseball memories, though, were of 1884, and he never tired of telling the story of Radbourn's extraordinary courage and endurance. "In my opinion, in those last 12 weeks of the season of '84 he did the greatest work ever performed by any pitcher," Bancroft told the *Cincinnati Enquirer* in late 1904. "He did it on his courage and nerve and by the intelligent use of his strength." In April 1905, when he was in Jacksonville, Florida, Bancroft ran into his team's old captain Joe Start, who had just sold his hotel at Oakland Beach, near Providence, for $16,000, ensuring him a pleasant retirement. "Capt. Joe Start is a fine figure of a man, hair white as snow, but cheeks as ruddy and form as erect as in the days when he led the Rhode Islanders on to victory," a *Cincinnati Enquirer* reporter observed. The two gossiped about the old team and what had become of the men. Radbourn's close friend Cliff Carroll was dead. Barney Gilligan was living in Lynn, Massachusetts, driving a garbage truck, and Jack Farrell was in Newark, prospering in business. Jerry Denny was doing well running a hotel in Derby, Connecticut. Paul Hines had, with the help of President William McKinley, a noted baseball fan, landed a comfortable berth as a clerk in the Agriculture Department in Washington, protected by the civil service. Cyclone Miller was retired, living in Pawtucket. Paul Revere Radford was back at his home in Hyde Park, Massachusetts. Arthur Irwin was still in baseball, managing the Kansas City Blues of the American Association. (Later he was a big-league scout.) "It will be seen that most of the champs have done pretty well for themselves in a worldly way," the reporter observed—though, perhaps tellingly, nobody seemed to bring up the name of Charlie Sweeney or his catcher Sandy Nava, another California man. (The *Sporting News*, in an 1897 story, noted that Nava had "dropped out of sight . . . Drink got the better of him.") As for his overall assessment of baseball, "Joe still thinks that the game was as fast twenty years ago as it is today, and that the peers of Pitcher Radbourn and Third Baseman Denny have yet to be discovered."

Arthur Irwin died on July 16, 1921, falling, or jumping, overboard from a steamer en route from New York City to Boston. He had seemed despondent to friends on the night he boarded, and had been diagnosed with an incurable disease. After his death it was discovered that he had been living a double life for thirty years, with a wife and child in Boston and a common-law wife and three children in New York.

Paul Hines, too, suffered a hard demise. He missed baseball terribly. "Do you know that every spring I have that baseball fever come over me?" he confessed to a newspaperman in 1908, when he was fifty-five. "When the grass gets green and I read of the players reporting to their training camps, I just feel like packing my grip and going with them, but, of course, I guess those are merely ideas, and I would not be able to keep up with the young fellows any more." In 1922, when he was seventy, the former baseball star was arrested in Washington on a pickpocketing charge. When police interrogated him, Hines reportedly broke down and exclaimed, "I have played my last game and lost." He died in 1935, at the age of eighty-three, poor, blind, and deaf, at the Sacred Heart Home in Hyattsville, Maryland.

On July 6, 1916, when the Reds visited Bloomington, Illinois, for an exhibition game, Bancroft made a point of bringing the entire team to Evergreen Cemetery, where he and his men decorated Radbourn's grave with flowers. Four months later, a reporter found Bancroft smoking a cigar in the lobby of his hotel, and informed him that John McGraw's New York Giants had just bested his ancient Providence streak of twenty straight wins, thought to be the record. Bancroft shook his head and laughed, noting it had taken thirty-two years to do that. He pointed out that, in the case of the Grays, unlike the Giants, just one pitcher—Old Hoss Radbourn—had won eighteen of those twenty games. "They haven't got iron men like that in these days," Bancroft observed. "Banny has seen all the great ball clubs come and go since that time," one reporter noted in 1918, "but he insists that the Providence club of 1884 was the greatest ball club he has ever seen and that Charley Radbourne was the super-pitcher of all time."

Bancroft, suffering the painful nerve disease of neuritis, finally quit after the 1920 season, when he was the oldest man still making a living in organized baseball. Out of respect, his club continued to pay his salary. He died of pneumonia in the hospital in Cincinnati on March 31, 1921, at the age of seventy-four, and was remembered as a picturesque figure with a wonderfully likeable personality. "Probably no man now connected with the National game has more friends," a reporter noted during his final season. "He makes scores of them every year and never has lost one."

Except, perhaps, for Charlie Sweeney.

Late in the 1884 campaign, the *Brooklyn Eagle*'s Henry Chadwick argued that Radbourn's stunning performance that season exposed one of baseball's dirty little secrets—that pitchers could, if they wanted to, pitch day after day without breaking down. Sweeney and Radbourn had merely been working a racket in trading off pitching duties, something that Radbourn quickly halted when he became jealous of Sweeney's success and drove him away, leaving himself "in command of the position." When pitchers claimed they were too sore to work, the *Eagle* asserted, they were merely being lazy and trying to avoid even their minimal duties. "What is the work of a first class pitcher during a season's campaign? Why nothing more than nine innings of pitching once a day—occupying less than two hours of labor out of the twenty-four—during an average of four days a week," Chadwick scoffed. "Why it is simply nonsense to assert that this is an arduous task for any man of the healthy class of athletics who compose the leading pitchers of the day. What Radbourne has done they can all do."

Except, of course, they could not. No pitcher ever again scaled the mountain to fifty-nine (or sixty) wins—not even Radbourn. The great John Clarkson came the closest one year later, with fifty-three. From 1885 through 1891, Radbourn averaged twenty wins a season—impressive by modern standards, but not magnificent for his day. Radbourn "continued to pitch good ball," Bancroft recalled, "but I have always thought that his arm was never as good again as it was in the last days of '84, when he won the pennant practically by himself." Indeed, neither Radbourn nor Sweeney nor Boston's Charlie Buffinton ever came close to matching their epic performances of 1884. The strain that they placed on their arms fighting for glory that season told for the rest of their lives.

But if his arm suffered the ravages of that season, his heart remained strong. Radbourn's Providence conquests included the woman he loved, Carrie Stanhope. During his years with the Beaneaters, at least through 1887, she was still listed in the *Providence City Directory* as Mrs. Stanhope, still the proprietress of her boardinghouse, though it seems she may have spent a fair amount of time in Boston, since she made friends there and became fond of the city. That year, Radbourn got locked into another bitter argument with his employers. The Boston owners had withheld part of his magnificent $4,500 salary, citing his "chronic poor play." Radbourn was not a man to be cheated with impunity. "One thing is very sure. If I am not treated squarely in money matters there will be trouble," he vowed with cold fury. Indeed, he was ready to quit over the slight. "They have driven me out of the business. You will never see me in another game of ball," he promised the *Globe* when the season ended.

At that point, Radbourn brought Carrie and her son, Charles, home to Bloomington, introducing her to family and friends as a widow and his wife. She was neither. Her first husband was very much alive, and Radbourn and Mrs. Stanhope had not married, though she filed for divorce that year, citing desertion by Charles Stanhope, with whom she had not lived since the early 1870s. The great pitcher and the woman he loved chose to live in sin, lying to everyone that they had wed back East.

That winter, Carrie Stanhope divulged in a letter to a woman friend back in the Athens of America that Radbourn was so serious about quitting baseball that he had purchased an interest in a Bloomington hotel and was discussing managing a semipro team in the city. That did not seem to please her. She preferred Boston, one of America's biggest, most culturally rich cities, to sleepy Bloomington. "Mrs. Radbourn says that she feels sorry her husband has made this business investment, as it means that he is determined not to play ball in Boston any more, and is preparing to settle down. She regrets the more because she likes Boston very much and so does he, but he is very sore on the club here."

After the season started the next spring, though, someone blinked. Radbourn cut a deal with management. "HE IS WID US," the *Boston Globe* headlined giddily, and his teammates formally welcomed him back with a lavish dinner. Jack Burdock and Billy Nash escorted him into the banquet room, as the orchestra struck up "For He's a Jolly Good Fellow." John Morrill presented Radbourn with a gold-headed walking cane, protesting that it was only a slight token of the high regard in which he was held. "You are with us again, Rad, and I hope you will remain a valued member of our club for many years to come," Morrill said. "God bless you, old boy, here's the cane." Radbourn stammered his thanks and said he hoped he would help Boston win the pennant in 1888. After more speeches and music, the evening broke up with three cheers for the pitcher. The late start hurt him, and his 7–16 record was the worst of his career. But Radbourn found his rhythm again in 1889, and, with a 20–11 season, very nearly helped secure the championship for the Beaneaters, who fell one game short after a thrilling chase. In 1890, Radbourn enjoyed a final blaze of glory, reuniting with his old shortstop Arthur Irwin on the Boston club of the Players' League, formed and run by the players themselves in a desperate attempt to break management control over the game. He pitched Boston to the pennant, winning twenty-seven against twelve losses, for a .692 winning percentage, highest in the league. "He had regained his old Providence form," the *Boston Globe* marveled in a wrap-up on the champions. "He is the 'king pitcher of 1890.'"

When the Players' League collapsed after one season, Radbourn left Boston and signed with the National League's Cincinnati Reds, reportedly for a whopping $5,000. On May 16, he beat his old Boston League team in Cincinnati, 8–3, in typical Radbourn fashion. He toyed with Boston "like a kitten with a ball of yarn until he had the game well in hand and then took things easy," the *Boston Globe* reported. "Rad pitched one of his seemingly careless games, underhand, overhand, fast and slow." Two weeks later, on Memorial Day afternoon, he made his celebrated return to Boston. Some fourteen thousand New England fanatics dutifully applauded when the Beaneaters took the field, but saved their loudest roar for the moment when Old Hoss walked from the bench to take his position in the pitcher's box. Radbourn tipped his cap to the people who had admired him for so long. "The bronzed old warrior of the diamond felt the blood come to his cheek when he stood on the spot he had made famous but a few years back when he was the main stay of that Rhode Island champion team," the *Globe* reported. "The Old Hoss is still in the ring with his perfect control of the ball and the sand to face the music."

Old Hoss lost that afternoon, though, 6–2 ("OFF HIS FODDER," the headline read), and it quickly became clear that his arm was worn down beyond redemption. After posting the third losing record of his career, 11–13, with a miserable 4.25 earned run average, he asked the Reds to release him. "He was too conscientious to take a five-thousand-dollar salary for five-hundred-dollar ball," the *Cincinnati Enquirer* reported. Many ballplayers of his time continued in the minor leagues when they were no longer up to playing in the majors, but Radbourn refused. "His proud nature could not stand for that," his former manager Sam Crane noted.

Over eleven major league seasons, Charles Radbourn had worked in 527 games, starting 502 times. He had won 309 games. Of the members of the elite 300-win club, Radbourn has the fewest strikeouts, with just 1,830. That reflected his strategy of ignoring all statistics but one: victories—saving his arm for the long season by throwing the ball over the plate, using his fielders to help record outs.

July 12, 1892, was a hot, muggy evening in Bloomington, the kind of night when perspiring people stripped down to their shirtsleeves, fanned themselves on the front porch, and sought relief with a tepid bottle of sarsaparilla or ginger beer. Mr. and Mrs. George Fletcher, who lived just west of the city, were paying a visit to the business district, running errands, their two-year-old child in tow. At about 7:30 p.m., George parked his buggy on West Washington Street and stepped down to go into a store, leaving the reins in Mrs. Fletcher's hands.

He had barely alighted when the horse acted up, gave a lunge, and started galloping wildly westward down the street. Mrs. Fletcher screamed and pulled on the reins but could not stop the careening beast, whose tantrum threatened to overturn the vehicle and kill both mother and child.

Suddenly, a young man in a white jacket dashed into the street. He had been on the sidewalk in front of Radbourn's Place, a local billiards hall, seeking a breeze and minding his own business, when the crisis unfolded before his eyes. He did not wait to act. "With the stride of a professional sprinter," the young man caught up with the horse's head. With his strong right hand he seized the bit, and with his left put a powerful clamp on the horse's nostrils. The moment was fraught with desperate danger; the man could easily have been trampled or thrown, his neck broken. Indeed, "the plunging horse dragged the man along with him, and would possibly have gotten away had not the man dexterously turned him so sharply as almost to upset the buggy, thus bringing the animal, suddenly almost to a standstill." Bystanders then rushed to assist, restraining the horse and helping down the terrified lady and child. The mysterious hero turned away from the scene and disappeared, as quietly and suddenly as he had appeared.

The next day's *Bloomington Pantagraph* broke the news of the identity of "the young man in the white jacket" who had saved two lives and silently returned to his business: "He was Charles Radbourne, the famous base ball pitcher." The *Pantagraph* gave Radbourn full credit for saving the mother and child. Summing it up in the last line of its brief news story, it attributed the rescue to qualities the ex-athlete seemed to possess in abundance, using words often employed to describe that particular young man: "His nerve and grit, combined with his muscular training, had averted a terrible accident."

Unlike his spendthrift fellow ballplayers, Radbourn had saved carefully, hoping to survive comfortably the rest of his life off his investments in his hometown. Radbourn "has sought a quiet nook at Bloomington, Ill.," one reporter noted, "to enjoy the fortune that was the fruit of a valuable baseball combination—a good arm and a wise head." In retirement, he opened his own saloon and billiards hall, just below his residence at 214 West Washington Street, and ran it with Carrie's help, no doubt relying on her business savvy. "Radbourn's Place. Chas. Radbourn, Proprietor," an ad in the 1891 Bloomington city directory proclaimed. "Billiards and Pool. Polite Attention. Pleasant Associates. Best of Everything in Wet Goods and Cigars." Yet he was never happy in that role. He sat in the corner, saying nothing, while young men, drinking and joking, racked up the billiard balls and broke them with a loud snap. The famous man refused to boast about his extraordinary baseball career. "He would talk about himself only when cornered, and then only for a few short words." A hole in his world had opened up, with nothing to fill it. He was no longer part of the fierce competition that gave his life meaning.

In 1892, he took his old Boston uniform out of storage and boarded a train for an exhibition game in nearby Chenoa, Illinois. Declaring he felt "as frisky as a young colt," Radbourn admitted his layoff from baseball had left him "a trifle rusty. But I'll show the boys how to split the plate with rifle shots yet. It does me good to get back on the diamond again." In January 1894, he wrote to the *Boston Globe*'s Tim Murnane, saying that he had sold his saloon business the previous June and had spent most of his time since hunting and fishing. Newspapers hinted that he had suffered painful financial reverses in the depression of 1893, one of the worst economic downturns in American history, which left unemployment soaring above 10 percent for half a decade. "I feel as if I would like to play this season," he wrote, claiming that Boston manager Frank Selee had written him the previous year asking for his terms to return. "I was not in first class shape at the time and refused the offer. I would like to have one more season with the champions." On March 28, Radbourn wrote a similar begging note to Christopher Von der Ahe, owner of the St. Louis Browns. "I am in good condition and would like to play with you this season. Have been in training and feel as I could play 'out of sight.' Please let me know if there is an opening for me." He pleaded with the New York Giants, as well. There were no openings, of course, and Radbourn seemed half-mad to even try. Perhaps the old pitcher was displaying delusions of grandeur, one of the symptoms of the illness that had begun to strip him of his mental and physical powers—advancing syphilis.

How Radbourn got the deadly venereal disease is not clear. Did he get it from a prostitute? Did he pass along the disease to Carrie? Did she, with her shadowy background, have something to do with his contracting it? We don't know. The nineteenth-century press was silent about such matters. Since the symptoms of syphilis can disappear for years, Radbourn or Carrie conceivably could have engaged in relations after infection without communicating the disease. But at some point, it became clear that he was infected. Unfortunately, his doctors failed to stop its ravages.

In any event, Radbourn's dreams of returning to baseball were soon blown away. In April that year, on Friday the thirteenth, Radbourn was out hunting with a friend when he stepped from behind a tree into the line of fire. He caught a portion of the shotgun load in his face, and the vision in his left eye was destroyed. Taciturn even in the best of times, Radbourn sank into depression, brooding over the loss of his eye and his money.

From then on, he lived as a recluse, shunning the open fields, drinking heavily in his house, gradually losing his faculties, while Carrie tended to him lovingly and turned away visitors who hoped to see the mighty pitcher. Plainly, Radbourn loved her and wanted to protect her even after his death, and he took legal steps to make sure that happened. On a frigid day in January 1895, they snuck off to Milwaukee, about 225 miles from home, and got married. They told no one, since they had led family and friends to believe they had been wed eight years earlier.

The minister who presided, Wesley A. Hunsberger, pastor of the Grand Avenue Methodist Church, ran a kind of marriage factory along the banks of Lake Michigan, popular with couples, many of them from nearby Chicago, who wanted to be wed quickly and quietly, no questions asked. Under Illinois state law, a reporter noted, there "are all sorts of difficulties to overcome when you want to get married, particularly if secrecy is desired. It is necessary to procure an expensive license and the publication in the daily papers of the names mentioned in the document makes secrecy almost impossible. That is why Milwaukee is popular with elopers. The boats that come up the lake, especially on Sunday, bring scores of unmarried couples who return home as brides and grooms in the evening." Charles and Carrie did not want to be shamed—or see Carrie's son shamed—by the widespread revelation that they were not already married.

One month later, on February 19, Radbourn completed his will. He directed that his debts and funeral expenses be paid off first. He left everything else, including property that was still worth tens of thousands of dollars, "to my beloved wife Carrie Radbourn," and in the event of her death, to *her* heirs, meaning her son. The great pitcher slowly, carefully signed "Charles Radbour" in a crabbed and shaky hand. Another hand finished the name for him.

As paresis slowly conquered his body, his nervous system began to give way, and he was robbed of feeling and movement. In time, his right arm— the mighty arm that had won fifty-nine games in one season—became paralyzed. He was quiet to the last. "Even when he was on his deathbed, few of his friends knew that he was ill," sportswriter Jacob C. Morse recounted. "The bitterness of senility had gripped him relentlessly."

On Wednesday, February 3, 1897, he suddenly went into convulsions and fell into a coma. Two days later, on Friday at 1:50 p.m., Charles Radbourn, forty-two, passed away without an apparent struggle, surrounded by his loved ones, including his wife, Carrie, and her son, whom he had reportedly adopted. "The heart, once the bravest and stoutest that baseball ever had known, broke at last under the strain of grief," one journalist later wrote.

His big family—his parents, three brothers, and four sisters—all survived him. Within weeks of his death, the Radbourns were contesting Carrie's claim to their famous relative's fortune. Clearly none too fond of Carrie and disgruntled over Radbourn's love for her, they had made the shocking discovery that the two had not been married in 1887 after all, and with valuable property at stake, they sent detectives to Providence to snoop around, looking for a marriage certificate. "The Radbournes allege that Mrs. Stanhope has no claim as a widow," one news story reported. "The detectives assert that no marriage ever took place in the West." But the Milwaukee marriage must have been discovered at some point, because Carrie was allowed to keep and sell the property.

One year and two months after Radbourn's death, Carrie's first husband, Charles L. Stanhope, passed away at the State Hospital for the Insane, in Cranston, Rhode Island. His death certificate could hardly have been more explicit: "General Paralysis of the Insane," also sometimes called general paresis, was the official designation for tertiary syphilis of the brain.

Carrie survived Radbourn by six years. After the bitter fight with Radbourn's family, she left Bloomington and moved to Vernon Avenue in Chicago with her mother and her son. She died in Chicago Baptist Hospital at 2:30 a.m. on August 3, 1903, of chronic myelitis—an agonizing inflammation of the spine that may have been a symptom of advancing syphilis. Her mother went home to Pawtucket.

Carrie's life might seem filled with pain, frustration, and misfortune, as well as love, but she had achieved something remarkable, something important to her: giving her son the start in life that seemed almost beyond her reach when she was a destitute shopgirl in Providence. Charles Stan-

Grave of Charles and Carrie
S. "Radbourne" at Evergreen
Memorial Cemetery,
Bloomington, Illinois

hope eventually found his way to Kenosha, Wisconsin, where he told his life story this way: He had gone to Bloomington with his "then widowed mother" (she was, of course, not a widow then), finished school, and got a job with the Central Union Telephone Company. (He did not mention his famous stepfather.) From there, he moved to Kenosha and ran a store, the Kenosha Hardware Company, at 221 Main Street. Census records show that subsequently he was a plumber, then a machinist and bookkeeper at a sheet metal company. None of these were spectacular jobs, but they were all honorable ones, and *his* son, Carrie's grandson, James "Clark" Stanhope, was educated at the University of Notre Dame, attended Marquette University Law School, served bravely as a technician in the U.S. Army in Italy and southern France in World War II, and became a prominent lawyer. Her family's rise tells a great American story in all its suffering, sacrifice, and achievement, and makes clear that Carrie's indomitable grit, as well as Radbourn's, had accomplished wonders.

Carrie was buried alongside her great husband at Evergreen Cemetery in Bloomington, their grave marked by a handsome monument that spelled the name, as so many people did, *Radbourne*, with an *e*. When the pitcher's father died in 1909 and was buried near his son, his gravestone spelled the name *Radbourn*. So even in the small family plot, the enigmatic name is spelled out both ways—a puzzle for eternity.

Charles Radbourn's hometown *Bloomington Pantagraph* noted the passing of the city's famous son with great pride: "He filled the nation with his praises. Not many men in American history up to his time faced so many people and received so many plaudits. His name was used as frequently as the president's." The nation's papers gave the news prominent play: "CHARLEY RADBOURNE DEAD," the *Philadelphia Inquirer* proclaimed. "The Greatest Pitcher Called

Out by the Inexorable Umpire." The *Sporting News* declared that "'Rad' was indisputably the greatest base ball pitcher the world has ever known." His death fell hard on the people of Providence, a correspondent reported to the *Sporting News* from Rhode Island, asserting that no one outside of his immediate circle of family and friends mourned his loss more keenly than the people who knew and admired him when he played in that city. Still, the *Providence Journal* remembered some peccadilloes along with the epic feats. "Radbourn was an eccentric fellow in some respects," it observed, "and one who had to be handled 'with gloves.'"

In the years that followed, as those of Radbourn's generation passed from the scene, the old men who had watched him play strove to recapture in words the brilliance they had witnessed. "Greatest Pitcher That Ever Lived," read the headline of a widely distributed 1908 story by Jacob C. Morse. "I have talked to many great ballplayers who have lamented to me the fact that baseball fame is so ephemeral that it was not worth the gaining; and while no doubt this is in a great measure true, there is one pitcher who has left a name that promises to roll on for many, many years," Morse wrote. Radbourn was "the great Hercules of baseball." As Old Hoss became a mythic figure, legends formed around his name. In 1907, an oft-told tale appeared in print about an incident during one of the famous Boston-Providence battles. Radbourn, running the bases, had sped around third when his leg cramped up and he had to limp home. Sandy Nava, "a Spaniard, who spoke broken English," piped up: "What's a malla you, Charley Hoss?" That's how the term "charley horse" entered sports lingo, supposedly.

In 1939, only three years after the first class was inducted, Radbourn was among a select group of nineteenth-century stars elected to the Baseball Hall of Fame. His plaque at the Hall—which spells his name *Radbourne*—depicts him with a bushy handlebar mustache, his head turned away from the viewer, presumably toward a batter, a scowl on his face. It calls him the "greatest of all 19th century pitchers."

A plaque installed a short time later at Evergreen Cemetery—"erected as a tribute to an illustrious son of Bloomington, Illinois by a group of baseball fans"—notes that no pitcher ever won more games over a three-year period than Radbourn did for the Grays in 1882, 1883, and 1884. Old Clark Griffith spoke at the dedication ceremony in May 1941:

Charlie Radbourn, you stand out in baseball history as one of the men who helped establish baseball as America's national sport. . . . We, of baseball, take off our hats to you. . . . And may those who look upon this plaque, as time goes by, be reminded of the fact that this plaque symbolized the love and devotion of all his loved ones, his friends and the people of baseball.

The plaque—just like the one at the Hall of Fame, just like his gravestone—spells his last name with an *e*. The distant and taciturn star had not bothered to make clear to the sportswriters of his generation how to spell his name, and history transmitted both versions. In a sense, it was fitting that his very name has remained an enigma, since so much else about the man did. But it seems doubtful he would have cared much one way or another. The brooding, intense son of a small-town butcher had always preferred to let his pitching—that supreme expression of his grit, talent, and brains—do the talking for him.

ACKNOWLEDGMENTS

Writing a book is a solitary occupation requiring years of work hunched over a computer—at least for me! Even so, this one could not have been written without the extraordinary kindness of many people. The errors, of course, are mine. Frederick Ivor-Campbell, probably the leading Radbourn scholar, carefully read through the manuscript, pointed me toward valuable sources, and prevented me from making some stupid mistakes. His articles on Radbourn piqued my interest many years ago; it was a joy to discover such a gentle, kind, and truly giving man behind the keen intellect. One of the thrills of my life was working with Elisabeth Kallick Dyssegaard at HarperCollins, a first-rate editor who improved the book enormously and seemed to love the story of Charles and Carrie from the start. My agent, David Miller, of the Garamond Agency, a superb editor himself, recognized the potential of a groundbreaking book on early baseball and helped me shape it into something that I hope is lively and readable. Thomas Wright, of Lexington, Massachusetts, used his skills as a genealogist to open a window on Carrie Stanhope and her family and graciously answered my many questions. Bill Kemp, librarian/archivist of the McLean County Museum of History in Bloomington, Illinois, sent me invaluable articles and information about Radbourn and his hometown, and kindly read part of the manuscript. Maury Klein of the University of Rhode Island, author of such wonderful works as *Days of Defiance*, went through an earlier version of the book with me, with a dog sprawled on his lap, and gave me a crash course in writing lively historical narrative. J. Stanley Lemons of Rhode Island College shared his invaluable insights about nineteenth-century Providence. Stanley M. Aronson, M.D., dean emeritus of medicine at Brown University, offered me guidance on medical issues, particularly the nature and treatment of syphilis. Priscilla Astifan spent hours digging into records in the Rochester, New York, area, looking for Radbourn's elusive birth records. Dr. P. J. Bendall, of Bath, England, shared genealogical work on the Radbourns in Bath and Prior Park and corrected some glaring misconceptions in the manuscript. Joan E. Barney of the New Bedford Free Public Library helped me find materials on Frank Bancroft. Candy Adriance read the manuscript, intrepidly aided with research, suggested shrewd structural changes and areas of development, and made the book much stronger and tighter. Richard Sullivan, an expert on nineteenth-century brothels in Providence, shared his insights and his copy of *Our Police*. The members of the Providence Grays vintage team, notably Tim Norton, shared their expertise about the nature of playing baseball barehanded, under 1884 rules. Maureen A. Taylor, author of the wonderful book *Picturing Rhode Island*, answered my questions about Providence in Radbourn's day and helped me find photographs. John Thorn, the great scholar of nineteenth-century baseball, pointed me in the direction of photographs. Robert Lifson of Robert Edward Auctions was unfailingly generous in helping me obtain images. Phil Swann offered endless insights and shared his knowledge of baseball. Howard Sutton, publisher, president, and CEO of the *Providence Journal*, was always supportive. My colleagues in the Editorial Department at the *Journal* were very helpful: Robert Whitcomb grasped the nature of baseball as a window on nineteenth-century American culture and offered the name of his agent, David Miller; Irving Sheldon and David Brussat contributed scanning and photographs. Don O'Hanley, the avuncular announcer at Newport Gulls baseball games, shared his wonderful collection of 1883 and 1884 scorecards. My sister, Nancy Engberg, an award-winning photographer, took the author photo and captured those early scorecards. Numerous institutions provided invaluable help: the Rhode Island Historical Society, the National Baseball Hall of Fame Library, the Library of Congress, the Boston Public Library, the *Providence Journal*, the Providence City Archives, and the Chicago Historical Society. My children, Jean, Matt, and Josh, put up with Dad's incessant labors in his study. My wife, Valerie, provided boundless support, encouragement, and faith, and told me early on that this was more than a baseball yarn; it was really a love story. To her the book is dedicated.

APPENDIX

RADBOURN IN 1884, GAME BY GAME

1884 PROVIDENCE GRAYS STATISTICS

RADBOURN IN 1884, GAME BY GAME

Game/Date	Opponent	Score	Decision
1. May 2	Cleveland	5–2	W (1–0)
2. May 5	Buffalo	5–2	W (2–0)
3. May 9	Buffalo	3–1	W (3–0)
4. May 12	Chicago	0–5	L (3–1)
5. May 14	Detroit	25–3	W (4–1)
6. May 17	Detroit	5–2	W (5–1)
7. May 19	Detroit	4–2	W (6–1)
8. May 21	@ New York	3–0	W (7–1)
9. May 23	@ Philadelphia	8–1	W (8–1)
10. May 26	@ New York	10–4	W (9–1)
11. May 30 (m)	New York	12–9	W (10–1)
12. May 30 (a)	Philadelphia	9–2	W (11–1)
13. May 31	Philadelphia	6–5	W (12–1)
14. June 3	New York	7–12	L (12–2)
15. June 6	Boston	1–1	None (12–2)
16. June 11	Boston	1–4	L (12–3)
17. June 14	@ Boston	4–3	W (13–3)
18. June 16	Philadelphia	13–1	W (14–3)
19. June 18	New York	15–0	W (15–3)
20. June 21	@ Detroit	10–0	W (16–3)
21. June 24	@ Detroit	1–0	W (17–3)
22. June 26	@ Chicago	8–6	W (18–3)
23. June 28	@ Chicago	13–4	W (19–3)
24. June 30	@ Chicago	4–5	L (19–4)
25. July 1	@ Cleveland	10–3	W (20–4)
26. July 2	@ Cleveland	2–4	L (20–5)

IP	H	R	ER	BB	SO
9*	5	2	0	1	4
9*	5	2	0	2	3
9*	5	1	0	2	3
8*	8	5	2	3	3
9*	5	3	2	4	5
9*	8	2	0	1	7
9*	3	2	~	2	7
9*	3	0	0	1	3
9*	7	1	0	0	6
9*	13	4	3	0	8
9*	12	9	3	2	7
9*	7	2	0	1	9
10*	18	5	4	0	2
8*	15	12	5	1	4
16*	4	1	~	0	8
8*	11	4	3	1	3
15*	7	3	0	2	13
9*	5	1	1	2	4
9*	1	0	0	1	0
9*	2	0	0	0	10
14*	3	0	0	0	14
9*	12	6	5	0	8
9*	10	4	3	1	4
8.2*	10	5	4	2	5
9*	10	3	2	3	1
9*	12	4	4	1	2

Game/Date	Opponent	Score	Decision
27. July 4	@ Cleveland	4–2	W (21–5)
28. July 7	@ Buffalo	14–9	W (22–5)
29. July 8	@ Buffalo	6–5	Save (22–5)
30. July 9	@ Buffalo	1–5	L (22–6)
31. July 11	Boston	2–0	W (23–6)
32. July 12	@ Boston	1–7	L (23–7)
33. July 14	Boston	9–6	W (24–7)
34. July 16	Boston	2–5	L (24–8)
35. July 23	New York	11–5	W (25–8)
36. July 26	@ Philadelphia	16–3	W (26–8)
37. July 28	@ Philadelphia	11–4	Save (26–8)
38. July 30	@ New York	8–5	W (27–8)
39. July 31	@ New York	3–3	None (27–8)
40. August 1	@ New York	7–3	W (28–8)
41. August 6	@ New York	1–2	L (28–9)
42. August 7	@ New York	4–2	W (29–9)
43. August 9	@ Boston	1–0	W (30–9)
44. August 11	Boston	3–1	W (31–9)
45. August 12	@ Boston	4–0	W (32–9)
46. August 14	Boston	1–0	W (33–9)
47. August 15	Cleveland	3–2	W (34–9)
48. August 19	Detroit	4–2	W (35–9)
49. August 21	Chicago	5–3	W (36–9)
50. August 23	Chicago	7–3	W (37–9)
51. August 27	Chicago	5–3	W (38–9)
52. August 28	Chicago	6–4	W (39–9)
53. August 29	Detroit	7–1	W (40–9)
54. August 30	Detroit	6–5	W (41–9)

IP	H	R	ER	BB	SO
9*	10	2	0	~	5
9*	13	9	4	0	2
1	0	0	0	0	0
9*	9	5	1	1	9
9*	4	0	0	1	8
8*	7	7	3	2	6
9*	6	6	~	2	8
8*	9	5	2	2	8
9*	9	5	1	6	4
9*	10	3	0	0	8
4	0	0	0	~	0
9*	6	5	2	3	6
9*	8	3	0	1	6
9*	7	3	3	0	6
11*	10	5	1	1	7
9*	4	2	0	1	1
11*	2	0	0	1	12
9*	2	1	0	2	3
9*	7	0	0	0	8
9*	6	0	0	1	5
9*	5	2	0	2	11
9*	5	2	0	2	10
9*	8	3	2	6	4
9*	6	3	0	2	2
9*	6	3	~	1	5
9*	11	4	3	1	2
9*	7	1	~	0	6
11*	10	5	1	1	7

Game/Date	Opponent	Score	Decision
55. September 2	Buffalo	4–0	W (42–9)
56. September 3	Buffalo	10–1	W (43–9)
57. September 4	Cleveland	3–1	W (44–9)
58. September 5	Cleveland	5–4	W (45–9)
59. September 6	Cleveland	3–0	W (46–9)
60. September 9	Buffalo	0–2	L (46–10)
61. September 10	Cleveland	5–3	W (47–10)
62. September 11	Cleveland	9–1	W (48–10)
63. September 12	Buffalo	8–2	W (49–10)
64. September 13	Buffalo	6–1	W (50–10)
65. September 15	@Cleveland	10–2	W (51–10)
66. September 16	@Detroit	4–2	W (52–10)
67. September 17	@Detroit	9–5	W (53–10)
68. September 18	@Detroit	9–6	W (54–10)
69. September 20	@Detroit	1–7	L (54–11)
70. September 24	@Chicago	3–5	L (54–12)
71. September 26	@Chicago	8–3	W (55–12)
72. October 4	@ Buffalo	4–1	W (56–12)
73. October 7	@ Cleveland	9–7	W (57–12)
74. October 11	@ Cleveland	8–1	W (58–12)
75. October 15	@ Philadelphia	8–0	W (59–12)

Source: Frank J. Williams and Frederick Ivor-Campbell

*   Pitched complete game. The mark (~) indicates there is some doubt about the number. Usually it means 0.

Radbourn's win-loss record against National League clubs: Boston, 7–3; Buffalo, 8–2; Chicago, 7–3; Cleveland, 12–1; Detroit, 11–1; New York, 8–2; Philadelphia 6–0. Tie games (2) against Boston and New York. Saves (2) against Buffalo and Philadelphia. Home record, wins, losses, ties: 33–5–1; away record: 26–7–1; versus Eastern clubs, 21–5–2; versus Western clubs, 38–7–0.

IP	H	R	ER	BB	SO
9*	3	0	0	0	10
9*	9	1	1	1	7
9*	8	1	~	0	3
9*	5	4	1	0	8
9*	6	0	0	1	8
8*	5	2	2	1	8
9*	9	3	2	2	~
9*	5	1	1	0	11
9*	6	2	0	0	4
9*	7	1	0	~	7
9*	9	2	2	0	2
9*	6	2	1	1	8
9*	7	5	0	2	5
9*	10	6	1	2	4
9*	9	7	~	3	8
9*	7	5	3	3	~
9*	6	3	2	2	7
9*	7	1	1	0	7
9*	10	7	2	2	2
9*	4	1	0	2	2
9*	5	0	0	2	2

Winning streaks: 18 games, August 7–September 6; 9 games, May 14–31; 8 games, September 10–18; 7 games, June 14–28. One-run decisions: 8–2.

THE 1884 GRAYS STARTING LINEUP

Batting order	Pos. played	Age*	G	AB	R	H
Paul Hines	cf	29	114	490	94	148
Jack Farrell	2b	26	111	469	70	102
Joe Start	1b	41	93	381	80	105
C. Radbourn	p	29	87	361	48	83
Cliff Carroll	lf	24	113	452	90	118
Arthur Irwin	ss	26	102	404	73	97
Jerry Denny	3b	25	110	439	57	109
B. Gilligan	c	28	82	294	47	72
Paul Radford	rf	22	97	355	56	70

Source: www.baseball-reference.com.

OTHER GRAYS PLAYERS

Batting order	Pos. played	Age*	G	AB	R	H
C. Sweeney	p	21	41	168	24	50
Sandy Nava	c	34	34	116	10	11
C. Bassett	if	21	27	79	10	11
Ed Conley	p	19	8	28	0	4
Miah Murray	ut	19	8	27	1	5
Cyclone Miller	p	24	6	23	3	1
J. Cattanach	of	21	1	4	0	0
Harry Arundel	p	29	1	3	2	1

Source: www.baseball-reference.com.

*   Age, as of midnight June 30, 1884.

2B	3B	HR	RBI	BB	SO	BA	OBP	SLG
36	10	3	31	44	28	.302	.360	.435
13	6	1	37	35	44	.217	.272	.277
10	5	2	32	35	25	.276	.337	.344
7	1	1	37	26	42	.230	.282	.263
16	4	3	54	29	39	.261	.306	.334
14	3	2	44	28	52	.240	.289	.304
22	9	6	59	14	58	.248	.272	.380
13	2	1	38	35	41	.245	.325	.313
11	2	1	29	25	43	.197	.250	.248

2B	3B	HR	RBI	BB	SO	BA	OBP	SLG
9	0	1	19	11	17	.298	.341	.369
0	0	0	6	11	35	.095	.173	.095
2	1	0	6	4	15	.139	.181	.190
0	0	0	0	0	9	.143	.143	.143
0	0	0	1	1	8	.185	.214	.185
0	0	0	0	1	10	.043	.083	.043
0	0	0	0	0	2	.000	.000	.000
0	0	0	1	1	1	.333	.500	.333

PITCHING

PLAYER	W	L	PCT.	ERA	G	GS	CG
C. Radbourn	59	12	.831	1.38	75	73	73
C. Sweeney	17	8	.680	1.55	27	24	22
E. Conley	4	4	.500	2.15	8	8	8
Cyclone Miller	3	2	.600	2.08	6	5	2
Paul Radford	0	2	.000	7.62	2	2	1
Harry Arundel	1	0	1.00	1.00	1	1	1
John Cattanach	0	0	—	9.00	1	1	0
Arthur Irwin	0	0	—	3.00	1	0	0
Paul Hines	0	0	—	0.00	1	0	0

Source: www.baseball-reference.com.

SHO	SV	IP	H	R	ER	BB	SO	H/9
11	1†	678.2	258	216	104	98	441	7.0
4	1	221.0	153	70	38	29	145	6.2
1	0	71.0	63	47	17	22	33	8.0
0	0	34.2	36	24	8	11	12	9.3
0	0	13.0	27	19	11	3	2	18.7
0	0	9.0	8	2	1	4	4	8.0
0	0	5.0	2	7	5	4	2	3.6
0	0	3.0	5	2	1	0	0	15.0
0	0	1.0	3	1	0	0	0	27.0

† Williams and Ivor-Campbell disagree on this point, awarding Radbourn 2 saves.

FIELDING

Player	Pos. played	PO	A
Paul Hines	of–1b-p	266	20
Jack Farrell	2b–3b	251	353
Joe Start	1b	939	21
C. Radbourn	p-of–1b-ss–2b	69	131
Cliff Carroll	of	206	11
Arthur Irwin	ss-p	99	308
Jerry Denny	3b–1b–2b-c	237	185
B. Gilligan	c–3b–1b	613	94
Paul Radford	of-p	146	29
C. Sweeney	p-of–1b	42	49
Sandy Nava	c-ss–2b	183	54
C. Bassett	3b-ss-of–2b	23	47
Cyclone Miller	p-of	2	7
Miah Murray	c-of–1b	44	11
Ed Conley	p	1	9
J. Cattanach	p-of	0	1
Harry Arundel	p	0	1

Source: www.baseball-reference.com.

E	DP	FA	PB
29	9	.908	
54	36	.918	
20	31	.980	
25	4	.889	
23	1	.904	
55	20	.881	
48	11	.898	1
55	7	.928	46
24	4	.879	
6	1	.938	
31	3	.884	16
15	1	.824	
0	0	1.000	
0	0	.814	14
0	0	1.000	
2	0	.333	
0	0	1.000	

Abbreviations and Short Titles Used in Notes

NEWSPAPERS AND MAGAZINES

AC: *Auburn* (New York) *Citizen*

BB: *Bloomington* (Illinois) *Bulletin*

BCA: *Buffalo Commercial Advertiser*

BDT: *Bismarck* (North Dakota) *Daily Tribune*

BE: *Brooklyn Eagle*

BG: *Boston Globe*

BH: *Boston Herald*

BM: *Baseball Magazine*

BMJ: *Boston Morning Journal*

BP: *Bloomington* (Illinois) *Pantagraph*

BRH: *Bridgeport* (Connecticut) *Herald*

CCG: *Cincinnati Commercial-Gazette*

CDIO: (Chicago) *Daily Inter-Ocean*

CE: *Cincinnati Enquirer*

CH: *Cleveland Herald*

CHH: *Chicago Herald*

CL: *Cleveland Leader*

CT: *Chicago Tribune*

DB: (Bloomington, Illinois) *Daily Bulletin*

DFP: *Detroit Free Press*

DI: *Daily Independent* (Helena, Montana)

DN: *Detroit News*

DNT: *Duluth* (Minnesota) *News-Tribune*

EG: *Evening Gazette* (Worcester, Massachusetts)

EN: *Evening News* (San Jose, California)

ET: *Evening Telegram* (Providence)

FRDEN: *Fall River* (Massachusetts) *Daily Evening News*

FWST: *Fort Worth* (Texas) *Star-Telegram*

GFH: *Grand Forks* (North Dakota) *Herald*

HC: *Hartford Courant*

IA: (Silver City) *Idaho Avalanche*

IS: (Boise) *Idaho Statesman*

KCS: *Kansas City Star*

KN: *Kenosha* (Wisconsin) *News*

LH: *Lexington* (Kentucky) *Herald*

LS: *Lincoln* (Nebraska) *Star*

MC: *Morning Call* (San Francisco)

MR: (St. Louis) *Missouri Republican*

MS: *Milwaukee Sentinel*

MT: *Macon* (Georgia) *Telegraph*

NBDM: *New Bedford* (Massachusetts) *Daily Mercury*

NBS: *New Bedford* (Massachusetts) *Standard*

NDN: *Newport* (Rhode Island) *Daily News*

NHP: (Concord) *New Hampshire Patriot*

NHR: *New Haven Register*

NM: *Newport* (Rhode Island) *Mercury*

NPG: *National Police Gazette*

NYC: *New York Clipper*

NYH: *New York Herald*

NYJ: *New York Journal*

NYT: *New York Times*

NYW: *New York World*

OP: *Oregonian* (Portland)

PDT: *Peoria* (Illinois) *Daily Transcript*

PEB: *Providence Evening Bulletin*

PEP: *Providence Evening Press*

PI: *Philadelphia Inquirer*

PMS: *Providence Morning Star*

PJ: *Providence Journal*

QDH: *Quincy* (Illinois) *Daily Herald*

RDC: *Rochester* (New York) *Democrat and Chronicle*

SEH: *Syracuse* (New York) *Evening Herald*

SFB: *San Francisco Bulletin*

SFC: *San Francisco Chronicle*

SJ: *Syracuse* (New York) *Journal*

SJMN: *San Jose* (California) *Mercury News*

SLGD: *St. Louis Globe-Democrat*

SLH: *Salt Lake* (Utah) *Herald*

SL: *Sporting Life*

SMT: *Sunday Morning Telegram* (Providence)

SN: *Sporting News*

TP: *Times Picayune* (New Orleans)

UDP: *Utica* (New York) *Daily Press*

USJ: *Utica* (New York) *Sunday Journal*

WBTL: *Wilkes-Barre* (Pennsylvania) *Times Leader*

WDS: *Worcester* (Massachusetts) *Daily Spy*

WP: *Washington Post*

WSG: *Williamsport* (Pennsylvania) *Sunday Grit*

WT: *Washington Times*

IMPORTANT MAGAZINE ARTICLES

Bancroft: Frank C. Bancroft, "'Old Hoss' Radbourn," *Baseball Magazine*, July 1908

Folsom: Lowell Edwin Folsom, "America's 'Hurrah Game': Baseball and Walt Whitman," *Iowa Review* 11 (Spring-Summer 1980)

Hanlon: John Hanlon, "First Perfect Game in the Major Leagues," *Sports Illustrated*, August 26, 1968

Holst: David L. Holst, "Charles G. Radbourn: The Greatest Pitcher of the Nineteenth Century," *Illinois Historical Journal* 81 (Winter 1988)

Ivor: Frederick Ivor-Campbell, "Extraordinary 1884," *National Pastime*, Vol. 13, 1993

Pierson: E. E. Pierson, "'Old Hoss' Radbourne," *Baseball Magazine*, August 1917

COLLECTIONS

CCR: Chicago Club Records, Chicago Historical Society

RF: Radbourn folder, National Baseball Hall of Fame Library

SS: Spalding scrapbooks, Albert G. Spalding Collection, New York Public Library

AGM: Abraham G. Mills Papers, New York Public Library

WFG: Thomas Wright, Wright Family Genealogy

BOOKS

Almeida: *Past and Present of Almeida County, California,* vol. II (Chicago, 1914)

Austen: Jane Austen, *Northanger Abbey, Lady Susan, the Watsons and Sanditon* (Oxford, 2003)

Beer: David Nemec, *The Beer and Whiskey League* (New York, 1994)

Benson: Michael Benson, *Ballparks of North America: A Comprehensive Historical Reference to Baseball Grounds, Yards and Stadiums, 1845 to Present* (Jefferson, N.C., 1989)

Boyce: Benjamin Boyce, *The Benevolent Man: A Life of Ralph Allen of Bath* (Cambridge, Massachusetts, 1967)

Burke: John Burke, *Buffalo Bill: The Noblest Whiteskin* (New York, 1973)

Carnegie: Andrew Carnegie, *Triumphant Democracy* (New York, 1886)

Catton: Bruce Catton, *The Coming Fury* (New York, 1961)

Chicago: *Chicago's First Half-Century, 1833–1883* (Chicago, 1883)

Clifford: Nathan Clifford and William Henry Clifford, *Reports of Cases Determined in the Circuit Court of the United States for the First Circuit, from May Term, 1867 to June Term, 1873* (Boston, 1878)

Dickens: Charles Dickens, *Nicholas Nickleby* (Oxford, 1998)

Epstein: Daniel Mark Epstein, *The Lincolns: Portrait of a Marriage* (New York, 2008)

Evers: Johnny Evers and Hugh S. Fullerton, *Touching Second* (Chicago, 1910)

Fielding: Henry Fielding, *Tom Jones* (Oxford, 1996)

Fleitz: David L. Fleitz, *Cap Anson: The Grand Old Man of Baseball* (Jefferson, N.C., 2005)

Foster: G. G. Foster, *Fifteen Minutes Around New York* (New York, 1854)

Goldsmith: Barbara Goldsmith, *Other Powers: The Age of Suffrage, Spiritualism and the Scandalous Victoria Woodhull* (New York, 1998)

History: *History of the State of Rhode Island* (Philadelphia, 1878)

Hyde: *The Hyde Park Historical Record,*
             Volume I, 1891–92 (Hyde Park,
             Mass., 1892)

Industries: *Industries and Wealth of the*
             Principal Points in Rhode Island
             (New York, 1892)

Judge: Mark Gauvreau Judge, *Damn*
             Senators (San Francisco, 2003)

Kaese: Harold Kaese, *The Boston*
             Braves (New York, 1948)

Kahn: Roger Kahn, *The Head Game:*
             Baseball Seen from the Pitcher's
             Mound (San Diego, 2000)

Kelly: Mike "King" Kelly, *"Play Ball":*
             Stories of the Diamond Field and
             Other Historical Writings About
             the 19th Century Hall of Famer
             (Jefferson, N.C., 2006)

Kessner: Thomas Kessner, *Capital City:*
             New York City and the Men Be-
             hind America's Rise to Economic
             Dominance, 1860–1900 (New
             York, 2003)

King: Moses King, *King's Pocket-book*
             of Providence, R.I. (Cambridge,
             Mass., 1882)

Kipling: Rudyard Kipling, *American*
             Notes (Boston, 1899)

Klein: Maury Klein, *The Flowering of*
             the Third America: The Making
             of an Organizational Society,
             1850–1920 (Chicago, 1993)

Lowry: Philip Lowry, *Green Cathedrals*
             (Reading, Mass., 1992)

Lyman: Frank H. Lyman, *The City of*
             Kenosha and Kenosha County
             Wisconsin: A Record of Settle-
             ment, Organization, Progress
             and Achievement (Chicago,
             1916)

Mann: Henry Mann, *Our Police: A*
             History of the Providence Force
             from the First Watchman to the
             Latest Appointee (Providence,
             1889)

Maynard: W. Barksdale Maynard, *Ar-*
             chitecture in the United States,
             1800–1850 (New Haven, 2002)

Mencken: H. L. Mencken, *Happy Days*
             (New York, 1936)

Nemec: David Nemec, *The Great Ency-*
             clopedia of Nineteenth Century
             Major League Baseball, 2nd ed.
             (Tuscaloosa, Ala., 2006)

Nourse: Henry S. Nourse, *The Military*
             Annals of Lancaster, Massachu-
             setts 1740–1865 (Lancaster,
             Mass., 1889)

Palmer: *Palmer House* (Chicago, 1883)

PCD: *Providence City Directory*

Paxon: Harry T. Paxon, ed., *Sport*
             U.S.A.: The Best from the Satur-
             day Evening Post (New York,
             1961)

Ritter: Lawrence S. Ritter, *The Glory*
             of Their Times: The Story of the
             Early Days of Baseball Told by the
             Men Who Played It (New York,
             1966)

Seymour: Harold Seymour, *Baseball: The*
             Early Years (New York, 1960)

Smith: Matthew Hale Smith, *Sunshine*
             and Shadow in New York (Hart-
             ford, 1869)

Social: *The Social Evil in Chicago* (Chi-
             cago, 1911)

Spink: Alfred H. Spink, *The National*
             Game (St. Louis, 1912)

Stars: Robert L. Tiemann and Mark
             Rucker, eds., *Nineteenth Cen-*
             tury Stars (Kansas City, Mo.,
             1989)

Stout: Glenn Stout, *The Dodgers: 120 Years of Dodgers Baseball* (New York, 2004)

Sullivan: Ted Sullivan, *Humorous Stories of the Ball Field* (Chicago, 1903)

Taylor: Maureen A. Taylor, *Picturing Rhode Island: Images of Everyday Life, 1850–2006* (Beverly, Mass., 2007)

Thorn: John Thorn and Pete Palmer, eds., *Total Baseball* (New York, 1989)

Ward: John Montgomery Ward, *How to Become a Player* (Philadelphia, 1888)

Whitman: *Specimen Days: The Complete Prose Works of Walt Whitman,* vol. 1 (New York, 1902)

Wright: Carroll D. Wright, *The Industrial Evolution of the United States* (Meadville, Pa., 1895)

★ ★ ★ ★ ★ ★ ★ ★ ★ ★ ★ ★ ★ ★ ★ ★ ★

NOTES

★ ★ ★ ★ ★ ★ ★ ★ ★ ★ ★ ★ ★ ★ ★ ★ ★

PREFACE

v *" 'I see,' writes a correspondent":* BG, September 2, 1924.

v *"To this day, I don't think":* DNT, March 20, 1920.

v *"He was brainy and game to the core":* MT, January 6, 1919.

v *"He will go down in the history of the game":* NYJ, January 12, 1912.

v *"Volumes have been written about Pitcher Charlie Radbourne":* FWST, January 22, 1911.

vi *"Radbourn's wonderful work":* WBTL, January 10, 1911.

vi *"Each year hundreds of pitchers claim attention":* OP, October 11, 1908.

vi *"He had a disposition that no one like him possessed":* SN, February 4, 1905.

vi *"Radbourne was a man of iron nerve":* RDC, January 2, 1905.

vi *"For dead gameness and grit":* SN, February 27, 1897.

vi *" 'Rad' was indisputably the greatest":* SN, March 6, 1897.

vi *"Radbourn was an eccentric fellow":* PJ, February 6, 1897.

vii *" 'Rad' is a peculiar fellow personally":* QDH, May 11, 1890.

vii *"He is a curious fellow":* BG, April 15, 1888.

vii *"Every fair-minded man":* ET, September 1, 1884.

vii *"Radbourn is the paragon of the season":* CH, September 16, 1884.

vii *"Radbourn pitches ball as if his very life depended upon it":* CL, September 16, 1884.

xi *Tip O'Neill's .492 batting average, Harry Stovey's 156 stolen bases in a single season:*

Modern statisticians have recalculated these once famous numbers: Tip O'Neill's batting average is now .485; Harry Stovey's 156 stolen bases have been sliced to 97.

xi   *A baseball writer named Brown Holmes:* WBTL, January 7, 1916.

xii   *"The real war will never get in the books":* Whitman, 140.

xiii   *"George Wright, the king of players a few years ago":* BG, September 17, 1904.

PROLOGUE: OLD HOSS IS READY

1   *paying hotel porters:* LS, "Nothing to Equal Radbourne Mark," January 7, 1923.

1   *Since his throbbing right arm would no longer cooperate:* Description of Radbourn's morning arm pain and warm-up practices drawn from CE, "Radbourn's Great Record," January 1, 1905; SJMN, "Radbourne a Game One Year He Won Pennant," March 1, 1908; DNT, " 'Old Hoss' Nearly Pitched Arm Off," January 13, 1913; OP, "Greatest Pitcher That Ever Lived," October 11, 1908.

2   *"He was of a silent, somewhat morose disposition":* SJMN, March 1, 1908.

2   *shoulder and stiff neck:* SL, October 8, 1884.

2   *the usual stories about the hazards and horrors of modern life:* CT, September 26 and 27, 1884.

3   *"during the chilly days of the spring and fall, and under a broiling July sun":* Ward, 47–48.

4   *"Old Hoss—that's what we always called Radbourne":* DNT, January 13, 1913.

5   *"Sometimes his face would be drawn up into contortions":* Spink, 150.

5   *"The 'Old Hoss' is ready and we can't be beat":* Bancroft, 13–14.

CHAPTER 1: THE IMPORTANCE OF GRIT

8   *some late news dispatches:* PEB, October 1, 1883.

10   *"Mr. Radbourn," Richmond cried out:* PJ, October 2, 1883. The details of the watch presentation are all drawn from that account.

10   *recipient of the gold watch had once pitched:* PDT, October 5, 1883.

10   *"a good, quiet chap":* PI, "Local Patrol Driver Hurled First No-Hit Fray in Big Leagues," January 26, 1922.

11   *"naturally jealous disposition . . . case of the sulks":* SL, June 22, 1887.

12   *"Radbourne was a man who never despaired of victory":* FWST, January 22, 1911.

12   *"never particularly wonderful in a physical way":* SL, May 11, 1912.

12   *"For dead gameness and grit":* SN, "Ted's Tribute," February 27, 1897.

12   *"sullen, dogged, and indifferent appearance":* SLH, April 5, 1903.

12   *five feet nine inches and weighed 168 pounds:* Statistics drawn from baseball-reference.com.

12   *obsessively firing at bottles:* WBTL, "Pitcher Who Has Good Control Is Most Valuable," August 28, 1912.

12   *"Any delivery without control":* Spink, 152.

12   *"Radbourne often appeared carelessly indifferent":* NYJ, January 12, 1912.

13   *"I'd say the two greatest things he showed me":* Kahn, 45.

14   *"The only difference between the league and slavery":* WSG, October 19, 1884.

14   *"He was a sort of anarchist":* RDC, January 2, 1905.

15   *"The greatest all-round pitcher in the League":* SL, October 29, 1883.

CHAPTER 2: I AM A PITCHER

16   *On an October day thirty-five years earlier:* I am indebted to Dr. P. J. Bendall of Bath, England, for his genealogical research into the Radbourns at Bath and Prior Park.

16   *creation of Ralph Allen:* Details of Ralph Allen's life drawn from Boyce.

17   *"There was an air of grandeur in it":* Fielding, 36.

17   *Roman Catholic bishop Peter Augustine Baines:* "History of Clifton Diocese," www .cliftondiocese.co.uk.

18   *hired a hardworking man from Chilton:* 1841 and 1851 censuses.

18   *Charles, had just married Caroline Gardner:* Marriage of Charles Radbourn to Caroline Gardner registered for 1848, third quarter, at Bath (volume 11, page 50).

18   *birth of their first child, on September:* Baptismal record, October 8, 1848, Sara Maria Radbourn, daughter of Caroli and Carolinae.

18   *living down below in the busy city:* 1851 census.

19   *arrived at the bustling port of New York City in 1854:* BB, October 3, 1909, cited in RF; letter from Red Ringeisen to Lee Allen, October 20, 1965.

19   *on December 11, 1854:* Cited in numerous sources, though the birth record has never been found.

20   *"speak the law to this nation":* Catton, 6–7.

20   *Before the end of the decade:* 1860 census.

20   *Charles senior taught his oldest boy how to hunt:* Pierson, 424.

20   *"didn't like people too well":* RF, letter by Red Ringeisen to Lee Allen, January 29, 1963.

21   *"anxious for another crack at Butte":* DI, April 24, 1884.

21   *"Radbourne's reserved, almost churlish disposition"* and *Radbourn captured a quail:* Pierson, 424.

21   *Charlie's schooling was perfunctory at best:* RF, letter by Red Ringeisen to Lee Allen, January 29, 1963.

22   *"Gee, Old Hoss, ain't you ever going to tire out?":* BP, November 27, 1915.

22   *brakeman on the Indiana, Bloomington, and Western Railroad:* Holst, 256.

22   *"Ever since Charley was big enough to toss a ball":* BP, January 15, 1883.

22   *On the night of August 30, 1876:* BP, September 2 and 4, 1876.

23   *"Charley was decidedly the best pitcher":* BP, January 15, 1883.

24   *relief pitcher against the National League's Chicago club:* Holst, 256.

24   *"Gentlemen, I have the strawberry shortcake team"*: SN, "Without an Equal," February
     4, 1905.

24   *"My heart was throbbing for fear"*: SN, February 27, 1897.

25   a *"defiant air" in the pitcher's box*: Sullivan, 57.

25   *"He was like the mighty oak"*: SN, February 27, 1897.

25   *"There was little of the dress parade"*: SN, February 4, 1905.

25   *"they would settle his ambition as a pitcher"*: SN, February 4, 1905.

26   *accusing Radbourn of pitching with a trick ball*: SN, March 19, 1898.

26   *"He said very little, but was a hard worker:"* NYJ, January 12, 1912.

26   *"The armory was like an ice house"*: NYJ, January 12, 1912.

27   *"I will show these Buffalo people this:"* NYJ, January 12, 1912.

27   *"especial delight in walloping the poor 'Bisons'"*: NYJ, January 12, 1912.

27   *"Radbourne was continually inventing some new delivery"*: IJH, 259.

27   *"He was as strong and sturdy as an oak:"* NYJ, January 12, 1912.

CHAPTER 3: RAGING, TEARING, BOOMING

29   *"an inveterate growler"*: Vaccaro, Frank, "Hugh Daily," The Baseball Biography
     Project, bioproj.sabr.org.

29   *sawed-off stump*: DN, June 29, 1883.

30   *"Don't speed them so hard at me"*: SL, March 19, 1898.

30   *"Only one man smelt first base"*: CCG, July 26, 1883.

30   *"raised a lump on his chest"*: CH, July 31, 1883.

31   *"Four straight defeats is a bitter pill"*: PEP, August 3, 1883.

31   *"The old nations of the earth creep on at a snail's pace"*: Carnegie, 1.

33   *"Charlie, how are you?"*: Smith, 428.

34   *"Avarice, duplicity, falsehood, corruption"*: Goldsmith, 428.

34   *The Ball once struck off*: From *A Pretty Little Pocket-book* (London, 1744). Digital
     image of 1787 edition, published by Isaiah Thomas in Worcester, Massachusetts,
     available on Library of Congress Web site.

34   *Jane Austen . . . named "base ball"*: Austen, 7.

35   *"Let us go forth awhile"*: Folsom, 70.

35   *"I see great things in baseball"*: Folsom, 73.

35   *"to them the highest happiness"*: Foster, 54.

36   *"rather more dangerous to play base-ball"*: NYT, "The National Game," August 30,
     1881.

36   *"The wolf, the snake, the cur"*: Folsom, 74.

36   *"I think base ball is a wretched game"*: SLGD, April 12, 1884.

36   *acts of "low trickery"*: SL, August 20, 1884.

36   *"Injuries were often intentionally inflicted"*: GFH, "Baseball Is Now Uplifted Sport,"
     April 7, 1910.

37   *"raging, tearing, booming nineteenth century!":* BG, April 9, 1889.

37   *"The ball is a combination of cast iron and India rubber":* SL, July 30, 1884.

37   *thrown ball shattered the left forefinger:* NYC, February 3, 1883.

37   *"they got hurt more":* AC, November 1, 1907.

37   *displayed his mauled and misshapen hands:* OP, May 30, 1911.

38   *"fruit cake":* PJ, "When Providence Won the First World's Championship," May 26, 1940.

38   *players had no union:* The first attempt at a union, the Brotherhood of Professional Base Ball Players, was not founded until October 1885. It was kept a secret for a year after that, for fear that owners would retaliate against the members.

38   *as Cleveland center fielder Al Hall discovered:* Nemec, 149.

39   *worthless, dissipated gladiator:* NYT, March 28, 1872.

39   *"more or less despised":* FWST, "Young Collegians Give Tone to Organized Baseball," June 26, 1910.

39   *"only one degree above grand larceny":* Paxon, 5.

39   *crushed, or horribly mutilated:* Klein, 88.

40   *a long, hard day's work:* Wright, 218.

40   *"small boy worships him":* BCA, "Lo! The Poor Player," 1885 clipping cited by baseballhistorian.com.

41   *"The pitcher would turn his back":* Paxon, 7.

41   *"The batter who has once been hit hard":* Ward, 120–21. The player hit by the pitch was Paul Hines.

41   *"It is absolutely necessary":* Ward, 127.

42   *"the batsman could stand and pound away":* BM, "Fans vs. Pitcher: John M. Ward on Baseball," February 1912, 33.

42   *"Striker-up! Low Ball! Play!":* SL, March 19, 1884.

42   *"a fierce-eyed, big-mustached warhorse":* BM, William A. Phelon, "Is Baseball Skill Improving?" June 1914, 54.

43   *visit to a local woodshop run by J. F. Hillerich:* The Louisville Slugger Web site, slugger.com.

43   *big, thirty-five-inch-long ash clubs:* Members of the Providence Grays vintage team use a replica of a bat once used by a Grays player. It is stamped Burlingame, with the Harrison Street address.

44   *"the play is delayed until extradition papers can be obtained":* SMT, June 8, 1884.

44   *"Tedious delays are thus avoided":* SL, September 24, 1884.

44   *ball turned into a wobbling oval of mush:* NYC, August 12, 1882.

44   *paid attendance of ninety-one:* WDS, August 21, 1880.

44   *"a leather bag filled with jelly":* BCA, August 21, 1880.

CHAPTER 4: LUCKY MAN

46   *decided to make a quick trip south:* SL, March 5, 1884.

46   *departed from Boston's Nickerson's Wharf at 3:00 p.m.:* BG, "100 Lives Lost," and NYT, "On Devil's Bridge Rocks," January 19, 1884.

47   *"proverbially a lucky man":* SL, March 5, 1884.

47   *enjoyed a busy and profitable winter:* SL, January 30, 1884.

47   *won a lottery:* SL, March 5, 1884.

48   *"works of art":* PEB, July 3, 1928.

48   *partnered with the Providence and Worcester Railroad:* PEP, April 1, 1884.

48   *"the most successful manager in the business":* SL, January 2, 1884.

49   *Sunday concerts at the Grand Opera House:* NYC, November 18, 1882.

49   *"as 'slick' as they make 'em":* DN, as quoted in ET, June 27, 1884.

49   *"Personally, he is a man of good address":* EG, April 9, 1879.

49   *"He was at his wit's ends":* ET, August 24, 1884. This may sound like a tall tale, but the fact that it was told less than a year after the incident weighs in its favor. Providence games in Cleveland on July 24 and 27 were indeed rained out.

50   *refused to drink even a glass of lager:* EG, April 9, 1879.

50   *"Boys, I'd rather pay the coin out of my own pocket":* SL, September 19, 1908.

50   *forced to fine:* NYC, August 5, 1882.

50   *On one road trip, the manager took a room:* PEB, June 16, 1928.

51   *"every man in the team is a clear-headed, sensible person":* SL, April 2, 1884.

51   *From the start:* Details of Frank Bancroft's life drawn from 1860 census; profile in EG, April 9, 1879; Henry S. Nourse, *Birth, Marriage and Death Register, Church Records and Epitaphs of Lancaster, Massachusetts 1643 to 1850* (Lancaster, 1890), 266; BM, May 1909, 35; RDC, "Frank Bancroft Had Interesting Diamond Career," April 2, 1921.

51   *enlisting under the alias of Henry F. Colter:* Nourse, 331.

52   *"felt prouder over having the famous shortstop":* SL, "Has Quite a Record," May 1, 1897.

52   *"Siberian Carnival":* NBS, "Baseball, Wild Men, and a Siberian Carnival," April 20, 1919.

53   *bluish gray uniforms:* BG, "Manager Bancroft's Southern Venture," December 14, 1879.

53   *"Invalid's Friend and Hope":* Web site of *Antique Bottle and Glass Collector Magazine*, glswrk-auction.com/bitter01.htm; *Time* magazine, "Life with Grandfather," July 25, 1955.

53   *"in every conceivable way but that of actual violence":* NYC, January 3, 1880.

53   *"encourage the Cubans to rebellion":* SL, "Sympathy for Cuba," January 2, 1897.

54   *"a good sprinkling of whom were ladies":* NYC, January 3, 1880.

55   *"Good ballplayers . . . make good citizens":* NYC, April 7, 1883.

55 *went on a drunken spree:* NYC, April 25, 1883.

55 *"Nine very gloomy men walked with Manager Frank Bancroft":* MR, "Cleveland's Collapse," September 11, 1883.

56 *"Wire lowest terms":* Undated and unattributed clipping from Spalding scrapbooks.

56 *thirty-one-year-old wife had died of pneumonia:* NYC, April 7, 1883.

56 *"To be near his boy":* CE, November 1, 1883, quoting a story from CH.

57 *"Mr. Bancroft . . . will always be remembered here":* CE, November 1, 1883.

57 *"a splendid baseball machine":* DNT, "Providence First World Champions," October 20, 1907.

57 *generating a meager profit of $3,098.19:* SL, February 6, 1884.

57 *"rumors swept the city":* PEB, June 30, 1928.

58 *"one of the very best men the League ever had":* AGM, letter to Jno. B. Jeffrey, March 8, 1884.

58 *"in your good Roman grip":* AGM, letter to Henry T. Root, February 2, 1884.

58 *"It is unnecessary to flourish any trumpets":* SL, April 2, 1884.

59 *"I made a bad error leaving Cleveland":* Harry Wright Correspondence, March 1884.

CHAPTER 5: TREASURE FROM THE GOLD COUNTRY

60 *Believing that I am best wing shot in the world:* BP, January 15, 1883.

61 *One W. D. Pearce:* BP, January 20, 1883.

62 *Charlie's Irish-born parents, Edward and Mary Sweeney:* 1860 census.

62 *"a crimson stream was gushing":* SFB, July 2, 1869.

62 *a teenager named Cornelius Dunn:* SFB, "Young Hoodlums Assault a Police Officer," June 7, 1871.

63 *"Parents who permit their sons to train with the Hoodlums":* SFB, June 12, 1871.

63 *subject of repeated complaints:* SFB, November 14, 1873; March 19, 1874; June 10, 1874.

63 *Sunday evening in June 1874:* SFB, June 10, 1874.

63 *vulgar language:* SFB, August 26, 1879.

63 *committing adultery:* SFB, April 2, 1869.

63 *disturbing the peace:* SFB, January 6, 1872.

63 *plunging a knife into a man's chest:* SFB, March 6, 1878.

63 *"was quite as much or more to blame than the officer":* SFB, June 10, 1874.

63 *drum him out of the force:* SFB, June 11, 1874.

64 *managed to get into one National League game:* PJ, May 12, 1882.

64 *"Under more favorable auspices":* PJ, May 13, 1882.

64 *Working for Frank Bancroft's Worcester club:* Hanlon, 76, 83.

65 *"has but one aim":* SFC, April 2, 1883.

65   *lost 8–2 because of his five wild pitches:* SFC, April 2, 1883.

65   *"throwing the game":* SFC, May 19, 1883.

66   *"His swift and deceptive delivery":* PJ, June 12, 1883.

66   *"He has great pace and good curves":* CH, July 31, 1883.

66   *"another treasure from the gold country":* PJ, June 12, 1883.

66   *"Sweeney was a bullheaded chap":* RDC, January 2, 1905.

67   *"One look at the real Sweeney":* PEB, June 21, 1928.

67   *"a mystery to the rest of the country":* PEB, June 29, 1928.

67   *"There is not a man in the Providence":* SS, undated article.

68   *"demonstrated that he is thoroughly competent to alternate with Radbourn":* NYC, January 12, 1884.

69   *"It seems unaccountable to me that the players who go to New Orleans":* CCR, letter by A. G. Spalding to George F. Gore, January 15, 1884.

69   *"Have already advanced you seven hundred dollars":* CCR, letter by A. G. Spalding to Ned Williamson, January 16, 1884.

69   *"Attempting to keep Williamson in funds":* CCR, letter by A. G. Spalding to Ned Williamson, March 7, 1884.

69   *"The fact is, I am heavily in debt":* American Sports, quoted in SL, November 5, 1884.

70   *"Now I do not want any trouble about it":* CCR, letter by A. G. Spalding to F. S. Flint, November 5, 1883.

70   *"It will be unpleasant for you":* CCR, letter by A. G. Spalding to F. S. Flint, November 5, 1883.

70   *"as you become more acquainted with Ball players":* CCR, letter by A. G. Spalding to Charles R. Jeffreys, November 5, 1883.

70   *rented a local gymnasium and got them working out:* SL, March 26, 1884.

70   *significant changes made by National League:* SL, February 27, 1884.

71   *"How pleasant it used to be to witness a game":* SL, January 30, 1884.

72   *"It will affect the batting very little":* SL, January 30, 1884.

CHAPTER 6: BRIMSTONE AND TREACLE

73   *There was something suspicious about them:* SL, April 9, 1884.

73   *an Irish lass named Nancy:* 1880 census.

73   *enlisting as a teenager:* Judge, 13.

74   *baseball matches on the White Lot:* Judge, 13; http://www.whitehouse.gov/baseball/.

74   *Scanlon roared with laughter when he learned:* SL, April 9, 1884.

74   *Central Pacific Railroad Company at Oakland Point:* SL, February 20, 1884.

75   *Gore Combination:* TP, December 17, 1883; SL, January 16, 1884.

75   *Arthur Irwin:* SL, January 23, 1884.

75   *Radbourn and Cliff Carroll arrived early, as did center fielder Paul Hines:* February 6, 1884.

75   *back for another year in the vital role of team captain:* SL., January 16, 1884.

75   *"peremptory order":* PEB, July 3, 1928.

76   *"digging fat Jack in the shins":* SL, April 9, 1884. The paper said the two had since become friends.

76   *Benjamin Franklin Radford:* Hyde, 57–58.

76   *"He is possessed of considerable wealth":* PJ, April 29, 1884.

77   *converted into a gymnasium:* SL, January 23, 1884.

77   *"swift and quite puzzling":* PJ, March 31, 1884.

77   *midnight steamship for a two-day trip:* SL, April 9, 1884.

77   *waded around the bases through mud, slush:* AC, February 18, 1908.

78   *"two motionless forms":* CT, "A Pair of Heroic Esthetes," April 6, 1884.

79   *"the vilest slush imaginable":* BG, April 4, 1884.

79   *massive explosions of the island volcano of Krakatoa:* Ivor, 16.

79   *"cold weather, with snow on the ground":* SL, "Sweeney Speaks," March 6, 1897.

79   *dose himself morning and night:* MT, "Three Most Remarkable Instances of Training," March 27, 1910; DMN, "Touching Second," May 16, 1910.

80   *starving students of Mr. Wackford Squeers's school:* Dickens, 86.

80   *"Whenever we would stop at a railroad station":* PI, "Local Patrol Driver Hurled First No-Hit Fray in Big Leagues," February 26, 1922.

80   *"proved such a success":* NYT, "Ball Players Who Won't Play," July 23, 1884.

80   *In Baltimore, some twenty-five hundred fanatics turned out:* PEP, April 14, 1884.

81   *landlord of the Stevens House in Lancaster:* PEP, April 16, 1884.

81   *Charles H. Byrne:* NYT, "Charles H. Byrne Dead," January 5, 1898; Stout, 18; http://www.theoldstonehouse.org/history.php.

81   *Fifth Avenue horsecars:* Benson, 57–58.

82   *"I feared there would be unpleasantness":* PEP, April 24, 1884.

82   *Bancroft met with Byrne's brother-in-law:* PEP, April 24, 1884.

82   *"pitches as a round-arm cricket bowler":* SL, April 30, 1884.

82   *In the presence of Providence club vice president Ned Allen:* PEP, April 24, 1884.

82   *splendid basket of flowers:* BG, April 20, 1884.

83   *uncharitably crushed the local team:* SL, April 30, 1884.

83   *angrily withdrew his permission:* PEP, April 24, 1884; "A Little Unpleasantness," SL, April 30, 1884; "An Exciting Scene at Washington Park," BE, April 22, 1884.

83   *Bancroft pulled the young pitcher aside:* PEP, April 24, 1884.

84   *He called Bancroft down from the rowdy grandstand:* BG, "Manager Bancroft on the Brooklyn Trouble," April 27, 1884.

84   *"The language used by this man":* BG, April 27, 1884.

85   *"lost prestige"* and *"deserved what they got":* BE, April 22, 1884.

85   *"While deploring any 'kicking' during a ball game:"* PEP, April 24, 1884.

85   *"This is not a question of dollars and cents":* SL, April 30, 1884.

85   *"I dislike very much to raise the cry":* SL, April 30, 1884.

86   *"out of pure mischief":* PEP, April 30, 1884.

86   *splendid gift of a gold-headed ebony cane:* NBS, May 1, 1884.

86   *"in fine trim" to start the home opener:* PEP, May 1, 1884.

CHAPTER 7: PNEUMONIA WEATHER

87   *"ushered in with a clear sunshine":* PJ, May 2, 1884.

88   *104,857 residents:* U.S. Census Bureau, "Population of the 100 Largest Cities and Other Urban Places in the United States: 1790 to 1990," Table 11: "Population of the 100 Largest Urban Places: 1880."

89   *the Rhode Islands made their debut:* PEB, June 5, 1928.

89   *secured a slot for it in the National League:* PEB, June 7, 1928.

89   *"Businessmen left their stores":* PEB, June 8, 1928.

89   *a delusional Providence man named Jimmy Murphy:* PEP, June 28, 1883.

90   *"I will get even with you yet!":* PEP, June 29, 1883.

91   *six-acre site enclosed by a twelve-foot-high board fence:* PMS, May 1, 1878.

91   *open seats at the Messer Street Grounds were filling up with black men:* AC, October 19, 1907.

91   *"one of the largest, grandest":* King, 71.

91   *"Every waiter in the place":* AC, October 19, 1907.

91   *Silver Flint drove a ball deep to center field:* NYC, January 20, 1883.

92   *"I do not want the boy (in an active state)":* HC, May 20, 1875.

92   *"They contained precisely the same rubbery, indigestible pseudo-sausages":* Mencken, 40.

93   *"there was a great shout of laughter from the crowd":* PEP, April 6, 1882.

94   *Testy spectators often yelled, "Louder!":* Kelly, 58.

94   *"constant rolling by heavy stone and iron rollers":* PMS, May 1, 1878.

94   *"the request for an extra pail":* FWST, "Young Collegians Give Tone to Organized Baseball," June 26, 1910.

94   *"these elegant grounds are unexcelled":* BG, April 28, 1878.

94   *"They are beautiful":* PMS, May 1, 1878.

95   *"Nearly the entire city government were present":* ET, May 2, 1884.

95   *admirers "of the lithe forms of the athletic-looking ball players":* ET, May 2, 1884.

95   *"the brilliant feature of the game":* PJ, May 2, 1884.

95   *"sea of pinched faces and blue, chattering lips":* ET, May 2, 1884.

96   *"Radford slid under Briody":* BG, May 2, 1884.

96   *The Sporting Life, the Journal, and the crowd all agreed:* SL, May 7, 1884; PJ, May 2, 1884.

96   *"infantile batting and careless base-running":* PJ, May 2, 1884.

97   *"a lamentable failure":* PJ. May 2, 1884.

97   *"He has lots to learn":* ET, May 2, 1884.

97   *"Well, he is a daisy":* PEP, May 2, 1884.

97   *"The way he dodged away from the ball":* PEP, May 2, 1884.

97   *"If you wouldn't curve 'em so much":* SL, July 23, 1884.

97   *"It isn't possible he has any admirers":* SMT, June 8, 1884.

98   *"predicted he would play his baby act":* FRDEN, May 2, 1884.

98   *working the turnstiles:* PEB, July 5, 1928.

98   *"Radbourn's return to the points":* PJ, May 3, 1884.

99   *a feeble tap by Dan Brouthers:* PEP, May 4, 1884.

99   *a dark, windy, and rainy afternoon:* ET, PJ and PEP, May 8,1884.

99   *"I am running this game, Glasscock; shut up":* ET, May 8, 1884.

99   *insisted the precipitation was a mere trifle:* PJ, May 8, 1884.

100   *"The game shall not be postponed":* ET, May 8, 1884.

100   *"Patrons remembered a game last season":* PJ, May 8, 1884.

100   *"It's no use; some one has got to secure a statue":* FRDEN, May 8, 1884.

100   *"pneumonia weather":* PEP, May 10, 1884.

100   *"could get no speed on the sphere":* ET, May 10, 1884. Source of other ailments cited
      as well.

101   *training all spring under Bancroft's tutelage:* PEP, April 30, 1884.

101   *beating Buffalo's Bisons:* PEP, May 10, 1884.

101   *riding the rumbling elevator in the plush Narragansett Hotel:* SL, May 21, 1884; SMT,
      May 25, 1884.

CHAPTER 8: SHE'S YOURS, RAD

102   *boardinghouse at the corner of Washington Street and Union Street:* PCD, 1884.

102   *"prominent figure in town":* SL, March 27, 1897.

102   *"was attractive and a fashionable dresser":* BG, "Bride Won on Baseball Field," Au-
      gust 7, 1903.

102   *"Billy looks upon it as a relic of friendship":* SL, September 24, 1884.

103   *banjo picking and southern songs crooned in a comical parody of black dialect:* NYT,
      "Billy Baxter, Old Minstrel, Dies," July 14, 1914.

103   *"She personally knew every man of the league teams":* BG, August 7, 1903.

103   *told everyone she was a widow:* PCD, 1879, 1880.

103   *married to a man named Charles Stanhope:* 1880 census; marriage certificate.

103   *said that she was deeply in love:* BG, August 7, 1903.

104   *Among her many fervent admirers was another man:* BG, August 7, 1903.

104   *"played ball with more grace and knowledge":* WP, "Discipline in Ball Team," July 17,
      1904.

104   *"They look like murderers":* Kelly, 25.

104   *"We had most of 'em whipped":* Kaese, 46.

105   *"the Napoleon of the diamond":* WP, "Bunting, team work," April 24, 1904.

105   *"let out a war whoop":* WP, "Was Aggressive Man," April 10, 1911.

105   *"I have got used to being hauled over the coals":* SN, January 7, 1888.

105   *"I've been on the ball fields with him"*: Kelly, 22.

106   *"And if anything stood in the way of his ambitions"*: WP, April 10, 1911.

107   *"Mr. Wright, I have played ball for a number of years"*: Kelly, 28.

107   *"It's a cold day [in hell]"*: CT, September 24, 1882.

108   *"If there was one thing that Carrie Stanhope loved better"*: BG, August 7, 1903.

108   *trooped all forty-two miles from Boston to Providence*: PJ, September 27, 1879.

108   *"Goaded by uncalled-for, as well as unexpected taunts"*: SL, May 7, 1884.

109   *"very clever and sociable off the field"*: DN, August 10, 1883.

110   *"seemed to be demoralized"*: PJ, May 11, 1884.

110   *"do the Chicagos to a nice brown"*: PEP, May 12, 1884.

110   *"using their 'lame' arms to good advantage"*: FRDEN, May 12, 1884.

110   *"the conspicuous sneak"*: PJ, May 13, 1884.

110   *umpire saw the whole thing*: PEP, May 13, 1884.

110   *"useless air agitation"*: PJ, May 13, 1884.

110   *"some of the liveliest leather chasing"*: PJ, May 15, 1884.

111   *Kelly . . . was in top form*: PJ, May 16, 1884.

111   *"made a great 'kick'"*: PEP, May 16, 1884.

112   *spat on his hands, grasped the bat, thumped the plate*: PEP, May 16, 1884.

113   *"Water never did agree with Kelly's complexion"*: FRDEN, May 19, 1884.

113   *"His Curves Puzzle Anson's Children"*: ET, May 17, 1884.

113   *"'Baby' Anson's pets"*: SMT, May 25, 1884.

114   *"thoroughly disgusted with the miserable exhibition"*: SL, May 28, 1884.

114   *"the crackling and flash of flames"*: PJ, May 20, 1884.

114   *Twenty-four years earlier, Stephen A. Douglas*: Taylor, 26; NYH, August 4, 1860.

114   *"several valuable presents"*: PJ, May 20, 1884.

114   *"the greater proportion of the Providence Club"*: CH, May 23, 1884, quoting the *Boston Herald*.

114   *"on being assured that all the boys were aroused"*: ET, May 19, 1884.

115   *"managed to make their escape in their night clothes"*: CH, May 23, 1884.

115   *"Men, women and children rushed to the street"*: ET, May 19, 1884.

115   *"A guest who had not felt well enough"*: PJ, May 20, 1884.

115   *"altogether too near to a sudden and awful death"*: CH, May 23, 1884.

115   *"The old players who have for so long had the entire monopoly"*: SMT, May 25, 1884.

116   *"one of the fiercest ever played"*: BG, August 7, 1903.

116   *"She's yours, 'Rad,' for you won her"*: BG, August 7, 1903.

CHAPTER 9: RED FIRE

118   *"rheumatism in the leg"*: PJ, May 31, 1884.

118   *discovered it and its extraordinary powers*: CT, June 10, 1883, quoting *Boston Herald*.

119   *Owen Winn's shoe*: DFP, June 10, 1883.

120   *Paul Hines began disappearing:* PEB, July 13, 1928.

120   *"The Imperial City of the American continent":* Kessner, 74.

120   *"The manner in which he fooled the New Yorkers":* NYT, May 22, 1884.

120   *"saw the New Yorks wilt away like hot-house plants":* PJ, May 25, 1884.

120   *"And do ye know that the howlers in Providence":* FRDEN, May 26, 1884.

121   *"showed up in their usual chicken-hearted style":* PEP, May 27, 1884.

121   *spectators wore heavy overcoats and wrapped carriage robes:* PEP, May 30, 1884.

121   *"owing to . . . rheumatic difficulty":* PEP, May 30, 1884.

121   *"he was either mad or sick":* PEP, May 30, 1884.

121   *"showed traces of his old strategic pitching":* PJ, May 31, 1884.

122   *"so lame . . . that he could hardly hobble":* SL, June 4, 1884.

122   *"A tall, energetic figure":* June 19, 1928.

122   *won both ends of a Memorial Day doubleheader:* PJ, May 31, 1884.

122   *"for prudential reasons":* PJ, June 2, 1884.

123   *"The Providences need to go in the dry dock":* FRDEN, June 2, 1884.

123   *A ten-by-twelve-inch group picture of the team:* SL, June 10, 1884.

124   *"still suffering with a lame arm":* SL, June 10, 1884.

124   *pugilist slugged him with a $10 fine:* PJ, June 4, 1884.

124   *"KALSOMINED":* ET, June 5, 1884.

125   *"Cattanach needs practice":* PEP, June 6, 1884.

125   *"These clubs may be justly termed the giants":* PJ, June 7, 1884.

125   *"It was scrap from start to finish":* BG, March 11, 1906.

125   *special excursion train to Providence:* BG, June 28 and 30, 1883.

125   *"The treatment of the Boston club at Providence yesterday":* BG, July 4, 1883.

126   *ringing cheers turned to roars of laughter:* BG, May 2, 1884.

126   *"He has a head about the size of a wart":* DN, August 10, 1883.

126   *"the fastest pitcher that ever lived":* CE, November 5, 1883, quoting interview in CH.

126   *"no pitcher in the league that is nearly as hard to handle":* BG, August 2, 1883.

127   *"full of pluck as an egg is full of meat":* BG, August 2, 1883.

127   *"After a player has faced him once":* NPG, August 18, 1883, quoting CE.

128   *"the hoodlum from the Far West:"* BCA, May 11, 1881.

128   *"double up like a jackknife":* BRH, "James H. O'Rourke, Grand Old Man of Base-ball, to Celebrate Forty-Second Year on Diamond," September 28, 1913. Mike Roer, author of *Jim O'Rourke: The Life of a Baseball Radical* (Jefferson, North Carolina, 2005), kindly located this quote for me.

128   *"As can be imagined, to be struck by one of Whitney's pacers":* BG, June 12, 1883.

128   *"dubbed the 'man-hitter' throughout the league":* NPG, June 2, 1883.

129   *Burdock's skull struck the pavement hard:* NYC, April 16, 1881.

129   *twice suffered collisions with other players:* NYC, February 3, 1883.

129   *"Sometimes the runner downs me":* CE, May 28, 1883.

129   *"as apropos as an umbrella for a frog":* FRDEN, June 6, 1884.

130   *between a thousand and fifteen hundred people poured:* PJ, June 7, 1884.

130   *"the finest exhibition of ball playing ever":* BG, June 7, 1884.

130   *"suspected that his right arm had forgotten its cunning":* PJ, June 7, 1884.

130   *"the opinion of gentlemen from Boston":* PJ, June 7, 1884.

131   *"deceptive drop ball":* PJ, June 7, 1884.

131   *"Whitney is a mere skeleton":* PMS, June 7, 1884.

131   *"It would be impossible to describe":* PJ, June 7, 1884.

132   *"Radbourne's days as a pitcher are not over":* PMS, June 7, 1884.

132   *"Outs and ins, drops and rises":* BG, June 8, 1884.

132   *"in magnificent form":* PJ, June 9, 1884.

133   *"the wildest excitement and confusion":* BG, June 8, 1884.

133   *"which Burns did not seem to see":* PJ, June 9, 1884.

133   *"at the sphere as if he would lift it over":* PJ, June 9, 1884.

134   *"Sweeney proved himself a jewel":* SMT, June 8, 1884.

135   *"streets were one vast blaze of red fire":* SL, June 18, 1884.

135   *"nagging him to 'break the record' ":* FRDEN, September 5, 1884.

CHAPTER 10: A WORKING GIRL

136   *came from solid, hardworking stock:* WFG. For the genealogical work on Carrie's
       family, I am indebted to Thomas C. Wright Jr., of Lexington, Massachusetts.
       Mr. Wright is distantly related to Carrie via her mother, who was an Allen; Mr.
       Wright's great-grandmother was an Allen. The Allens lived on what is Allen Av-
       enue in North Attleboro, Massachusetts, which is where Mr. Wright spent much
       of his youth.

136   *Josiah Allen:* WFG.

137   *Henry A. Clark:* WFG.

137   *Harriet Allen:* WFG.

137   *burgeoning family he tried to raise with Harriet:* WFG.

138   *Charles's father, born in 1824, went to sea as a teenager:* NM, "Death of Mr. Stan-
       hope," May 25, 1889; Gravestone at the Common Grounds Cemetery in New-
       port, Rhode Island, records his birthdate as May 16, 1824; Seaman's Protection
       Certificate Register Database, http://library.mysticseaport.org/initiative/Pro-
       tectionDetail.cfm?id=30277.

138   *lawsuit detailing the events:* Clifford, 417–29.

139   *married in Providence:* Marriage certificate, City Registrar's Office.

139   *Carrie on her own in Providence, using her maiden name:* Listed as Carrie S. Clarke,
       Providence City Directory 1873.

139   *at some point contracted the fearful malady of syphilis:* Charles L. Stanhope, death
       certificate, Rhode Island. He died on April 23, 1898, at the State Hospital of
       the Insane in Cranston, of "General Paralysis of the Insane." Stanley M. Aron-

son, M.D., dean of medicine emeritus, Brown University, tells me the certificate "could not have been more explicit." That was the official designation for tertiary syphilis of the brain, sometimes called general paresis.

140 *"she had been married in extreme youth to an engineer":* BG, August 7, 1903.

140 *In its preliminary stage:* Epstein, 19–25. I owe much of this description to his summary of the disease.

140 *"went to Beardstown and during a devilish passion":* Epstein, 19.

140 *"blue mass," three times a day:* Epstein, 19.

141 *"THE GLORY OF A MAN IS IN HIS STRENGTH":* PEB, October 1, 1883.

141 *at 34 Randall Street: Providence City Directory 1873.*

141 *worked long hours in a store called the Japan Switch Company:* Her working address was 169 Westminster Street, *Providence City Directory 1873.*

141 *"Patronized by the best people in the city":* Industries, 144.

141 *bursting with stores in the 1870s:* History, 253–59.

142 *"The number of young girls, from twelve years of age":* Mann, 70.

143 *"She enumerated different articles of clothing":* Social, 204.

144 *"Is it any wonder these girls in sheer desperation":* CDIO, "Women's Kingdom," March 5, 1881.

144 *"She resisted all his persuasion":* NHR, "A Shocking Wife Murder," October 20, 1884.

144 *Merchant H. Weeden:* NHP, "Sad Tragedy at Providence, R.I.," April 26, 1876.

145 *"she only taunted him by daring him to lay a finger on her":* Mann, 321.

145 *had also banked a small fortune of $7,000:* Social, 97–98.

146 *"love of easy life and love of dress":* Fifteenth Annual Report of the Massachusetts Bureau of Labor Statistics (Boston, 1884).

146 *catch a glimpse of him:* NDN, December 20, 1876.

146 *Broad Street boardinghouse as a "widow": Providence City Directory 1879.*

146 *running her own boardinghouse downtown, at 1 Beverly Street:* 1880 census, *Providence City Directory 1880.*

147 *"Charming Carrie Stanhope":* BG, August 7, 1903.

147 *"quiet, order and taste abound":* Smith, 375.

147 *"As the evening wanes and wine flows":* Smith, 376.

147 *"She knows who comes and goes":* Smith, 377.

147 *"poorer houses, meaner dresses":* Smith, 377.

148 *rented a mansion at 51 Washington Street: Providence City Directory 1883.*

CHAPTER 11: AN UGLY DISPOSITION

149 *clutching a big basket brimming with fresh flowers:* PJ, June 10, 1884.

149 *"in tribute to the skill and ability of the young pitcher":* PJ, June 10, 1884.

150 *"sending in a swift, puzzling ball":* PJ, June 10, 1884.

150   *"Too Much Red Fire Maketh the Heart Sink"*: PMS, June 10, 1884.

150   *"The 2306 people rose like one person"*: BG, June 11, 1884.

150   *"did not find a band of music and carriages awaiting their return"*: FRDEN, June 11, 1884, quoting *Boston Herald*.

151   *"Radbourn was in no condition to pitch"*: BG, June 12, 1884.

151   *"lameness . . . has now extended to his shoulder and back"*: PEP, June 12, 1884.

151   *"Radbourn is lame"*: FRDEN, June 12, 1884.

151   *"There are times when we weep"*: PEP, June 14, 1884.

151   *"fruitless wind agitation"*: PJ, June 14, 1884.

152   *"yelled and applauded until it became tired"*: BG, June 15,1884.

152   *"a nasty grounder"*: PJ, June 16, 1884.

153   *"Yeth, but you thee, the whole trouble ith"*: ET, June 10, 1884.

153   *safe to release his failed project*: PJ, June 17, 1884.

153   *Sweeney threw his second near-perfect game*: PJ, June 18, 1884.

153   *"Welch good-naturedly submitted to the slugging"*: PJ, June 19, 1884.

153   *"not many of them had their apparel spoiled"*: PEP, June 20, 1884.

154   *ended up breathing ash and getting singed by hot cinders*: Lefty O'Doul describes what that was like in Ritter, 244.

155   *Gothams arrived in Philadelphia without their trunk*: SL, July 23, 1884.

155   *returned to Cincinnati's Grand Hotel*: NPG, August 25, 1883, quoting CE.

155   *"Both men were bleeding profusely"*: SL, July 9, 1884.

156   *"helpless as so many school boys"*: ET, June 27, 1884, quoting DN.

156   *"Sweeney is surely doing the most effective pitching"*: FRDEN, June 26, 1884.

157   *Jack Manning turned his ankle*: BG and CT, June 22, 1884.

158   *"If you step your foot upon the Boston base ball grounds"*: CHH, June 29, 1884.

158   *"Sir, you are a coward"*: CL, July 2, 1884.

158   *"I expect abuse and am prepared for it"*: CHH, June 29, 1884.

158   *a new kind of bat*: SL, July 9, 1884.

159   *at the Clifton House*: SL, July 2, 1884.

159   *"Here everything is quiet, genteel"*: Chicago, 63.

159   *appetizers, fish courses, main courses, and desserts*: Palmer, 17.

159   *"lighted by the Edison System"*: Palmer, 44.

159   *"overmuch gilded and mirrored"*: Kipling, 92.

159   *"the only thoroughly fireproof hotel in the United States"*: Chicago Historical Society, http://www.chicagohistory.org/fire/queen/pic0521.html.

160   *long whitewashed fence along Michigan Avenue*: Lowry, 127.

160   *main grandstand accommodated two thousand*: Benson, 81–83.

161   *"very cool and witty"*: SL, July 16, 1884.

162   *"What makes you sick, Goldsmith?"*: SL, July 2, 1884.

162   *"He has all the curve he ever had"* and *"$5 bat"*: CT, June 27, 1884.

162   *"a small, quiet player in a brown cap"*: CH, June 28, 1884.

162 *"A cord in his arm above his elbow"*: CH, July 2, 1884.

163 *"to show an ugly disposition"*: NYT, July 23, 1884.

163 *"What work I did, from the opening of the championship season"*: SL, March 6, 1897.

163 *"got a finger knocked out"*: CT, July 1, 1884.

164 *"Providence has no use for McLean"*: CH, June 29, 1884.

164 *"Billy has since got the specs, though"*: SL, June 18, 1884.

164 *"He delivered a slow drop"*: PJ, June 30, 1884.

164 *cranked it over the right-field fence*: CT, July 1, 1884.

164 *"Chicago may be sick but it is a dangerous foe"*: SL, July 9, 1884.

164 *seventeen-hour train journey*: CH, July 2, 1884.

164 *"he said he wasn't earning anybody's salary for them"*: SL, March 6, 1897.

165 *prime example of the "cliqueism"*: SL, October 1, 1884.

165 *the longest hit anyone had ever seen on the grounds*: CT, July 2, 1884.

165 *"a pestiferous little varmint"*: CH, July 2, 1884.

165 *"until he looked hurt and surprised"*: CH, July 3, 1884.

166 *Sweeney had thrown some practice pitches*: CL, July 5, 1884.

166 *"climbed on the roofs and roosted on the fences"*: CL, July 5, 1884.

166 *"he refuses to associate to any extent"*: ET, July 17, 1884.

166 *"he had no expectation of winning"*: SMT, July 6, 1884.

166 *"his arm partially gave out"*: PJ, July 8, 1884.

167 *"Had you not better let Radbourn go in, Charlie?"*: SL, March 6, 1897.

CHAPTER 12: RENDEZVOUS OF THE WAYWARD

168 *a massive Norman-Gothic pile*: King, 89.

168 *"Was struck by the Providence depot"*: Maynard, 269.

169 *staggering cost to taxpayers of $1 million*: King, 28.

169 *Soldiers' and Sailors' Monument*: King, 103–4.

169 *six-story Butler Exchange*: King, 16.

169 *Providence Telephone Company*: King, 110.

169 *demonstrated the magic of his telephone*: BG, April 6, 1877.

170 *Shattuck's Exchange*: King, 77.

170 *stagecoach runs*: King, 76–77.

171 *sharing her block: Providence City Directory 1884*.

171 *"It is adorned by fine shade-trees"*: King, 33.

171 *"one of the most eccentric characters of Providence"*: NYT, "Death of a Providence Character," March 2, 1879, reprinting a story in PEP, February 24, 1879.

172 *"the apple of the eye of Providence"*: Mann, 109.

172 *"filth heaps"*: PEB, October 1, 1883.

172 *'"the beautiful Cove' stinketh to Heaven"*: SMJ, July 13, 1884.

173 *"a rendezvous of the scum"*: Mann, 223.

173   *"They pushed every person they met":* ET, "Capture of Roughs," June 4, 1883.

174   *wife spent hours skulking:* BG, ' "That Other Woman,' " September 11, 1886.

174   *Irish-born:* 1880 census.

174   *"Addicted to drink":* "Through a Panel," BG, December 14, 1894.

174   *"several white girls of youthful age":* ET, "Broken Up," May 31, 1884.

174   *"run out of town":* ET, June 2, 1884.

175   *"Queen Victoria reputation":* Mann, 1884.

175   *"rendezvous of the wayward":* KCS, "The Jumping Off Place," May 27, 1885.

175   *rivers and factories of the industrial revolution:* I owe much of my general knowledge
        of nineteenth-century Providence to historian and professor J. Stanley Lemons
        of Rhode Island College, who very graciously shared his insights and pointed me
        in the direction of useful research.

176   *ten arc lights had been installed:* King, 108.

176   *forty million cubic feet of gas a year:* King, 47.

176   *employed sixty-two lamplighters: Providence City Manual 1880.*

177   *Park Garden:* King, 77.

177   *Sans-Souci Garden:* King, 99.

177   *"on account of the filthiness":* King, 10.

178   *"In summer, when the bay is filled with sailing-craft":* King, 71.

178   *"considered the finest in the country":* King, 10.

CHAPTER 13: CRACKUP

179   *club had provided him a stove:* SL, "Sweeney Speaks," March 6, 1897.

179   *"crude petroleum remedy":* SL, July 9, 1884.

180   *"done him lots of good":* BG, April 15, 1888.

180   *"One thing is evident":* FRDEN, July 8, 1884.

181   *Buffinton's "slow drops":* SL, July 16, 1884.

181   *"foxey to a finish":* BG, "Murnane's Baseball," December 3, 1905.

182   *"insubordination and neglect of duties":* SL, "Bond and Brown," July 16, 1884.

182   *frantically shot off a series of telegrams:* SL, "Another Squabble," July 16, 1884.

182   *"a hit from Burdock would have been most acceptable":* BG, July 12, 1884.

182   *"Just see that Buffinton":* FRDEN, July 15, 1884.

183   *"greatly to his disgust":* PJ, July 12, 1884.

183   *"received with an icy coldness":* FRDEN, July 14, 1884.

183   *"If Blaine is elected":* SL, July 16, 1884.

183   *"Neither Cleveland nor Chicago":* SL, August 6, 1884.

183   *6,137 paying customers:* BG, July 13, 1884.

183   *"it is weak and refuses to obey him":* SL, July 16, 1884.

184   *"Radbourn acted careless and indifferent":* PJ, July 14, 1884.

184   *"to pitch ball for Charlie Radbourne, and not for the nine":* ET, July 17, 1884.

184   *"Radbourn seemed to find it very agreeable"*: SMT, July 13, 1884.

184   *"It is hinted that Radbourne was cranky"*: FRDEN, July 14, 1884.

184   *attributed the defeat Saturday:* NBDM, July 14, 1884.

185   *Charlie downed a quart of whiskey every day:* RF, letter from Red Ringeisen to Lee Allen, January 29, 1963.

185   *"It is best for none of you fellows to say anything to Rad"*: BG, January 5, 1890.

185   *"as a result he was not exerting himself"*: SEH, February 12, 1897.

185   *"plainly showed the effects of his indisposition"*: PJ, July 15, 1884.

186   *"muffing, fumbling and wild-throwing exhibition"*: BG, July 15, 1884.

186   *one Joseph "Cyclone" Miller:* SL, August 6, 1884.

186   *beating Boston's Unions soundly:* BG, July 12, 1884.

186   *paid $150 for Miller's release:* SL., July 23, 1884.

186   *"vast crowd, almost to a man"*: BG, July 16, 1884.

187   *"while hats went into the air"*: Ibid.

188   *"in no condition, physically or mentally"*: BG, July 17, 1884.

188   *"His nerves were unstrung"*: PEP, July 17, 1884.

188   *"almost enough to make an angel weep"*: PEP, June 2, 1883.

188   *"The scorers were consulted"*: BG, July 1, 1883.

188   *compelled to offer Decker protection:* BMJ, July 2, 1883.

188   *police escorted him from the Messer Street Grounds:* PJ, July 2, 1883.

188   *five feet away from the runner:* PI, June 19, 1883.

188   *cries of "Shoot him!" and "Hang him!"*: BG, July 13, 1883, quoting NYH.

189   *"bare-faced robbery of that burlesque"*: BG, August 12, 1883.

189   *"not a bad umpire"*: BG, August 12, 1883, quoting CL.

189   *"Decker, the alleged umpire"*: CT, May 20, 1883.

189   *drew a line of sawdust:* ET, July 17, 1884.

189   *"that he was going to see how far out of the box he could go"*: Ibid.

189   *Radbourn "took the sphere"*: Ibid.

189   *"Radbourn became vexed and slammed the ball"*: PJ, July 17, 1884.

189   *"Then Radbourne gave Gilligan the wrong sign"*: ET, July 17, 1884.

190   *Bill Crowley began to shout:* Ibid.

190   *"Again Gilligan went in and faced the cannon ball delivery"*: Ibid.

190   *"with reckless haste and wildness"*: PJ, July 17, 1884.

190   *"Morrill felt as bad as anyone"*: ET, July 17, 1884.

191   *"exhibited his hands"*: Ibid.

191   *"greatly exercised"*: PJ, July 17, 1884.

191   *"ungentlemanly and unprofessional conduct"*: ET, July 17, 1884.

191   *"feelings of utter disgust at the exhibition"*: PJ, July 17, 1884.

191   *"it had got so bad that he was forced to strike out twenty-seven men"*: ET, July 17, 1884.

191   *"general verdict is that the management should let him go"*: Ibid.

191   *"He has been served with a summons"*: PJ, July 17, 1884.

191   *"sudden lameness, which was set down as rheumatism"*: ET, July 17, 1884.

192   *"dark insinuations afloat"*: PJ, July 17, 1884.

192   *"A 'pitcher' that goes to the well too often"*: ET, July 15, 1884.

192   *"cursed with a bad temper"*: PEP, July 18, 1884.

192   *"Radbourn's popularity with the Providence people is ruined"*: BG, July 18, 1884.

192   *"If Radbourne leaves Providence good-bye any hope"*: FRDEN, July 18, 1884.

CHAPTER 14: DRUNK ENOUGH TO BE STUPID

193   *"It looks as though the base ball craze"*: SL, August 6, 1884.

193   *"The skillful player is constantly dwelling"*: SL, August 27, 1884, quoting the CHH.

193   *Jack Farrell had turned down a $1,000 offer*: ET, July 15, 1884.

193   *"strips splendidly, showing a well-proportioned physique"*: PEP, April 7, 1882.

193   *"cigarette fiend"*: BCA, September 1, 1882.

194   *"It does seem to me that there can be no possible objection"*: AGM, July 15, 1884 letter to J. Edward Allen.

194   *The UA was a new league*: Seymour, 149.

195   *"A rich man like Lucas"*: SL, July 16, 1884.

195   *"Onion" Association*: Seymour, 150.

195   *"very glad indeed" to learn*: AGM, July 18, 1884, letter to J. Edward Allen.

195   *"I'll not only go into the business"*: SL, July 9, 1884.

196   *"on perfectly reliable authority"*: PJ, July 21, 1884, quoting BH of July 20, 1884.

196   *"Radbourn is an old player, and a good pitcher"*: Ibid.

196   *"The end of the Unions cannot be far distant"*: ET, July 22, 1884.

196   *"If a player is to be reprimanded"*: FRDEN, July 21, 1884.

196   *"overworked last year"*: Ibid.

197   *"If Miller had been weakening"*: BG, July 18, 1884.

197   *"will cure Radbourne's perversity quicker"*: ET, July 18, 1884.

198   *"looks more as if he were studying for holy orders"*: PEP, July 21, 1884.

198   *twenty-one of the Stars of Bristol*: ET, July 2, 1884.

198   *"twirls the sphere with swiftness and accuracy"*: PJ, July 20, 1884.

199   *fortifying himself with whiskey*: ET, July 23, 1884.

199   *half-drunk player arrogantly refused to do so*: NYT, "Ball Players Who Won't Play," July 23, 1884. The ET of the same date reports that Sweeney's catcher, Sandy Nava, refused to come home as well.

199   *"If you want to know why I was not here"*: ET, July 23, 1884.

200   *"evincing jealousy of young Miller"*: NYT, July 23, 1884.

200   *"Sweeney was a bull-headed fellow"*: WP, "Radbourne's Great Record," January 1, 1905.

200   *disrespectfully "surly tone"*: SL, March 6, 1897.

200   *"came nearly a fight on the field"*: WP, January 1, 1905.

200   *"You go out to right field and let Miller come in":* SL, March 6, 1897.

200   *"I give you a tip. I finish all the games I start":* ET, July 23, 1884.

200   *"Gentlemen, you now see":* Ibid.

201   *"most villainously abused":* NYT, July 23, 1884.

201   *"It is true I called him names":* SL, March 6, 1897.

201   *"he had a place to go, and could make a living away from Providence":* ET, July 23, 1884.

201   *"just drunk enough to be stupid":* Ibid.

201   *actually stood there:* Ibid.

201   *"face brightened up like a luminous match":* FRDEN, July 24, 1884.

201   *"foolish pitcher left the grounds in the company of two women":* SL., July 30, 1884.

201   *"very bad company":* ET, July 23, 1884.

202   *knew Sweeney's nature so well:* WP, January 1, 1905.

202   *"in order to retain the respect of the base-ball public":* CT, July 24, 1884.

202   *"one of the most disgraceful exhibitions":* SMT, July 27, 1884.

202   *"knocked around like corn in a popper":* FRDEN, July 29, 1884.

202   *"The club was going to disband":* DNT, January 13, 1913.

202   *"There are no pitchers to be had":* NYT, July 23, 1884.

203   *"Disbandment would be crowning triumph of scoundrels":* AGM, July 23, 1884 telegram to Henry T. Root.

203   *"Don't give up the ship":* AGM, July 23, 1884 telegram to J. Edward Allen.

203   *"Will run a nine [even] if we put amateurs":* AGM, letter by A. G. Mills to each league club president, July 23, 1884.

203   *"wooden cigar-store Indians to represent the club":* BG, July 24, 1884.

203   *"A watch is to be kept on 'funny players'":* CHH, July 24, 1884.

203   *"I am proud of the Providence club":* AGM, letter by A. G. Mills to each league club president, July 23, 1884.

203   *"There seems to be something cyclonic":* FRDEN, July 24, 1884.

204   *"The conduct of the fellow is shameful":* SL, July 30, 1884.

204   *"rum killed Sweeney's chances":* FRDEN, July 25, 1884.

204   *"There are just two sides to each story":* FRDEN, July 29, 1884.

204   *"He claimed that in Boston his arm was lame":* ET, July 17, 1884.

205   *"with uncommon speed":* PJ, July 24, 1884.

205   *"It was a gratifying exhibition to the spectators":* Ibid.

205   *"Radbourn had been pitching great ball":* WP, January 1, 1905.

205   *Sweeney's salary as well as his own:* The *New York Journal,* in an article reprinted in ET on August 25, 1884, reported that Providence gave Radbourn $2,000 on top of his own salary, "and if he gets it an honest and manly player will be rewarded." That would have meant the stupendous sum of $5,000 for the year.

205   *"If you will strike out the reserve clause":* WP, January 1, 1905.

206   *"I can jump a contract with the league":* WSG, October 19, 1884.

206 *"I can win the flag all right"*: Spink, 150.

206 *"Nobody believed 'Rad' could make good"*: PEB, July 11, 1928.

206 *"He said he'd pitch his arm off"*: DNT, January 13, 1913. In WP, January 1, 1905, Bancroft offers a less emphatic response from Radbourn: " 'I will do the best I can,' he said, 'if I can go free when the season is over.' "

207 *"Sweeney was getting all the credit for everything"*: SL, March 6, 1897.

207 *"All the boys are down on him"*: ET, July 25, 1884.

207 *" 'Served him right,' seems to be the unanimous verdict"*: PEP, July 24, 1884.

207 *"Charley Sweeney's temper throttled his good judgment"*: USJ, July 16, 1898.

207 *"Radbourn is himself again"*: PEP, July 24, 1884.

207 *"I candidly believe he never had any intention of skipping the nine"*: ET, July 24, 1884.

207 *"THE CRISIS OVER"*: Ibid.

CHAPTER 15: THE SEVERE WRENCHING

208 *staggered down Eddy and Point streets:* ET, July 25, 1884.

208 *going into the enemy's camp, capturing their guns:* ET, August 13, 1884.

208 *Grays had it coming to them:* SL, July 30, 1884.

208 *"All the harm I can wish the Unions":* ET, July 24, 1884.

208 *"splendid service in the early part of the season":* SL, August 6, 1884, quoting MR.

209 *igniting a controversy a century later:* The esteemed baseball historian Frederick Ivor-Campbell has studied this issue of victories closely and dispassionately, inspiring baseball to change its official records to reflect the more accurate number.

210 *On July 19, when Van Court was working in Boston:* BG, July 20, 1884.

210 *deep cut above his left cheek could be covered with court plaster:* NBDM, July 24, 1884.

210 *"the champion roller skater of the Pacific coast":* SL, April 15, 1885.

210 *"His decisions were wretched":* PJ, August 1, 1884.

210 *"highly indignant" mob hooted and hissed:* Ibid.

210 *"their umpire came to the rescue":* NYT, August 1, 1884.

210 *Miller "looked out for 'number one' ":* FRDEN, August 1, 1884.

210 *"All the pitchers are now showing the effects . . . the severe wrenching":* SL, August 13, 1884.

211 *his father a laborer, his brother a bakery worker:* 1880 census.

212 *Will Salkfeld, catcher of the aptly named Painsville Club:* SLGD, August 17, 1883.

213 *"battered, bruised, crippled and blood besmeared catcher":* SN, April 23, 1887.

213 *"On a hot day, when the blood circulated freely":* WBTL, "Rusie was the best," March 7, 1910.

214 *his hard hands cracked open:* CE, November 18, 1883.

214 *"with blood dripping from his fingers' ends":* Ibid.

214 *"the most intense agony":* Spink, 91.

214 *"His fingers have been battered almost to pieces:"* SN, November 12, 1887.

214 *heavy cork chest protector:* DFP, May 1, 1883.

214 *"Oh! get a bed!":* CH, May 22, 1884.

214 *foul tips sometimes snapped the wire:* As happened repeatedly to Jack Rowe, reported in BCA, August 13, 1880, and SL, April 30, 1884.

215 *"wriggled over about 10 square feet of grass":* CDIO, May 18, 1883.

215 *"There is something radically wrong":* NYW, August 6, 1884.

215 *"the agility of a cat and the fleetness of a deer":* NYT, August 7, 1884.

216 *"This gentleman was in the worst humor possible":* NYT, August 9, 1884.

216 *"umpired fairly and impartially, if anything":* SL, August 13, 1884.

216 *"Call the game. What can they do?":* NYT, August 9, 1884.

217 *"forgot themselves":* BG, August 9, 1884.

217 *"a stunning blow":* NYT, August 9, 1884.

217 *"A regular pitched battle ensued":* SL, August 13, 1884.

217 *"Things have reached such a state in New York city":* Ibid.

217 *"We have been shabbily treated by the umpires":* NYT, August 9, 1884.

217 *On September 24, a dark, rainy afternoon:* SL, October 8, 1884.

219 *a big, rugged-looking man arrived:* PJ, August 7, 1884.

219 *"Down to its smallest details, the show is genuine":* Mark Twain, letter to Buffalo Bill Cody, September 10, 1884, quoted in Burke, 164.

220 *"Everyone rides in that coach":* PJ, August 7, 1884.

220 *"sadly dilapidated":* BG, May 14, 1884.

220 *"a disgrace to the city and the club":* BG, July 8, 1883.

220 *"the poorest and most shabbily fitted-up":* NYC, September 29, 1883.

220 *some three hundred people had watched a game from outside:* BG, May 30, 1882.

221 *more "screen work":* BG, May 30, 1883.

221 *painted the poles with a slow-drying brand of sticky black paint:* SL, July 30, 1884.

221 *"It was one of those games":* BG, August 10, 1884.

221 *"the great game of the season":* PJ, August 11, 1884.

221 *"so close that he must have heard it sing":* BG, August 10, 1884.

221 *"the great gathering roared with laughter":* Ibid.

221 *"the entire Boston team simply stood and looked at it":* IS, "Cliff Carroll First Player to Bunt Ball," February 19, 1921.

221 *"A vigorous striking out is preferable:"* FRDEN, August 14, 1884.

222 *"Crowley! Crowley!":* BG, August 10, 1884.

222 *after his wife gave birth:* ET, June 17, 1884.

222 *"set his eye on that hole, and aimed for it":* SJ, "Went Through Hole in Fence," June 3, 1911.

222 *"Now that would depend":* FRDEN, August 11, 1884.

223 *"With Whitney in the 'box'":* BG, August 12, 1884.

223 *"But while they were in ecstasy in this inning":* Ibid.

223   *"the scoring of one run meant fully as much mischief"*: Ibid.

224   *"girded up his loins, dashed for the plate"*: PJ, August 12, 1884.

224   *"his thorough mastery of the sphere"*: Ibid.

224   *betting ran 2 to 1 against Providence*: ET, August 13, 1884.

224   *"Sure . . . I'm all right"*: SJMN, November 1, 1908. Irwin was confused over some
       of the details; Radbourn had not pitched four straight days, as he asserted, and
       the 4–0 game did not take place on a Saturday. But the story seems to contain
       a kernel of truth in capturing the public's surprise that Radbourn was pitching
       day after day.

224   *"he believes he can hold out against any and all League teams"*: ET, August 13,
       1884.

224   *"There is a tradition among the oldest inhabitants"*: Boston Post quoted in ET, August
       13, 1884.

225   *"If me was out of debt"*: PEB, July 13, 1928.

225   *one actually looked up Hines's "good Hibernian parents"*: SL, December 17, 1884.

225   *"Paul is very deaf when he wants to be"*: Ibid.

225   *"I found Paul at work on it, with a carpenter's pencil"*: Ibid.

226   *"while Paul was admiring the gift"*: ET, August 15, 1884.

226   *"playing Fox on Hines"*: BG, August 15, 1884.

227   *"John Morrill stepped to the plate"*: PJ, August 15, 1884.

227   *"Now, Joe!"*: BG, August 15, 1884.

227   *"A shout went out from those Providence throats"*: FRDEN, August 18, 1884.

227   *"Good-by, Fall River delegation"*: PMS, quoted in FRDEN, August 18, 1884.

227   *"The Providence scribes are lubricating Irwin all over"*: FRDEN, August 14, 1884.

228   *"Boston audiences are behind the times"*: FRDEN, August 18, 1884.

228   *"Even if Gilligan throws back a ball high"*: FRDEN, August 27, 1884.

228   *"Too bad! It were better that they enter the big sewer"*: FRDEN, August 26, 1884.

228   *"for a better-played string of games"*: BG, August 15, 1884.

228   *"magnificent contests, and fortunate indeed"*: SL, August 20, 1884.

229   *"Providence people have great cause to thank him"*: ET, August 25, 1884.

229   *"Will the Providences go through the season"*: FRDEN, August 18, 1884.

CHAPTER 16: INWARD LAUGHS

230   *informed their poor manager, Charlie Hackett*: SL, August 20, 1884.

231   *"had used him 'white'"*: SL, August 20, 1884, quoting CH.

231   *"They wanted me to go, and Mac asked me"*: SL, September 24, 1884, quoting CH.

231   *"Disbandment now would seriously injure League"*: AGM, August 9, 1884, telegram
       to C. H. Bulkley, president, Cleveland Ball Club.

231   *"the unscrupulous gang of thieves"*: AGM, August 26, 1884, letter to H. Chadwick.

231   *"supply the places of the traitors"*: BG, August 14, 1884.

232   *"it was evident that the spectators accorded the Clevelands much sympathy"*: PJ, August

16, 1884.

232   *"seized with a hemorrhage of the bladder"*: BG, August 16, 1884.

232   *"the grandest short stopping in the League"*: SL, August 20, 1884.

232   *proudly burned the number 448:* PJ, "When Providence Won the First World's Championship," May 26, 1940.

233   *"We do not like the idea of these exhibition games"*: ET, August 25, 1884.

234   *"brainiest pitcher that ever delivered a ball across the plate"*: SJMN, "Radbourne's Records Are Likely to Stand," April 12, 1908.

234   *"But Radbourne, as sure as you live"*: Spink, 151.

234   *"hundreds of would-be pitchers"*: SL, September 10, 1884.

234   *"This was the basic secret of his great success"*: WBTL, August 28, 1912.

234   *"I want the men behind to have something to do"*: RDC, January 2, 1905.

234   *"Radbourne, in some games, deliberately tossed the ball"*: FRDEN, May 5, 1885.

235   *"would bear the most careful watching"*: NYJ, January 12, 1912.

235   *One of his most devastating pitches:* SL, September 10, 1884.

235   *"It seemed impossible"*: Evers, 107.

235   *imparted the secret pitch to his friend Clark Griffith:* Evers, 108.

235   *liable to spring some new pitching wrinkle:* NYJ, January 12, 1912.

235   *"They may get used to his delivery today"*: BG, May 9, 1887.

235   *"Pitchers in his day had the privilege"*: NYJ, January 12, 1912.

236   *"the least exertion possible"*: Ibid.

236   *"One secret of his success"*: SL, September 10, 1884.

236   *"The best pitcher"*: SN July 26, 1886.

236   *"his inward laughs must have been immense"*: NYJ, January 12, 1912.

236   *"Keep in the box!"*: FRDEN, August 26, 1884.

237   *Gore went on the field "so drunk"*: FRDEN, August 28, 1884.

237   *put on the Grays togs of little Sandy Nava:* PJ, August 28, 1884.

237   *"Go in, even if they make a thousand runs!"*: ET, August 28, 1884.

237   *"sent a boy on the roof after the sphere"*: Ibid.

238   *offered Clarkson a cool $400 a month:* SL, August 27, 1884.

238   *"showed him to be a player of much value"*: PJ, August 29, 1884.

238   *"lost his head completely"*: PJ, August 29, 1884.

238   *"with glaring eyes"*: SMT, July 6, 1884.

239   *"did not know whether they were muffing"*: SL, September 10, 1884.

239   *"This year it has been impossible to discipline"*: SL, November 5, 1884.

239   *"for having abstained from intoxicating drinks and orgies"*: WP, October 7, 1885.

239   *"It was a straight whiskey"*: Fleitz, 139.

240   *"Radbourn's easy delivery"*: ET, August 30, 1884.

240   *tying Larry Corcoran's major-league record:* Thorn, "Streaks and Feats," 484.

240   *dirty tricks scorned by their moral superiors:* FRDEN, quoted in SL, September 17, 1884.

241   *"These hints and innuendos are all wrong"*: SL, September 17, 1884.

241 *a life-sized crayon portrait of Radbourn:* PJ, September 3, 1884.

241 *"a monument of skill and strategy":* Ibid.

242 *"you have such demon pitchers here":* PEB, July 11, 1928.

243 *"one of his old-fashioned three-baggers":* PJ, September 5, 1884.

243 *"took up his little bat, spat upon his hands":* ET, September 6, 1884.

243 *"the like of which was never seen":* FRDEN, September 9, 1884, quoting PMS.

243 *"several miles over the Connecticut boundary":* FRDEN, September 9, 1884.

244 *"LAST GAMES OF SEASON 1884":* PJ, September 6, 1884.

244 *"He put out his man, however":* SMT, September 7, 1884.

244 *"Radbourn pitched with his old-time effectiveness":* PJ, September 8, 1884.

244 *"20TH STRAIGHT":* SMT, September 7, 1884.

245 *"an infant in the tall hat of its father":* SL, September 17, 1884, quoting the *Boston Courier.*

245 *about 60,000 for the season:* SL, September 24, 1884.

245 *"rather see the pennant go to Providence":* Ibid.

245 *"in prime form":* PJ, September 8, 1884, quoting *Boston Herald.*

245 *"Radbourne might get disabled in the meantime":* FRDEN, September 1, 1884.

245 *"Radbourn is in splendid trim at present":* PJ, September 8, 1884.

246 *"The whole country had been looking":* PEB, July 12, 1928.

246 *"putting Eggler out, as every person who witnessed":* PJ, September 10, 1884.

246 *"This thing was getting monotonous":* ET, September 10, 1884.

247 *the crowd roared and cheered:* Ibid, citing the *Boston Journal.*

247 *pledged that Providence would not lose again at home:* Ibid.

247 *"strong right arm . . . has not 'forgotten its cunning'":* PJ, September 12, 1884.

247 *several members of the Beaneaters:* PJ, September 13, 1884.

248 *"I looked for him to give up the job":* DNT, January 13, 1913.

248 *"a bulky envelope containing lawful currency":* PJ, September 15, 1884.

249 *"in excellent spirits and fine physical trim":* Ibid.

250 *Radbourn was "not alarmed":* Ibid.

250 *boardinghouse kept by Mary Larvin:* Ibid.

CHAPTER 17: A PROMISE KEPT

252 *"How about Buffinton now, Mr. Boston Herald?":* ET, September 17, 1884.

253 *"Does that account for his weak pitching?":* SL, September 24, 1884.

253 *"The Providence Club may just as well":* SL, September 24, 1884.

254 *"cripples, bums and bigheads":* CT, September 27, 1884.

254 *"disgraceful exhibition":* CHH, September 27, 1884.

255 *"THE PENNANT WON":* PJ, September 27, 1884.

255 *"W-H-O-O-P!":* PMS, September 28, 1884.

255 *"earned in fair play the right to take the largest":* SL, October 8, 1884.

255 *"wreckers' association"* . . . *"contemptible trick"*: PMS, September 28, 1884.

255 *"suffering from a fit of 'temporary' hostility"*: PJ, September 29, 1884.

256 *"This has been Radbourn's year"*: PJ, September 29, 1884, quoting *Boston Herald*.

256 *"many with a knowing smile"*: BG, September 28, 1884.

256 *"the acknowledged king of the box"*: SL, October 8, 1884.

256 *"The happiest man in the profession"*: Ibid.

256 *"That club was certainly a hummer"*: DNT, October 20, 1907.

256 *"lucky horseshoe find"*: SL, October 8, 1884.

256 *"It is to be regretted that the championship"*: PJ, September 29, 1884, quoting BH.

257 *"as scarce as politeness among the Providence spectators"*: SL, October 1, 1884.

257 *dash from Chicago to his home in Bloomington:* Ibid.

258 *"Radbourn is feeling the effects"*: September 30, 1884.

258 *"Radbourne, Gilligan and Denny resume"*: SL, October 8, 1884.

258 *"They left him to get up and withdrew all sympathy"*: SL, October 15, 1884, quoting the CH.

259 *"But that reminds us that 'Rad' must be consulted"*: FRDEN, October 11, 1884.

259 *"worst exhibition of thick-headed bull playing"*: PJ, October 12, 1884.

259 *"was regarded of more importance than the game"*: PMS, October 18, 1884.

259 *"but Bancroft and Radbourn wouldn't have it"*: SL, October 22, 1884.

259 *"The weather was cold, and the crowd was small"*: PI, October 16, 1884.

261 *"a 'little bird' has whispered"*: PJ, October 18, 1884.

CHAPTER 18: THE BEST ON EARTH

262 *some seven thousand citizens packed downtown:* Description drawn from PMS, ET, PJ, October 18, 1884; SL, October 22, 1884; and BE, October 26, 1884.

262 *"pyramid of humanity"*: PMS, October 18, 1884.

263 *"As Radbourne left the cars and began to walk"*: BE, October 26, 1884.

264 *"Everybody was on the street; in fact"*: SL, October 22, 1884.

264 *"Some men are born great, some achieve greatness"*: ET, October 18, 1884.

264 *"three times three for Bassett and Radbourne"*: Ibid.

264 *"than would have been tendered either of the Presidential candidates"*: Ibid.

264 *"in the best of health and spirits"*: PJ, October 22, 1884.

264 *"at League prices"*: SL, October 29, 1884.

265 *"three phenomenal catches"*: PJ, October 21, 1884.

265 *"a present from a lady friend"*: Ibid.

266 *"Coats were thrown aside"*: PJ, October 22, 1884.

266 *ran into some barbed wire:* Ibid.

266 *"savory bivalve could hardly maintain its supremacy"*: PJ, October 22, 1884.

267 *"I would rather wear that badge than be president"*: PMS, October 22, 1884.

267 *Jim "Smilin' Jeems" Mutrie:* NYT, "Manager Mutrie Confident His Men Will Win

the Championship," August 31, 1885; NYT, "Tales of Tim Keefe," April 25, 1933.

267   *"Championship of America":* ET, October 17, 1884, October 16 letter by Frank Bancroft.

267   *"world's championship":* SL, October 29, 1884.

268   *"the poor of the city":* ET, October 1, 1884.

268   *"getting up some free advertising":* FRDEN, August 4, 1884.

268   *"But, while the project strikes me unfavorably":* AGM, letter to "Friend [Henry] Chadwick," August 4, 1884.

269   *privately to Root on the same day:* letter to Henry T. Root, August 4, 1884.

269   *"I regret very much that any one would misinterpret our intentions":* SL, August 13, 1884.

269   *proposed a best-of-five set:* ET, October 1, 1884.

269   *talked Mutrie instead into a three-game series:* ET, October 17, 1884.

269   *"how easily his Metropolitan crew":* DNT, October 20, 1907.

270   *"The boys were hardly in shape to play":* Ibid.

271   *"six months of malaria":* Beer, 62.

271   *the Mets lost $8,000:* NYT, "Bothered About the Mets," March 8, 1888. The *Official Base Ball Record,* August 11, 1885, had the Mets losing even more money, $20,000. See Harold Seymour, "The Rise of Major League Baseball to 1891," Ph.D. thesis, Cornell University, June 1956, 351n.

271   *"These will probably be the greatest games ever played":* SL, October 22, 1884.

272   *"A cold, raw wind blew across the grounds":* PJ, October 24, 1884.

274   *"One may see, therefore, that Mets patterns are firmly imbedded":* NYT, "Nostradamus and Herodotus," August 1, 1965.

275   *"masterly exhibition of strategic skill":* BE, October 24, 1884.

275   *"they were afraid of Radbourn":* BG, October 24, 1884.

275   *"Radbourne struck terror to their hearts":* NYT, October 24, 1884.

275   *"AFRAID OF RADBOURN":* BG, October 24, 1884.

276   *suspended their "free list":* BE, October 25, 1884.

276   *"Both teams, especially the Mets":* NYT, October 25, 1884.

277   *"Radbourne . . . was an insurmountable obstacle":* Ibid.

278   *"turned up their noses and said they would not play":* NYT, October 26, 1884.

278   *"he would not disappoint his patrons":* Ibid.

278   *"A keen northwest wind swept across":* PJ, October 26, 1884.

278   *"The Metropolitans played most wretchedly":* BG, October 26, 1884.

278   *"CHAMPIONS OF THE WORLD":* SL, October 29, 1884.

279   *'"Champions of this Mundane Sphere'":* FRDEN, October 27, 1884.

279   *"He was as strong in the third game":* BG, October 12, 1915.

279   *"just about broke Mutrie's heart":* DNT, October 20, 1907.

279   *"Allen almost fell on his neck and wept for joy":* Spink, 150.

279 *"to fulfill a boast of his prowess"*: BE, September 14, 1884.

280 *"They knew there was a girl in Providence who was pretty sweet"*: RF, undated clipping, no headline, featuring Bancroft's recollections.

EPILOGUE: CALLED OUT BY THE INEXORABLE UMPIRE

281 *How swiftly grows the laurel:* BG, September 11, 1915.

282 *"the greatest pitcher in the country"*: UDP, January 3, 1888.

282 *Sweeney's equal never existed:* Ibid.

282 *"the most difficult man to hit"*: BG, December 3, 1905.

282 *"a man of great strength and power"*: Spink, 157.

282 *"Well, Seery, old man"*: NYC, November 21, 1885.

282 *"whiskey-guzzling cowardly nincompoop"*: Beer, 76.

282 *"carry a small arsenal in his back pocket"*: SN, July 12, 1886.

283 *"in the coolest manner possible"*: Ibid.

283 *"a worthless girl of fifteen years of age"*: SJMN, "About a Girl," July 1, 1891.

283 *"in a familiar manner"*: SFB, "A Ball-Player's Wrath," July 1, 1891.

283 *"Grim Death is likely to punch his ticket"*: CDIO, July 18, 1891.

283 *odd jobs:* MC, July 16, 1894.

283 *circle of San Francisco mobster Frank "King" McManus:* KCS, "Once a Famous Ward Boss: Death of 'King' McManus, a Power in San Francisco Politics and Fist Fights," November 1, 1896.

284 *shot in the left breast in a bar brawl:* CDIO, "They Will Both Die," June 26, 1892.

284 *"I never knew him in such an ugly mood"*: RF, Transcription of *San Francisco Post* article, per SL, August 4, 1894.

284 *"called me all the names he could think of"*: Ibid.

285 *"I'm sorry for what I have done"*: MC, July 16, 1894.

285 *sought out the Reverend Peter J. Grey:* KCS, "Once a Famous Ward Boss," November 1, 1896, reprint of *San Francisco Chronicle* story.

285 *seventy-four-year-old:* 1880 census.

285 *"an earnest and stern man of the old school"*: Almeida, 269.

285 *reports that he bribed four jurors:* IS, "Jury Bribing in San Francisco," December 6, 1893.

285 *Sweeney's wife fainted in the courtroom:* SJMN, "Fate of Sweeney," November 1, 1894.

286 *"and I know that he will be amply repaid"*: SL, March 6, 1897.

286 *"he ought to have been rewarded for the killing"*: BM, "The Critics' Corner," January 1914, 89.

286 *Budd granted him a formal pardon:* NHR, April 5, 1898.

286 *arrested the ex-con for assault:* EN, "Umpire Sweeney Ran Away," August 2, 1898.

286 *slip to officers there:* EN, "Sweeney Escaped," August 3, 1898.

286   *"await the final summons of death"*: SJMN, "Death Waits at Final Goal for Old Time
       Coast Ballplayer," February 11, 1902.

286   *broken man, Radbourn's old adversary died:* Stars, 123.

287   *"Next year will be the time when his arm will show"*: FRDEN, September 30, 1884.

287   *"handsome woman"* and *"pronounced brunette"*: MS, "Frank Bancroft Wedded,"
       March 30, 1885. Marriage also reported in *The Whalesman's Shipping List* (New
       Bedford, Mass.), March 31, 1885.

287   *"Mr. Bancroft seemed to regard the defeat"*: NYT, September 12, 1885.

287   *"You have got the best pitcher in the world"*: NYC, December 19, 1885.

288   *"and this is not croaking, either"*: Ibid.

288   *"deterred them from attending later games"*: PJ, "When Providence Was in the Na-
       tional League," January 24, 1904.

288   *"I have kissed Mr. Allen hundreds of times"*: PEB, "Mrs. Pepper Says She Kissed J.
       Edward Allen," September 12, 1907.

288   *Allen literally died of shock:* PEB, "J. Edward Allen, Ill Only a Night, Dies from
       Shock," September 13, 1907.

289   *"Every human being in the hotel"*: OP, July 9, 1911.

289   *"Do you think I'm a fish?"*: DNT, "Tersely Told Tales of Ball Field," August 1, 1915.

289   *handled the cash in more than four thousand ball games:* BG, May 8, 1917.

289   *"Father of Baseball in Cuba"*: GFH, "Cuba to Figure in World Series," December 30,
       1911.

290   *taking the world champions to Japan:* WT, "Johnson Opposes Trips," December 30,
       1910.

290   *as conspicuous as a full-bloom peach tree:* BG, "Paid Pitcher $90 a Month," February
       8, 1920.

290   *"a kid at 71"*: BG, October 12, 1915.

290   *"the greatest work ever performed"*: WP, January 1, 1905.

290   *"Capt. Joe Start is a fine figure of a man"*: WP, "Old Providence Champions," April
       30, 1905.

291   *"dropped out of sight . . . Drink got the better of him"*: SN, "Providence Champions,"
       February 20, 1897.

291   *seemed despondent to friends:* BG, "Loved Figure in Baseball for Years," July 17,
       1921; Stars, 67.

291   *"every spring I have that baseball fever"*: AC, January 11, 1908.

291   *"I have played my last game and lost"*: PI, "Former Baseball Star Is Arrested for
       Theft," November 15, 1922.

291   *poor, blind, and deaf, at the Sacred Heart Home:* Stars, 60.

291   *bringing the entire team to Evergreen Cemetery:* LH, "Flowers Are Strewed on the
       Grave of Charley Radbourne," July 7, 1916.

291   *"They haven't got iron men like that in these days"*: BM, "The Secret of the Giants'
       Twenty-Six Straight Wins," January 1917, 45.

292 *"the super-pitcher of all time":* WBTL, "Frank Bancroft Is World's Oldest Man in Baseball," May 9, 1918.

292 *"Probably no man now connected":* BG, February 8, 1920.

292 *"What is the work of a first class pitcher":* BE, "The Pitching of the Season—Speed and Strategy," September 14, 1884.

293 *"One thing is very sure. If I am not treated squarely":* BG, September 8, 1887.

293 *"They have driven me out of the business":* BG, September 25, 1887.

293 *"Mrs. Radbourn says that she feels sorry":* BG, January 22, 1888.

294 *"HE IS WID US":* BG, May 9, 1888.

294 *"You are with us again, Rad, and I hope you will remain":* BG, "Present for Radbourn," May 12, 1888.

294 *"He had regained his old Providence form":* BG, "Emblem of Glory," October 11, 1890.

294 *"like a kitten with a ball of yarn":* BG, May 17, 1891.

294 *"The bronzed old warrior of the diamond":* BG, May 31, 1891.

294 *"He was too conscientious to take":* CE, February 6, 1897.

295 *"His proud nature could not stand for that":* NYJ, January 12, 1912.

295 *a hot, muggy evening in Bloomington:* BP, July 13, 1892.

296 *"sought a quiet nook at Bloomington":* BDT, October 8, 1891.

296 *"He would talk about himself only when cornered":* Spink, 152.

297 *felt "as frisky as a young colt":* DB, July 20, 1892.

297 *"I feel as if I would like to play this season":* BG, "Boston's New Men," January 28, 1894.

297 *"I am in good condition and would like to play":* SN, March 31, 1894.

298 *caught a portion of the shotgun load in his face:* BG, "Pitcher Loses an Eye," April 14, 1894.

298 *lived as a recluse:* Spink, 152.

298 *Wesley A. Hunsberger:* IA, "A Marriage Market: Milwaukee Has One and Business Is Lively," November 19, 1897.

298 *"to my beloved wife Carrie Radbourn":* Charles Radbourn's will.

299 *"Even when he was on his deathbed, few of his friends knew":* Spink, 152.

299 *"The heart, once the bravest and stoutest that baseball ever had known":* IS, "Great Pitcher Succumbs to Broken Heart," by Frank G. Menke, July 13, 1922.

299 *"The Radbournes allege that Mrs. Stanhope has no claim":* SL, "Radbourne's Widow: Is Not Recognized by His Relatives, Hence a Contest," March 27, 1897.

299 *Vernon Avenue in Chicago:* BG, August 7, 1903.

299 *died in Chicago Baptist Hospital at 2:30 a.m.:* Department of Health: City of Chicago: Bureau of Vital Statistics, Report of Death in Chicago Baptist Hospital, August 3, 1903.

300 *with his "then widowed mother":* Lyman, 285; WFG.

300 *Carrie's grandson, James "Clark" Stanhope:* KN, obituary, October 28, 1985.

301   *"He filled the nation with his praises"*: BP, "Radbourn Is Dead," February 6, 1897.

301   *"Greatest Pitcher Called Out by the Inexorable Umpire"*: PI, February 6, 1897.

301   *"Radbourn was an eccentric fellow in some respects"*: PJ, February 6, 1897.

301   *"Greatest Pitcher That Ever Lived"*: OP, October 11, 1908, for example.

301   *"What's a malla you, Charley Hoss?"*: MT, " 'Charley Horse': How Did the Popular Baseball Term Spring Into Being?" January 27, 1907.

302   *"Charlie Radbourn, you stand out in baseball history"*: SN, "Home Town Pays Homage to Radbourne and Griffith," May 8, 1941.

PHOTO CREDITS

Grateful acknowledgment is made to the following for permission to reproduce illustrations in the text:

Frederick Ivor-Campbell: pages 134, 272, 276

Library of Congress: pages 69, 78, 90, 100, 105, 107, 119, 127, 129, 157, 190, 213, 223, 226, 243, 254, 268, 273

Hugh Mason: page 17

Don O'Hanley: pages 75, 83, 212, 265

From *Picturesque Rhode Island, 1881*: page 143

Providence Journal archives: pages 170, 173

Vintage Providence Grays: page 257

INDEX

Page numbers in italics refer to illustrations.

Index